Secularization
and
Fundamentalism
Reconsidered

SECULARIZATION AND FUNDAMENTALISM RECONSIDERED

Religion and the Political Order Volume III

Edited by Jeffrey K. Hadden and Anson Shupe

A New Era Book

PARAGON HOUSE

New York

First edition, 1989

Published in the United States by

Paragon House
90 Fifth Avenue
New York, NY 10011

A New Ecumenical Research Association Book

Library of Congress Cataloging-in-Publication Data

The Politics of religion and social change / edited by Jeffrey K. Hadden
　　and Anson Shupe.—1st ed.
　　　　p.　　cm.—(Religion and the political order : v. 2)
　　Rev. versions of papers originally presented at a conference at Hilton
　　Head Island, S.C., in 1985.
　　Includes bibliographies and index.
　　ISBN 0-913757-76-4.　ISBN 0-913757-77-2 (pbk.)
　　1. Religion and politics—Congresses.　2. Religion and state—
　　Congresses.　3. Religion and sociology—Congresses.
　　I. Hadden, Jeffrey K.　II. Shupe, Anson D.　III. Series.
　　BL65.P7R433　1986 vol. 2
　　291.1'77 s—dc19
　　[322'.1]　　　　　　　　　　　　　　　　　　　87-24480
　　　　　　　　　　　　　　　　　　　　　　　　　　　CIP

Manufactured in the United States of America

Dedicated to
BARBARA HARGROVE
FRIEND, COLLEAGUE, AND SCHOLAR
(1924–1988)

Contents

Introduction

Jeffrey K. Hadden
and
Anson Shupe

From Gnawing Skepticism Toward
New Conceptualizations

This is the third in a series of volumes designed to explore the role of religion in the transformation of the political order. Drafts of most of the papers for these three volumes were written first for scholarly conferences convened in 1984 and 1985. Scholars representing several intellectual disciplines and expertise on most of the major world religions were present at each conference.

The personal biographies of the editors as well as events unfolding in the world were both significant in the genesis of the project. Both of us have studied religious groups struggling to effect social change. And we have both paid more than passing attention to the seemingly worldwide explosion of religious groups in political conflict. This combination of personal research experience and attentiveness to religion in the modern world left both of us uncomfortable with the conventional sociological wisdom that postulates that the influence of religions is eclipsing; that, at best, faith can have no significant impact beyond the private realm. In scholarly literature, this perspective is known as secularization theory.

As we told our colleagues in the opening session of the first conference, held on the remote Caribbean island of Martinique, the project was born of a gnawing skepticism about the efficacy of secularization theory to account for all the apparent anomalies of religious influence in the modern world.

In retrospect, it is clear that one of our motivations for organizing the conference was to provide a context where we could join with other scholars for the purpose of open and candid discussion of the theoretical heritage of the social sciences. We were interested in learning whether others shared our skepticism and misgivings about the adequacy of secularization theory for understanding religion in the modern world. We expressed our concern in telephone conversations and in our letters of invitation. Also in retrospect, our candor may have skewed the composition of the conference. Although we had hoped to assemble staunch defenders of secularization theory and the parallel idea of "modernization," those scholars closely identified with the conventional social science perspective expressed little interest in "rethinking secularization." The writings of many of the people who accepted our invitation seemed to suggest reservations about secularization theory, but none had assaulted this intellectual orientation head-on.

From the onset, we were also interested in exploring the potential productiveness of the idea of "global fundamentalism." The sudden politicization of American fundamentalists and the revolutionary rise to power of the Ayatollah Khomeini in Iran, both occurring as we moved into the 1980s, gave cause to speculate about the possibility of a broader global phenomenon. The mass media quickly dubbed Shi'ite Muslims "Islamic Fundamentalists," and religious historian Martin Marty (1980) wrote a thought-provoking piece for *Saturday Review* in which he endorsed the global character of fundamentalism.

If skepticism toward secularization theory and a curiosity about the prospect of global fundamentalism were underlying concerns as we proceeded to organize an international conference on religion and politics, the intellectual products of the first conference demonstrate our own timidity about putting these issues up front as the main agenda for the conference. We opted, rather, for a more conservative or conventional scholarly theme. Our stated conference charge was to reexamine the relevance of the historical and theoretical work of Max Weber on the role of the prophet in politics and religion.

Thanks to a splendid opening conference paper by Theodore Long (1986), which both assessed and reinterpreted Weber's classic studies of prophecy and charisma, we achieved a considerable measure of success with this conference objective. But most of the conference papers served another purpose—the mapping of a broad comparative scheme for conceptualizing how religion and politics interface.

The papers published in the first volume of this series, *Prophetic Religions and Politics* (Hadden and Shupe, 1986), make abundantly clear the efflorescence of religion in the political arena around the globe. The authors of the papers in Volume I addressed various issues central to the relationship between religion and politics. Traversing the globe—the United States, Canada, India, Jamaica, Central and Latin America, the Caribbean, Poland, Scotland, Ireland, Malaysia, China, Japan, Eastern Europe and the Soviet Union, Egypt, Iran, and Western Europe—scholars found religion deeply entangled in the political process.

The scholarly papers and, even more importantly, the formal and informal discussions at this first conference heightened our confidence in the legitimacy of our skepticism toward secularization theory. While there was not a single paper that directly critiqued secularization theory, neither was there a single paper that suggested that religion was drifting toward the political irrelevance implied in classic secularization theory. Buoyed by this outcome, we left Martinique determined to pursue the quest to understand the interface between religion and politics in the modern world. And, in particular, we wanted to explore more directly the issues of secularization and global fundamentalism.

The site of our second conference, in the fall of 1985, was Hilton Head Island, South Carolina. A slightly larger number of participants, as well as circumstances that resulted in the production of additional papers directly germane to the proceedings, suggested the publication of two additional volumes rather than one. The second volume, *The Politics of Religion and Social Change* (Shupe and Hadden, 1988), focused in more depth on three broad issues that were introduced in papers during the first conference: (1) world-transforming religious movements, (2) liberation theology, and (3) religious minorities. We also had the very good fortune of having in attendance at the conference scholars who were able to explore three very different religiopolitical issues in the state of Israel. For each of these issues, we were able to build upon the baseline of knowledge established during the first conference.

One of the challenges we encountered in the first conference was establishing communication between, on the one hand, area or faith specialists who tended to focus on the *unique* aspects of "their group" or "their religion" and, on the other hand, scholars who sought pathways to comparative analysis. There was a healthy tension, with the specialists properly warning against premature generalizations and the comparativists insisting that our task was to seek out and discover patterns of hidden similarity.

Perhaps the single most important breakthrough at the Hilton Head conference, compared with the Martinique conference, was the ease with which participants were able to simultaneously elaborate the unique aspects of case studies of religion and politics while openly exploring comparative dimensions. Richard Rubenstein helped get us off on the right foot during the first plenary session. In his opening comments, he abandoned the subject of his paper, "God and Caesar in Conflict in the American Polity," and discussed, instead, parallel issues in Japan. Even before we got to the question "Is there a global fundamentalism?" our thinking was synchronized and operating at the global level.

We all owe much to our colleague Roland Robertson for helping us transcend the particular to see the many ways in which planet earth is becoming a global culture. Understanding this reality has not been easy. Most of us have only very limited knowledge about cultures other than the one in which we live and religious groups other than the ones we study. The mass media have heightened our awareness of global confrontations of religion and politics and, hence, have challenged us to attain greater knowledge. But the mass media have not been very helpful in meeting this challenge. As we have noted elsewhere (Hadden and Shupe, 1988: 42), between 1982 and 1986 we videotaped fourteen "depth" segments on Islamic Jihad from network television newscasts. Except for an expanding chronicle of events attributed to "Jihad," a viewer learns little more from watching all of the segments than from careful study of a single segment selected at random.

The mass media do not significantly broaden the depth of our knowledge about religion around the globe, or any other subject for that matter. And because the career commitments of scholars leave limited discretionary time, the challenge to broaden our comparative knowledge is effectively a challenge to do something different with our scholarly careers. Roland Robertson has challenged us to "think globally," and the papers in this volume are testimony to our collective inching toward a comparative analysis of religion and politics.

Another problem in "thinking globally" is that the concept of "globalization" has strong ideological overtones. Particularly among leaders of the New Christian Right, the concept of "globalization" is often confused with the idea of "globalism." From our perspective, the idea of globalization is to be understood as an empirical process. There is clearly evidence of the emergence of global markets, global cultural traits, global icons, global architecture, global consumer products, and so forth. How far this process may go in transcending and/or replacing traditional cultures and regional characteristics is, at this point in history, unknown. Globalization is, nevertheless, an empirical reality.

Globalism, on the other hand, is an ideological commitment to achieving a highly integrated global community. It is an idea associated with "one worlders," "internationalists," and the "Trilateral Commission." From the point of view of conservative Christians, this process is synonymous with the erosion of Christian values and Western culture and, like communism, must be resisted.

A difficulty in sorting out the nuances and distinguishing between globalization and globalism is that the former is intellectually associated with the idea of "world systems" theory. World systems theory, in turn, is intellectually aligned with and informed by Marxist economic theory. Indeed, some of the leading proponents of world systems theory are ideologically neo-Marxists. Hence, even to profess interest in exploring the process of globalization is to suggest alignment with those who are intellectually Marxists or neo-Marxists and ideologically committed to globalism. The problem is similar to the difficulty of disassociating liberation theology from "Marxist analysis" from being a Marxist.

Again, Roland Robertson has been very helpful in sorting out and clarifying the issues. His critique of world systems theory pivots on Marxist assumptions which dismiss religion as a significant factor in the modern secular world. The process of globalization does tend to debunk traditional belief systems, but, as Robertson and others (e.g., Stark and Bainbridge, 1985) have argued persuasively, the erosion of values and belief systems sets in motion the search for a new universal meaning. The irony and contradiction of secularization destroying religion, even as faith and meaning are being rekindled, is one of the truly remarkable paradoxes of civilization.

Following Robertson, we seek to understand the globalization process, and particularly its impact on religion. We eschew any suggestion or implication that inquiry into the globalization implies *any* ideological posture toward the phenomenon. In this, the third volume in the Religion and the Political Order Series, *Secularization and Fundamentalism Reconsidered,* we seek to address the two key issues that motivated us to pursue the comparative study of religion and politics from the onset. Our conclusion, which we think the papers appearing in this volume substantially support, is that secularization theory is certainly not to be dismissed, but its intellectual foundations are not completely solid. In a word, secularization, as the leading integrative idea of social change in the modern world, is seriously flawed. Secularization as a powerful global force in the modern world is a reality that cannot be challenged. We do, however, seriously challenge the intellectual underpinnings of secularization theory, which equate secularization with the erosion of religious influence in the world.

Our second conclusion, which again we think the weight of evidence appearing throughout the three volumes of the Religion and the Political Order Series supports, is that fundamentalism is flourishing and is likely to continue to be a driving force in the world. We think that conventional scholarly wisdom, which sees fundamentalism merely as an archaic cultural form that is destined to extinction, is seriously at odds with the preponderance of evidence.

The papers presented in this volume were in no way commissioned to drive home these two conclusions. Conference participants were asked to prepare papers commensurate with their interests and intellectual perspectives. Our conclusions are an interpretation of the evidence as we read it. Others reading the papers from the conference may reach different conclusions. Most importantly, we believe the conference achieved some focusing of the debate over the efficacy of the theories social scientists evoke to claim understanding of the modern world. With the publication of this volume, we hope the debate will broaden even further.

We must emphasize that we are not suggesting that secularization theory be scrapped. Our concern is to develop a more reflective understanding of the theory, including its origins, so that the unspoken assumptions about how the process of secularization works can be examined afresh. If the theory's unspoken assumptions about faith in a secular age are understood, overhauling the theory so that we can account for the sacred in the midst of the secular will become an easier task.

The papers on fundamentalism in this volume add to a growing body of literature that begs for a reinterpretation of conventional understanding of the phenomenon. Conference participants found the broader concept of globalization helpful in thinking about the prospects of some underlying generic process which might be labeled "global fundamentalism." The mass media, and particularly television, have scarcely transcended simple two-dimensional communication. Television is a natural medium for the marketing of the absolutist and simplified worldviews of fundamentalism. Hence, rather than witnessing the erosion of fundamentalist strength in the world, we see it on the rise. Stimulated by lively discussions of the idea of global fundamentalism at Hilton Head, we have written a paper for this volume that makes a case for the utility of the concept and we also develop an agenda for research.

In addition to the general assessments of secularization theory and fundamentalism that appear in this volume, a third significant contribution is the presence of theory and analysis that proceeds without reference to or dependence upon secularization theory. This, perhaps more than the critique of secularization theory, is better testimony of the waning importance of this long-established way of thinking about religion in the modern world. Part III, "New Perspectives on Religion and the Modern World," provides stimulating examples of theory and analysis that proceed comfortably and creatively without the assumptions of secularization theory.

In a sense, we have come a long way since our gnawing skepticism led us to seek others who could help us rethink some of the basic theoretical ideas about the interface of religion and politics in modern culture. But in another sense, the quest has just begun. The evidence manifest in the scholarship presented in this, the third volume of the Religion and the Political Order Series, suggests we are on our way toward creative new conceptualizations of the problem.

Organization and Content of This Volume

The essays in this volume are organized into three parts, following the themes discussed above. Part I presents six papers that contribute to a reconsideration of secularization theory. Part II follows with five papers that help rethink the importance and meaning of fundamentalism. Finally, Part III presents exemplars of new directions in theoretical analysis.

Secularization Reconsidered. The lead paper in this section, by Jeffrey K. Hadden ("Desacralizing Secularization Theory"), examines the historical context in which secularization theory has emerged. The theory of secularization is seen as a product of the social and cultural milieu in which it emerged. Specifically, the intellectual milieu of Europe expected religion to vanish, either quickly or gradually, and this expectation fit well with the evolutionary model of modernization.

Critical reexamination, Hadden argues, reveals secularization to be an orienting concept grounded in ideological preference rather than in systematic theory. Inertia, neglect, and an enduring ideological preference, rather than confirming evidence, have kept the theory more or less intact, at least until recently.

Four discrete types of evidence are examined to account for the present challenge to the theory. First, careful scrutiny reveals the absence of a systematic theoretical statement. Secularization is, at best, an orienting posture toward the role of faith in the modern world. Second, there is no substantive body of data confirming that secularization is eroding belief and participation in religious activities. One reason the data confirm the theory may simply be the absence of adequate indicators. Where data do exist, they seem to suggest that quite the opposite is happening. A recently published paper (Finke and Stark, 1988) adds important evidence to confirm this reasoning. Third, the emergence of new religious movements in the United States and Europe during the late 1960s and 1970s triggered research that offers theoretical models representing a frontal assault on the secularization theory. The fourth general type of evidence cited is the widespread entanglement of religion in the political process. How can religion, which is such a vital force around the world, be dismissed as impotent or close to extinction?

Karel Dobbelaere ("The Secularization of Society? Some Methodological Suggestions") has devoted more effort than any other scholar in the world toward the goal of clarifying the meaning of the concept of secularization (Dobbelaere, 1981, 1984). While he clearly has an intellectual commitment to the utility of the concept of secularization, his research has laid bare the laxity with which the concept has been used in scholarly literature.

In his paper for this volume, Dobbelaere analyzes research literature to reveal general processes underlying the secularization process and the religious interventions aimed at checking it. He hypothesizes that the higher the degree of functional differentiation in a society, the more advanced secularization will be, and the less impact religious organizations will be able to exert on the culture.

Dobbelaere sees secularization emerging within the context and as a consequence of the evolutionary process of functional differentiation. This process produces internal social subsystems—such as polity, the economy, and the family—which have become increasingly autonomous and specialized in their functions. For Dobbelaere, religion is substantively reduced to a subsystem of society rather than an overarching system of values and beliefs. Secular values increasingly replace religious values. In an effort to preserve control over their members and protect believers from the secularized world, religious organizations seek to establish institutions that provide the same social functions as secular ones. Dobbelaere refers to this process of creating separate schools, hospitals, youth movements, senior citizens' homes, social welfare movements, newspapers, and so forth as pillarization.

While the Catholic Church in Belgium and the Netherlands has made valiant attempts to establish this pillarized world apart from the secular world,

Dobbelaere is skeptical about the prospects of the church staying the tide of secularization. Cracks in the strong Catholic pillars in Europe have caused the church to adopt a "new collective consciousness" position which focuses on aggregate human needs and social justice rather than on a purely Catholic mission. Dobbelaere views this development as "internal secularization" and sees it as a necessary move for the church to adapt to the changing world.

Dobbelaere then examines the New Christian Right movement in America as a revitalization of religious defense against secularization. NCR members, feeling their life-style and sacred values threatened by secular humanism, have initiated new forms of political action. The power of this religious movement to overcome the effects of secularization depends on the size of the constituency the leadership can mobilize to defend its stance.

Is secularization inevitable? Are the various efforts of the religious to shore up their positions in the face of an evolving secularization futile? One may deduce that Dobbelaere's response to these questions is affirmative. But, in his conclusion, Dobbelaere hedges, returning to the role of methodologist. We lack adequate indicators to measure the critical concepts. For example, Dobbelaere argues, if we had more satisfactory definitions of functional differentiation *and* concrete measures of its societal consequences, then we could design research that would yield answers and not mere speculation.

William M. Wentworth ("A Dialectical Conception of Religion and Religious Movements in Modern Society") views classic secularization theory as a powerful, if flawed, statement of sociocultural change. The theory gained popularity, he believes, because of its ability to describe some of the prominent features of modern society, but it lacks specificity.

"Modern secularity is a fact," writes Wentworth, "[but] the character of the process behind this fact has yet to be portrayed in a theoretically appropriate manner." Wentworth joins Robertson ("A New Perspective on Religion and Secularization in the Global Context") and Walsh ("Religion, Politics, and Life Worlds"), both in this volume, in rejecting the classical conception of the transformation of society from *Gemeinschaft* to *Gesellschaft*. Rather, the two worlds of simple and complex, sentimental and rational, private and public, coexist in a societal dialectic.

The modern political economy and the administrative imperatives of the modern nation-state tend to push the sacred to the periphery. But the microsociological communal world and private biography are the epicenters from which flows a *commonsense* understanding of the world. Social change, which tends to destabilize commonsense understandings of the world, produces a counteractive mobilization of resources to restore balance, equilibrium, or normality.

Drawing creatively upon Thomas Kuhn's concept of the structure of scientific revolutions, and William McLoughlin's theory of revivals and great awakenings, Wentworth develops a conceptual model for tracing the cyclical process from normal society to revolutionary society to the reestablishment of normal society. The revolutionary cycle involves five phases: (I) discontent, (II) loosening of traditional rules, (III) moral exhaustion, (IV) tightening of the moral structure, and (V) the redefinition of common sense.

Wentworth sees the private sphere and common sense as the fundamental elements of revolutionary society. And, in turn, religion holds the potential to exert enormous influence over these spheres. The moment of its greatest potential influence is during Phase IV. The specific role of religion in this cyclical process will vary depending upon a variety of factors including the power differentials among the competitors peddling "common sense" in a pluralistic marketplace and the alliance or absence of alignment between church and state.

Wentworth's analysis is a valuable contribution toward finding balance between, on the one hand, a refusal to question the secularization hypothesis and, on the other, an overreaction to the buoyancy of religion which leads to the conclusion that secularization is a myth. "Contrary to both these contentions," Wentworth argues, "the sacred and the secular can apparently coexist in mutual good health."

Roland Robertson ("A New Perspective on Religion and Secularization in the Global Context") conceptualizes secularization in a new and theoretically promising way. He views the process as an unfolding dialectic in which pressures for universality (toward globality, or global consciousness) vie with persistently reasserting pressures for particularism (toward redefinition of religion along sectarian and even nationalistic lines).

Thus, for Robertson, secularization is not a one-way, nonrecursive movement on a unilinear evolutionary continuum of increasing *Gesellschaft* urbanization/industrialization/desacralization. Rather, both *Gemeinschaft* and *Gesellschaft* modes of societal style continue to emerge in counterpoint, with important implications for religion when it surfaces as a factor in global relations.

Robertson is careful to differentiate the global level from the merely international in his distinction between a process of many different nations/cultures ascending on parallel trajectories toward a homogeneous "convergence" (the international) and a transformation of planet Earth's human condition as the fate of an entire species (the global).

The key point of his essay is that a truly global view of the human condition cannot evade telic (i.e., "ultimate") concerns any more than organized religions can avoid being caught up in the inevitable search for answers to such questions concerning meaning and identity.

Most globalization theory is, as Robertson points out, admittedly secular, even Marxist, in its cut-and-dried focus on political and economic convergence. But such trends create structures that eventually confront larger questions of meaning and purpose and existence (and goals for the future). And religion becomes a powerful tool for legitimacy, definition, and counterdefinition. In this way, the question of identity—both internally for a nation as well as externally in that nation's relations to peers in the global community—becomes crucial.

Robertson understands the dialectic of *Gemeinschaft* and *Gesellschaft* interfacing at a theoretical level. Indeed, the logic of this ironic mix is the message of his article. The globalization process confronts men and women with both the need to transcend national boundaries for the sake of unity (perhaps even survival) and the wish to reassert or revitalize particularistic identities. There is no end to this dialectical dynamic. For this reason, as Robertson argues here and in previous works, religion is continually integrated into evolving questions of global order.

Calling contemporary sociological theory's failure to recognize the importance of the religious factor in macro affairs an "embarrassment," John H. Simpson ("Toward A Theory of America: Religion and Structural Dualism") uses the United States to illustrate that "there is an enduring link in societies between religion, religious expression, and authoritative public action, but it is variable in terms of its effective potency and forms at any given time."

Simpson locates this linkage in the organization of power in societies. Starting from a fourfold neofunctionalist typology of centrifugal and centripetal forces in social systems, Simpson argues that America is what he terms "an oscillating dualistic system." That is, in American society "neither the purposes of the whole nor the interests of the parts ever gain the upper hand on a permanent basis, although one or the other dominates from time to time as the system oscillates between periods in which the purposes of the whole command attention and resources and periods in which the interests of the parts are paramount." Watershed political events marking such important oscillating shifts, Simpson suggests, would be Thomas Jefferson's presidential election in 1800 and Ronald Reagan's victories in 1980 and 1984.

Most importantly for this volume, Simpson delineates a correspondence between such alternations in American politics and religious movements. For example, Hamiltonian federalism paralleled Calvinist assumptions of immoral, depraved humans unfit to govern themselves. But then Jeffersonian and, later, Jacksonian forms of democracy were accompanied by the Arminianist "salvation-by-choice" thrust of the Second Great Awakening. The contemporary Reagan era, with its vociferous New Christian Right, is yet another example. Such groups as the Moral Majority lend legitimacy to the recent political oscillation in American society of the 1980s: a movement toward a concern with the "parts" of the system and away from the centralization of systemic power.

Simpson's interest is comparative, and his argument is "pitched" at a theoretical, rather than strictly historical, level. The fruitfulness of his approach for comparative analysis appears promising, and begs for early application in other Western and non-Western societies, particularly in the many existing varieties of democracies.

Thomas Walsh ("Religion, Politics, and Life Worlds: Jurgen Habermas and

Richard John Neuhaus") addresses afresh the classical question of the proper relationship between religion and the political order.

Whereas Max Weber, one of the founding fathers of modern social science, viewed religion as instrumental in the development of the modern rational state, religion itself was judged by the rational social order to be insufficiently rational to have a viable place in the modern political process. In the modern rational state, the problem of pluralism and cultural diversity has been resolved by assigning religion to the private realm and creating value-neutral, rationally established procedures for guiding the operations of the political order. Weber's separation of religion and such a state has served as a paradigm of Western liberal democracy. But rationality, which separates process and procedure from values and meaning, has a strong propensity toward creating alienation from the modern state.

Walsh critically examines the scholarly efforts of Jurgen Habermas and Richard John Neuhaus to overcome this vexing problem of alienation. Habermas's work pivots on restructuring the classic *Gemeinschaft-Gesellschaft* dichotomy of society with the distinction between *system* and *life world*. Departing from Tönnies, who viewed the contemporary social order as being transformed from the intensely personal *Gemeinschaft* community to the impersonal and highly rational *Gesellschaft,* Habermas sees the modern world as simultaneously comprising *both* system and life world. For Habermas, the crisis of contemporary society is to prevent the "colonization" of the life world by the system. To prevent the occurrence of this pathological state, Habermas conceptually "decouples" system and life world. His goal for the structuring of a viable life world, free from the rational and technological effects of the modern world, is effective communication, free from the domination of the imperatives of system.

Walsh is intrigued by Habermas's endeavor to create a normative world regulated by dialogue grounded in communicative competence. But in the end, he rejects Habermas's formulation for two fundamental reasons. First, Walsh finds the theory lacking an effective means whereby the life world can participate in the political process—which has been relegated to the system. Second, Walsh argues that Habermas's theory "does not indicate the way in which values and norms communicatively generated and reproduced in the life world might infuse the system." Like secularization theory from which it derives many precepts, Habermas's theory affords no place for religion. Habermas's sociology of religion, Walsh argues effectively, amounts to the "linguistification of the sacred," wherein "God . . . comes to be known immanently as a communicative structure."

In effect, Walsh argues, Habermas has created a structure for the achievement of universalistic norms without grounding in any particular tradition or mechanisms for infusing these norms into the (political) system.

Uncomfortable with this outcome, Walsh turns to a critical examination of neoconservative Neuhaus's treatise, *The Naked Public Square*. Neuhaus argues that religion has always defined and given substance to the core of culture; when religion is removed from the "public square," religion by other names will be "bootlegged" into the public square. Neuhaus is critical of the capability of civil religion to critique and check its theocratic tendencies.

Walsh finds Neuhaus's writings sensitive to the regressive concerns Habermas has expressed about neoconservative writings and concludes that Neuhaus provides "a way of both distinguishing and relating spheres of morals, religion, and politics." He concludes not with a rejection of Habermas, but by calling for a revision of his theory in a way that incorporates the concerns of persons such as Neuhaus.

Fundamentalism Reconsidered. Historically, fundamentalism dates only to the early part of this century. Fundamentalists take their name from a series of twelve paperback books that sought to put forth the *fundamentals* of the Christian faith in the face of the onslaught of "modernism." During the 1980s, the concept of fundamentalism has been more broadly, but loosely, used to characterize conservative religious fanatics with a political agenda regardless of the faith tradition.

In this broader usage, fundamentalism has nothing to do with theological belief per se, but rather refers to a zealous commitment to act in radical ways because of religious conviction. It was first commonly applied to identify the Shi'ite Muslim followers of the Ayatollah Khomeini, but soon the term was used to characterize other Islamic radicals. A little later, the term was used to describe the radical Sikhs who assassinated Indian Prime Minister Indira Gandhi. And, occasionally, zealous Jewish groups in Israel would be designated as fundamentalists, although more frequently they have been characterized as "ultraorthodox." This provides a significant clue to the biased political overtones of the concept. This bias is clearer still with press coverage of the Afghanistan rebel forces who successfully conducted guerrilla warfare against the Soviet army and the Soviet-controlled Afghan army. Portrayed as brave patriots fighting against the Soviet invaders, the *mujahideen* are Muslims engaged in a holy war (jihad). But because the Western world feels greater sympathy with these Muslims and their cause, the press has not characterized the *mujahideen* as fundamentalists.

Anson Shupe and Jeffrey K. Hadden ("Is There Such a Thing as Global Fundamentalism?") attempt to dig beneath the loosely conceived concept to ask if it makes sense to apply the idea of fundamentalism in a global context. Their answer is a cautious yes, with the important caveat that serious research is required to better understand the phenomenon. In pursuit of this objective, Shupe and Hadden offer a formal definition of global fundamentalism and identify some guidelines for systematically examining the efficacy of the concept.

Daniel Pipes ("Fundamentalist Muslims in World Politics") explores the utility of the concept of global fundamentalism in the context of one major world religion: Islam. Pipes believes that the concept of Islamic fundamentalism viably describes a phenomenon now spreading throughout the world regardless of Muslim sect (e.g., Sunni versus Shi'ite) or region (e.g., Iran versus Pakistan or Malaysia).

Fundamentalist Muslims ostensibly orient their reform movements according to a strict interpretation of the Sharia—Islamic law based on the Qur'an and other sacred writings—which, they believe, reveals normative prescriptions and proscriptions both about private and public affairs, from culinary and sexual habits to economic and military practices. As Pipes points out, no historic society has ever operated, practically speaking, under the Sharia's unforgiving restrictions. In fact, all Islamic societies have existed under what he terms "traditionalist Islamic," or pragmatic, compromises of the ideal.

In the face of Western encroachment, new cleavages have split Islam. Pipes identifies three broad subgroupings. He terms one variation Secularized Islam, a Westernized accommodationist form that abandons much of traditional Islamic culture. The second subgrouping, Reformist Islam (perhaps better termed Conservative Islam), seeks to preserve much of Islam while not rejecting Western technology and innovations out of hand. Fundamentalist Islam, however, is dogmatic and reactionary.

The appeal of Islamic fundamentalism, as Pipes sees it, is its creation of a mythic past; in the long run, it is essentially unrealistic and unworkable. Writes Pipes, "Although aiming to recreate what they think of as an ancient way of life, fundamentalists in fact espouse a radical program that has never been implemented." In other words, there is a reclamation of moral/spiritual authority in the name but not necessarily in the form of the older tradition.

Pipes elaborates on how the cultural traditions of both the Soviet Union and the United States are anathema (but not equally) to fundamentalist Muslims. In particular, the liberal Western tradition, with its emphasis on individual liberties, is further removed from fundamentalist Islam than is Marxism's collectivist, statist, universalistic thrust. "Other things being equal," Pipes argues, "radical Muslims understand Marxists better than [they understand] liberals."

Pipes's essay is a valuable case study for the comparative validation of the concept of global fundamentalism. It fits within the conceptual purview we have sought to establish, and helps render what might be dismissed superficially as "fanaticism" into something more understandable, less emotional, and theoretically more useful.

For most of this decade, the Southern Baptist Convention (SBC) has been locked in a fierce tug-of-war between newly vocal fundamentalists who have now substantially overthrown the traditional moderate leadership. Nancy T. Ammerman ("Organizational Conflict in the Southern Baptist Convention") focuses on the dynamics of that struggle, using the controversial issue of abortion as a case study to illuminate the larger drama. Specifically, Ammerman examines the Sanctity of Human Life Sunday proposal presented at the 1984 SBC meeting in Dallas, and the ensuing debate.

The Sanctity of Human Life Sunday issue for the first time provided the forum for fundamentalists to confront the laissez-faire stance of the moderate leadership. Aligning themselves with the pro-life philosophy of the New Christian Right, the dissenting fundamentalists forced Southern Baptist clergy to reassess their position on abortion. The unobtrusive "personal moral choice" ethos of the establishment could not compete with the cries of the outspoken charismatic fundamentalist leaders for action against the "slaughtering of millions of unborn babies."

The moderate leadership's tolerance of diversity and "gray areas" in moral choice has faltered under the single-minded moral absolutism of the fundamentalist religious right. Tradition and loyalty are crucial political resources for the moderate leaders, but, as Ammerman suggests, they may not be enough to bind together the divisive forces within the denomination. For the moderates, the mere acceptance of ambiguity diminishes the strength to communicate effectively and to mobilize human and financial resources.

The fundamentalists of the SBC have built an expanding and powerful network of communication within the larger New Christian Right social movement. And their increasing control over Southern Baptist institutions has provided new leadership opportunities. Furthermore, the fundamentalist faction has actively capitalized on mass media access to present goals and generate national support.

W. Barnett Pearce, Stephen W. Littlejohn, and Alison Alexander ("The Quixotic Quest for Civility: Patterns of Interaction Between the New Christian Right and Secular Humanists") examine the seemingly hostile impasse reached in the dialogue between conservative (evangelical/fundamentalist/charismatic) Christians and liberal secularists.

Focusing on the example of a debate between liberal Massachusetts Senator Edward Kennedy and the Moral Majority's irrepressible Reverend Jerry Falwell, the authors demonstrate that these two spokesmen operate on the basis of *incommensurate worldviews*. Their definitions and criteria for truth, evidence, and logically primary assumptions are light-years apart. There is virtually no way to reconcile their opposite views. In fact, each side's attempts to understand or convince the other are "*in principle* interminable: There is no criterion by which both sides will agree to let it stop."

The authors see the liberal secularists as having passed beyond the initial condescending phase of simply dismissing the New Christian Right as insignificant into a second, more unpleasant, phase of "reciprocated diatribe." Stereotypes, caricatures, and crude sloganeering substitute for reflective criticisms. Some spokespersons in the controversy, however, are trying to move into a third phase: the quest for civility. Kennedy and Falwell, in a spirit of friendly antagonism in which each agrees to disagree with the other, have tried to pursue this civility, but Pearce, Littlejohn, and Alexander pessimistically regard the attempt (like all such attempts) as ultimately doomed. Such civility must rest on a modicum of shared understanding about the sources of morality and truth, but so far the debate lacks this bare modicum.

No one can ever "win" in a debate format that presupposes rational discourse and competing logic if the terms of victory are not agreed to beforehand. The actors cannot terminate the debate (through the supremacy of one side over the other) "by finding some mutually acceptable criterion for adjudicating conflicting claims."

The authors' message touches on a fundamental point of mass communications, with implications for politics, religion, and conflict on a global scale. Superficial notions that we simply need *more* communication and contact with one another as citizens of planet Earth in order to lessen tensions are quixotic. As long as the paradigms, or models, within which peoples interact are dramatically different as well as unexamined, attempts at dialogue will be frustrating, not to mention futile.

Benton Johnson and Mark A. Shibley ("How New is the New Christian Right?") utilize General Social Survey data from the National Opinion Research Center (NORC) to examine the question of the recency of conservative evangelical political expression in the United States. Utilizing data from 1974, 1977, and 1982 surveys, Johnson and Shibley conclude that the antecedents of conservative political thought and action were well established before the emergence of the Moral Majority in 1980.

The paper is based on data gathered for other purposes. Nontechnical readers will find this paper difficult reading, as a significant proportion of the space is devoted to delineation of the methodological and statistical procedures. Data gathered for other purposes are "reconstructed," as it were, to address the questions raised by Johnson and Shibley. The advantages of this kind of secondary analysis are obvious; one can retrospectively ask questions that otherwise could not be addressed. The disadvantage is that one has no option but to use data that already exist, and seldom do the existing data directly match the researchers' precise interest. In this case, the authors use eight questions about conservative issues to create an index that will approximate New Christian Right sentiment. Recognizing that the items selected might also provide a measure for "libertarianism," the authors incorporate an indicator of church attendance as part of their measure of the New Christian Right.

Johnson and Shibley conclude that the New Christian Right "has been built on the foundation of a distinctive, regionally differentiated [i.e., Southern], evangelical political culture of long standing. . . ." While they view this thesis as plausible, they believe that it requires further research before the generalization can be "fully accepted." The tentativeness of their conclusions stems very much from the statistical manipulations of the secondary data. Other scholars might create alternative indices, utilizing the same data, and come up with different conclusions.

The one apparently stable finding is that the values which Jerry Falwell's Moral Majority championed were clearly present in the United States before the high visibility of the New Christian Right during the early part of the 1980s. And it seems evident that the high visibility of NCR leadership did not have an immediate and dramatic impact in attracting public sentiment toward their conservative position.

New Perspectives on Religion and the Modern World. Richard L. Rubenstein ("God and Caesar in the American Polity") examines the perplexing relationship between religion and the American capitalist system of free enterprise. In recent years, several national trends in the American economy and society have intensified the conflict, with two of the most influential religious institutions, the Roman Catholic Church and the New Christian Right, adopting polar ideological stances.

Traditionally, the Roman Catholic Church has criticized the capitalist system for creating a "morally unacceptable" situation of extreme economic inequality in America and the world at large. The free enterprise market, church authorities maintain, encourages egocentric individualism without any regard for moral or spiritual values, or for the suffering poor who have failed to prosper in the marketplace.

In 1984, the U.S. Bishops' Ad Hoc Committee on Catholic Social Teaching and the U.S. Economy published a draft letter sharply criticizing the current economic and public-policy decision making. To remedy the injustices created by capitalism, the Bishops proposed a reemphasis on human needs rather than on military and consumer progress. They cited the welfare system as the highest national priority, followed by the establishment of federal programs to reduce unemployment. Furthermore, they called for the curtailment of the nuclear arms race, "which diverts energy and resources away from the economic problems besetting the nation and the world."

Rubenstein faults the bishops for their failure to offer a realistic plan for implementing a social and economic program to diminish poverty and the injustices it creates. Although he affirms the religious and social commitment of the Roman Catholic Church, Rubenstein believes that the New Christian Right exerts more influence and power in American politics.

The political program of the New Christian Right can be characterized by three distinct concerns: economic libertarianism, social traditionalism, and militant anticommunism. Protestant evangelical and fundamentalist leaders promote the pursuit of individual economic self-interest and material prosperity. They view government intervention in the marketplace as a threat to personal freedom and progress. Instead of government efforts toward economic redistribution, the New Christian Right leaders favor restoration of moral and religious values to the American society to alleviate injustices. And, as a divinely sanctioned morally and economically prosperous nation, the Christian Right leaders stoutly believe that the United States should implement a firm anticommunist foreign policy, supplemented by increased military expenditures.

Rubenstein believes that the New Christian Right, more than the Roman Catholic Church, has been politically active in making influential and concrete changes in the public arena. But he offers a serious challenge to both major religious powers. Both, he believes, have blindly focused on American poverty and communism, and both have dangerously neglected to consider the impact of Japan on the economy as a potent economic competitor.

Japan is a society in which government and industry cooperate intimately and effectively in long-range planning. Furthermore, the sacred and public realms are inextricably intertwined, providing spiritual support for economic and social programs. Rubenstein questions whether the traditional Roman Catholic power or the emerging New Christian Right will be able to provide the nation with the spiritual and cultural leadership to confront the Japanese challenge.

The complexity of postmodern industrial societies requires leaders who can transcend the chaos and organize the changing social, economic, and political order. Barbara Hargrove ("Religion and the New Mandarins") traces the rise of a class of intellectual elites who are filling these leadership roles. The power of the "New Class," as they have been called in social science literature, derives from expertise and control of information. Educational qualifications and professional certifications grant cultural status to its members.

Hargrove compares the ascendancy of this new cultural elite with the ruling mandarin class of old China. In ancient China, tremendous prestige was associated with the knowledge of precedent, ritual, and scripture. In contrast to the traditional claims to power by kinship and royal connections, the old mandarins achieved political authority and social acceptance by establishing learning as a cultural value. They were masters of intellectual accomplishments, as indicated by their ability to pass examinations measuring knowledge of precedent, ritual, and scripture.

In addition to opposition from traditional forms of leadership, Hargrove notes that religion posed a threat to the ideology of the old mandarins. The somber rationality and bureaucratic rigidity of the mandarin structure could not accommodate religion's orgiastic fervor, nor its celebration of kinship identity. The inability of the mandarin authority to incorporate or supplant religion's strength in China was a leading element of its downfall.

In a parallel argument, Hargrove believes the resurgence of a new charismatic religious right to be a potent threat to the New Class. Criticized for its substitute of a rational scientific base for a moral, expressive foundation, Hargrove argues that it is essential for the professional elite to align itself with a revitalization movement to gain legitimacy and identity. The decline of the New Class may be imminent if it refuses to merge its impersonal, factual stance with an appreciation for the affective side of human culture.

Jeffrey K. Hadden ("Religious Broadcasting and the Mobilization of the

New Christian Right") argues that religious broadcasters are utilizing their access to the airwaves to mount a social movement of significant proportions. Indeed, he sees them as having "the potential of changing American society in ways that are revolutionary in character."

Utilizing social movement analysis, Hadden traces the roots of the contemporary New Christian Right social movement to the reoccurring view of America as a providential land set aside by God with a special mission in world history. Periodic crises of dominion set off social movements that attempt to return America to the Godly principles upon which the nation was founded.

The theology, organizational resources, and managerial techniques of contemporary televangelists are traced to nineteenth-century urban revivalism. Hadden also explores the historical circumstances which have led evangelical broadcasters to develop a near monopoly on religious broadcasting.

The potential success of the New Christian Right social movement rests, in part, on the failure of liberal leadership to achieve the ideals, visions, and goals of the civil rights and human rights movements of the 1960s and 1970s. Movements are not easily sustained over long periods of time. Entropy has replaced the dynamism of the liberal agenda, and this now provides the conservative Christian movement an opportunity to assure its agenda.

John Colamen's essay (*"Raison d'Église:* Organizational Imperatives of the Church in the Political Order") provides insight into how churches (in the Weber-Troeltsch meaning of *ecclesia*) act to inhibit and even reverse what might otherwise be a unilinear secularization trajectory.

Much has been made of the accommodation of large, worldly churches' secular culture. Few scholars have examined another basic dimension of the churches' *raison d'église:* the "cooling off" or co-optation of sectarian fervor. The prevailing wisdom in the sociology of religion has it that routinized charismatic fervor is best contained and co-opted to prevent an assumed threat to the legal-rational authority of ecclesiastical bureaucracies.

True enough, but the skill to contain charisma also means the power, under certain conditions, to release it. Such experiential religion, as opposed to ritualistic religion, can be a vehicle for religious renewal and even prophetic actions (in the strictest Weberian sense; see Long, 1986, 1988) by the church. The secularization paradigm, in other words, cannot safely assume that the religious factor is removed as a core ingredient of much social change simply because a mainstream religious tradition has become more comfortable with a wide variety of life-style issues and social institutions. Coleman's analysis of the Roman Catholic Church in this regard is a valuable corrective to much thinking on the future of mainstream religious traditions, the secularization process, and religious renewal.

Barbara Strassberg ("Religion and Patriotism: Poland, France, Great Britain, and the United States") examines the interdependent relationship between the development of religious and national identities. A central component of this interaction is a country's "central zone." Following Edward

Shils, Strassberg defines the "central zone" as "the center of order, of symbols, of values and beliefs, which govern the society." The cultural values affirmed in this zone are generally those of the elite or ruling authorities. In contrast, cultural "peripheries" are values and beliefs espoused by the common culture.

The social and cultural integration of a country depend on the extent to which cultural "peripheries" and the central zone overlap. Contributing factors include government acceptance by the people, a thriving economy, a well-developed educational system, and a folk culture endorsed by the mass media and other social institutions.

Strassberg proposes that the religious factor will play a significant role in the development of a national consciousness in sociocultural contexts in which the scope of the central zone is small and the gap between this zone and the cultural peripheries is large. When common patriotic values are incorporated into the cultural zone, religious identity will be less significant.

To explore this hypothesis, Strassberg identifies four culturally distinct countries in which either the Roman Catholic (Poland and France) or the Protestant (Great Britain and the United States) culture has traditionally dominated. Each country is examined independently with regard to the content of the central zone, the degree of political and economic unity, and the celebration of peripheral values in the educational and mass media systems.

Strassberg concludes that in countries with exploitive political, economic, and social systems, such as Poland, religious identity is manifested in patriotism. In France, where there is economic and social stability, the religious culture is not aligned with the national one. Mutual respect exists between the national and religious factions in Great Britain because of its unique joint political and religious structure. The United States situation involves a combination of the French and British contexts in that religious identity has been integrated in the national identity, yet its significance in American culture has declined with the advent of secularization.

In the final paper in this volume, John T. S. Madeley ("Religion and Political Order: The Case of Norway") examines the apparently anomalous case of the Christian People's Party (CPP) in Norway. Christian Democratic parties have thrived primarily in countries with either a majority or a large minority of Catholics. The CPP is the only significant Christian Democratic party in Scandinavia. It is, furthermore, a party whose right to exist has been challenged.

While scholars have not ignored the religious dimension of Norwegian politics, they have tended to interpret religion as one among many peripheral protests against the nation's cultural and political center. Madeley seeks to account for the presence and vitality of the CPP in terms of a unique set of "church-state-society" relations that can be traced at least to the Reformation.

The Reformation thoroughly eradicated any loyalty to the Roman Catholic Church. Madeley notes that "[t]he church and its property was taken over by the crown and the clergy reduced to its royal ecclesiastical servants. . . ." The

Eidsvol constitution of 1814 significantly altered relations between the crown and the people, but left intact the sole and absolute jurisdiction authority of the monarchy over the church. The failure of constitutional reform to grant people sovereignty over matters of faith resulted in a "threefold religious monopoly": (1) Lutheranism as the national religion, (2) the control of the faith by the crown, and (3) the monopoly of the exercise of religious practice by the clergy.

Madeley argues that this unusual heritage contains the structural roots of intrafaith conflict, and he traces three major religious conflicts that have been translated into national political movements during the nineteenth and twentieth centuries. Religious revivalism is the central thread that accounts for the genesis of each conflict. Conflict has been initiated within the church and, for reasons unique to the Norwegian situation, has been worked out by toleration and even accommodation of religious dissidents. But in each case, the conflict spilled over into national political action.

Formation of the Christian People's Party in 1933 is the most recent manifestation of this reoccurring conservative religious movement. The CPP tends to draw about ten percent of the electorate and represents the third largest party. Its agenda is dominated by traditional moral issues, similar in nature to the conservative agenda of the New Christian Right movement in the United States. In 1981, the CPP was in a position to join a coalition that would have produced a majority coalition of nonsocialists, but it refused to join because the other parties would not agree to its goal of reforming liberal abortion legislation.

Madeley's case study is interesting in its own right, but it also provides valuable comparative data for understanding "the role of religion in the construction and management of the political order."

References

Dobbelaere, Karel. 1981. *Secularization: A Multi-Dimensional Concept.* Current sociology series, vol. 29. Beverly Hills, Ca.: Sage Publications.

———. 1984. "Secularization Theories and Sociological Paradigms: Convergences and Divergences." *Social Compass* 31:199–219.

Finke, Roger, and Rodney Stark. 1988. "Religious Economies and Sacred Canopies: Religious Mobilization in American Cities, 1906." *American Sociological Review* 53 (February): 41–49.

Hadden, Jeffrey K., and Anson Shupe, eds. 1986. *Prophetic Religions and Politics.* Religion and the Political Order Series, vol. 1. New York: Paragon House.

———. 1988. *Televangelism: Power and Politics on God's Frontier.* New York: Henry Holt.

Long, Theodore E. 1986. "Prophecy, Charisma, and Politics: Reinterpreting the

Weberian Thesis." In *Prophetic Religion and Politics*, edited by Jeffrey K. Hadden and Anson Shupe, 3–17. New York: Paragon House.

———. 1988. "A Theory of Prophetic Religion and Politics." In *The Politics of Religion and Social Change*, edited by Jeffrey K. Hadden and Anson Shupe, 3–17. New York: Paragon House.

Marty, Martin. 1980. "Fundamentalism Reborn: Faith and Fanaticism." *Saturday Review* (May): 37–42.

Shupe, Anson, and Jeffrey K. Hadden, eds. 1988. *The Politics of Religion and Social Change*. Religion and the Political Order Series, vol. 2. New York: Paragon House.

Stark, Rodney, and William Sims Bainbridge. 1985. *The Future of Religion*. Berkeley and Los Angeles: University of California Press.

PART I
SECULARIZATION
RECONSIDERED

1

Desacralizing Secularization Theory

Jeffrey K. Hadden

FEW FORECASTS have been uttered with more unshakable confidence than sociology's belief that religion is in the midst of its final death throes.[1] Writes Gerhard Lenski in the introduction to *The Religious Factor* in 1961: "From its inception [sociology] was committed to the positivist view that religion in the modern world is merely a survival from man's primitive past, and doomed to disappear in an era of science and general enlightenment. From the positivist standpoint, religion is, basically, institutionalized ignorance and superstition" (3).

This view, of course, is not sociology's alone, but rather is the legacy all social sciences inherited from the Enlightenment.[2] Rodney Stark and William S. Bainbridge (1985) note: "At least since the Enlightenment, most Western intellectuals have anticipated the death of religion. . . . The most illustrious figures in sociology, anthropology, and psychology have unanimously expressed confidence that their children, or surely their grandchildren, would live to see the dawn of a new era in which, to paraphrase Freud, the infantile illusions of religion would be outgrown" (1).

This forecast is anchored in a broad sweeping theory of secularization, which, in turn, is nested in an even broader theory of modernization. It is a compelling model; for a long time one could say it was *the* master model of sociological inquiry. From this theory of modernization emanated our understanding of bureaucratization, industrialization, rationalization, secularization, and urbanization. It was a general theory that embraced all that was to be explained about the transformation of human societies from simple to complex entities. And having accounted for that process, it provided a comprehensive set of conceptual tools for an ongoing analysis of modern society.

Various components of this linear view of history have come under critical

3

scrutiny over the past two decades, but until quite recently, the challenge to secularization theory has been more implicit than explicit.

A central idea of this paper is that secularization theory has not been subjected to systematic scrutiny because it is a *doctrine* more than it is a theory. Its moorings are located in presuppositions that have gone unexamined because they represent an *ideology* that is taken for granted rather than a systematic set of interrelated propositions.

The conceptual tradition that orients this inquiry is found in Thomas Kuhn's (1970) celebrated work *The Structure of Scientific Revolutions*. Ideas, indeed our very thought processes, are grounded in and shaped by the scholarly communities in which we labor. Except in periods of "scientific revolutions," our work takes place within a conceptual, or paradigmatic, framework that is generally taken for granted.

According to my interpretation of the history of sociology and the social sciences, our understanding of how the process of modernization has unfolded has carried paradigmatic status right from the dawn of the social sciences. Secularization has always been an integral part of this paradigm; its status was so obvious that it scarcely constituted a problematic issue requiring empirical investigation. In a word, secularization went beyond merely being taken for granted; *the idea of secularization became sacralized.*

This paper seeks to achieve two objectives. The first is to understand how the idea of secularization came to be sacralized. Utilizing a sociology of knowledge perspective, I argue that the process of sacralization began even as the social science disciplines were being born. Belief in secularization has been sustained by a deep and abiding antagonism to religious belief and various expressions of organized religion.

The second objective is to trace several critical developments which have recently led social scientists to challenge secularization theory. I argue that before the mid-twentieth century essentially no empirical research and, hence, no foundation for challenging secularization theory existed. Two decades of vigorous data collection and the recognition of a theoretical stalemate provided the foundation for a critical reassessment of the theory.

The Sacralization of Secularization

George Santayana's simple but eloquent exhortation, "Those who do not remember the past are condemned to relive it," is a powerful reminder to us that our past is an important key to understanding where we are and where we may be going. In the Introduction to Karl Mannheim's (1959) *Ideology and Utopia*, Louis Wirth wrote, "The most important thing . . . that we can know about a man is what he takes for granted, and the most elemental and important facts about society are those that are seldom debated and generally regarded as settled" (xxii–xxiii). It is my thesis that sociologists have forgotten the history out of which the idea of secularization emerged. In a broader sense, they have forgotten the context of the larger corpus of modernization thought as well.

The European Heritage. Sociology was born in the midst of profound tension between religion and liberal culture in Europe, and only in this context can we understand the discipline of sociology's understanding of religion. The spirit of the Enlightenment flooded over from the eighteenth into the nineteenth and then into the twentieth century. Reason was king, and science would pave the way to a world that would soon rid itself of superstition and tyrants. The tension between ecclesiastical authority and the emerging new order was evident at three discrete levels.

The first source of tension was an emerging evolutionary worldview. Even before the publication of Charles Darwin's theory of evolution, historical and philosophical thought abounded with nascent theories postulating the unfolding of the world in a series of progressive stages. These perspectives not only challenged the established religion's meaning of history, they postulated religion to be an archaic form standing as an obstacle to progress.

A second source of deep division involved a struggle over status and power. After the Counter-Reformation and during the period of emerging nation-states, clergy exchanged monopoly for legitimation. During this period, ecclesiastical authorities lost much power, but they retained considerable autonomy. The French Revolution was a revolt not only against the crown, but against the religious authority that legitimated the monarchy.

A third source of conflict emerged by virtue of reason and science challenging religion's claim to monopoly over understanding the working of the mind and human consciousness. The nascent model of consciousness which was emerging viewed the mind as an unbounded resource to be understood and to be used for the betterment of mankind. Clearly the mind is not like a bird battered back and forth between angelic and satanic forces.

In the late nineteenth century, the emerging order was at war with the old order, and the Catholic Church was an integral part of the latter. Reason and science were destroying the foundation of superstition and ignorance upon which the church rested. Anticlericalism was rampant. The church fought back. Pope Pius IX began his reign as a liberal, but after Rome experienced revolutionary violence he condemned the French Revolution, issued his Syllabus of Errors, and led the First Vatican Council to declare the Doctrine of Papal Infallibility (Madeley, 1986:11). The church seemed engaged in a losing battle. Writes Anthony Rhodes (1983): "The enemies of the Church in 1870 bore little resemblance to her traditional enemy in the preceding millennium. . . . In 1870 her enemies were atheists, radicals, anarchists, communists, socialists of all kinds, using weapons which were more effective than the swords and scimitars of the Turk—speeches and writings propagated all over Europe by printing press and pamphlet" (13).

The founding generation of sociologists were hardly value-free armchair scholars, sitting back and objectively analyzing these developments. They believed passionately that science was ushering in a new era that would crush the superstitions and oppressive structures the church had promoted for so many centuries. Indeed, they were all essentially in agreement that traditional forms of religion would soon be a phenomenon of the past.

But many of the founding generation of European social scientists were deeply concerned about the place of religion in the emerging social order. For many, the vision of society without religion was hardly more tolerable than the reality of society with religious dominance. Some thought it would be necessary to "reinvent" secular forms of religion. Frank Miller Turner (1974) captures the tension and cultural dilemma of late nineteenth- and early twentieth-century intellectuals who know "that they have outgrown the church as exemplified in Christianity, but who have not therefore been brought to deny the fact that a religious attitude to life is as essential to have as a belief in the authenticity of science" (247).

One such person was Auguste Comte, who gave our discipline its name. He postulated in the mid-nineteenth century that society had passed through two stages, the religious and the metaphysical. We were on the verge, Comte believed, of a new stage, which he called the positive stage. In this third stage, science and reason would replace belief in the supernatural.

But Comte (1852) could not envision moving into a religionless society. Often missing from contemporary textbook discussions of Comte is the fact that he attempted to found a religion.[3] Called the Church of Humanity, Comte's religion did not include a supernatural force, but it was grounded on the assumption of the necessity of religion as a mechanism of social control. Social rituals, designed to socialize and reinforce commitment, were central to the doctrines of Comte's religion. He established a Positivist Society and recruited a small cadre of disciples. They, in turn, organized the Church of Humanity.[4]

I used to think it terribly important that every significant figure in the founding generation of social scientists wrote at length about religion. But when one recognizes that they lived in a world that had been dominated by religion for centuries, one can readily ask how could they possibly have written a theory of society without considering religion.

What now seems more significant to me is that it has taken so long to consider the social context in which they wrote. Theirs was a world in transition no less than is ours. It was a world that Charles Dickens portrayed as the best of times and the worst of times. Where they were going may not have been clear, but they were on their way. And there was an almost universal certainty that when they arrived the ecclesiastical authorities would not be in charge. And that was not bad news.

The American Heritage. The American experience is different in some important particulars. Perhaps most important, the American intellectuals attracted to sociology were more concerned with the pragmatic and practical aspects of developing a science of sociology than were their European counterparts. Some saw this as a means to the ends of social reform; others were interested in developing a pure science. Notwithstanding important differences, the outcomes in Europe and America were similar.

No less than Europe, America was feeling bombarded by industrialization and urbanization. In addition, she experienced the onslaught of millions of immigrants and was torn at the seams by civil war. Despite these strains, there was a sense that the problems of America could be solved without resorting to a radical restructuring of society. This view was almost universally shared by the founding generations of American sociologists.

The founding generations of American sociologists were not, on the whole, so antagonistic to religion as were their European counterparts. All the available evidence indicates that a significant proportion of the founding generations of American sociologists were clergy or sons of clergy (Carey, 1975; Faris, 1970; Reed, 1975). Many of the American founders were committed to social reform and viewed sociology as a moral science. Albion Small, founder of the Department of Sociology at the University of Chicago and of the *American Journal of Sociology (AJS)*, was the leading proponent of this view. The early volumes of *AJS* contained nine articles by Shailer Matthews, a leading figure in the Social Gospel movement. *Social Forces* and *Sociology and Social Research,* the other two major sociological journals through 1925, were also edited by reform-minded churchmen (Reed, 1975: 112).[5]

While Christian sociologists occupied important roles in the early years of the discipline, there is significant evidence to suggest that their views were not the dominant point of view in the discipline. A remarkable study conducted by psychologist James Leuba (1916) in 1914 found that only 29 percent of the sociologists in his sample believed in God and, among a subsample judged to be the elite of the discipline, only 19 percent were believers (264). The credibility of these data is enhanced by a replication Leuba (1934) conducted in 1933, which produced very similar results.

Frank Lester Ward, who was the most influential theorist among the founding generation of American sociologists, believed religion to be an archaic institution, and he often expressed antiecclesiastical views (Reed, 1975:100).[6] And Herbert Spencer, the non-American most widely read by the first two generations of American sociologists, was adamantly antagonistic to religion.

Notwithstanding religious origins, it seems clear that a very large proportion of both first- and second-generation sociologists were doubters or disbelievers. It is also clear that the second generation was concerned with the institutionalization of sociology as a science.

The association of some prominent first-generation sociologists with the Social Gospel movement, social work, and other forms of social reform was viewed as a threat to their scientific claim. The second generation grew increasingly bold in their antagonism toward those who viewed sociology as a handmaiden to religion or as an instrument for "doing good." Indicators of tension between the "scientists" and the "do-gooders" are not difficult to locate in the *Proceedings* of the American Sociological Society (ASS) and the journals of the discipline. The formation in 1928 of the Sociological Research Association, a sociometrically self-selected elite, was an important step in differentiating the "real" scientists from the rank and file of the ASS, which still harbored social workers, preachers, and just about anyone else who paid their dues and called themselves sociologists.

William F. Ogburn's presidential address to the ASS in 1929 reflects a mood he expressed often: "Sociology as a science is not interested in making the world a better place. . . . Science is interested in only one thing, to wit, discovering new knowledge" (Reed, 1975:122). The creation of the American Catholic Sociological Association a decade later, in 1938, was testimony that the ASS was not particularly accommodating to the religious interests or perspectives of Catholic sociologists.

Leuba's (1916, 1934) data tell us that the great majority of sociologists did not believe in religion, and there is ample evidence to indicate that they didn't want to mix the religious agenda of social reform with the development of a science. But we have only limited insights as to how they felt about religion. In his autobiography, E. A. Ross expressed a view about clergy in the discipline that may have been rather typical among first-generation American sociologists: "For years I felt bitter toward the clergy for 'bulldozing' me. But after I found that I could ignore the preachers and still hold a university chair I made a mute pact, 'You leave me alone and I'll leave you alone' " (Reed, 1975:108).

Another view that is prominent in sociological archives is the sentiment that religion is unprogressive in creed and deed. Writing for the first volume of the *American Sociological Review,* Harry Elmer Barnes (1936) reviewed an edited volume entitled *Varieties of American Religion.* The ontological superiority of his sociological wisdom for judging religious creed is abundantly evident: "One of the strongest impressions derived from reading the work is that of cultural lag. While a few of the more advanced thinkers present a point of view thoroughly in harmony with up-to-date secular thinking, there are a number of chapters which depart in no important manner from the fundamental notions of the Middle Ages or early modern times. Modern science and critical scholarship have not left the slightest impression upon wide sections of religious opinion" (1025). But properly reorganized, religion has the potential to benefit mankind, Barnes thought. He continued: "Religion, purged of its antiquated trappings of theology, ceremonialism, and absolutism, may be the sovereign quality in human life, integrating the social and emotional urges by gathering them and focusing them in the service of our highest ideals" (1025).

Far less shrill, Howard Odum (1936) expressed frustration that religion in the South was not a progressive resource for social change. Odum's treatment of religion in *Southern Regions* is brief, but it is clear that he felt religion functioned largely to reinforce southern political demagoguery. "Like politics," wrote Odum, "religion is closely interwoven in the fabric of southern culture" (141). There is an implicit undercurrent of outrage in Odum's writing that the "mighty influence [and] power of the church" had not been used in a constructive manner (525–27).

A further look at the Leuba (1916, 1934) studies is instructive for understanding the milieu of early twentieth-century sociological thought about religion. Both studies involved national samples of scientists in physics, biology, sociology, and psychology. Each sample was subdivided between greater and lesser scientists. In each group, the elites were less likely to profess belief in God and immortality. Also for all groups, the proportion rejecting belief in God declines among elites from the first to the second surveys. From these surveys, and two less satisfactory samples of college students, Leuba (1934) concludes that knowledge is an important cause of the decline in beliefs and, presumably, so long as knowledge increases, religion will be on the wane (300). The one proviso that might prevent oblivion would be if religions were "to organize themselves about ultimate conceptions that are not in contradiction with the best insight of the time" (300).

Leuba's studies merely confirmed what a large proportion of sociologists and intellectuals believed in the early twentieth century. Religion had fallen on hard times and, quite possibly, it had weakened beyond the point of resuscitation.

I have argued that sociology emerged in Europe and America during a period of social upheaval that left intellectuals personally disillusioned with religion. The overwhelming influence of Darwinian thought during that period quickly shaped a theoretical perspective that postulated the imminent demise of religion. Our heritage, bequeathed by the founding generations, is scarcely a theory at all but, rather, a *doctrine* of secularization. It has not required careful scrutiny because it is self-evident. We have sacralized our commitment to secularization.

Notwithstanding the centrality of religion in the theories of the European founding generations and the historical centrality of religion to value formation, the overwhelming proportion of nonbelievers among American sociologists found religion uninteresting or unworthy of their attention. Religion offered nothing problematic, nothing useful for the development of sociology. It was not even necessary to study the process of secularization, because the disappearance of religion was not very important.

The nature and quality of attention devoted to the study of religion is an important indicator of this proposition. Myer Reed's (1975) diligent investigation of studies of religion published in the leading sociological journals from 1895 to 1970 reveals that only a small proportion of these articles were authored by secular scholars. Overwhelmingly, sociologists not only abandoned belief, they also turned their backs on religion as a bonified topic for sociological investigation.

Examining the three major journals from the inception of the *American Journal of Sociology* in 1895 through 1919, Reed found that 71 percent of the articles on religion were authored by persons he could positively identify as religious (1975: 81). Recall that Leuba (1916) found in 1914 that only 29 percent of sociologists believed in God, and the figure was 19 percent for his group of elites, the group more likely to be publishing. Thus, a group of believers, who constituted roughly one-quarter of all sociologists, produced nearly three-quarters of the articles on religion.

Reed (1975) carried his analysis through 1970. The proportion of articles written by religionists declines gradually, but for the first seventy-five years of American sociology, 51 percent of virtually all journal articles on religion were authored by persons Reed could identify as religious. His argument is that those who are ideologically undifferentiated from the subject of their inquiry are likely to let those extrascientific commitments intrude into their analyses. While his conclusion is debatable, Reed mounts substantial evidence to support his argument.

Eroding Belief in Secularization

The ideological bias against religion, so deeply internalized in the minds of our European and American founding fathers, is still firmly entrenched in the minds of contemporary sociologists. This is understandable. If the discipline has not systematically recruited persons of a secular worldview, the socialization process has loosened whatever beliefs in the sacred many aspiring sociologists may have held when they entered graduate education.

To understand how our belief in secularization theory was gradually eroded, we need to go back to Leuba (1916, 1934) one more time. An important motivation for his investigation was to offer a counterpoint to "modernist" propaganda asserting that there was no conflict between religion and science. His work caused some fury, but not as much as one might have anticipated. William Jennings Bryan, the fundamentalists' champion defender of American education against the theory of evolution, used Leuba's data in his unrelenting tirades against the godless universities. And Catholics used the data to argue for more aid to parochial education. But among liberals, there was mostly a conspiracy of silence. The modernist church tradition, having chosen to accommodate rather than fight science, maintained that, properly understood, there was no conflict between religion and science. With fundamentalism on the rise, many educators felt it best to just leave matters that way (Reed, 1975:111).

Through 1960, the four leading journals of the discipline had published approximately 400 articles on religion representing 5 percent of all articles published (Reed, 1975: 81). If one seeks a unifying character to describe this corpus of literature, I would simply note that one does not find any of them reprinted in sociology of religion readers and very few of them are cited in textbooks.

There are exceptions to the generalization that sociology of religion was neither a theoretically robust nor empirically worthy area of inquiry. During the 1950s, these exceptions become more numerous. Joseph Fichter's (1951) study of a southern parish is a case in point. Russell Dynes's (1955) empirical church-sect typology is another. And Paul Harrison's (1959) study of the exercise of power in the American Baptist Convention is quite sophisticated. But, in general, the theoretical and empirical legacy inherited through the 1950s was very thin. So rare were empirical studies that the likes of Gordon Allport (1950), Joseph Fichter (1951), and J. Milton Yinger (1957) wrote lengthy introductions or appendices defending the proposition that religion *could* be studied empirically.

Gerhard Lenski's (1961) monumental study, *The Religious Factor,* represents a critical turning point in the development of the social scientific study of religion. His study provided a dense mountain of empirical data and the first solid evidence suggesting the need to reassess the theoretical foundations of the sociology of religion.

Among the reasons Lenski offered for his interest in studying religion in Detroit was the fact that America was perceived to be experiencing a religious revival during the post–World War Two era. The issue of whether we were or were not experiencing a religious revival was hotly debated, and the validity of the secularization thesis became a part of that debate. Defenders of the secularization model argued against the presence of a revival; critics cited the revival as evidence that the theory was wrong.

For the most part, this debate was carried on by religious leaders, not social scientists. But in 1959, Seymour Martin Lipset entered the debate and concluded that "by far the most striking aspect of religious life in America is not the changes which have occurred in it—but the basic continuities it retains" (cited in Lenski, 1961: 43). Writing that same year, Charles Y. Glock concluded that "none of the work done to assess the state of religion in America currently or historically meets even the minimum standards of scientific inquiry" (Glock and Stark, 1965: 84). In a word, Glock insisted, it is hard to conclude much of anything.

As to the theory of secularization, Glock found "nothing in the literature that would constitute a serious and systematic defense of the secularization hypothesis" (Glock and Stark, 1965: 83). Its advocates, he believed, tended to be non–social scientists. Among the ranks of social scientists, Glock believed that supporters of secularization theory "tended to be oriented to qualitative rather than quantitative observation" (83).

Glock seriously underestimated the grip of secularization thought on the social scientific study of religion, but he was right in asserting that most of the ardent advocates of secularization theory were qualitatively oriented. Faced with a dearth of data and what he believed to be inadequate theory, Glock began a systematic program of research. A significant research grant from the Anti-Defamation League in the early 1960s provided him with the opportunity to fill the void of empirical data about religion. That initial five-year grant became the foundation for two decades of research at the University of California at Berkeley and the training of more than a dozen graduate students.

Initially, it was perceived that Glock's influence was strictly in the area of empirical research. Glock and his students, along with their students, have come a long way toward developing a foundation of empirical research. But Glock's imprint on the development of a new theoretical foundation is also evident. Influenced by Paul Lazarsfeld and Robert Merton while a student and then a faculty member at Columbia, Glock's initial contributions can be identified as theories of the "middle range." But from his first entrance into the scientific study of religion, Glock was interested in moving beyond the classic statements of secularization theory.

In conjunction with the Twentieth Anniversary of the Society for the Scientific Study of Religion, Glock and Phillip Hammond (1973) commissioned a series of "stock-taking" papers, with the objective of examining just how far the social sciences had come since the classic statements of the founding generation. Contributors included luminaries like Talcott Parsons, S. N. Eisenstadt, and Paul W. Pruyser. In an epilogue to the published volume, Glock and Hammond wrote: "There can be little doubt, based on these essays, that the accumulative record is meager indeed" (410). And in recognition of this conclusion, the editors of *Beyond the Classics?* inserted a question mark in order to accurately communicate the tone and substance of the volume. Reflecting upon that volume more than a decade later, Hammond (1985) noted: "The founders had identified the links connecting religion to culture, society, and personality, but subsequent investigations showed little in the way of systematic elaboration or development. . . . It was as if those founders had said it all; by early in the twentieth century the social scientific study of religion had received the model bequeathed by these giants but had not gone importantly beyond it" (2).

The substantive essays of *Beyond the Classics?* were probably never widely read, but the message was aptly summarized, if only slightly obliquely, in the epilogue by Glock and Hammond: Secularization theory is a dead end.

Challenging Secularization Theory

With the benefit of hindsight, it is easy to understand how the presuppositions of the discipline have radically affected our thinking about religion. But only of late have scholars begun to explore how the discipline's theoretical presuppositions, emanating from the secularization model, have clouded clearheaded observation of the data as well as theory construction.

Phillip Hammond (1985) has edited a volume of essays entitled *The Sacred in a Secular Age*. Each of its twenty-two chapters focuses on some fairly discrete aspect of the relationship between the sacred and the secular. The essays well document the degree to which the study of religion has been, and continues to be, influenced by secularization theory. The volume does not add up to a systematic critique of secularization theory; nevertheless, in chapter after chapter, one finds many of the most productive scholars in the scientific study of religion raising doubts about the utility of secularization theory.

Perhaps the most significant aspect of the volume is the fact that this sweeping assessment and critique carries the imprimatur of the Society for the Scientific Study of Religion. It represents, in effect, an "official" beginning of the process of challenging the assumptions of the secularization paradigm that has reigned since the mid-nineteenth century. If it is premature to announce the passing of this long tradition, the essays in *The Sacred in a Secular Age* bear testimony that the search for alternative models has begun.

My own assessment of the status of secularization theory reveals four important challenges. First, a critique of secularization theory itself uncovers a hodgepodge of loosely employed ideas rather than a systemic theory. Second, existing data simply do not support the theory. Third, the effervescence of new religious movements in the very locations where secularization appears to cut deeply into established institutional religion suggests that religion is perhaps truly ubiquitous in human cultures. Fourth, the number of countries in which religion is significantly entangled in reform, rebellion, and revolution is continually expanding. This reality challenges the assumptions of secularization theory that would relegate religion to the private realm.

Critique of the Theory. C. Wright Mills (1959, 32–33) once translated Talcott Parsons's 555-page tome, *The Social System,* into four short paragraphs. Following in Mills's tradition, here's a translation of secularization theory in three short sentences: "Once the world was filled with the sacred—in thought, practice, and institutional form. After the Reformation and the Renaissance, the forces of modernization swept across the globe and secularization, a corollary historical process, loosened the dominance of the sacred. In due course, the sacred shall disappear altogether except, possibly, in the private realm." Secularization, thus understood, is more properly described as a general orienting concept that causally links the decline of religion with the process of modernization. That is, it is more appropriately described as a proposition than as a theory.

Beyond its use as a general orienting proposition, secularization has been used in many ways ranging from the "decline" or "loss" of religion (Yinger, 1957: 119) to the "differentiation" of the religious from the secular (Parsons, 1963) to an Enlightenment myth "which views science as the bringer of light relative to which religion and other dark things will vanish away" (Bellah, 1970: 237).

In the mid-1960s, David Martin (1965) argued for the abandonment of the concept. Later, Larry Schiner (1967) reviewed the uses of the term secularization and found six discrete meanings. Noting that several of these meanings were infused with polemical and ideological overtones, Schiner too considered abandonment a reasonable way to deal with the problem.

Encased within this general orienting proposition are the elements of a theory. Many scholars have highlighted one or more of these elements, but for all that has been written about secularization, probably only Martin (1978), who decided not to abandon the concept, has written a treatise that would qualify as a theory.

More recently, Karel Dobbelaere (1981, 1984) has achieved a remarkably thorough and systematic review of secularization literature which reveals the absence of a general theory. Dobbelaere's review (1981) differentiates three distinct levels of use: (1) societal, (2) organizational, and (3) individual. A Belgian, Dobbelaere sees the evidence of secularization all around him and is reluctant to challenge the utility of the theory. Rather, he concludes that we need to be more conscious of the fact that different theorists, working with different paradigms, mean different things by the term. "All classifications of secularization theories," he writes, "should also take into account the sociological paradigms used by the builders of these theories" (1984: 217).

Dobbelaere's analysis is extremely useful. More clearly than anyone else, he has illuminated the sad fact that, in the lexicon of sociological inquiry, "secularization means whatever I say it means." But Dobbelaere's solution to the problem seems ill-advised. He seems prepared to give the idea of secularization a life of its own, free to yoke or splinter in as many directions as there are sculptors with molds and chisels. I believe a sounder conclusion to be drawn from his work is the same that Martin (1965) and Schiner (1967) reached in the 1960s.

To summarize, the idea of secularization is presumed to be a theory, but literature reviews support this assumption only in a very loose sense. This, however, does not diminish its importance. It is believed to be a theory and is treated as such. The fact that the theory has not been systematically stated or empirically tested is of little consequence. It has dominated our assumptions about religion and guided the types of research questions scholars have asked. Its imagery is powerful, and it is unlikely that it will disappear from our vocabulary or thought processes. But developments in the social scientific study of religion have begun to erode its credibility.

I turn next to the empirical evidence we have about secularization in support of this prediction.

Examining the data. Charles Glock (1959) not only warned us about the limited utility of data on religion, he further counseled that "It is extremely doubtful that accurate statistics can be produced through manipulating the unreliable ones" (82). A decade later, N. J. Demerath III (1968) thoroughly documented the point that Glock had only asserted. In a ninety-five page contribution to Eleanor Sheldon and Wilbert Moore's *Indicators of Social Change,* Demerath meticulously examined indicators of church membership, religious belief, organization, and ecumenical activity.

Some types of data are more reliable than others, Demerath concluded, but for every argument that can be made in defense of a data set, there exists a rebuttal. The result of Demerath's extensive evaluation and critique of many data sources leaves us with a single plea: "If there is a single recommendation that emerges from this review," Demerath (1968) pleaded, "it is that *the Census should include questions concerning religion in its regular enumerations*" (368–69). "Indeed," Demerath continued, "this recommendation is so urgent . . . that it deserves a postscript of its own" (369).

In the face of such a passionate admonition, one must be cautious in trying to build a case either for or against secularization with existing data. But if we must not throw caution to the wind, neither are we compelled to silence, or forbidden from examining and interpreting the data.

To me, the data, with all their recognized faults, speak clearly. And their most important message is that the data cannot confirm the historical process predicted by secularization theory. One must also add the caution that neither can the data disconfirm the process. But when one examines the large corpus of literature that provides some longitudinal perspective, I don't see how one can fail to conclude that religion stubbornly resists the prophecies of its early demise. If that simple proposition is entertained, then we open the door for alternative ways of thinking about religion in the modern world.

Marking 1935 as the beginning of scientific polling, the Gallup Organization's annual *Religion in America* report for 1985 highlights a half-century assessment of religion. In the introductory essay, George Gallup, Jr. (1985) concludes: "Perhaps the most appropriate word to use to describe the religious character of the nation as a whole over the last half century is '*stability*.' Basic religious beliefs, and even religious practice, today differ relatively little from the levels recorded 50 years ago" (5).

Unfortunately, early polling included only sporadic questions about religion, and when they were included, the wording was frequently changed just enough to leave one wary about comparability. Most of the items for which Gallup now provides trend data were not available in the early years of polling. But when one picks one's way through the poll data, plus other types of data that permit some inferences, Gallup's conclusion of stability seems to me a prudent assessment.

Still, within the general context of stability, there are some important changes. I shall briefly identify six significant variances to the theme of stability.[7]

(1) The most reliable indicators we have confirm the existence of a religious revival in the post–World War Two era. We can't precisely pinpoint the beginning, but it seems to have lost steam by the end of the 1950s.

(2) During most of the second half of this century, the "mainline" or liberal church traditions have struggled and mostly have lost membership and influence.

(3) During this same time period, conservative religious traditions, evangelicals and fundamentalists, have experienced sustained growth. Growth continues within these groups, although there is some evidence of a slowing of the process.

(4) The Second Vatican Council dramatically affected the beliefs and behavior of Roman Catholics in America. Attendance at mass and confession fell dramatically. Catholics were much less likely to report that religion was "very important" in their lives. But these indicators of decline now seem to have leveled off and stabilized.

(5) While Catholics now seem positioned to fight among themselves over the essentials of belief and the meaning and purpose of the church, and the authority of their leaders, the authority of the Roman Catholic leadership is now greater than at any point in American history.

(6) Primarily as a result of immigration from Central America and the Caribbean, Catholics have increased their proportion in the American population from roughly 20 percent in 1947 to almost 30 percent in 1985, and their proportion in the total population can be expected to continue to grow.

Each of these patterns of change either has had or will have important implications for the future of religion in America. Nested within these trends and countertrends are social forces that portend changes which could alter the face of religion during the next fifty years. But the indicators of stability also provide clues to the future. I shall identify five among many possible indicators of stability.

(1) The overwhelming proportion of Americans report that they believe in God, and that proportion has fluctuated very little over the forty years for which we have data. The proportion professing belief in God has never dipped below 94 percent and has moved as high as 99 percent during the revival period of the 1950s (Gallup, 1985: 50).

(2) Church membership statistics have fluctuated only a little over the past forty years. Self-reported membership surveys consistently run a little higher than statistics reported by religious organizations. By Gallup survey estimates, church membership was 73 percent in 1937 and 68 percent in 1984. A high of 76 percent was reached in 1947, and the low was 67 percent in 1982 (Gallup, 1985: 40).

(3) Church attendance has fluctuated in some religious sectors, but the overall picture of church attendance is amazingly stable. Essentially the same proportion reported attending church in 1984 as was the case in 1939. After the revival of the 1950s, reported church attendance dropped back to the range of 40 percent and has remained at that level since 1972 (Gallup, 1985: 42).

(4) Some differences in personal devotion can be noted, but the bigger picture is again one of stability. In 1985 almost as many people reported that they pray (87 percent) as they did in 1948 (90 percent). Whereas fewer people report frequent prayer (twice a day or more), the proportion who read the Bible at least daily is half again as great in 1984 as in 1942 (Gallup, 1985: 48). And religious knowledge has grown significantly between 1954 and 1982 (Gallup, 1985: 57), this during a period when most types of cognitive skills seem to be declining.

(5) Contributions to charitable or voluntary organizations are higher in the United States than in any other country in the world. And there is only scant evidence that either proportional or per capita giving to religion has declined. In 1955, 50 percent of all charitable contributions were given to religious organizations. That proportion slipped to 44 percent in 1975, but has since climbed back to 46.5 percent. On a per capita basis, in constant dollars, Americans gave almost twenty percent more to religious organizations in 1982 than they did in 1962 (Jacquet, 1984: 259)

During the period for which we have data, some dramatic shifts in people's perceptions about religion have occurred. For example, the proportion believing that the influence of religion was increasing in society peaked at 69 percent in 1957 and then plunged to only 14 percent in 1970. Since that date, the figure has risen steadily to 48 percent in 1985 (Gallup, 1985: 16). Also, people are less likely to report today that religion is "very important" when compared to the revival period of 1950s (Gallup, 1985: 16). But after a significant plunge following the revival period, these figures have now stabilized and have even risen slightly.

Other short-term trends may be interpreted as supporting the secularization hypothesis. Space permitting, I could comment on each. In the absence of that opportunity, I offer two general conclusions. First, there is abundant evidence to support the conclusion that *what* people believe and *how* they practice religion is a dynamic, ever-changing process. For example, over the past twenty years we have experienced a significant decline in the proportion of Americans who believe that the Bible is the actual word of God and is to be taken literally, word for word (Gallup, 1985: 48). But, as we have seen, rejecting biblical literalism does not mean that people cease to believe. Similarly, weekly attendance at mass has fallen dramatically for Roman Catholics in the quarter of a century since the Second Vatican Council. But this is not *prima facie* evidence that people are ceasing to be Catholic or that they are "less religious" because they don't go to mass every week.

Second, it is clear that some indicators are affected by the broader cultural milieu. Demerath (1968) noted this possibility in his essay on religious statistics: "There may be a self-fulfilling prophecy crescendoing as the phrase 'religious revival' is trumpeted from steeple to steeple. The tendency to conform artificially to this newly religious image in a poll response may be a factor in documenting the image itself" (368). It should be equally obvious that downside trends may be triggered by media-pronounced prophecies of religious demise. The Gallup question on the perception of the importance of religion seems to support the self-fulfilling prophecy generalization.

Claims about trends in religions are not likely to be sustained and reinforced for long in the face of contrary evidence, but we can hypothesize that any trend is likely to get some self-fulfilling action from mass public perceptions. But the general conclusion this suggests is that we can expect indicators of religious behavior to continue to fluctuate.

To summarize this all-too-brief assessment of trends in religious behavior, I would say that the balance of data supports the proposition that religion is changing within a context of broad stability. There is a general absence of indicators which would support the long-term secularization hypothesis. Religion is dead in the minds, hearts, and feet of large sectors of American society. But just as certainly, religion is alive for other broad sectors. There is no evidence to support a decisive shift either toward or away from religion.

New Religious Movements. A third factor which has served to challenge the secularization thesis has been the emergence of new religious movements. The countercultural movement of the late 1960s involved a wholesale rejection of our materialistic world and its concommitant secularized ethos. The search for a "new consciousness" took many bizarre turns, but there was a profoundly religious quality to the search for new meaning.

This happened on the heels of a radically different perception of what was happening in America. In the early 1960s, a small group of theologians proclaimed the "death of God," and their proclamation captured substantial national media attention. Arguing that man is by anthropological nature a religious animal, Harvey Wheeler (1971) concluded that "a death-of-God era is also a god-building era" (8). And certainly the late 1960s and early 1970s were an era of frantic "god-building."

The growth of new religions was stimulated in part by Lyndon Johnson's repeal of the Oriental Exclusion Acts in 1965. The disoriented but searching counterculture became a missions' field for gurus of Eastern religions (Melton and Moore, 1982: 9). Their seeds multiplied, as did the seeds of many new sectarian visions of the Christian faith and the indigenously manufactured religions and quasi-religions.

Midway through the 1980s, many of the more prominent new religions have collapsed. Most of the others are struggling. At the moment, it does not seem likely that any of the new religions of the 1960s and 1970s will experience the kind of sustained growth that has characterized the Mormons, the most successful of several surviving new religious movements of the nineteenth century.

In the final analysis, the significance of the new religious movements of the 1960s may lie not so much in their contributions to religious pluralism in America as in the fact that their presence stimulated a tremendous volume of scholarly inquiry. And the result of this inquiry has been an enrichment of our understanding of the process of sect and cult formation and dissolution.

Many scholars have contributed to this literature. The single most important development to emerge out of these studies has been the comparative study of new religions over time and across cultures. Research teams, such as David Bromley and Anson Shupe (Shupe, Bromley, and Oliver, 1985) and Rodney Stark and William S. Bainbridge (1985), need to be singled out for their important contributions. Bromley and Shupe pioneered historical investigations of the patterns of sect and cult formation. Stark and Bainbridge have creatively utilized archival materials to add empirical breadth to the stock of knowledge, even as they have contributed a significant attempt at theoretical integration.

I offer here four important generalizations that are emerging from the research on new religious movements:

(1) Historical investigations have led us to understand much more clearly that sectarian fissures (splintering from established traditions) and cults (newly created or imported) have been forming for the whole of human history (Shupe, Bromley, and Oliver, 1985).

(2) Furthermore, the parallelisms in the patterns and process of sect and cult formation appear to be highly similar over a very long period of time (Shupe, Bromley, and Oliver, 1985).

(3) "Religious schisms are inevitable" (Stark and Bainbridge, 1985: 124). In a free marketplace, new religious organizations will spring abundantly from established traditions. Even under conditions of an established state church and the suppression of unsanctioned religions, new groups spring forth.

(4) Cults (new inventions or exports from another culture) flourish where traditional established religions are weakest (Stark and Bainbridge, 1985: 454).

There is less documentation with cross cultural evidence for the last proposition. Nevertheless, the comparative ecological research of Stark and Bainbridge (1985) for the United States during the nineteenth and twentieth centuries, with more limited data for Canada and several European nations, provides some provocative conclusions. "Secularization, even in the scientific age," they argue, "is a self-limitation process" (454).

Referring to the West Coast region as the "unchurched belt" in America, Stark and Bainbridge demonstrate that this pattern has persisted for a century. Cults, thus, do not automatically "fill the void" in areas that have experienced a high degree of secularization. But cult activity is greatest in those areas with the lowest levels of "established" religious activity. With but a slight twist on Egyptian mythology, the phoenix may be consumed by the fires of secularization, but it is sure to rise again from its own ashes.

The study of new religious movements introduces a certain irony to the view that our heritage from the founding generations provides ample evidence that religion will eventually fade from our collective consciousness. Durkheim (1961), perhaps more than any other founding scholar, took us into the abyss which follows the discovery that society itself is the object of collective worship. How can we believe once we have discovered that we are the creators of the Gods?

In the context of skepticism, if not open antagonism toward religion, perhaps we sociologists have parted from our guide before the journey was finished, presuming we had learned all there was to learn. "There is something eternal in religion," concluded Durkheim (1961), "which is destined to survive all the particular symbols in which religious thought has successively enveloped itself" (474).

Religion and Political Authority in Global Perspective. One way that secularization theorists have accounted for the persistence of religion in the midst of the secular is with the notion of privatization. Within Kuhn's (1970) conception of "normal science," this concept may be viewed as a "mopping-up" operation, filling in details and accounting for anomalies.

According to this reformulation, religion becomes a personal matter in the modern world, anchored in individual consciousness, rather than a cosmic force. Religion may be capable of maintaining its traditional function as a mechanism of social control, at least in some sectors of human societies. But religion is certainly not to be taken seriously as an earth-moving force.

This assignment of religion to the private sphere is rather like having one's cake and eating it too. One can hold steadfastly to the Enlightenment image of the demise of religion and still account for its embarrassing persistence. It is not necessary to establish a timetable for the disappearance of religion. In due course it will happen. And in the meantime, its only significant effects are in the private sphere.

The anomalies have been ignored for a long time. Notwithstanding the omnipresence of religious leadership during the civil rights movement of the 1960s, we did not tend to view this as a religious movement. The periodic outbursts of violence in Northern Ireland have something to do with the historical conflict between Protestants and Catholics. The present conflict involves only a small minority of fanatics. We got over our differences earlier this century, and surely they will too.

Jews have been fighting Arabs since the establishment of the state of Israel, but that's a struggle over turf. After all, the Zionist leaders of Israel were highly secularized. What do their quarrels with their neighbors have to do with religion? Mohandas Gandhi was a religious leader, of sorts, but the nation he led in revolt against colonialism was hardly a modern secular state. And besides, with Hindus and Muslims and Sikhs all fighting one another, it didn't make much sense. And if one thought about it at all, India's ongoing unrest was grounded in the great ethnic diversity of the Asian subcontinent.

One thing is for certain—the Europeans know how to have a good brouhaha without bringing religion in. Remember World War Two?

Examples of such myopic analysis could go on and on. Because of our assumptions about secularization, we have systematically engaged in a wholesale dismissal of the religious factor when considering sociopolitical events in the modern world.

In 1979 and 1980, the United States encountered two nearly simultaneous developments that radically altered our consciousness about religion. In 1979, fanatical Muslims culminated their drive to overthrow the Shah of Iran, a man and government believed to symbolize the modernization of the Middle East. That same year, Jerry Falwell heeded the call of secular right-wing leaders and formed the Moral Majority. In 1980, a small band of the Ayatollah Khomeini's followers held hostage more than four hundred Americans from the diplomatic and military corps. And Falwell held captive the attention of the mass media with claims that his organization had registered millions of conservative voters.

Since these developments at the beginning of the 1980s, our consciousness has been bombarded almost continuously with evidence of religious entanglement in the political sphere. The Roman Catholic Church played a central role in the overthrow of the corrupt regimes of Ferdinand Marcos in the Philippines and Jean-Claude Duvalier in Haiti. Pope John Paul II is a tormented man who has tried to curb ecclesiastical involvement in the praxis of liberation theology in Nicaragua and Brazil while tacitly encouraging political engagement in Poland and the Philippines.

The remarkable Kairos Document signed by more than 150 South African clergymen confesses prior timidity even as it charts a bold course of engagement in the political crisis of that nation. Like Martin Luther King, Jr., Nobel Peace Prize winner Bishop Desmond Tutu is but a symbol of courageous religious leadership.

Not all of the religion and politics stories of the 1980s involve courageous voices speaking out for peace and justice. And in many tension spots, discerning the heroes from the villains is very much an ideological issue. In Lebanon, Egypt, Iran, and Iraq, most Americans agree that the Muslim extremists are villains. But when the same Islamic zealotry is unleashed against Soviet invaders in Afghanistan, most Americans see its adherents as heroes and seek to minimize the similarities with their brothers in the Middle East. Turning to Central America, if you are a "liberal," you're likely to admire the courage of the priest brothers Ernesto and Fernando Cardenal. If you are a "conservative," you see them as traitors to their church and dupes of the Sandinista regime.

In many tension-ridden areas, there is the tendency to reduce religious conflict to "ethnic hostilities," and there are no heroes at all: Sikhs assassinate Hindu leaders, Hindus do battle with Muslims, Buddhists oppress Tamils, and Tamils strike back with guerrilla warfare tactics; all of these are seen as part of a complex mosaic of ethnic conflict.

Such simplistic explanation by labeling reduces our need to come to grips with one of the most important developments of the second half of the twentieth century. But the extent of political entanglement around the globe is simply too great to be ignored. Each episode cries out for explanation, not as an isolated event, but as part of a global phenomenon. The present data base for comparative analysis consists mostly of case studies. We do not yet have a very good conceptual model, much less a theory, to account for the tumultuous entanglement of religion in politics all around the globe. The one thing that is clear is that the classical imagery of secularization theory is not very helpful.

Summary and Conclusions

Let me turn now to a summary of the argument I have advanced and attempt to draw a few conclusions. My basic thesis is that the theory of secularization is very much a product of the social and cultural milieu from which it emerged. The expectation that religion would vanish, either quickly or gradually, fits well with the evolutionary model of modernization, which attempted to account for the transition of human societies from simple to complex forms. But beneath the theoretical statement is a silent prescriptive assertion that this is good.

Unlike biologists who scramble to learn all they can about vanishing species before they become extinct, most sociologists have not been motivated in the slightest to understand the "archaic" belief systems of mankind. The result of this neglect was the absence of data or alternative hypotheses that might have challenged secularization theory. Neglect, rather than a body of confirming evidence, has kept the theory intact. That is, until recently.

I have offered four explanations to account for the challenge that secularization theory now faces. Two of the explanations are indigenous to the theory itself; the other two are exogenous. First, careful scrutiny of the theory reveals that there really is not much of a theory at all. Secularization is, at best, an orienting posture toward the role of faith and religious institutions in the modern world. Second, although the data are less satisfactory than we would like, there is no substantive body of data confirming the secularization process. To the contrary, the data suggest that secularization is not happening.

Third, the emergence of new religious movements in the United States and Europe during the late 1960s and 1970s triggered research that offers theoretical models that directly assault the secularization theory. Finally, there is abundant evidence at home and around the world that religion is deeply entangled in politics. This religious vitality not only challenges the secularization model, it begs for a theoretical model that would explain why and how this has happened.

But what of the future? Patrick Henry, one of the founding fathers of this nation, once stated: "I know of no way of judging the future but by the past." As the substance of this paper suggests, I feel more comfortable peering into the past than trying to speculate about what is yet to come. If religion has stubbornly refused to accommodate the secularization theorists in this past, will this trend continue? I think so. Let me conclude by identifying six trends that flow logically from the thesis I have advanced.

(1) Religion will not be dead in the twenty-first century, but forecasts of its imminent demise will be less frequent in social science literature.

(2) Secularization theory will be radically revised or relegated to the category of a marginally useful heuristic pedagogical device, not unlike the theory of "demographic transition." The secular is not going to disappear from modern cultures any more than the sacred. But if secularization is to be a useful construct for analyzing a historical process, it will have to be significantly refined.

(3) The increased global visibility of religion will not dissipate quickly, with the result that there will be a significant propagation of interest in the scientific study of religion.

(4) With the grip of secularization theory having loosened, and interest in the study of religion heightened, we can look forward to greater interest in theory construction with, I believe, a significant accretion of understanding.

(5) The development of a sound data base will remain a problem in the United States and most of the world. Scholarly interest in systematic data collection stands little chance against the coalition of secular bureaucrats who are not interested in religion, and religious leaders who fear the misuse of religious data.

(6) Finally, I would return once more to the past to see the future. Max Weber's search for clues about the place of religion in human society took him deeply into the study of the world's major religions. The future will take us back to where Weber began. Indeed, I think the development of a comparative social scientific study of religion will become an extremely important intellectual thrust over the next half-century.

To this prediction, I would add one final note. In reviewing Alvin Toffler's best-selling book *Future Shock* in the early 1970s, an astute observer noted that one of the problems in trying to predict the future is that the future will be determined in part by events that have not yet happened. We have only scant resources for even trying to imagine what these might be. My informed guess is that those who will be most surprised by the future are those who still refuse to discard the crystal balls bequeathed by the founding generations.

Notes

1. This paper was initially presented as the author's presidential address to the Fiftieth Annual Meeting of the Southern Sociological Society (New Orleans, Louisiana, April 10, 1986). A slightly different version was subsequently published in *Social Forces* 65 (March 1987). Through their writings, private conversations, and comments on an earlier draft of this paper, many persons contributed to the author's understanding of the subject. He gratefully acknowledges the following: Randall Collins, N. J. Demerath III, Karel Dobbelaere, Charles Y. Glock, Phillip E. Hammond, Gerhard Lenski, Theodore Long, Myer Stratton Reed, Jr., Anson Shupe, Rodney Stark, and William Wentworth. This acknowledgement of gratitude to these scholars, of course, implies no responsibility on their part for the author's conclusions regarding the status of secularization theory.
2. Baumer (1960) has traced the history of skepticism over four centuries. The seventeenth century was characterized by attacks on specific doctrines, the eighteenth century by attacks on the church, and the nineteenth century by attacks on the concept of God. The twentieth century, Baumer argues, "combines [skepticism] in a new way with 'longing' for the God who is dead or for a God who is not yet born" (24). Auguste Comte (1852), the acknowledged founder of sociology, sought to fill this vacuum by creating a nontheistic "Religion of Humanity." Most of the founding fathers of European sociology pondered deeply the implications of nonbelief but, in time, the vexing problem was lost. To successive generations of skeptics, the doctrine of secularization "explained" all that needed to be known.
3. Most sociologists have downplayed Comte's efforts to found a religion, but Comte was very serious. In one of his last major works (1852), he signed his foreword "Auguste Comte, Founder of the Church of Humanity."
4. The first volume of the *American Sociological Review* carried a lead article (June) which attempted to explain why Comte's Religion of Humanity failed to take root in England (Bryson, 1936). With only a little effort, this article could be translated into the language of the resource mobilization theory of social movements.
5. Reed's (1975) research identifies Howard Odum, founding editor of *Social Forces*, as a reform-minded churchman. Guy and Guion Johnson, who knew Odum from the 1930s, recall that he was a member of the local Methodist church, but that he almost never attended local services (personal communication, 1986). Resolution of this apparent discrepancy may be inferred from Odum's (1936) celebrated treatise *Southern Regions*. Odum perceived that the churches did not use their considerable power to effect constructive change (525–27), and this was disconcerting to him. Perhaps his institutional involvement waned over the years as the result of his disillusionment.
6. Reed (1975) reports that both Ward and Spencer ran into "considerable resistance because of their outspoken contempt for theism" (100). Albion Small was interested in protecting Ward's general corpus of intellectual inquiry from criticism because of his atheism. When Small counseled him to be more circumspect so as not to offend the religious, Ward snapped back: "I do not write for the feebleminded!" (Reed, 1975: 100).

7. For a different approach to discussing patterns of religious change in America, see Marty (1979, 1985).

References

Allport, Gordon W. 1950. *The Individual and His Religion*. New York: Macmillan.

Barnes, Harry Elmer. 1936. Review of *Varieties of American Religion*, Charles S. Barden, ed. *American Sociological Review* 1 (December): 1025–26

Baumer, Franklin L. 1960. *Religion and the Rise of Skepticism*. New York: Harcourt, Brace.

Bellah, Robert N. 1970. *Beyond Belief*. New York: Harper and Row.

Bryson, Gladys. 1936. "Early English Positivists and the Religion of Humanity." *American Sociological Review* 1 (June): 343–62.

Carey, James T. 1975. *Sociology and Public Affairs*. Beverly Hills, CA: Sage Publications.

Comte, Auguste. 1852. *Catachisme Positiviste*. Paris: Dalmont.

Demerath, N. J., III. 1968. "Trends and Anti-Trends in Religious Change." In *Indicators of Social Change*, edited by Eleanor Barnert Sheldon and Wilbert E. Moore, 349–445. New York: Russell Sage Foundation.

Dobbelaere, Karel. 1981. *Secularization: A Multi-Dimensional Concept*. Current Sociology Series, 29. Beverly Hills, CA: Sage Publications.

———. 1984. "Secularization Theories and Sociological Paradigms: Convergences and Divergences." *Social Compass* 31: 199–219.

Durkheim, Emile. 1961. *The Elementary Forms of Religious Life*. New York: Collier.

Dynes, Russell. 1955. "Church-Sect Typology and Socio-Economic Status." *American Sociological Review* 20: 555–60.

Faris, Robert E. L. 1970. *Chicago Sociology: 1920–1931*. Chicago, IL: University of Chicago Press.

Fichter, Joseph. 1951. *Southern Parish*. Chicago, IL: University of Chicago Press.

Gallup, George, Jr. 1985. "Fifty Years of Gallup Surveys on Religion." *The Gallup Report* 236 (May): 4–14.

Glock, Charles Y. 1959. "The Religious Revival in America?" In *Religion and the Face of America*, edited by Jane Zahn. Berkeley: University Extension, University of California. Reprinted in *Religion and Society in Tension*, edited by Charles Y. Glock and Rodney Stark, 68–85. Chicago, Il: Rand McNally.

Glock, Charles Y., and Phillip E. Hammond. 1973. *Beyond the Classics?* New York: Harper and Row.

Glock, Charles Y., and Rodney Stark. 1965. *Religion and Society in Tension*. Chicago, IL: Rand McNally.

Hammond, Phillip E., ed. 1985. *The Sacred in a Secular Age*. Berkeley and Los Angeles: University of California Press.

Harrison, Paul M. 1959. *Authority and Power in the Free Church Tradition*. Princeton, NJ: Princeton University Press.

Jacquet, Constant H., Jr., ed. 1984. *Yearbook of American and Canadian Churches, 1984*. Nashville, TN: Abingdon.

Kuhn, Thomas S. 1970. *The Structure of Scientific Revolutions*. 2d ed. Chicago, IL: University of Chicago Press.

Lenski, Gerhard. 1961. *The Religious Factor*. Garden City, NY: Doubleday.

Leuba, James H. 1916. *The Belief in God and Immortality*. Boston: Sherman, French.

———. 1934. "Religious Beliefs of American Scientists." *Harper's Magazine* 169 (August): 291–300.

Madeley, John T. S. 1986. "Prophets, Priests and the Polity: European Christian Democracy in a Developmental Perspective." In *Prophetic Religions and Politics*, edited by Jeffrey K. Hadden and Anson Shupe. New York: Paragon House.

Mannheim, Karl. 1959. *Ideology and Utopia*. Translated by Louis Wirth and Edward Shils. New York: Harcourt, Brace.

Martin, David. 1965. "Towards Eliminating the Concept of Secularization." In *Penguin Survey of the Social Sciences*, edited by Julius Gould, Baltimore, MD: Penguin.

———. 1978. *A General Theory of Secularization*. New York: Harper and Row.

Marty, Martin E. 1979. Foreword to *Understanding Church Growth and Decline: 1950–1978*, edited by Dean R. Hoge and David A. Roozen. New York: Pilgrim Press.

———. 1985. "Transpositions: American Religions in the 1980s." *The Annals of the American Academy of Political and Social Science*. 480: 11–23.

Melton, J. Gordon, and Robert L. Moore. 1982. *The Cult Experience*. New York: Pilgrim Press.

Mills, C. Wright. 1959. *The Sociological Imagination*. New York: Oxford University Press.

Odum, Howard W. 1936. *Southern Regions of the United States*. Chapel Hill: University of North Carolina Press.

Parsons, Talcott. 1963. "Christianity and Modern Industrial Society." In *Sociological Theory, Values and Sociocultural Change*. Edited by Edward Tiryakian, 33–70. Glencoe, IL: Free Press.

Reed, Myer Stratton, Jr. 1975. "Differentiation and Development in a Scientific Specialty: The Sociology of Religion in the United States From 1895 to 1970." Ph.D. diss., Tulane University, New Orleans, Louisiana.

Rhodes, Anthony. 1983. *The Power of Rome in the Twentieth Century*. New York: Franklin Watts.

Schiner, Larry. 1967. "The Concept of Secularization in Empirical Research." *Journal for the Scientific Study of Religion*. 6: 202–20.

Shupe, Anson D., Jr., David G. Bromley, and Donna L. Oliver. 1985. *The Anti-Cult Movement in America*. New York: Garland.

Stark, Rodney, and William S. Bainbridge. 1985. *The Future of Religion*. Berkeley and Los Angeles: University of California Press.

Turner, Frank Miller. 1974. *Between Science and Religion*. New Haven, CT: Yale University Press.

Wheeler, Harvey. 1971. "The Phenomenon of God." *The Center Magazine*. 4: 7–12.

Yinger, Milton. 1957. *Religion, Society and the Individual*. New York: Macmillan.

2

The Secularization of Society? Some Methodological Suggestions

Karel Dobbelaere

IN THEIR INTRODUCTION to *Prophetic Religion and Politics,* Hadden and Shupe (1985) wrote that the "volume was born out of a gnawing skepticism about the efficaciousness of secularization theory to account for all the apparent anomalies of religious influence in the modern world" (3). And they referred to "the role of religion in the Civil Rights movement in America," "the rise of Soka Gakkai Buddhists to political power," "the Moral Majority in the United States," and "the stormy rise to power of Shi'ite Muslims led by Ayatollah Khomeini in Iran." And after having mentioned many other events that bombard us in the news, Hadden and Shupe stated: "These events [e.g., liberation theology, interreligious conflict, the resistance of the Catholic Church to authorities in Poland, the struggle of churches against apartheid, and the new religious movements], and many more, point increasingly to religion as a phenomenon to be taken seriously if one is to understand national and world developments" (5).

The scholarly work of the 1960s and 1970s that "uncritically incorporated the linear secularization/modernization/functionalist theoretical models" did not, according to Hadden and Shupe, seem to be capable of explaining religious influence in the modern world. New "dramatic events involving religion and social structural/political change have occurred even in the so-called 'secularized' industrial nations, that the need for a new assessment on a global scale has become glaringly apparent" (3–7). Others have written about the 1980s in the same vein, stating: "The face of religion is now more securely recognized" (Marty, 1985: 19).

For lack of objective verification in social theory, we should be ready to falsify our theories on the basis of new empirical material. But sound methodological practice demands an evaluation of the facts in light of the theory. Because secularization theory describes an evolutionary sequence, we should try to compare countries and events along an ordinal scale. In order to do this, we must first consider the criteria we might use to build such a scale. In this paper, I will discuss some building blocks with which we might construct a degree of falsification that is superior to hunches.

Before doing so, I want to stress that the notion of "evolutionary sequence" is only a condensed way of suggesting that universal processes underlie and promote secularization, other things being equal. But as Martin (1978) has pointed out, these processes operate very differently depending on the nature of the sociocultural complex within which they operate. He describes different aspects of the sociocultural complex that check and foster the general processes underlying secularization, such as the degree of religious pluralism, the inherent character of different religions, the size of religious minorities and their territorial dispersion, the framework in which a society emerges, the relationship of center to periphery and the linking of religious groups to it, ethnic composition, and so forth (Martin, 1978: 3–69).

Although the particular sociocultural complex is important in the unfolding of the secularization process, so also are the evaluations of this process by individuals, groups, and quasi-groups, and their consequent actions. Thus, we must divest our thinking about secularization of its *mechanical,* straightforward character. In former publications I have already developed this idea (Dobbelaere, 1981: 60–72). Let me now turn to the task I have set myself in this paper.

Secularization and Functional Differentiation

As Luhmann has pointed out, secularization is a consequence of the structural changes of society, in other words, of its functional differentiation (Luhmann, 1977: 228–29). This process is also evident, at least implicitly, in the secularization theories of other sociologists, such as Berger, Luckmann, Fenn, Martin, and Wilson (Dobbelaere, 1984: 213–14, 1985). Consequently, we may safely say that sociologists generally agree that secularization has resulted from the process of functional differentiation, which has produced internal societal subsystems. Such subsystems—the economy, polity, family, education, and science—have become increasingly specialized in their functions, and some have developed increasingly rational organizations. This process has led to a sharp "segmention of the several institutional domains" (Luckmann, 1967, 1975), and the institutional norms have increasingly become functional, rational, and autonomous within the separate institutional domains. In other words, a differentiation of role systems and role expectations has developed between the different subsystems. Secularization then, is the repercussion of these changes on the religious subsystem and its societal environment. It denotes a societal process in which an overarching and transcendent religious system—religion as substantively defined—is reduced to a subsystem of society alongside other subsystems, the overarching claims of which have a shrinking relevance.

Consequently, we can talk about secularization only in those societies in which a process of differentiation has already set in to segregate several institutional domains, for example, the political from the religious. This is only partially the case in most Islamic countries, and certainly not in Khomeini's Iran. The latter regime can even be considered a reaction to the functional differentiation process stimulated by the previous one. Of course, these things are matters of degree, and even in the West certain aspects of the sociocultural complex have checked that process. Martin (1978) has labeled them "statist regimes of the right ... where a pressured Catholic right succeeds in taking over for a period the reins of power." Obvious instances, according to him, "are Spain, Portugal, Croatia, [and] pre-war Fascist Italy." He points out that as more and more segments of the church perceive that there is a cost for its own specific mission, they respond to functional differentiation and even initiate it (Martin, 1978: 46; for a more extensive analysis: 244–77). Consequently, a comparison of countries should first of all take into account the degree of functional differentiation between politics and religion.

Functional Differentiation and the Individuation of Decisions

Some authors have stressed that so-called privatization of religion and not secularization is typical of modern societies. According to Luhmann (1977), the privatization or individuation of religion is a particular instance of the individuation of decisions, which is a structural consequence of the functional differentiation of society (232–48). Both aspects of modernization, namely, secularization and individuation, are a consequence of the same process of functional differentiation, and are complementary processes.

Indeed, Luhmann correctly stated that functionally differentiated societies cannot "ascribe" people to subsystems, as was done in segmented societies (e.g., in clans) and status-differentiated societies (e.g., in estates). Each person should have equal access to every subsystem, which implies that the individual's entry into one subsystem may not be restricted by the other roles he has. This is called inclusion. For example, taking a role in religion cannot be restricted by other roles one occupies and vice versa. From this point of view, enforced celibacy and the exclusion of women from the priesthood is a problem.

These requirements of a functionally differentiated society are clearly formulated in the core civic values of liberty and equality. But it is impossible that everyone should be equally qualified for every function. Consequently, specialization is needed, and professional roles emerged. It follows, then, that the inclusion requirement can only be met if complementary roles emerge in each and every subsystem alongside professional ones, which allow individuals to participate, even if only for a short period of time, in all subsystems. In this way, each person can participate professionally in one subsystem, and as part of a *Publicum* (his complementary roles) in all subsystems. For example, he can be a manager (his professional role) as well as a voter in the polity, a consumer in the economy, a member in a church, and so on (his complementary roles). Consequently, specific "publics" emerged for each subsystem: voters, consumers, students, believers, and so on. But functional differentiation is also needed between complementary roles which means, for example, that people do not have to vote as consumers, nor consume as members of a church. We should not forget, however, that this is a new situation. Before the emergence of democracy, for example, people were allocated to political roles on the basis of their social ranking. A strict separation of complementary roles being difficult to control and enforce, the *Privatisierung des Entscheidens* (i.e. the individuation of decisions) serves as a functional equivalent. Through the individuation of decisions a statistical neutralization of certain role-combinations, which are possible in complementary roles, is aimed at. Such combinations should only occur, however, at the personal level, and should hold only for personal motives; otherwise, they would destroy functional differentiation.

It must be clear from the above that individuation is *not* a private option. It is a *structural* consequence of the societal structure, which forces society to react to the consequences of this structure. As personal motives cannot be controlled by general symbolic or normative codes of conduct, only an adaptive, correcting, and compensating reaction is possible in view of the fact that one cannot react in a causally adequate way. This has consequences on the subsystem religion. In religion, churches, denominations, and sects cannot control the micromotives of their members. Consequently, an adaptive policy is pressed upon them; and Luhmann refers to Wilson for examples of this: ritual renewal, restressing the sacraments, and remystification (Wilson, 1969: 160). Furthermore, just as caring agencies may link the members better to the religious system than religion itself, so religious organizations venture more and more into ancillary functions and the establishment of pillarized structures. But here, too, there are problems: Pillarized structures have difficulty in typifying and enforcing their religious character.

Pillarized Structures Differentiation. Indeed, in Belgium and the Netherlands—to mention only the most obvious cases—organizations have been founded and run by committed church members or committed party members to provide all kinds of social functions on a religious or ideological basis. Such organizations were centralized in pillars, for example, the Catholic pillar in Belgium. This pillar embraces schools, hospitals, old people's homes, youth movements, social welfare organizations, newspapers, libraries, and more. It also runs a federation of sick funds, a trade union, and a political party—the Christian People's Party (*Christelijke Volkspartij*, or CVP). Although this party has officially been nondenominational since 1945, it continues to play a central role in organized Catholicism. The other two traditional parties, however, have developed similar structures, so we can readily identify both a "socialist" and a "liberal" pillar as well. In other words, in Belgium, pillarization characterizes the institutionalization of segregated and opposing *religious* and *ideological* systems, in which political parties play a central role. In the Netherlands, we can identify a Catholic, a Protestant, a socialist, and a humanist pillar.

Religious pillarized structures have been developed to protect believers from secularization. This trend started at the end of the last century as an attempt to differentiate of the public schools from the church: Catholic schools were erected to ensure a Catholic education for Catholic children (1879–1882). And when socialism tried to organize the workers in support of a socialist (i.e., Marxist and antireligious) ideology (sick funds, a trade union, a party, etc.), the church and part of the Catholic elite stimulated the establishment of independent Catholic organizations to provide the same social functions. These different Catholic organizations were, in the first half of this century, organized into an increasingly centralized pillar, and gradually became a state within the state, or an isolated Catholic life world within a state that continued to provide for its population more and more social functions differentiated from the church: hospitals, old people's homes, libraries, and so forth. Functional differentiation produced in Belgium—and also in the Netherlands, Austria, Germany, and other European countries—a "defense reaction" from the churches, which established "dikes" to prevent the secularization of their flock. If the state and the differentiated subsystems could no longer be organized along a Catholic, *casu quo* Christian, ideology, then the new civic liberties provided the opportunity to establish religious organizations to protect believers from a secular ideology. Depending upon the sociocultural complex (e.g., the degree of religious pluralism), a more or less complex structure of pillars was established.

About a century after the emergence of the pillar structures in the Netherlands, studies have demonstrated that they had begun to "totter" (Thurlings, 1978). Factors responsible for the decline in strength of pillarization in Holland include the crisis in the Catholic culture itself which started among the nuclear Catholics; the disorganization of Dutch Catholics under the pressure of the permissive society that surrounded them; the integration of the elites at the top of the societal system; the slow permeation downward of objections by intellectuals to the system; the successful conclusion of the emancipation process giving Catholics greater self-confidence, which stimulated openmindedness; financial needs, which, for example, stimulated mergers in the world of the press; legal regulations, for example, in the world of education;

and an intensification of social and economic conflicts (Martin, 1978: 190; Thurlings, 1978: 170–81 and 222–25; and Van Heek, 1973: 205–57).

In Belgium, the Catholic pillar did not appear to "totter" under the pressures affecting it in the Netherlands. Indeed, the regular Sunday Mass attendance also dropped drastically at the end of the 1960s and the early 1970s in Belgium (2 percentage points a year), indicating a crisis in the Catholic world similar to that of the Netherlands (Dobbelaere, 1985a: 194, 196, 211–13). But, in Belgium, there were no mergers between Catholic and other organizations, nor was there, in the long run, a reduction in the membership of Catholic organizations or in the volume of services provided by them.

There was, however, a slight crack in the Catholic pillar: Catholic Action groups for youth (i.e., organizations for the apostolate of the laity) have seen a constant decline in membership since the late 1960s, and such groups for the middle class have completely disappeared. There also wasn't any extension of pillarization into new fields; instead, new kinds of social services are now provided by pluralistic organizations, for example, the Federation of Neighborhood Centers (Dobbelaere and Billiet, 1983: 150–57; Voyé, 1979). But the bulk of the organizations making up the Catholic pillar seem to be as strong as they were before the crisis in the church of the late 1960s and early 1970s, if not stronger. How can this be explained?

As a consequence of functional differentiation, the organization of the services of the Catholic pillar—for example, in the schools and hospitals— became more and more specialized, and an increasing number of lay professionals replaced a vanishing number of religious personnel. Organizationally, religion was marginalized and privatized. Consequently, the control of the church over the membership and the clients was reduced to influencing their micromotives. On the other hand, the control over the professionals was also greatly diminished because of the low visibility of the interaction between professionals and clients. All that remains is a strict control over the orthodoxy of public standpoints and the public formulation of ethical norms by the overarching organizations of the Catholic pillar; these are still enforced (Dobbelaere and Billiet, 1983: 158–77; Dobbelaere, 1982a).

At the same time, a new "collective consciousness" was established, which J. Billiet and I have called "Sociocultural Christianity." Its core values are the legitimation of vertical pluralism on the basis of the constitutional freedom of assembly and choice, on the one hand, and, on the other hand, the articulation of the Christian identity in so-called evangelical values, including a humane approach toward clients and patients, or the *Gemeinschaftlichkeit* of the Christian institutions; the solidarity between social classes, with special attention to marginal people; a rational economic use of the available resources (i.e., the elimination of luxury and the promotion of thrift); and the realization of social justice (Dobbelaere, 1982b: 144–51). This "sacred canopy" is symbolized by a "C," referring more and more to Christian (i.e., evangelical) rather than to Catholic, which is considered to have a more restricted appeal and to be more confining. This "collective consciousness" functions internally: It is used to promote different programs, for example, a program for the humanization of Christian hospitals. It is also proclaimed externally and used to attract a large number of clients and patients (Billiet and Huyse, 1984: 133–36) of whom a great percentage are not regular churchgoers.

Specialized services have difficulty in typifying their so-called religious, or Christian, character, and professionals have difficulty in giving a typical religious answer to the problems that confront them. Social workers of the Confederation of Catholic Sick Funds, for example, expressed a tension between the professional approach to clients and the Catholic worldview of the organization. Their deontology implies the acceptance of the worldview of their clients, which could confront them with conflicting values when working on such specific problems as abortion, euthanasia, homosexuality, and so forth (for more examples, see Dobbelaere, 1979: 55–61). The church tries to influence the micromotives of its members, and consequently of its professionals, but, as we pointed out, its social control is very limited.

Confronted with a sharp decline of involvement in the Catholic Church, the pillar has cast off its clerical character and replaced it with a Christian aura. In other words, in order to promote its services, the pillar adapted itself to the "secularization" of the Belgian population with an "internal" secularization, or religious change. But it promotes values—*Gemeinschaftlichkeit,* or solidarity, thrift, efficiency, and social justice—which are typical Western values, and which could also be claimed by groups other than the Christian pillar. Recent reactions of particular groups in the Church and its hierarchy support this interpretation since they wish to reestablish stricter boundaries by stressing again typical "Catholic" ethical norms, beliefs, and practices (Dobbelaere, 1982a: 126).

By the mid-1980s, it appeared that the "secularized" collective consciousness had been able to maintain a flourishing corporate channel: The increase of clients made the pillar eligible for increased state subsidies, which enabled it to promote even better services. But, as Rokkan (1977) suggested, an institutionalized pillar has two channels: one corporate and the other electoral. Since 1980, the electoral channel has been crumbling. Billiet has demonstrated that, having recuperated its losses from the early 1970s by the end of the decade, the Christian People's Party lost 25 percent of its electorate in the 1981 election. This loss was confirmed by the results of the 1984 election (Billiet and Dobbelaere, 1985: 135). The electoral channel not only lost 25 percent of its electorate, but many people working in the corporate channel have also contested the privileged relationships between the Christian People's Party and the corporate channel. Consequently, the majority of clients and members of the Christian corporate channel and many of its executives have rejected the Christian People's Party as a valid expression of the Christian corporate channel. In a study of a Flemish town, Van de Velde (1985) demonstrated very clearly that members of the boards of the organizations making up the

Christian corporate channel were related not only to the Christian People's Party, but also to the Flemish Nationalist Party and to Agalev, the Flemish Green Party (166–71). Is this the beginning of the desinstitutionalization of the Christian pillar, or will the Christian corporate channel be able to adapt to the new political preference and affiliation of its membership and the members of the boards of its component organizations? The least we can say is this:

(1) The Catholic Church and its elite set up Catholic organizations to protect its flock from the areligious and antireligious influence, as they defined it, of the functional differentiation of modern society. Gradually, these organizations were coordinated and centralized in a Catholic pillar.

(2) The process of secularization resulting from the functional differentiation of Belgian society also had its impact on the Catholic pillar. The services became more and more specialized, and lay professionals took over from religious personnel in schools, hospitals, old people's homes, and so forth. Consequently, a declericalization set in and the pillar also adapted its collective consciousness to the "secularized" Catholic world. Symbolically, this was expressed by the "C" of Christian replacing the "C" of Catholic. This "internal" secularization of the pillar also had its consequences for the political channel.

(3) Indeed, more recently, the electoral channel started to crumble, and this may well be the definite beginning of the deinstitutionalization of the Christian pillar.

(4) This situation is not unique to Belgium. In the Netherlands, the confessional parties have also lost much of their appeal.

(5) It seems then that the functional differentiation of society has its secularizing consequences even in those organizations that were set up to prevent it.

Religion and Politics. Pillarization was a radical reaction to the process of functional differentiation, which accelerated in Belgium in the second half of the nineteenth century. It was a reactive policy: The church and part of the Catholic elite started creating a Catholic world segregated from the secular world. In fact, they reverted to an older process of differentiation: segmentary differentiation (i.e., the duplication of services in those sectors that were differentiated from the church), to check the impact of functional differentiation and to preserve control over the Catholic part of the Belgian population. The same process occurred in other European countries. But as we have seen, the pillarized structure also had to adapt to the process of functional differentiation. In other countries, however, less radical policies were used to check the processes of secularization: Denominational leaders started new social movements, but could not organize their followers into corporate and political channels. This is another indication of the diminished influence of religious bodies. They are no longer in a position to mobilize their flock into pillars, which proves again the advance of secularization.

Recently, the New Christian Right (NCR) was heralded as such a new social movement, and was seen by some as the reverse of the secularization process. First of all, such involvement in politics is not new: "Liberal Protestantism and Catholicism have long been politically active" (Hadden and Swann, 1981: 151). The leaders of such movements try to mobilize individuals to use their influence on political incumbents: Declarations are drafted, letters are written to senators and representatives, and rallies are organized; leaders along with followers show up at conventions, use the media, oppose some candidates and endorse others, and are endorsed by candidates (Hadden and Swann, 1981: 133); "Congressional Report Cards" are produced showing scores that reflect the number of times a member of congress has voted correctly on so-called "key moral issues" (139); and so forth. The type of tactics used by the New Christian Right were not new; however, its involvement in politics was new (Wuthnow, 1983: 168–74). Several studies were published about this new social movement. Of the different aspects that were analyzed, I am interested here only in the emergence of the NCR, the issues it is concerned with, and its impact.

It is clear from the available material that the NCR's cultural framework and life-style, its so-called "cultural fundamentalism," is opposed to "secular humanism." This value and life-style clash manifested itself in issues related to television (because secular humanism was being implanted in modern consciousness by TV, the NCR planned to expand televangelism, or the electronic church, to propagate its own countermythology); the public school (the NCR firmly supports Bible reading and prayer in the public schools, opposes evolutionism, and fights to have creationism taught; it also defends Christian schools); and the family (the NCR sternly opposes casual sex, pornography, homosexuality, living together out of wedlock, abortion, and the Equal Rights Amendment) (Heinz, 1983: 137–43). In the NCR, fundamentalists express familiar values through new forms of action (Liebman, 1983: 237); it emerged as a consequence of this value and life-style clash, conducive circumstances, and sociopsychological conditions (see also Harper and Leicht, 1984; Wuthnow, 1983).

Concerning the impact of the New Christian Right, the NCR has claimed responsibility for the crushing defeat of many liberal candidates in the 1980 elections, and some defeated senators and congressmen agreed with their claims. But, according to Hadden and Swann (1981): "It may be very difficult to locate unequivocal evidence of its decisiveness" when all postelection analyses are completed, and when all the other factors that affected the election are taken into account (164). Yinger and Cutler (1984) also concluded that "the political impact of the moral majority in the 1980 election remains difficult to measure" (88). Subsequent studies also made clear that "public support for the New Christian Right could hardly be described as widespread" (Bromley and Shupe, 1984: 61), and in his introductory remarks Hammond suggested: "For all the political rhetoric and enthusiasm expressed by the New Religious Right, its potency is not sizable" (xi). Shupe and Stacey (1983) concluded: "Our analysis suggests that the constituency of the New Religious Right is much more limited and much less unified than the Reverend Falwell and others would lead us to believe" (114).

On the basis of these studies, we may conclude that conducive circumstances—among others, the Watergate episode, which blurred the distinction between private morality and public good; the Carter election, which increased public recognition of evangelicals; the new political conservatives, including Reagan, who saw the NCR as a potent source of electoral support; the perception that the liberal welfare state policies had failed; the legitimation by the state and courts of nonconventional life-styles; and the relativism of mainline theology and ethics (Wuthnow, 1983: 175–80; Harper and Leicht, 1984: 106–9)—stimulated the emergence of the NCR movement, which organizationally was backed by the development of the electronic church (Hadden and Swann, 1981) and local fundamentalist churches (Liebmann, 1983: 69–73). They reacted against "secular humanism," which is human-centered rather than God-centered, and which is contrary to the American Christian tradition as they see it. Several studies use the term "secular" or "secularization" to describe the enemy the NCR is fighting (e.g., Simpson, 1983: 203–5; Heinz, 1983: 143–46).

Here we have a good example of my statement at the beginning of this paper: Secularization is not a mechanical process with a straightforward character. The process is analyzed and evaluated by individuals, that is, by ministers and members of churches, who use available channels to make their evaluation known. The NCR objects to "secular humanism" and uses legitimate means to protest against a life-style that denies its sacred values. The success of such social movements will, to a large extent, depend upon the number of people who are mobilized and their unanimity about issues and means.

In the United States, only the evangelicals seem to be growing in recent years. In 1984, they represented 22 percent of the American population (Gallup, 1985: 38). This group supports the NCR, but, according to a study on the buckle of the Southern Bible Belt, "Where support should logically be strongest and where the electronic church is most heavily syndicated," the constituency of the NCR is much more limited and much less unified than its leaders proclaim (Shupe and Stacey, 1983: 103, 114). Consequently, it may be regarded as a rear guard action, which will not alter American society. The growth of the NCR does prove, however, that a substantial number of people still oppose "secular humanism," and it certainly is capable of slowing down the process of secularization, most probably in these regions where a substantial number of fundamentalists live.

In a functionally differentiated society, the power of religion rests, at least in part, on the number of people it can mobilize to defend its views. Except for the evangelical churches, in the United States the prospects are not great. Indeed, the number of self-declared members of churches or synagogues has declined by about 5 percent since the mid-1960s. But over the last six years, the percentage has been quite stable, at about 68 percent. The percentage is substantially lower with young people: in 1984, 58 percent versus 75 percent for those fifty and older. If, as most studies suggest, this is a generational trend, then the prospects for the churches and synagogues are rather dim. The involvement in churches and synagogues has diminished, especially in the so-called liberal denominations, but, since 1968, also in the Catholic Church. Since 1972, however, the global figures for church attendance have not varied by much more than one percentage point around 40 percent in the United States. Again, the rate of churchgoing is higher among older persons than younger (Gallup, 1985: 40–44). And these trends are confirmed for Europe as well (Stoetzel, 1983: 94–95, 229–30).

What can we conclude from this example? Secularization is not a mechanical process, and it allows for religious groups to react. Their power is restricted, however, to the motivation and eventually the mobilization of individuals. In the long run, it seems that churches and synagogues are losing potential recruits, especially among the young. Should we wish to evaluate the effect of such movements on matters concerning the family, education, and ethics, we might measure the impact on legislation, or on court decisions, rather than simply accepting their self-proclaimed victories, or listening to the noise that they are making. Such an evaluation is, of course, very difficult to make; it may take years of study, and the outcome will certainly vary according to regions and countries.

It seems that, in the long run, functional differentiation will further promote individuation and secularization. Pillarized structures were unable to hold back these processes, and the churches and synagogues are losing too many members, especially among the young, to fight back effectively. This does not mean that religious groups give up. Some new religious movements have the resacralization of society on their banner, but their recruitment is very low, for example, that of the Unification Church. Nor have most of the churches fully accepted secularization. The evangelicals in particular fight it, and some church groups want to promote the resacralization of society and its subsystems. In the Catholic Church we can point to liberation theology, Opus Dei, and so forth. Here again, we should evaluate the impact of these trends, and not merely point out their existence. The position of churches in Eastern Europe is quite different. There, functional differentiation is prevented by the "party" for ideological reasons, and the population has to accept the primacy of the political "subsystem." It is only natural that opposition to an agnostic system can be voiced solely through religion, for example, the resistance of the Catholic Church to the authorities in Poland.

The Falsification of Secularization

Unlike Martin, I have not looked for aspects of the sociocultural complex that check or foster the general processes underlying secularization. On the contrary, I have used the above-mentioned studies to look for general processes underlying the secularization process, to discover the building bricks we should use to scale societies in order to predict degrees of secularization. In this way, our studies might become more than hunches, and might allow more reliable falsification.

First, we should try to develop measures to scale functional differentiation (sometimes called "institutional differentiation"). We should look for indicators measuring the degree of segregation of role systems and role expectations between the different subsystems of society. This should lead us to analyze the development of professional and complementary roles in the different institutional domains, and we should try to establish what degree of inclusion is achieved in the different subsystems. The level of functional rationalization of the different institutions and the individuation of decisions would be another indicator of the degree of functional differentiation that had been achieved.

We might then check our hypothesis empirically: Our hypothesis, that the higher the degree of functional differentiation, the more advanced secularization will be, means that religion—churches, synagogues, denominations, sects, and cults—would first of all have no impact, or at least a diminishing impact, on the rules governing the different institutional domains. In other words, traditional religious rules, or norms based on religious values, would increasingly have been replaced by secular norms or simply have fallen into disuse in the different subsystems of education, family, polity, economy, and science. Secondly, in more highly differentiated societies, the impact of religion on the micromotives of the citizens should also be less than in less highly differentiated societies. This would not exclude the existence of a vocal religious minority. It is not their presence which should count, however, but only their impact on the enactment and application of laws, on court decisions, and on the preservation of traditional mores. In order to study this impact, we might look for inspiration and models in the studies on power and influence. I am thinking especially of Dahl's (1957) approach to "power," measuring the increased probability of alter's actions being influenced by ego, and "scope of power," measuring the domains in which power is exercised (1957: 203–5). In this context, the problem of inter- and intrasystems comparisons has also been raised and some solutions offered (Harsanyi, 1962). Finally, the

Resource Mobilization Theory also offers valuable suggestions, since it examines "the structure of [social] movements and how resources are mobilized and managed to achieve goals" (Hadden, 1985: 6).

Epilogue

Is this paper an argument for the inevitability of secularization in the long run? Our conception allows for ebb and flow but seems to argue that we "cannot react causally adequately" on the general process. Indeed, it is argued that "only an adaptive, correcting, and compensating reaction is possible" (Hadden, 1985: 6). The basic idea is that the resacralization of "modern" societies can be achieved only through a new process of differentiation or the blocking, and eventually the reversal, of functional differentiation. If this process continues, however, then its outcome will be the secularization of society and the privatization of religion. Such an approach, however, does not exclude the possibility of social change. The history of mankind proves such possibilities: After segmentary differentiation status differentiation was developed, and later the process of functional differentiation set in. In the light of this evolution, a new type of differentiation is always possible, and its characteristics will allow us to evaluate the chances for religion in such a new type of society.

Wuthnow's (1976) study, *The Conscious Reformation,* has ascertained ongoing experimentations that represent "a conscious attempt to either halt or to reverse the process of differentiation": agrarian communes reflecting "an interest in reuniting economic and familial functions in one institution" and "political militancy of some of the new mystical religious cults" (197). And Wuthnow suggests that "diversification may be replacing differentiation as the major process of social evolution of our time" (198). First of all, there were only a few examples given of reversing the process of functional differentiation by reintegrating institutions. And what do they represent "statistically"? Are these not examples of retreatment in the Mertonian sense of the term? It seems to me that Wuthnow is more correct is stating, "In some respects, of course, diversification and differentiation are not entirely separate processes" (197). Most of his examples are indeed the outcome of segmentary and status differentiations *within* functionally segregated institutions: for example, in religion, in the family, and even in the economy and polity. Such a process of diversification is linked to the privatization of decisions and allows for a wide range of family styles: living together without marriage or in homosexual and heterosexual combinations, serial monogamy, communes, and so forth.

Such diversification as a consequence of experimentation at the individual level creates greater possibilities of disintegration of the social order, as Wuthnow (1976) has correctly stated. But Wuthnow then looked for integration through consensus, or cohesion on the basis of new and/or old meaning systems (201–2, 211–14), and analyzed "other mechanisms [that] have rushed in to fulfill this function"—that is, integration—"in the meantime" (202). The real question, however, is: Are these new integrative mechanisms Wuthnow described—privatization, isolation, and commercialization and ritualization of nonconventional behavior (205–11)—which are structural rather than cultural ones, not better adapted to a functionally differentiated society? Indeed, functionally differentiated societies can no longer be integrated on the basis of consensus or collective meaning systems.

In a functionally differentiated society, according to Luhmann (1977), the grip of the total societal system on the subsystems has changed (242–46). A subsystem belongs to a societal system not because it is guided in its structural choices by requirements, values, and norms applying to all subsystems, but because it is oriented toward the other social subsystems. Integration is mediated by the fact that all subsystems are an inner-societal environment for each other, and have to prevent their operations from producing insoluble problems in other subsystems. Hence, integration is based on the prevention of the intersystem consequences of subsystemic actions. All subsystems should, of course, also know and respect the functional specialization of every other subsystem; they should respect each other's boundaries. Furthermore, to the extent that integration is based on cognitive rather than normative mechanisms, those subsystems of society that are primarily based on cognitive processes, such as science and economy, will have better chances of development.

What, according to Luhmann (1977), is the further impact of this evolution on religion (246–48)? First of all, religion is only a subsystem of society, and it can neither block nor change the evolution of society. It is also clear that, contrary to what Durkheim thought, religion will no longer integrate society, nor will it express societal integration. However, being an autonomous subsystem of society, religion has the possibility of formulating its own original responses to this new situation. But, to the extent that society is secularized, it forces religion to focus on its primary function. Consequently, it must now be possible to find answers to religious questions uncontaminated by secondary considerations stemming from the economy, the polity, the family, or science. But it is not self-evident that in society these solutions to the problems will be accepted. It is even possible for people to deny religion entirely without losing credit in other subsystems.

Luhmann's system approach also throws new light on the civil religion debate (Dobbelaere, 1981: 41–49), and may possibly explain the precarious construction of civil religion in a functionally differentiated society (Fenn, 1978: 41–53). His approach questions Bellah's exclusively cultural analysis of the broken convenant (Bellah, 1975: 142–63), and allows a new approach to the problem of the integration of society, in contrast to Parsons's stress on a "value pattern." Parsons simply integrated Bellah's notion of civil religion into his theory without analyzing its precarious nature (Parsons, 1974: 203–9). According to Luhmann, civil religion offers on the level of the total society—

and consequently not on the level of the religious subsystem—an *implicit* consensus on basic values. It is very difficult to formulate the so-called *Grundwerte,* the value consensus, explicitly. On the one hand, each and every specification leads toward dissension; on the other hand, although it is possible to refer to them and to try to operationalize basic values in such special functional contexts as law and politics, there are, according to Luhmann, problems of "translation." For example, how can core values be operationalized in party platforms and political conduct? Concrete political programs cannot logically be inferred from such core values as freedom, solidarity, and justice. There is no way of deducing them on the basis of rational decisions (Luhmann, 1981: 303–5).

These problems of making *explicit* the core values of society and *translating* them into concrete action point to the fact that value integration is only one mechanism, and in our differentiated society a minor mechanism, for the integration of society. To speak in Durkheimian terms: Modern societies are now integrated; they are not cohesive (Wilson, 1981: 358–59; Fenn, 1982: 17). In more "traditional" societies, cohesion was achieved through a collective consciousness that provided a powerful source of feelings of solidarity or shared moral obligation (Durkheim, 1960: 99–100). In "modern" societies, integration is mediated by the fact that all subsystems form an inner-societal environment for each other. They should know and respect the functional specialization of every subsystem; they should respect each other's boundaries and prevent their own operations from causing insoluble problems in other subsystems (Luhmann, 1977: 242–46).

Consequently, one can question the importance of the study of meaning systems for the integration of society. They are important, however, for the motivation of individuals who "man" society. Taking up roles not only implies knowledge and skills, but also motivation. And Wilson (1982) has pointed out in several studies that, on the societal level, there are signs of breakdown (pretext, absenteeism, nepotism, corruption, vandalism, hooliganism, and violence) manifesting a lack of public responsibility, civic virtue, commitment, trust, mutuality, and goodwill, and signs that the traditional agencies invoking these virtues, such as religion and education, are becoming weaker and weaker (Wilson, 1982: 50–52, 176–78). But, to understand the development of our modern societies, it seems to me that we should look toward those subsystems based primarily on cognitive processes, such as science and economy, and see if we are heading toward new types of differentiation. Such studies could better help us to evaluate the prospects of a resacralization of modern societies. On the other hand, we should also study, as Wuthow did, the ongoing experiments, and look for attempts to either halt or reverse the process of functional differentiation. Such studies could reveal to us new *structural* devices that are being developed to diminish the felt negative impact of functional differentiation on interpersonal relationships and culture. These studies might also inform us about the prospects of religion in the near or more distant future. But again, we should try to study the prospect of such experiments on the restructuring of those institutions that mold our societies most forcefully: the economy, science, and so forth. Hitherto, too many studies in the sociology of religion have been interested in meaning systems. It is my contention that the study of structural changes is more important and is in closer alignment with the great sociological traditions.

References

Bellah, R. N. 1975. *The Broken Covenant: American Civil Religion in Time of Trial*. New York: Seabury.

Billiet, J., and K. Dobbelaere. 1985. "Vers une désinstitutionalisation du pilier chrétien?" In *La Belgique et ses Dieux: Eglises, mouvements religieux et laiques*. edited by L. Voyé et al., 119–52. Louvain-la-Neuve: Cabay.

Billiet, J., and L. Huyse. 1984. "Verzorgingsstaat en verzuiling: een dubbelzinnige relatie." *Tijdschrift voor Sociologie*. 1–2 (5): 129–51.

Bromley, D. G., and A. Shupe, eds. 1984. *New Christian Politics*. Macon, GA.: Mercer University Press.

Dahl, R. A. 1957. "The Concept of Power." *Behavioral Science*. 3 (2): 201–15.

Dobbelaere K. 1979. "Professionalization and Secularization in the Belgian Catholic Pillar." *Japanese Journal of Religious Studies*. 6: 55–61.

———. 1981. *Secularization: A Multi-Dimensional Concept*. Current Sociology Series, 29. Beverly Hills, CA: Sage Publications.

———. 1982a. "Contradictions Between Expressive and Strategic Language in Policy Documents of Catholic Hospitals and Welfare Organizations: Trials Instead of Liturgies as Means of Social Control." *The Annual Review of the Social Sciences of Religion*. 6: 107–31.

———. 1982b. "De katholieke zuil nu: Desintegratie en integratie." *Belgisch Tijdschrift voor Nieuwste Geschiedenis*. 13: 119–60.

———. 1984. "Secularization Theories and Sociological Paradigms: Convergences and Divergences." *Social Compass*. 2–3 (31): 199–219.

———. 1985a. "La dominante Catholique." In *La Belgique et ses Dieux: Eglises, mouvements religieux et laiques*. edited by L. Voyé et al., 193–220. Louvain-la-Neuve: Cabay.

———. 1985b. "Secularization Theories and Sociological Paradigms: A Reformulation of the Private-Public Dichotomy and the Problems of Societal Integration." *Sociological Analysis*. 46: 377–87.

Dobbelaere, K. and J. Billiet. 1983. "Les changements internes du pilier Catholique en Flandre: D'un Catholicisme d'Eglise à une Chrétienté Socio-culturelle." *Recherches Sociologiques* 2(14): 141–84.

Durkheim, E. 1960. *De la division du travial social*. Paris: Presses Universitaires de France.

Fenn, R. 1978. *Toward A Theory of Secularization*. Storrs, CT.: Society for the Scientific Study of Religion Monograph Series,.

————. 1982. *Liturgies and Trials: The Secularization of Religious Language.* Oxford: Basil Blackwell.

Gallup, George, Jr. "Fifty Years of Gallup Surveys on Religion." *The Gallup Report.* 236 (May).

Hadden, J. K. 1985. "Religious Broadcasting and the Mobilization of the New Christian Right." Presidential Address delivered to the Society for the Scientific Study of Religion, 26 October, Savannah, Georgia.

Hadden, J. K., and A. Shupe. 1985. Introduction. In *Prophetic Religions and Politics.* edited by J. H. Hadden and A. Shupe. New York: Paragon House.

Hadden, J. K., and C. E. Swann. 1981. *Prime Time Preachers: The Rising Power of Evangelism.* Reading, MA: Addison-Wesley.

Harper, C. L., and K. Leicht. 1984. "Explaining the New Religious Right: Status Politics and Beyond." In *New Christian Politics.* edited by D. G. Bromley and A. Shupe, 101–10. Macon, GA: Mercer University Press.

Harsanyi, J. C. 1962. "Measurement of Social Powers, Opportunity Costs, and the Theory of Two-Persons Bargaining Games." *Behavioral Sciences.* 1(7): 67–80.

Heinz, D. 1983. "The Struggle to Define America." In *The New Christian Right.* edited by R. C. Liebman and R. Wuthnow, 133–48. New York: Aldine.

Liebman, R. C. 1983. "Mobilizing the Moral Majority." In *The New Christian Right,* edited by R. C. Liebman and R. Wuthnow, 49–73. New York: Aldine.

Liebman, R. C., and R. Wuthnow, eds. 1983. *The New Christian Right: Mobilization and Legitimation.* New York: Aldine.

Luckmann, T. 1967. *The Invisible Religion: The Problem of Religion in Modern Society.* New York: Macmillan.

————. 1975. "On the Rationality of Institutions in Modern Life." *Archives européennes de sociologie.* 1(16): 1–15.

Luhmann, N. 1977. *Funktion der Religion.* Frankfurt am Main: Suhrkamp Verlag.

————. 1981. "Grundwerte als Zivilreligion." In *Soziologische Aufklärung 3: Soziales System, Gesellschaft, Organisation.* edited by N. Luhmann. Opladen: Westdeutscher Verlag.

Martin, D. 1978. *A General Theory of Secularization.* Oxford: Blackwell.

Marty, M. E. 1985. "Transpositions: American Religion in the 1980s." *The Annals of the American Academy of Political and Social Science.* 480: 11–23.

Parsons, T. 1974. "Religion in Postindustrial America: The Problems of Secularization." *Social Research.* 2(41): 193–225.

Rokkan, S. 1977. "Towards a Generalized Concept of Verzuiling: A Preliminary Note." *Political Studies.* 4: 563–570.

Shupe, A., and W. Stacey. 1983. "The Moral Majority Constituency." In *The New Christian Right.* edited by R. C. Liebman and R. Wuthnow, 103–16. New York: Aldine.

Simpson, J. H. 1983. "Moral Issues and Status Politics." In *The New Christian Right.* edited by R. C. Liebman and R. Wuthnow, 187–205. New York: Aldine.

Stoetzel, J. 1983. *Les Valeurs du Temps Présént: Une Enquête Européene.* Paris: Presses Universitaires de France.

Thurlings, J. M. G. 1978. *De wankele zuil. Nederlandse katholieken tussen assimilatie en pluralisme.* Deventer: Van Loghum Slaterus.

Van de Velde, V. 1985. "Zuilstructurele determinanten van de politieke besluitvorming in een locale samenleving: Een case study in Kontich." Licentiate thesis, K. U. Leuven, Department of Sociology.

Van Heek, F. 1973. *Van hoogkapitalisme naar verzorgingsstaat. Een halve eeuw sociale verandering, 1920–1970.* Meppel: Boom.

Voyé, L. 1979. "De l'adhésion ecclésiale au catholicisme socio-culturel en Wallonie." *Religion et Politique.* (Actes 15 ème Conférence Internationale de Sociologie des Religions): 293–321.

Wilson, B. 1969. *Religion in Secular Society: A Sociological Comment.* Baltimore, MD: Penguin Books.

———. 1981. "Morality and The Modern Social System." *Acts 16th International Conference for the Sociology of Religion: Religion, Values, and Daily Life.* (Paris): 239–360.

———. 1982. *Religion in Sociological Perspective.* Oxford: Oxford University Press.

Wuthnow, R. 1976. *The Consciousness Reformation.* Berkeley and Los Angeles: University of California Press.

———. 1983. "The Political Rebirth of American Evangelicals." In *The New Christian Right.* edited by R. C. Liebman and R. Wuthnow, 167–85. New York: Aldine.

Yinger, J. M., and S. J. Cutler 1984. "The Moral Majority Viewed Sociologically." In *New Christian Politics.* Edited by D. G. Bromley and A. Shupe, 69–90. Macon, GA: Mercer University Press.

3

A Dialectical Conception of Religion and Religious Movements in Modern Society

William M. Wentworth

Secularization: Society Against Religion?

THE SECULARIZATION THESIS states that religion and the world were once one. Since that mythical time, the two have been divided by powerful social forces; in our hearts and in our minds, Creation now pales before human creation. Religion and modernity are in basic contradiction, and the result can only drive religion into oblivion. With an occasional regret, we are all to become technicians, scientists, and bureaucrats: "Specialists without vision, sensualists without heart; this nullity imagines that it has attained a level of civilization never before achieved" (Weber, 1930: 182).

The personal significance of this great divorce between worldly and religious interests is the loss of a conduit to things ultimate. For society, it means the loss of a source of irreproachable legitimacy, the draining of a unifying Meaning from the world. The secularization hypothesis has seemed accurate to many, from frontline Protestant preachers to the most abstract theologians and theorists.

Despite the embattled tradition and the "official wisdom" of the secularization thesis, religion has refused all invitations to its demise. Religious denominations might decline (e.g., Dutch Catholicism), but others rise up (e.g., the
United States Southern Baptist Convention, the Mormons). Where church
membership in conventional religions is "low" for various demographic,
political, and historical reasons, unconventional religious beliefs and cults
seem to abound (Bainbridge and Stark, 1980, 1981; Stark and Bainbridge,
1985).

Religious change and change in the place of religions in society, far from
signaling the demise of "religion," encourage a variety of religious persuasions
to sprout and flourish, each appealing to a different segment of society. But
because "my" religion is always better than "yours," and "old" religion is
almost always better than "new," changes are often seen as the moral decay of
secularization by pundits, theologians, social scientists, and preachers. Indeed,
their voices sometimes make apparent many ideological tensions that would
otherwise remain privatized, unseen social facts of life. As Mary Douglas
(1982) put it: "The privilege of modernization is for a culture to view itself
from the meta-level" (18). Notwithstanding this "privilege," there is no implication of greater objective understanding.

In terms of the conceptual scale of events, and because secularization was
long depicted as a blanket fact of modern society, its study has paralleled that
of the emerging nation-state. The relations of church and state and the rise or
decline of certain conventional institutions of religion tell but a partial and
distracting story of religion in the world. For example, in European studies,
we might be asked to witness the current dissolution of church-state relations
whose basic format was established near the time of the fall of the Roman
Empire. Is this secularization, or an example of remarkable institutional tenac-
ity finally worn down by relations in industrial democracies? In United States
studies, we see membership demographics shifting to favor more evangelical
churches and the (now waning) political turbulence of the so-called New
Christian Right. Is either of these an example of resacralization, or are they
symptoms of more complex structural phenomena that happen at this
moment in history to involve a halo of "religious" language and issues?

We are hardly prepared empirically to answer these questions in a definite
way because our global sensitivities and our measures of religiosity are so
firmly tied to a mainline base of aggregate data on individuals.[1] Although this
mold has been broken by a number of researchers (e.g., Stark and Bainbridge,
1985), whether it is New Age or age-old paganisms, one senses an enormous
underground religious economy whose productions are scarcely counted in
our statistical surveys.

The current strength of religion has been called a paradox by those who
cannot force themselves to reevaluate the secularization hypothesis, while
Andrew Greeley (1972) has called the secularization thesis a myth. Contrary
to both these contentions, apparently the sacred and the secular can coexist in

mutual good health. This has certainly been the case in America. Ladd (1986), relying on Martin Marty, has said in this regard:

> My argument is that America is today what it has always been: a highly religious, intensely secular society. . . . Martin Marty has suggested (correctly, I believe) that the kaleidoscopic shifts in religious belief and institutional experience in the United States during the past several decades have occurred "within the borders of an 'all pervasive religiousness' and a concurrent and 'persistent secularity.' " (Ladd, 1986: 23)

And while the United States may have a unique structural configuration, the basic structural processes that allow for mutuality are not unique.

Modern secularity is a fact. The character of the process behind this fact has yet to be portrayed in a theoretically appropriate manner. However biased or simplistic, the secularization hypothesis offers a better description of certain intrinsic developments of "modernizing" society than the opposite contention starting to form in some quarters (cf. Caplow et al., 1983; Douglas, 1982; Greeley, 1972; Hadden, 1986). After all, the notion of modern secularity directs us to the undeniable emergence of totally secular economic, scientific, and educational institutions, vastly secularized Western governments, mass media, and various atheisms (including communism).

Since there are shortcomings in the old view of secularization, it is fortunate that the pieces of a new viewpoint are starting to fall into place (cf. Chirot, 1985; Dobbelaere, 1981, 1985; Fenn, 1978; Habermas, 1979; Martin, 1978; Seidler, 1986; Wilson, 1982). Taking these studies synthetically, we may postulate that our reconceptualization of secularization should be multidimensional and absolutely value neutral. "Modern society" should be understood as multilevel, differentiated, "societalized" (Wilson, 1982), and as allowing for degrees of structural autonomy among its constituent elements. Societal relations among constituent components, furthermore, should be seen as dialectical. Societal relations wax and wane in their complementarity such that, provoked by structural changes, occasional periods of noticeable cultural readjustment are required to sustain a general sense of order, meaning, legitimacy, and community.

Any useful study of secularization must start with some assumptions about the sources and location of religion in modern society. It must also address the social processes that put the *experiential* part of religion at risk (not only established religious institutions and organizations) *and* those processes that expand opportunity for religious experience. My contention is that no theoretical matrix currently exists to order adequately the complex facts of actual secularization. The goal of this paper is to sketch an outline of religion, society, and secularization that is less troubled by the biases of past inquiries.

In what follows, three of Durkheim's (1965) insights will form a broad matrix for the aspects of my argument pertaining directly to religion: (1)

religion in whatever form is important for any society, (2) the relations among societal institutions and the individual are agencies of value production, and (3) religious belief has society as its object.

Religion. Religion is a communal and affilative phenomenon. In this micro-level social context, religion encourages and lends shape to a panoply of individually varying "human needs." Whether these needs are for emotional arousal, affiliation, "Truth" (and hence, certainty and permanence), or power and purpose, they find room for their satisfaction within a religious community. Whenever religion occurs, it is collectively self-contained, legitimately experiential and, by degree, charismatic and mystical. By this phrasing, I wish to emphasize two ideas. One is that the religious motive, if not universal, is nonetheless a fundamental aspect of communal construction. The second is that religion—here I mean *the religious experience*—is a derivative of the communal level of societal structure.

Intending no pejorative interpretation, religion is not very civilized, that is, not "civilized" in its typical usage as a referent for modern, large-scale, deper-sonalized, and functionally rational organizational linkages. Civilization may contain and channel religion by theology, bureaucracy, law, and liturgical form, but such an architecture only administers some contexts of religion. Church and state influence the religious market, but they neither create nor subsume it.

Society. Modern society is not an organic whole like some biological system. It is, rather, a composition of sometimes cooperating, sometimes competing, and sometimes conflicting constituents held together by an integument of accountability (agencies, commerce, and laws) and by representations of the collective. The latter, a symbology of the whole, when felt strongly blurs actual structural cleavages with feelings of unity such as loyalty and patriotism. Structural cleavages remain, however, and create a constant antinomic tension that fluctuates in relation to the salience of "unity" among members.

For present conceptual purposes, the constituents of society may be divided into those belonging to the public sphere and those belonging to the private sphere. The public sphere contains macrosociological elements organized in relation to principles of functional rationality. Public institutions belong to and act as the principals of society-as-a-whole. The private sphere exists interstitially, as it were. It contains microsociological, communal, and inter-personal relations.

As a matter of intellectual presumption, the public sphere has been the theoretical shibboleth for "Modern Society"—a fallacious synecdoche. The private sphere, by contrast, has remained in the shadow of the grand sociologi-cal tradition: accepting the notion of the total transition of social life from *Gemeinschaft* (private) to *Gesellschaft* (public). In this scheme, secularization was *Gesellschaft* rationality dissolving the custom and sentiment of religion.

The problem with this model is that the community did not *transform* to society. Rather, the public sphere grew alongside the private and penetrated it. By degree, communities came to be placed in the context of and connected by an integument of *Gesellschaft* relations. Habermas (1979) calls this process the "colonization of the life-world." But the process is not so one-sided. Each part retains a *relative* structural autonomy, and each acts dialectically to delimit the other. The dialectic occurs among institutions and organizations acting (insofar as they have the power) to insure their own interests. But the values, norms, and interests of the public and private spheres are also directly juxtaposed by the daily, massive migration of members across these sociological borders.

The dialectic of structural relations creates the grounds for what members understand about their everyday lives, that is, their common sense. Some of the major producers of components for the commonsense market are public religion (church), state, economy, school, and various communal associations, including folk religions.

The sources of common sense purposefully or coincidentally compete with each other for their part in shaping the symbology of reality. But all realities are not similar in their appeal for sovereignty, their claim to pervasive validity, or their power to create a desired effect in the world. The dialectics of society that create history produce shifts in the relative contribution of the sources of common sense.

Changes in commonsense knowledge, thus, are founded on shifts in the operative sovereignty of their structural source. The outcome of the competition is in the images, metaphors, and language members use to understand their very lives. Weber (1958) describes the relationship between ideas and interests with a cogent metaphor: "Not ideas, but material and ideal interests, directly govern men's conduct. Yet very frequently the 'world images' that have been created by 'ideas' have, like switchmen, determined the tracks along which action has been pushed by the dynamic of interest" (280). Market share in the symbology of common sense can act as a valuable resource in furthering the interests of a group by creating alternative realities (Heinz, 1983).

Change may well be a ubiquitous feature of modern society. However, change is not always passively accepted by individuals. Common sense is biographically stabilized and is perceived from that perspective. Against the standard of individual biography, change that appears by speed or direction to threaten collective interests may be counteracted by a mobilization of protective resources (either conservative or progressive). When this occurs, the result may be the reorganization of the societal dialectic, the course of change, and the balance of sacred and secular, private and public, components to common sense (Mauss, 1975). There is, then, a "normal" ebb and flow in the production of ever-modified commonsense knowledge. To be winning the competition for common sense at one point in history is far from deciding the balance at the next moment.

Secularization. Secularization is the peculiar creature of modern society because of the latter's juxtaposition of the communal and the societal, the penetration of community by society, the dialectic of its many constituents, and the dynamic pace of its change. As implied by our discussion of the dialectics of common sense, secularization is far from an irreversible process. This is not to deny the fact that religious knowledge undergoes historical change to keep "society as its object."

Secularization is change perceived as problematic for the religious components of common sense, against a background of biographically stabilized knowledge. Mere accommodation to the world is not, then, necessarily enough to be perceived as the social problem of secularization. Indeed, theological accommodation may occur as acts of *sacred incorporation.* By insight and reason, adherents to a creed may reinterpret their traditions to incorporate new secular elements of the world: Godless capitalism with its poverty amidst plenty is new, but economy is old and part of scripture; the nation-state is new, but Caesar is not, and so forth.

Specific practices that belong only to recent times (widespread pornography, birth control and abortion, or the banning of school prayer) become religious issues when they threaten the religious monopoly of moral authority over communal groups in everyday life. These too, receive their scriptural sanctions by way of accommodative interpretation. And so, various modernisms, attitudes toward the world, and even modern rationality itself may become a part of a religious interpretive scheme—by either nihilation or incorporation. Secularization is not nearly the threat to religion that would be posed by irrelevance in the dialectics of society.

Let me give several general examples of secularization that are fairly inclusive of the species, if not exhaustive. First, when a religious organization is seen by its membership as having gone too far in its attempts at incorporation, such efforts become understood as *problematic accommodation* that cannot be grasped as religious Truth. Such feelings were aroused when the Roman Catholic Church began using the vernacular as the language of the Mass and when the Episcopal Church accepted the latest revision in its Book of Common Prayer. If divine inspiration is claimed in such cases, as with the Mormon switch from polygamy, fears of profanation may thus be allayed.

Second, when there is an outside threat to the sovereignty of religious knowledge because secular knowledge is produced more rapidly than it can be legitimately accommodated by sacred incorporation, the balance of common sense shifts accordingly (e.g., the various modernisms of the nineteenth century: liberalism, pragmatism, "higher criticism" of the Bible, the organized atheism of the 1890s, Darwin's evolutionary theory, and the peculiar cocksureness of nineteenth-century science).

Third, as the religious and secular institutions of the public sphere have grown more societalized, their functional knowledge recedes from that of the private sphere, at first causing sharp challenges to common sense and then irregularities in the distribution of common sense. This effect began with the disruptions of the industrial revolution and continues through such means as the loss of truly local economies (conversely, growing economic interdependencies) and the state's expanding sphere of moral concerns. Regarding the latter, a concomitant concentration of sovereignty in the state increases the immediacy of the challenge to communal sentiments. In essence, "legitimate" alternatives are forced upon communities through the twin channels of enormous growth in government employment and the spectacular increase in service agencies (cf. Caplow et al., 1982: 26ff.). These agencies' purpose is to standardize the rights, opportunities, protections, and benefits of all citizens despite diversity of communal traditions. However, what is newly installed justice for some appears to others as amoral intrusion and threat: a damnable evenhandedness that brings with it busing, legal abortion, First Amendment rights to pornographers, and a host of other ties to a hyperexpanded common good.

The structural emergence of the public sphere and its subsequent sharp differentiation (a process at the very heart of the modern composition of society) have become interpreted by a theological tradition as a sign of secularized society. This ongoing critique—a virtual theological staple—and any subsequent political action help to defend the sovereignty of an endangered communal boundary for those protestant traditions first formed in response to modernization, urbanization, and industrialization. Such religions have reacted to the depersonalization of knowledge as the community is penetrated by society.

Biography as a Gauge of Change. Society is not an organic whole, yet we may perceive it as a unity via the representations of the collective carried in common sense. Two things are crucial to common sense from the interpretive perspective of a member: (1) Is it currently adequate for the understanding of everyday life? (2) Do its categories allow for the presumption of societal unity and cohesion? When these conditions hold, members have the advantage of conventional or folk wisdom.

New structural contradictions (e.g., democratic pluralism recently societalized by the growth of the state) give rise to patterns of events that are implausibly dealt with by the prevailing distribution of common sense. If structural changes occur such that both of the conditions of common sense are violated in (at least) some segment of society, an anomic crisis ensues that affects a grouping from the individual up. Society seems to be falling apart (cf. Fenn, 1978). Such crises take generational time to mount and to be resolved (McLoughlin, 1978). In relation to recognizing these changes as patterns, private unease is raised to the level of public debate (McLoughlin, 1978: 12–13; Mauss, 1975).

Although the usage of "secularization" has been cemented to historical time, I have tried to make it relative to biographical, generational time. Using biography as a gauge, an anomic crisis is a "rapid" and pervasive threat to the very fabric of common sense. Responses are evoked from both secular and religious sources. The crisis at hand heightens levels of dialectical competition, because considerable energies become directed toward redefining society (cf. Kuhn, 1970: chap. 8). As the crisis mounts, therefore, the three types of secularization become more apparent when segments of society rush headlong to produce and monopolize new symbols of legitimate social coherence (Heinz, 1983). Nothing less than the "conventional wisdom" is at stake.

Let us now examine the sociological characteristics of these crises.

Change, Common Sense, and Religion in Normal and Revolutionary Society

Overview. History brings about new competitive relations among segments of society and carries the whole toward unforeseen structural consequences.[2] In *normal* times, the organizations of the public sphere—because they *are* organized—carry much of the burden of these competitive dialectics. Alone, or by coalition, they seek to further their competitive advantages in what are mere boundary adjustments over established territory. After all, many churches in making peace with modernity have become virtually established. Church, state, and economy exist in relative complementarity with a few merely policy-level differences. Whatever the competitive hustle within society, the margins hold.

Despite the surface normality, structural changes can be stirring with significance beyond the immediate personal awareness or relevance to biographically stabilized common sense. To give some examples of such change, we have witnessed in the United States: (a) rapid suburbanization, (b) the rise of the middle class and new population segments moving into it, (c) the fall of the underclass with all its (especially urban) consequences, (d) the industrialization of the South with its attendant increase in affluence, (e) population shifts by migration and natural increase, (f) shifts in the locus of employment from industry to services, and (g) legal enfranchisement and other operative additions to pluralism. Such changes amount to shifts in the available resources for competition, thus allowing the introduction of new competitors or new advantages into the competitive market.

The utilization of massive new resources disturbs the everyday grounds of common sense. Existing rules lose their legitimacy, social control weakens, and the old matrix of rules, roles, and resources is overpowered by circumstance. The anomic crisis of *revolutionary* society is at hand. Eventually, major social movements arise to add their participation to the historical dialectic of competition. "Everyman" is affected in manners, fashion, opportunities, and beliefs—or so it feels at the time. The margins cannot be made to hold. And all along, the relative competitive advantages of the segments change.

Let me summarize. Change in societal relations leads to unaccounted structural contradictions. Contradictions lead to threatening shifts in the field of competition that resolve into specific public issues. Once made public, threats to the everyday logic of common sense force accommodative changes.[3] Accommodations appear at the structural level, the common sense level (the creation of a social "theodicy" that blurs structural differences), or on both levels. Accommodated positions form the grounds for a new period of normal society.

"Normal" Society Described. Normal society describes a period in which issues are well defined by established symbologies. Competition among the hundreds of components in a modern society may be generally cooperative, or competition may have escalated locally to conflict; one side may gain advantage or relations may be more stable. In any case, the issues at hand are parochial, and the rules for competition, while perhaps occasionally strained, are still forceful and clear. Concerning the progress of secularity (or of sacralization), what outcomes can be expected within the modern normative framework?

In the short term, for example, the accumulated effects of economic structural change or rapid growth in the administrative capacity of the state make it appear that the competition is to be won by the forces of secularity. Up to a point, these changes appear legitimate in their own right and, in any case, difficult to resist or to know that they *ought* to be resisted. The benefits of employment, of economic diversity, and the general sense of well-being evoked by a robust economy are indubitable "facts of life"—and they are powerful secular influences on common sense. The penetration of the state into society, while occurring in the name of the Common Good, is nonetheless backed by bureaucratic form, taxable affluence, and other resources for control and power. The cunning allure and day-by-day, all-consuming demands of material security easily distract one from spirituality. Law and the Common Good are manifest sources of authority, perhaps second only to religion. Still, the availability of religious language categories to everyday speech, religion's claim to absolute sovereignty, the ultimate nature of religious authority, its appeal to certain "human needs" (communal perquisites), and the cooptive power of sacred incorporation provide religion with strong resources for free competition. Encroachments by economy or state notwithstanding, religion retains a steady long-term advantage.

The very long-term advantages, however, lie with the secular components of society. They are likely both to remain secular and (perhaps imperceptibly) to gain in symbolic preponderance over traditional symbologies.[4] Unlike the revolutionary pace of eighteenth- and nineteenth-century secularity, I foresee a deliberate rate of mundane influence in the future because a far more established barrier to societalization exists in contemporary society: the structural autonomy of the private sphere. The private sphere is currently a social location of established and expanding rights, freedoms, and practices, catered to by customary expectation and enhanced by economic market power.

According to Weberian logic, the very trend of secularity, by narrowing the acceptable range of public expression, stirs countertrends. And in the relatively safe haven of the private sphere, where the appeal and authority of religion is persistent, routes to the expression of religious needs go beyond existing religious institutions. An active subterranean religious economy engenders cults, quasi-religions, and religious movements. Occasionally from this source a new religious group will rise to international significance (Mormons, Moonies). So, too, religious movements may rise to prominence and become the origin of powerful societal turbulence.

"Revolutionary" Society and Great Awakenings. Revolutionary society described. Normal society is constituted when there exists dialectical complementarity among societal components. Revolutionary society is a complex societal incoherence during which common sense itself is in grave question. The worse the incoherence, the greater the struggle for change and redefinition. The usual competitive rules are deemed temporarily irrelevant, or, in really bad times, major changes are implemented in the structure of competition.

Revolutionary society is marked by two characteristic positive activities: (a) it is a time for reassessment and reorientation; and (b) it becomes used as the reason for a sometimes painful restructuring in the outlay of societal resources. A revolutionary society is a historical moment when society turns to examine itself, then proceeds with a new "wisdom" in an altered direction. I agree with Weber's conclusions that although historical trends are powerful, they do not demonstrate an inexorable unfolding of an immanent logic. Nor are they predetermined as to duration (because they engender counterforces); furthermore, epoch-to-epoch directionality is indeterminant (Weber, 1958: 54).

Another concern related to directionality may be summed up with the word chosen by Thomas Kuhn (1970): *commensurability.* Are instances of normal society, as punctuated by revolutionary society, commensurable? Or, is there a clean break with any preceding common sense? McLoughlin (1978) would insist that a certain core of culture is carried forward across periods (e.g., xiii–xv, 96–105). I believe McLoughlin to be only partly correct. A dialectical translation occurs as culture is transmitted across periods. That is, the new framework of rules, resources, and competition acts to contextually redefine the meaning of any "received" wisdom.

Marx should be allowed an interjection here on the relation of pre- and postrevolutionary societies. With the exception of the *ideal* communist revolution, Marx (1972) conceived that at the birth of an epoch, just as it is on the verge of being something truly new, it falls back and resurrects some of the heroes and beliefs of the past (437). The revolutionary period will "burst asunder" contemporary relations that have regulated all spheres of human endeavor. Surviving pieces become woven into a new societal motif. Epochs, then, can be said to demonstrate degrees of commensurability. A period of revolutionary society and its eventual resolution into normal society mimics McLoughlin's (1978) historical account of an awakening-renewal model. And secularity as a trend, despite an awakening-renewal pulse, does not die.

At a general theoretical level, it is possible to provide some of the preconditions and the career trajectories of dialectical movements in revolutionary society.

Empirical generalizations and rules of thumb. Because common sense is biographically stabilized, some individuals with definite interests in the status quo come to define themselves by rebellion against changing conditions. These persons may resist, complain, or engage in prophetic critique. In their acts of rebellion, they seek support from others and from established bases of power. Therefore, the very salience of the state in modern consciousness will almost inevitably involve it with religion in times of massive cultural accommodation. Even if the state is initially perceived as a source of threat, it is also a concentration of real power and a potential means to contain or redirect menacing change.

Religion, among all the life-ways, may be the most fundamentally conservative concerning threats to its interests, and, hence, it is an institution with a great tendency to react. However, different religions have different tolerance for change—depending on their own interests, traditions, the segment(s) of society to which they appeal, and, of course, the salience to them of specific changes. (Cf. Hadden, 1980: 103). The likely collective responses provoked or legitimated by religion vary in their intensity according to the place of a religion in a society.

An established religion is least likely to be violent and most likely to seek various accommodative changes. Those religions whose adherents are structurally marginal or who have been pushed to the margins of society by structural change are most likely to rebel or become violent. Thus, knowing their rough structural location, we are chagrined but not surprised by the activities of Posse Comitatus or by abortion clinic bombers. Similarly, we would not be surprised to hear of Episcopal or Catholic bishops gathering in committees to write out a position paper on the same public issues that provoked violence in others.

Where power differences between competitors are overwhelming, religious groups may, in the Mertonian sense, "retreat" on a permanent course of divergence (e.g., the Amish). Otherwise, any divergence will be temporary and later be dialectically driven toward mutual accommodation. Some hypothetical rules of thumb may serve to specify the above generalizations relative to particular configurations of competition.

(1) "Rapid" change is defined relative to (probably some portion of) a sociological generation.

(2) Rapid change in competitive advantage will raise various social issues and lead to popular unrest in affected segments of a society.

(3) As a mechanism of *societal* power and order, the state will become involved in any confrontations concerning threats to sociological boundaries. In highly societalized nations, the state (in its courts, agencies, and political capacities) would probably not be allowed irrelevancy even if not compelled by law to protect the common good. To that extent, society is irrevocably secularized.

(4) Where church and state have overlapping and complementary interests (e.g., where religion is "established"), any divergencies are temporary; convergence will occur. Overall, relations will again be normalized. However, the establishment of religion, by law or by practice, will politicize religion to the degree that it is converged with the state. Whatever material strengths religion might thereby gain in law and force, a "state" religion will eventually appear profaned and its moral hold on adherents will be diminished. Such religion will either become irrelevant or be made to carry the same political burdens as the state (cf. Tocqueville, 1969: 297). Sects, cults, and associations will form to sustain "traditionalist" sentiments and perspectives, although these will slowly evolve in the changed social climate.

(5) Where a church has little societal investment, divergence will lead to retreat and secret societies or alternative subsocietal life-ways will be produced (e.g., communes).

(6) Where interests between church and state are overlapping and contradictory (e.g., where religion is unestablished), where there are large but not overwhelming imbalances of power or both, reactions to rapidly changed competitive advantage will be extreme, conflictive, and possibly violent. Social movements and organizations will be involved that act to redress power imbalances and to reestablish competitive stability.

As a result of these social movements, either convergence will occur or a more or less unintended commonsense "theodicy" will emerge from the dialectic that (at least temporarily) blurs the salience of structural contradictions. The latter outcome will appear where power imbalances and overlapping interests remain after the period of ferment.

The sociological conception of interests as defining the territory of authority is the key to applying these rules of thumb to empirical events. Such applications may include analyses of shifting class positions and other pertinent aspects of private sphere differentiation.[5]

The anatomy of revolutionary society. I would now like to suggest the anatomy of a revolutionary period. Although periods of revolutionary society are structurally caused, contradictions engender bottom-up patterns of engagement.[6] This is so because the anomic crisis characteristic of the time throws individuals back on their own biographies for interpretive schemes and (creative) recipes for action.

The private sphere and common sense are the fundamental elements of revolutionary society. Millions of individual concerns and activities outline the period from beginning to end. The organizational structure of the public sphere, however, may serve to focus and define some of the underlying discontent.[7] Organizations influence, but do not constitute or dominate, common sense; until new presumptions about Order, Meaning, and Community are reached at the bottom, they cannot be legitimately instituted at the top (cf. McLoughlin, 1978: 213).

The career of revolutionary society I outline below is a complex specification of McLoughlin's work within the context of a dialectical society and in relation to the career of a social movement. Such a model better fits the historical pattern, even as he describes it. During the course of unrest and eventual accommodation, the moment which should be noted is when religion can have its greatest influence (i.e., Phase IV).

(1) Phase I (Discontent): Change produces contradictions that in turn influence the plausibility of common sense. The "natural attitude" is difficult to sustain in the face of heretical representations of the collective. Anomic forces emerge.

(2) Phase II (The Loosening): Public issues are raised. Normal rules for competition break down and social control deteriorates. A variety of new contenders rush into the competition seeking their special interests in the chance of writing these into a revised common sense and thereby influencing the organization of rules, reasons, resources, and rituals.

The voice of religion is raised but may be either on behalf of another contender or one voice among many contenders for secular place and power. Secularity seems to be winning a permanent advantage. Contenders may appear in successive waves, in clusters, or both. Any social movements by these contenders act more to *expand* legitimacy and enfranchisement than to contract them.

(3) Phase III (Moral Exhaustion): Order, Meaning, Destiny, and a sense of Community all seem lost. The "natural attitude" is one of skepticism; there is little *esprit de corps*. Individuals begin to seek anchorage in ultimate, religious sources of authority and the discipline and certainty of authoritative life prescriptions. A variety of new religions and cults arises.

(4) Phase IV (The Tightening): "Nativistic" or "traditionalistic" sentiments arise and support conservative social movements. The competitive dialectic of these movements begins the reformation of common sense, but the elements of the conservative voice are a blend of the old ways and the new conditions realized in Phase II (new wine in old bottles!). There is a general effort to restore the presumption of Order and Meaning. Excesses of conservatism (demands for orthodoxy, even before the nature of that orthodoxy is well defined publicly) appear, just as excesses of pluralism were earlier apparent. The degrees of extremism will be determined in both cases by the balance of resources for social power, including access to the arena of public debate (the

means of symbol production). Imbalances of resource arrays are likely to bring extremism (cf. Gusfield, 1963). Thus, if one competitor rapidly expands its advantages (e.g., the state), the reaction is likely to be extreme.

Liberal religions decline; highly prescriptive religions gain.

The position of religion is changed as a result of its increased salience for subjective and intersubjective activity. Where it once may have been a voice for itself or for another special interest, it now appears as a superordinate voice of moral authority, a legitimate and uplifting or uniting representation of the collective.

The presence of religion in this role will become accommodated in the dialectic, and any excesses of orthodoxy will eventually fall before the dialectically driven convergence. This is a time of rapid, legitimate, sacred incorporation because of the pervasive salience of religious authority and the strong motivation for religious legitimation. Thus, religion becomes an atypically influential ingredient in the creation and administration of policy and as a contributor of components to common sense. Society is *briefly* sacralized in a diffuse way, but symbols of this sacralization (e.g., a special covenant) may find a variety of institutional niches and thereby society may survive beyond its temporary place in common sense.

(5) Phase V (The Redefinition of Common Sense): Once the social movements of Phase IV have begun the repositioning of segments of society, new patterns of resources, new rules, and new reasons are defined in this final phase of revolutionary society. A new "theodicy" is established that allows, in its various expressions across the diversity of differentiated society, existing contradictions to be blurred as operative sources of widespread discontent. The role of religion is "normalized" by convergence, and the pace of sacred incorporation slows; secularization continues.

The presumption of Order and Meaning, along with the sense of community, is reestablished. There is a return to "normal society" and a new conventional wisdom of commonsense understanding.

Conclusions

The concept of the *societal dialectic,* as captured metaphorically with the notion of competition, has the advantage of escaping a classical view of the simple transition of society from *Gemeinschaft* to *Gesellschaft* and all that that entails for morality and sentiment. Rationality is thus considerably more confined to the public sphere (and secularization is open to analysis as a *complex* phenomenon). The barrier to rationalization and secularization is the reservoir of communal structures and the individually stabilized common sense of the private sphere.

Across this great divide of the public and private spheres, the primary dialectic meshes and molds interests in a periodically intense pulsation of religiosity and societal sacralization. Let it be granted that however extensive the religiosity of the private sphere, the public sphere operates mostly without functional reference to, or sanction from, religion as a social institution. A "godless" and "amoral" modern economy is arguably the progenitor of massive secular influence—an influence lent legitimacy by a positivistic, humanistic materialism.

Not far behind the secularizing effect of economic structures are the administrative requirements of societalized nations. But the Western state is no simple force for secularity. Although enormously powerful and driven by bureaucratic imperatives, the state is a hodgepodge of values and impulses, a hub for the conflicting demands of the polity.

If left alone, which it rarely is, the state would no doubt tend toward totalitarian bureaucracy. Insulated but in no way isolated from the polity, the state remains an intensely moral agency, which is nevertheless swayed this way and that by its schizophrenic desires to manage impartially and to respond to public needs.

In the not-too-distant past, the state's internal tensions, while no doubt somewhat reduced, were disguised far better than they are today by what has been called a "common moral language." Accordingly, believers could be comforted against secularity in the bosom of the state. Little recognition was given to the fact that this common moral language was sustained at the expense of those who were simply left out of public discourse.

Since those good old days, the Western state has been forced to meet the challenge of a growing democratic pluralism, a veritable galloping inclusiveness. This time, left nearly alone and unprodded by focused public sentiment, the state resolved its internal schizoid tensions by treating all religious beliefs as equally important (as opposed to trivializing them, as would be expected of a fully "rational" entity) and by simultaneously privatizing religion by treatment in law (a public process mirroring what had already become sociological fact). This legal practice of a damnable evenhandedness, as I earlier phrased it, has yet to find any philosophical room for sectarian exceptionalism in the public sphere. This causes agony for those believers who look to the state to mirror and amplify their religious perspectives.

Still, following its queer ways, the state remains a strong respecter of religion, thus keeping very much open that dialectical relationship; however, it need respect no particular religious expression.

Without the comfort of a "common moral language" and the supression of pluralistic structures, the state at best *appears* to throw itself completely into the secular tide. When the threat of this additional influence toward secularity is absorbed into the biography along with the realization that the state has been further depersonalized, religious movements may seek control over the power of the state. At such a historical moment of revolutionary "awakening," the state becomes the forum for religious interests. But more action than that is possible. Indeed, if the correct judicial equation can be discovered, or if enough lawmakers can be induced to sympathy, specific religious interests can be made a part of societal practice. In the 1970s and early 1980s, the world seemed filled with the resurgence of various "traditional" cultures into the public sphere. Modernization is simply not the all-defeating demon that the old secularization hypothesis portrayed.

Secularization is no straightforward process, and the state is no mere conduit for rationality and imposed secularity. The competition for common sense, resting as it does on the interests of various societal components, produces considerable change, even in the highly traditional corridors of religion. For the purpose of clear analysis, change cannot *ipso facto* be equated with secularity. Conversely, the period of revolutionary awakening and renewal that currently seems to be upon us should not be treated myopically as a postmodern shift to a sacralizing ethos—not so long as society remains in conversation with itself.[8]

Notes

1. Such measures fail to offer any kind of historical gauge for, or comparative balance between, individual religiosity and the institutional secularity of the public sphere.
2. The useful framework outlined in this section was adapted to the whole of society from Thomas Kuhn's (1970) historical account of scientific revolutions.
3. These accommodations are "forced" at the pain of societal disintegration—an event rare in recorded history. People work hard to avoid total anomie and, indeed, the destruction of the means for survival.
4. It is impossible to imagine a permanent sacralization of capitalism or the agencies of Western democratic polities, whereas their continued reshaping of society is palpable.
5. These rules of thumb are in broad consideration of Davis, 1979; Mauss, 1975; Smelser, 1962; and Turner and Killian, 1972: 289–98.
6. In keeping with the economic metaphor used throughout, the bottom-up response could be called a demand-side action to redefine the market.
7. Organizations often long outlast the actual ferment. This is the danger of highly institutionalized means of violence. Such institutions may not know when to stop (e.g., the IRA, the *ton ton macoutes*.)
8. Neuhaus (1987) is especially sure that a postmodern, sacralized, age is dawning (cf. others mentioned in the paper who reflect the belief that secularization is dead, or maybe never happened at all).

References

Bainbridge, W. S., and Rodney Stark. 1980. "Client and Audience Cults in America." *Sociological Analysis* 41: 199–214.

———. 1981. "Suicide, Homicide, and Religion: Durkheim Reassessed." *Annual Review of the Social Sciences of Religion* 5: 33–56.

Caplow, Theodore, Howard M. Bahr, Bruce A. Chadwick, Reuben Hill, and Margaret Holmes Williamson. 1982. *Middletown Families*. Minneapolis: University of Minnesota Press.

Caplow, Theodore, Howard M. Bahr, and Bruce A. Chadwick. 1983. *All Faithful People*. Minneapolis: University of Minnesota Press.

Chirot, Daniel. 1985. "The Rise of the West." *American Sociological Review* 50: 181–95.

Davis, James Chowning. 1979. "The J-Curve of Rising and Declining Satisfactions as Causes of Revolution and Rebellion." In *Violence in America,* edited by Hugh Graham and Ted Gurr, 411–36. Beverly Hills, CA: Sage.

Dobbelaere, Karel. 1981. *Secularization: A Multidimensional Concept*. Current Sociology Series, vol. 29. Beverly Hills, CA: Sage Publications.

———. 1985. "Secularization Theories and Sociological Paradigms." *Sociological Analysis* 46: 377–87.

Douglas, Mary. 1982. "The Effects of Modernization on Religious Change." *Daedalus* (Winter): 1–19.

Durkheim, Emile. 1965. *The Elementary Forms of the Religious Life*. New York: The Free Press. (originally published, 1915)

Fenn, Richard K. 1978. *Toward a Theory of Secularization*. Storrs, CT: Society for the Scientific Study of Religion Monograph Series, no. 1.

Greeley, Andrew. 1972. *The Denominational Society*. Glenview, Il: Scott Foresman.

Gusfield, Joseph R. 1963. *Symbolic Crusade*. Urbana, IL: University of Illinois Press.

Habermas, Jurgen. 1979. "Legitimation Problems in the Modern State." In *Communications and the Evolution of Society*. Boston, MA: Beacon.

Hadden, Jeffrey K. 1980. "Religion and the Construction of Social Problems." *Sociological Analysis* 41: 99–108.

———. 1986. "Toward Desacralizing Secularization Theory." *Social Forces* 65: 587–611.

Heinz, Donald. 1983. "The Struggle to Define America." In *The New Christian Right,* edited by Robert C. Liebman and Robert Wuthnow, 133–48. New York: Aldine.

Kuhn, Thomas. 1970. *The Structure of Scientific Revolutions*. 2d ed. Chicago, IL: University of Chicago Press.

Ladd, Everett Carll. 1986. "Secular and Religious America." In *Unsecular America,* edited by Richard John Neuhaus, 14–30. Grand Rapids, MI: Eerdmans.

Martin, David. 1978. *A General Theory of Secularization*. New York: Harper and Row.

Marx, Karl. 1972. *The Marx-Engels Reader,* edited by Robert C. Tucker. New York: Norton.

Mauss, Armand. 1975. *Social Problems as Social Movements*. Philadelphia, PA: Lippencott.

McLoughlin, William G. 1978. *Revivals, Awakenings and Reform*. Chicago, IL: University of Chicago Press.

Neuhaus, Richard John. 1987. *The Catholic Moment*. New York: Harper and Row.

Seidler, John. 1986. "Contested Accommodation: The Catholic Church as a Special Case of Social Change." *Social Forces* 64: 847–74.

Smelser, Neil J. 1962. *The Theory of Collective Behavior*. New York: Free Press.

Stark, Rodney, and W. S. Bainbridge. 1985. *The Future of Religion*. Berkeley and Los
    Angeles: University of California Press.

———. 1986. *A Theory of Religion*. New York: Peter Lang.

Tocqueville, Alexis de. 1969. *Democracy in America*, edited by J. P. Mayer. Translated
    by George Lawrence. Garden City, NY: Anchor.

Turner, Ralph, and Lewis M. Killian, eds. 1972. *Collective Behavior*. 2d ed. Englewood
    Cliffs, NJ: Prentice-Hall.

Weber, Max. 1930. *The Protestant Ethic and the Spirit of Capitalism*. New York: Charles
    Scribner's Sons.

———. 1958. *From Max Weber*, edited and translated by H. H. Gerth and C. Wright
    Mills. New York: Galaxy.

Wilson, Bryan R. 1982. *Religion in Sociological Perspective*. Oxford: Oxford University
    Press.

4

A New Perspective on Religion and Secularization in the Global Context

Roland Robertson

GLOBALIZATION HAS TWO main components, which are often thought of as standing in a contradictory relationship.[1] The first consists of a tendency toward homogeneity and universalism; the second involves a thrust in the direction of heterogeneity and particularism. The former has to do with an increasing sense of the systemicity of the modern world and the wholeness of mankind, while the latter is centered upon the generalization of the value of civilizational and societal uniqueness. Modern social science echoes and reinforces this paradox, in that much of it is predicated upon the assumption of both the unity of mankind and the uniqueness of all sociocultural circumstances.[2]

The tendency toward homogeneity and universalism is captured in part by the so-called convergence thesis—namely, the argument that there is a worldwide trend in the direction of what Alex Inkeles calls a common "sociocultural system."[3] Inkeles specifies that trend in terms of increasing global homogeneity with respect to (1) modes of production and patterns of resource utilization; (2) institutional arrays and institutional forms; (3) structures of patterns of social relationships; (4) systems of popular, individual attitudes, values, and behavior; and (5) systems of political and economic control.

Inkeles emphasizes that the convergence of which he speaks has to do primarily with "certain specific qualities identified as part of the syndrome of individual modernity" and with organizational characteristics of the economic and political realms. While claiming that "as human life experience becomes

63

more alike, attitudes, values, and basic dispositions will also become alike," Inkeles maintains that such "processes are . . . subject to countervailing and contradictory trends that greatly mute the force of the tendency toward the emergence of a uniform world culture." Among the most significant of the "brakes" on the process of homogenization are, he says, "distinctive cultural traditions" and specific arrays of "historically determined institutional arrangements" deriving from the precontemporary era.

The degree to which it is fruitful to think of such factors as contradicting or inhibiting the homogenization process is an issue to which I will return shortly. A more immediately relevant matter is the problem of the degree to which we regard the processes of homogenization as deriving primarily from intrasocietal or societally bounded experiences and developments, on the one hand, or from global developments, on the other. This involves our adopting a position along a continuum which at one end stresses *ontogeny* (convergence of individual societies toward a common point) and which, at the other, emphasizes *phylogeny* (referring to the world *as a whole*, as opposed to a mere aggregation of sociocultural entities, evolving in a particular direction).

In specific reference to much of the argument about convergence, we thus have to be aware of the possibility that whatever convergence there may be results more from the constraints of the global system *as such* than from the diffusion across societal boundaries of common values and beliefs and/or the endogenous development of separate societies, or clusters of societies, toward a common point. In that connection, it has to be emphasized that the latter alternatives (diffusion versus sameness resulting from endogenous change) refer to the familiar debate concerning internalist in contrast to externalist explanations. However, the global approach—which is advocated here and involves emphasizing the phylogenous treatment of the modern world—lies "beyond" that issue.

Much evidence has recently been produced to show that during the past few centuries individual societies have become more and more constrained on an increasingly planetary scale—in their internal functioning and in their external relationships—by the autonomization of "the world." Virtually all of that substantial work has been accomplished, however, in reference to the idea of a world *economy*,[4] with a smaller amount being accomplished with respect to a world *polity*.[5] Both of these approaches have for the most part emphasized the theme of the increasing strength of the bureaucratic apparatuses of the modern state and the demise of the individual to the point of being only a "shadow" in the modern world. The general image, then, is one of an increasingly autonomous system of *interstate* and *trans-state* relations which dominate the affairs of individual societies and bifurcate the individual into a bureaucratic cog, on the one hand, and a societally residual self, on the other.

One item which is missing (and, indeed, which is explicitly disavowed in the case of the economistic approach) is regard for the ways in which *meaning* is being given, or might be given, to contemporary "globality." No way is provided for seeing any links of ongoing significance between the undoubted trend toward globality in material and political respects, on the one hand, and the idea of shared global experience (for example, the threat of the end of the human condition through nuclear annihilation or the threat of AIDS) and the rapid increase in such themes as "world theology," on the other.[6]

The issue of the meaningfulness of the experience of global interdependence facilitates consideration of the nature of the involvement of societies and individuals in the globalization process. In one sense, this matter may be looked at in terms of the *reactions* of societies and individuals to the trends toward global homogeneity and interdependence. Those trends are likely at one and the same time to exacerbate, first, concern with the *identities* of particular societies and, second, predicaments concerning the meaningfulness of individual attachment to particular societies, on the one hand, and their sense of global involvement, on the other.

With respect to both the exacerbation of concern with societal identities (synchronically in relation to other societies and diachronically in relation to the historical "mission" of the particular society) and the nature of individual attachment to one's "own" society, it would be expected that societies in the modern world would experience fundamentalist movements which make special claims to exhibit the "real" identity of the society in question and also, perhaps, the "true" meaning to be given to the entire global circumstance. Indeed, we have witnessed the proliferation of such movements across the globe in recent years—some of them being explicitly concerned not merely with the identity of the societies in which they have arisen but also with the positive and negative identities of *other* societies in the international system—indeed, with the meaning of the global condition itself. My argument is that the fundamentalist and absolutist religious (and nonreligious) movements of our time should be seen in terms of *global* developments and not simply in terms of their being reactions to particular *Gesellschaft* trends which a large number of societies have in common.[7]

The rise of fundamentalist and absolutist movements directed at the declaration of societal identity and the presentation of a kind of mythology of international relations is sociologically understandable in these terms.[8] Such understanding does not, however, exhaust the task of the social scientist, who is, as Louis Dumont has put it, "poised between a value-free science and the necessity to restore value to its proper place."[9] Dumont speaks specifically of the discipline of anthropology, but his argument surely has strong implications for social science and social theory generally. Social scientists (as modernists) have fallen victim to the Western-Christian tendency to regard values as referring to values-as-held-by-*individuals*. This leaves *societies* (and other collectivities) without values. The modern world exhibits, says Dumont, "a break-up of the value relation between element and whole," a circumstance which applies both to the relationship between individual and society and between the society and the world as a whole.

There is some similarity between Dumont's view and that of Bryan Wilson. Both see Christianity as having become entangled with secular matters, having promoted inner-worldly individualism, having encouraged artificialist conceptions of society, and having thus attenuated value (Dumont's term) or morality (Wilson's). In spite of this similarity, Dumont is much more sensitive to the *Gemeinschaft-Gesellschaft* dilemma in the entire history of the Christian West (indeed in human history as a whole) and, even more important in the present context, deeply concerned with confronting directly the relativistic implications of nostalgia for the world of closed communities.

Wilson concedes that *Gesellschaft* has brought us a number of benefits—such as the rule of law and the principles of abstract justice—but he offers only a sense of resignation concerning the seeming impossibility of overcoming the cleavage between the allegedly desirable state of *Gemeinschaft* and those benefits of *Gesellschaft* that we should not relinquish. Dumont, however, has warned us severely on more than one occasion of the totalitarian and/or racist form which conscious programs for restoring *Gemeinschaft* relative to modern individualism are almost bound to take.[10] The search for absolute values is, then, not an attractive strategy in the modern world—neither with respect to locally bound societies or communities binding themselves to such nor to the globe as a whole. How then can we, to use Dumont's phrase again, restore value to its "proper place"?

Returning to Wilson's argument, we see in fact that it is not any *particular* set of substantive values that he advocates. Rather, the consequences of the substantive-value aspect of communal life (which he regards as lost to the West and now to be found only in a few Eastern contexts, notably Japan) constitute his major interest. Specifically, Wilson's concern about the decline of value rationality appears to inhere in the claim that such a trend brings in its train a severe attenuation of the principles of civility, piety, trust, love, and so on.

This is a problematic argument. For a start, it takes little effort to show that the modern concern with what have been called the *secondary* virtues arose precisely in order to meet the challenge of the decline and/or to *promote* the decline of values seen to be external to the individual.[11] This is, indeed, one of the critical points where the question of the relevance of religion to "the crisis of modernity" becomes acute. For if one maintains that the secondary virtues are inextricably tied to the primary virtues (value rationality) and that those virtues have invariably taken a religious form then, clearly, secularization will bring with it a decline of the secondary virtues. In *those* terms, religion in the conventional sense is a desideratum of a society which operates on more than purely instrumentally rational principles; for without religion there can be no value rationality and thus no morality (in the sense of the secondary virtues).[12]

Toward the end of his life, Emile Durkheim became increasingly interested in what might be called extrasocietal matters. This interest, I believe, followed closely upon his older interest in the themes of the cult of the individual and humanity. In any case, Durkheim did not merely speak in *The Elementary Forms of Religious Life* about the emergence of "an international life," we know that it was his intention to follow his comments in that respect with a book on a new moral universalism.[13] I take from Durkheim's concerns in this regard the simple idea that the problem of *Gesellschaft* has to be comprehended in a global context as opposed to at the level of the national society.

The idea that there are concerns of modern humanity that lie clearly beyond the community or society raises a crucial question. Is religion as conventionally understood being transformed or superseded with respect to its foci by some other form of concern, so that we should in some respects speak securely of secularization but in others of the crystallization and generalization of "ultimate concerns"—concerns centered upon the grounds of human existence and the fundamental contingencies in terms of which individuals and societies function and interact?

I have, in the past, found it necessary to invoke rather harsh judgment upon the religion-as-ultimacy perspective.[14] However, rejection of the proposal to define religion as having to do with "ultimacy" is entirely compatible with the proposition that religion itself becomes more constrained by consciousness of and discourse about the human condition, while matters pertaining to the latter are increasingly thematized in ways which do not derive from or are not easily linked to ostensibly religious contexts. In the modern world, there is an increasing constraint upon religious movements and, indeed, religious traditions—such as Islam, Christianity, and Judaism—to justify themselves with respect to, and present themselves in terms of, criteria which are, as we might say, extrareligious—or, at the very least, transdoctrinal. Extrareligious questions of moral quality, perspectives on the nature and value of human life, the viability of communal and societal life, the relationship between humanity and nature, the needs of individuals, and so on, increasingly affect the evaluation and vicissitudes of religious doctrine and practice (as does the substantial thematization of such ideas as *world* mythology, *world* theology, and so on).

We have seen that arguments about the nature and degree of secularization can quickly involve matters relating not so much to religion per se but to the nature and viability of ways of life, morality, the quality and resilience of forms of communal and/or societal order, and so on. In a sense, then, arguments which involve bemoaning the loss of religion (in the traditional sense) in reference to the functions which religion has in the past allegedly performed are symptomatic of the very point which I have just made—namely, that issues revolving around the nature, purpose, and form of human life are basic cultural themes of the modern world. Do we, then, speak of the modern tendency to find the everyday world (which traditional religion has, for the most part, addressed) a highly problematic aspect of a *more inclusive* circumstance (what we may call the telic-existential aspects of the human condition) as "the second secularization"?[15] Do we accept the substance of that idea but call it a form of *de*secularization, since it might be argued that fundamental concern with the human condition *is* religious concern? Or do we, as a third possibility, attempt conceptually to escape the choice between the first and second alternatives and talk in terms of simultaneous processes of secularization and desecularization? Or do we, fourthly, talk simply of religious change (thus bypassing the secularization problem)? Or do we, finally, speak simply of such developments as an extension of "normal" secularization—that is, the loss of significance of religion in social life, which Wilson and others have claimed to be the pivot of the secularization process?

In the context of the overall thrust of the present argument, three of these proposals must be rejected. Specifically, I reject the desecularization, religious change, and secularization proposals. We have only to accept a modicum of Durkheim's claim that religion has to do with "the serious life" in order to indicate the liabilities of any facile form of the desecularization thesis, because it is fairly clear that thinking about life "seriously" is not on the wane. The religious-change argument—although it has its attractions—is insufficiently adventurous in the face of the momentous circumstances suggested by the idea of the differentiation of ultimate concerns from conventionally religious ones, although one would surely expect there to be conventionally religious changes *attendant upon* those circumstances. The normal-secularization contention must be rejected because it relies upon the claim that normal secularization involves a loss of social relevance of non-immediate, "higher concerns." Transparently, forms of consciousness of the kind which I have been pointing to cannot be regarded as socially insignificant, even though they may involve the transcendence of concern with societies as such in some of their modalities.

Thus we are left with the "second-secularization" and desecularization-*and*-secularization arguments. Taken together, they appear to meet certain requirements suggested by the considerations I have introduced so far.

The notion of the second secularization makes particular sense because it draws attention to the relativization of particular religious forms and of "communal" religion, which has itself been facilitated by the crystallization of consciousness of a global-human condition. It indicates both the secularization which is inevitably attendant upon our increasing consciousness of the positive and negative functions of religion, and the problem of the form a mode of discourse concerning the contemporary and future human condition may take. It also assists in our putting firmly behind us a nostalgia concerning communal religion ("absolutism on a local scale") and pushes us toward the recognition of the significance of the Durkheimian program of a mode of moral discourse which at one and the same time addresses the global circumstance and is sensitive to the theme of the uniqueness of societies (as well as of other social entities, including individuals). Whether we perceive such as a religious development in conceptual terms is not of *vast* importance. In any case, we should be extremely sensitive to the observations of those, such as Robert Jay Lifton, who have noted that there is a paucity of symbolic forms in terms of which global-human predicaments *can* be expressed. On the other hand, consciousness of those predicaments is likely, as we have seen, to *increase* fundamentalist and/or absolutist responses from within societal, continental, or civilizational contexts which interpret the global-human condition in their own particularistic terms. These are likely to be religious but not necessarily so.

In sum, there is an emerging problem of "the definition of the global-human situation." The increasing sense of shared fate in the modern world rests primarily upon *material* aspects of rapidly increasing global interdependence, and conflicts associated with the distribution of material and political power. On the other hand, notwithstanding recent developments relevant to the embryonic crystallization across national boundaries of modes of discourse concerning, in the broadest sense, the *meaning* of the modern global-human circumstance, global *consciousness* is indeed relatively unformed in comparison with mere sense-impression of material interdependence. However, in order that the global circumstance may be rendered meaningful both for purposes of analysis and for the "members" of the modern world it has to be conceived in an "orderly" manner. This does not, of course, mean that there is no possibility of dispute about conceptions of global order.[16] It is merely to say that by simply acknowledging the materiality of the globe as "a single place" and by recording the variety of mainly particularistic conceptions of the meaning of the latter, the sociologist evades the predicament Dumont has described—namely his/her being "poised between a 'value-free' science and the necessity to restore value to its proper place."

Not to provide a conception of the wholeness of the modern world results, intentionally or not, in the sociologist subscribing to the idea of individuals/societies holding values vis-à-vis the global-human circumstance but denying that there are values implicated directly in that circumstance per se. The attempts Dumont has made to map a program for the establishment of what might loosely be called a hermeneutic of the modern human condition raise a special problem with respect to the significance of religion in our time. His enterprise cannot itself be called religious. Indeed, it transcends the domain of particular religious faiths. At most, it is in this respect what Wilfred Cantwell Smith has called—in a broadly theological context—a context *for* faith. It is an aspect of what I have called, following Ernest Gellner, the second secularization—but a secularization which, in Dumont's case at least, promotes the idea that the world, the modern global-human circumstance, is rendered possible (in the neo-Kantian sense) partly in terms of a "transcendent glance." Let me quote Dumont at some length:

> Is it possible that what is true of particular entities or wholes . . . is also true of the great Whole, the universe or whole of wholes? Is it possible that the Whole in its turn needs a superior entity from which to derive its own value. . . . Clearly religions have a place here, and one could even try to deduce what the Beyond

should be like in order to be final. Then we could say not only that men feel a need
for a complement to the "empirically" given, as Durkheim supposed, but that the
need bears on an apex of valuation.[17]

Dumont attempts to clinch his point by arguing that "a transcendent glance
has been historically necessary to the understanding of the world as a
whole. . . ." The beyond is not, Dumont maintains, simply a refuge. It is "a
distant place from which . . . one looks back with detachment upon human
experience in the world; it is finally a transcendence that is posited and in
relation to which the world is situated." Thus, otherworldliness has powerful
effects on worldly life. Dumont conveys his ambivalence on one point of
significance which concerns us here—namely, when he says "religions have a
place here." That may simply mean that historically the different world religions have been differentially interested in the problems Dumont makes
explicit in "secular" terms. Or it may mean that a globewide "transcendental
reflection" would constitute the core of a global civil religion in the sense that
Durkheim approached religion at the societal level. My own preference is to
see the kind of concern with the human condition exhibited in Dumont's work
as an exemplification of what Victor Lidz has called "the building up of new
elements of secular moral doctrine."[18] Dumont can thus be seen as one of a
few who are concerned with what Lidz describes as "speculation about the
transcendent groundings of moral culture," which have, at least in the West,
become increasingly differentiated from religious doctrine and commitment.

Thus, we are faced with the fundamental problem of complexity.[19]

The complexity of the modern world, particularly since the incipient phase
of the Industrial Revolution in the late eighteenth century in the West, has
been met by a variety of attitudes, which can be clustered into four extreme
types. The *communistic* response has been to see the problem of complexity in
basically economic terms, and to consider the political transformation of
economic circumstances as the primary path to achieving a desired outcome of
radical equality. The *communalistic* response has been to regard "the problem
of the modern world" as centered upon the intrusion of individualism and
impersonality, and to see the cultivation of piety and civility as the path to the
desired outcome of communal authority. The *economistic* response has been to
regard the modern world as basically economic in character, and to consider
"undue" complexity the result of a failure to see the world "economically,"
thus advocating the removal of structural and cultural impediments to the
ideal condition of economic individualism. Finally, the *psychologistic* response
has been to emphasize that the problem of complexity is largely in the mind of
the individual and that it can be overcome by psychic adaptation, or what
Weber called hygienic utilitarianism, leading to the ideal condition of widespread psychic well-being.[20]

I argue that these ideal-sketched responses to the "big leap" in complexity
can and should be seen as attempts to grapple *fundamentalistically* with the

problems of a world in which religion, as we tend in the narrow sense to define it, no longer performs or is regarded as performing the function of binding individuals to relatively cohesive, taken-for-granted universes. They are, in a word, absolutisms. I tend to think that we should not call them religious responses in and of themselves. They may, on the other hand, be considered forms of rejection of the (modern) world in the same analytical spirit that Weber spoke of "religious rejections of the world." Moreover, they have on occasion been given straightforwardly religious expression or have been expressed in conjunction with claims concerning the extrareligious benefits of religion—the latter being true, for example, of the communalistic response with which I am particularly concerned in the present content. As far as direct religious expression of these rejections of the world is concerned, Latin American liberation theology has affinities with the communistic response; some of the more "familial" of the new religious movements are closely related to the communalistic attitude; the economistic response has been expressed religiously in militant forms of the work ethic and "money worship"; and the psychologistic response has found religious representation in the more "expressive" of the new religious movements.

There is, however, a fifth nonextreme response to the problem of complexity. It is constituted by the core of the classical-sociological tradition which first crystallized with Durkheim and Weber (and some of their contemporaries) and which was cultivated by Talcott Parsons. That response is one which I would characterize as taking complexity as a moral issue in its own right. Such an attitude is indeed the basis upon which sociology arose and which made the study of religion so central a part of classical sociology. The leading question in the overall endeavor was, in effect, that concerning how we, collectively and individually, should now live, given the assumption that religion had in the Western past both constituted a rationale with respect to what we now see secularly as complexity and functioned to restrain the "forces" which promoted complexity. Weber, in particular, showed more than anybody had before that Christianity, notably since the Reformation, had been greatly involved in the production of complexity. Nevertheless, both his and Durkheim's view was that the latter should be *faced*. Durkheim insisted early in his academic career on the social facticity and thus, for him, the *moral* significance of an increasingly complex division of labor. Durkheim's conception of organic solidarity may in that regard be seen most fruitfully as a moral response to the pessimistic implications of the emergent *fin-de-siècle* characterization of a predominantly *Gesellschaft* world. While Weber can be sociologically faulted for failing, unlike Durkheim, to explore thoroughly the problem of the normative binding of the increasingly differentiated spheres of life, he did, nonetheless, become increasingly preoccupied with the *ethical* dilemmas and options of men and women as individuals in relation to that circumstance.

In returning both to Durkheim's conceptions of a realm of modern life beyond the societal and to his conception of humanity, I note initially that these themes constitute vital ingredients of what I have been calling complexity, since they add significantly to the contingencies of the modern world. More specifically, I argue that the modern world—on a global scale—can be characterized as involving, on the one hand, a rapid shift away from the communal intimacy of earlier periods and, on the other, a rapid bringing together of that which was previously separate.[21] In the latter respect, I think of both the consciousness of the unity of mankind and the globalization of many aspects of our lives, which have been largely facilitated by, but which now speed the fading of, traditional *Gemeinschaft*. And yet, both societies and humankind as a whole clearly face the normative problems of linking the separate spheres of human life, linking individual and society, linking societies, and so on.

Undoubtedly, many of the religious tendencies which we have witnessed in recent years have crystallized in reference to such contingencies; and many of the more fundamentalist and/or absolutist of them have been guided essentially by a *Gemeinschaft* conception of religion. Thus, we can indeed follow Wilson in regarding many recent religious trends as *Gemeinschaft*-inspired responses to *Gesellschaft* trends—as communalistic responses to complexity as I have outlined that phenomenon. However, to see such responses simply as negative reactions, for the most part doomed to marginality in the face of the triumph of *Gesellschaft*, is, I believe, uninsightful. Rather, it is the way in which *Gemeinschaft* and *Gesellschaft* tendencies may be *combined* at a "level" that is "higher" than both which is the crucial modern, moral-sociological (as well, perhaps, as religious) issue.

More specifically, as I have noted, it would seem that many modern societies have recently encountered the problem of defining their identities in reference both to the global circumstance as a whole and to their internal cohesion and vitality. In other words, the pressure to *revitalize* societies has become a major feature of the modern world. If that is indeed the case, then Durkheim's argument that societies have, above all, moral-religious significance becomes particularly relevant to the *modern* (or postmodern) world. It follows also that in such a circumstance many religious movements—old and new—become implicated in revitalization phenomena precisely because of their concern with "deep-life" issues.

Thus, in an increasingly global form of life, the society as such experiences both internal and external pressures to define its "vital core," and at the same time individuals are faced with both the consciousness of their humanity and their membership in specific societies. This is a new world in which not merely does the old tendency to think of *Gemeinschaft* and *Gesellschaft* as mutually exclusive become antiquated but also one in which concern with "ultimacy" becomes increasingly conspicuous.

We do not have to define religion in reference to ultimacy to see, on the one hand, that religion in the narrow sense is encouraged by this new circumstance and, on the other, that it is highly misleading to label the new form of life as straightforwardly secular. We would expect the boundaries between the secular and the sacred to become intense (hence the proliferation of church-state tensions) once we have acknowledged that *Gesellschaft* in the conventional sense never had the dominance which many sociologists have awarded it. By that I mean to say that the very idea of *Gesellschaft*—the world of the strong state, the bureaucratic ethos, highly differentiated spheres of life, and individualism—involves the idea of a *world* of societies and individuals. The more, however, that that world becomes a "single place," the more *its* functional imperatives constrain the operation of societies. This occurs not merely in the well-documented sense that the state-centered *Gesellschaft* has itself crystallized and proliferated around the globe under the constraint of a world-systemic political culture of the modern state, but also in the even more profound sense that modern societies are increasingly under constraint to reproduce or regenerate their identities in reference to the global-human condition.

I offer a set of concluding observations. First, I think we should talk of a shift to a new, global stage in respect of the *Gemeinschaft-Gesellschaft* dilemma, in terms similar to the way in which Donald Black has talked of a *synthesis* of "the communal" and "the situational" forms of life. Black's extrapolation is that we are, as part of a global trend, on the verge of a widespread condition of low stratification, high differentiation, low organization (in the sense that individuals regard "organization" more as an external instrument and less as an encumbrance), and great cultural diversity. I suggest that Black's speculations imply a global circumstance in which *the sense of human primordiality* is promoted by distantiation from "organizational reality," on the one hand, and simultaneous "pulls" toward both the communal cores of particular societies and the communal aspects of humanity, on the other.

Second, it would seem that students of "religion" would gain more from, and contribute more to, the understanding of the modern world were they to concern themselves less directly with religion "as such" and more with the kind of phenomena to which I have been drawing attention. In particular, the issue of the constraints upon many societies to engage in processes of revitalization is one which both transcends the conventional foci of the sociology of religion and is clearly relevant to it. The increasing thematization of issues having to do with humanity, the nature and purpose of human life, and so on—the trend toward concern with "the ultimate" in global context—may be similarly regarded.

Third, it follows from much of what I have said that we should be more conscious of and, for that matter, more adventurous in respect to the hermeneutical bases of our inquiries—our starting points, *Problemstellungen,* and intentions. In that connection, I cannot see a way in which an interest in whether the world is getting more or less religious can be sociologically or, indeed, morally grounded. Whether, like Weber, we are primarily interested in clarifying how the modern world was made and the nature of modern discontents, or whether, like Durkheim, we are concerned with making the modern world possible—in the sense of facing sociologically its *complexities* and arguing for particular cognitive-moral ways of dealing with that complexity—we will not get far by starting with religion and *then* moving on to other sociocultural matters.

Benjamin Nelson cogently argued that one of the central features of Max Weber's analytical approach was its adherence to the *social*-reality principle, and he might well have said the same of Durkheim.[22] Both men, in seeking not to be, in the everyday sense, merely realistic, sought also to promote subscription to the social-reality principle in a critical phase in the history of the Western world. Theirs was a moral as much as a sociological endeavor, one which was predicated on the idea of the end of absolute values and the consequent attempt to reach for morally effective ways of living in the face of ever-increasing societal and individual complexity. I have more than hinted that they—particularly Durkheim—saw the latter in terms of a new form of global-human complexity. I have also said that Parsons was the main recent interpreter along such lines. In any case, my overall argument may be summarized in the contention that we ought now to see the new globality and its attendant human predicaments as the late–twentieth century equivalent (but, in many ways, the extension) of the passage from the pre-industrial to the industrial form of life which gave rise to the modern critical sociology of religion and of morality.

Notes

1. A number of the ideas expressed in this paper have been published previously along similar lines in two other contexts: first, in the postscript to *The Sociological Interpretation of Religion* (Tokyo: Kawashina-shoten, 1982.) (The original, English-language version was published by Oxford: Blackwell; and New York: Schocken, 1970); and, second, in a paper entitled "Religion, Global Complexity and the Human Condition," published in the *Proceedings of the Eleventh International Conference on the Unity of the Sciences* (New York: International Cultural Foundation Press, 1983). Jeffrey K. Hadden and Anson Shupe have been of great help in reshaping and shortening the latter.
2. Cf. Louis Dumont, "The Anthropological Community and Ideology." *Social Science Information* 18 (1979): 785–817. See also Roland Robertson, "Globalization Theory and Civilization Analysis," *Comparative Civilizations Review* 17 (Fall 1987): 20–30.
3. Alex Inkeles, "Convergence and Divergence in Industrial Societies," in *Directions of Change,* edited by Mustafa O. Attir et al. (Boulder, CO: Westview Press, 1981): 3–38. Cf. Rainer C. Baum, "Beyond Convergence: Toward Theoretical Relevance in Quantitative Modernization Research," *Sociological Inquiry* 44 (4) (1974): 225–40; and Rainer C. Baum, "Authority and Identity: The Case for

Evolutionary Invariance," in *Identity and Authority: Explorations in the Theory of Society,* edited by Roland Robertson and Burkart Holzner (New York: St. Martin's, 1980), 61–118.

4. See in particular Immanuel Wallerstein, *The Modern World-System* (New York: Academic Press, 1974); and Terence K. Hopkins, Immanuel Wallerstein et al., *World Systems Analysis* (Beverly Hills, CA: Sage Publications, 1982).

5. See in particular John Boli-Bennett, "Global Integration and the Universal Increase of State Dominance, 1919–1970" and John W. Meyer, "The World Polity and the Authority of the Nation-State," in *Studies of the Modern World-System,* edited by Albert Bergesen (New York: Academic Press, 1980): 77–108 and 109–38. The article by Meyer does indeed touch upon issues of world culture and consciousness, issues which are of particular concern in the present context. See Roland Robertson, "Globality, Global Culture and Images of World Order," in *Social Change and Modernization,* edited by Hans Haferkamp and Neil Smelser (Berkeley and Los Angeles: University of California Press, 1989).

6. On the idea of world theology, see Wilfred Cantwell Smith, *Towards a World Theology* (Philadelphia, PA: Westminster Press, 1981). Smith's notion of world theology as "a context for faith" may be regarded as an aspect of a possible world civil religion. For the symbolic void that exists in relation to the allegedly generalized, global fear of technologically induced annihilation, see Robert Jay Lifton, *The Broken Connection* (New York: Simon and Schuster, 1981).

7. There can be little doubt that the modern sociology of religion relies considerably on the pioneering work of Emile Durkheim and Max Weber. However, sociologists of religion have, on the whole, never come to terms with the fact that the interest of Durkheim and Weber in religion was developed in very specific reference to the problem of the viability of *Gesellschaft,* or at least the type of society that manifests strong *Gesellschaft* tendencies. Religion was a focal interest of Durkheim and Weber because they sought to understand the degree of uniqueness of this form of life, how it had emerged, and how it was possible. Moreover, the discipline of sociology itself was regarded as a product of the shift from the dominance of *Gemeinschaft* to the dominance of *Gesellschaft* (or from mechanical to organic solidarity). If we take that view seriously, then we have to acknowledge that sociology is embedded in the *Gesellschaft* circumstance and that the pursuit of the sociology of religion is—or was, at least in the minds of its modern founders— geared positively toward the primary puzzles and problems of *Gesellschaft.* What, then, are we to make of the strong tendency not merely to define religion in relation to *Gemeinschaft* and secularity in relation to *Gesellschaft* (which is not significantly at odds with the views of either Durkheim or Weber) but also to see the problems of *Gesellschaft*—the aspects of modern society which need sociological treatment—as centered specifically on its lack of *Gemeinschaft* attributes? Neither from Durkheim nor Weber can one draw such a policy for the modern sociology of religion. Both Durkheim and Weber argued that such was the nature of the modern world that nostalgia for old-style *Gemeinschaft* should be taken both as symptomatic of the ills of the modern world and as a form of misinterpretation of modern society. Moves to reestablish it as the dominant form of life were ill-advised and likely to have quite disastrous outcomes. Ironically, however, the thematization of religion in political and constitutional terms is a distinctively

modern move, involving the attempt to keep religion in its privatized place, which itself has become the locus of contemporary nostalgia for *Gemeinschaft*. See Roland Robertson, "Modernity and Religion: Towards the Comparative Genealogy of Religion in Global Perspective," *Zen Buddhism Today* 4 (1988).

8. This should be read in comparison with Bryan Wilson's claim that "a modern state does not need a creation myth of the kind ubiquitous among tribal or communal peoples.... Much less ... does a league of states ... need such a device to symbolize unity and co-ordination. The creation myth of the new state, or the new league of states, is a document with articles, clauses, and provisions that are ... amendable. As with every increase in rationality, the partners expect better to manage their incidental irrational consequence...." (Bryan Wilson, *Religion in Sociological Perspective* [New York: Oxford University Press, 1982]: 158). This argument, I suggest, flies in the face of various religiously linked movements concerned with national identities which have come into prominence in recent years. While few states may actually manifest creation myths in their constitutions, the concern with the religious identities of nations and with the religious or quasi-religious aspect of relations between nations has surely increased greatly in recent years.

9. Louis Dumont, "On Value," *Proceedings of the British Academy* (Oxford University Press, 1980): 207–41. Cf. Wilson, *Religion in Sociological Perspective*.

10. See also the sharp polemic against the contemporary wish for *Gemeinschaft* in Ernest Gellner, "Accounting for the Horror," *Times Literary Supplement,* August 6, 1982: 843–45. For a different perspective on "destructive *Gemeinschaft*," see Richard Sennett, *The Fall of Public Man* (New York: Vintage, 1978).

11. Cf. the highly provocative discussion in Alasdair MacIntyre, *After Virtue* (Notre Dame, IN: Notre Dame University Press, 1981).

12. For another viewpoint involving, as I see it, a claim as to the civil-religious significance of the secondary virtues—most notably civility—see Phillip Hammond in *Varieties of Civil Religion*, edited by Robert N. Bellah and Phillip E. Hammond (San Francisco: Harper and Row, 1980): 188–205.

13. Cf. Daniel Bell, *The Winding Passage* (Basic Books, New York, 1980): p. 327. For Durkheim's statements on what I have called extrasocietal life, see Emile Durkheim, *The Elementary Forms of the Religious Life* (New York: Collier Books, 1961), 493; and Emile Durkheim and Marcel Mauss, "Note on the Notion of Civilization," *Social Research* 38 (4) (1971): 809–913. See also Roland Robertson, "Individualism, Societalism, Worldliness, Universalism: Thematizing Theoretical Sociology of Religion," *Sociological Analysis* 38 (4) (1977): 281–308.

14. See in particular Roland Robertson, *The Sociological Interpretation of Religion* (New York: Schocken Books, 1970): 34–77.

15. I take the notion of the second secularization from Ernest Gellner, *The Legitimization of Belief* (London: Routledge, 1973). On the significance of the idea of telos in discussion of virtue and morality, see MacIntyre, *After Virtue*. Telos also figures, in a very different form, in Parsons's discussion of the human condition; see Talcott Parsons, *Action Theory and the Human Condition* (New York: Free Press, 1978). My invocation of MacIntyre's ideas is severely tempered by my view that his is basically a *Gemeinschaft* conception of morality. MacIntyre—not unlike Wilson—characterizes the modern world as "Weberian" with respect to its utilitarian individualism and bureaucratic ethos. However, unlike Weber (and, even more

clearly, unlike Durkheim), MacIntyre and Wilson do not truly morally engage with *Gesellschaft*—let alone take cognizance of the possibility of its being overtaken. Rather, they *moralize about* it.

16. See Robertson, "Globality, Global Culture and Images of World Order." See also Roland Robertson and JoAnn Chirico, "Humanity, Globalization and Worldwide Religious Resurgence: A Theoretical Exploration," *Sociological Analysis* 46 (3) (1985): 219–42.

17. Dumont, "On Value," 223.

18. Victor M. Lidz, "Secularization, Ethical Life, and Religion in Modern Societies," *Sociological Inquiry* 49 (1979): 191–217.

19. For a somewhat different approach, see Frank J. Lechner, "Modernity and its Discontents," in *Neofunctionalism*, edited by Jeffrey C. Alexander (Beverly Hills, CA: Sage, 1985), 156–76. See also Roland Robertson and Frank Lechner, "Modernization, Globalization and the Problem of Culture in World-Systems Theory," *Theory, Culture, and Society* (3) (1985) 103–18.

20. Here and in the following paragraph I draw upon François Bourricaud, *The Sociology of Talcott Parsons* (Chicago, IL: Chicago University Press, 1981), 189–203; and Talcott Parsons, "Religious and Economic Symbolism in the Western World," *Sociological Inquiry* 49 (1979): 1–48. See also Talcott Parsons, "Law as an Intellectual Stepchild," *Sociological Inquiry* 47 (2–3) (1977): 11–58.

21. Cf. Donald Black, *The Behavior of Law* (New York: Academic Press, 1976) 123–37.

22. Benjamin Nelson, "Discussion on Industrialization and Capitalism," in *Max Weber and Sociology Today,* edited by Otto Stammler (Oxford: Blackwell, 1971).

5

Toward a Theory of America: Religion and Structural Dualism

John H. Simpson

AS WE NEAR THE END of the twentieth century, it is becoming increasingly clear that secular culture in both its modernistic and Marxist forms is playing a considerably more modest role in the development and dynamics of nation-states than was once thought would inevitably occur. Indeed, the theory and establishment of popularly based national sovereignty in the post-modern period seems to require a religious or, at least, a religiously informed framework, as the cases of Iran, Libya, Nicaragua, and the Philippines suggest. Elsewhere in the world, significant separatist/nationalist movements are fueled by religious sentiments (in India, Sri Lanka, and Poland), while governments in Egypt, Malaysia, Indonesia, and Tunisia face sustained pressure from religiously based opposition groups. The Soviet invasion of Afghanistan can, at least in part, be understood as a preemptory move against a state which, if infected with the Islamic zeal of Iran, could abet insurgence among the Muslims of Soviet Central Asia. Finally, it is clearly impossible to understand the chaos in the Middle East without considering the religious factor, including the religious complexities embedded in Zionism and the foundation and development of the state of Israel.

The contribution of religion to the movement of contemporary world history is, in fact, something of an embarrassment to general sociological theory. Among sociologists who count themselves heirs of Comte and/or Durkheim, and who reluctantly or otherwise subscribe to the view that religion is a fundamental aspect of human systems of action, there can only be bewilderment that traditional religion with transcendent/supernatural refer-

78

ents continues to appeal to the masses, while humanistic religion in its various guises remains esoteric and enfeebled. On the other hand, those whose sympathies lie with the withering-away-of-religion point of view in either its Marxist or Weberian forms must be genuinely surprised that one of the most successful movements for social change in the contemporary situation is guided and justified by a liberation *theology* and that secularization in the West has created conditions that have led to an increase in cult and sect formation (Stark and Bainbridge, 1985).

One reason we are puzzled, bewildered, or simply wrong in our theoretical understanding of religion in the contemporary situation is that we have failed to understand that there is an enduring link in societies between religion, religious expression, and authoritative public action, but that it is variable in terms of its effective potency and forms at any given time. Especially in highly differentiated Western societies with great institutional autonomy, it is tempting to conclude that religion has no public face and is thoroughly and inescapably privatized. Recent events in the United States, however, suggest otherwise. What, then, encourages religious expression and participation in the contemporary public domain?

At the most general level, the answer to that question involves a specification of the ways in which power is organized and expressed and an understanding of the relationship between power and religion in societies. Since that task encompasses both a classic sociological question—what is the relationship between religion and power—and a vast amount of historical and empirical material, it is legitimate to ask: What can be accomplished within the modest confines of this paper? The answer is that this paper is an attempt to bias the contemporary discussion about religion and politics in a particular direction by proposing a simple general framework for classifying the organization of power in societies and by using that framework to examine the religion-politics nexus. While the proposed framework is explicitly comparative, I will, as the title indicates, focus in this paper on the United States as an empirical case. That choice is, in part, dictated by the current interest in religion and politics in America but, it must be emphasized, the analysis can and should be extended to other units in the world system, with somewhat different results to be expected in each case. We would then be in a position to understand the range of conditions that specify the relations between religion and politics at the nation-state level and, furthermore, would have additional insight into the contributions that religion makes to the "behavioral" propensities of nations acting in the contemporary world system.

Classifying the Organization of Systems

In the late 1960s, sociologists in America retreated from "grand theory" in favor of a number of narrower theoretical approaches, including a variety of Marxisms. However, even before the decline of the hegemony of Parsons,

Merton, et al., some theorists were making suggestions that enhanced the usefulness of systems theory as a tool for understanding societies. Ironically, some of the more notable suggestions were made by Alvin Gouldner (1959), who, later on, would eschew the reformation of functional systems theory and would devote himself to its demolition and replacement.

In his constructive analysis of functionalism, Gouldner (1959) underlines the tendency in systems theory and, especially, in Parsons's perspective, to dwell on the needs and stabilization of social systems as wholes while assuming or taking for granted the interdependence of system parts. Although Parsons recognizes the existence of system parts, he tends, as Gouldner points out, to treat both independence and interdependence (of system parts) as "constants" while emphasizing the contribution of parts to the maintenance of a system qua system and the equilibration of systems through shared value elements.

This analytic approach, as Gouldner observes, obscures the fact that the elements in a system may have little need, as well as great need, for one another, and that the mutual needs of parts (that are satisfied through reciprocal exchanges) need not be symmetrical. Because reciprocity is not symmetrical (that is some parts get better "deals" than do others) and, furthermore, because the striving of a system to satisfy its needs as a whole may impair the autonomy of its parts, tension will exist between system elements, and between parts and the system as a whole. According to Gouldner (1959), then, the organization of a system is "shaped by conflict, particularly by the tensions between centripetal and centrifugal pressure, as limiting control over parts as well as imposing it, as establishing a balance between their dependency and interdependency, and as separating as well as connecting the parts" (264).

Although the point should not be forgotten, I have not referred to Gouldner simply as a reminder that functionalism does not exclude conflict from its domain of analysis. Rather, the intent is to underscore Gouldner's point that systems should be analyzed from both the perspective of the interests and purposes of the whole—stabilization, maintenance, value consensus—and from the perspective of the interests and purposes of system parts—the striving of elements for autonomy, social desiderata, and returns in the economy of resources. At the same time, it should be pointed out that there are models other than Gouldner's for what might be called the "organizational settlement" of a system.

Gouldner assumes that there is a tendency to move through conflict toward a state of balance or equilibrium between the interests and purposes of the whole and the interests and purposes of the parts in a system. However, in some systems, the outcome of conflicts between centripetal and centrifugal forces might be best described as resulting in the periodic ascendance of either the interests and purposes of the whole or the interests and purposes of the parts, the temporary dominance of one creating the conditions for the subsequent rise of the other. In contrast to Gouldner's proposal, this model assumes that there is no equilibrium point where tensions are in balance. Neither the interests and purposes of the whole nor the interests and purposes of the parts ever gain the upper hand on a permanent basis, although one or the other dominates from time to time as the system oscillates between periods in which the interests and purposes of the whole command attention and resources and periods in which the interests and purposes of the parts are paramount.

Within the parts-wholes perspective, there are other configurations in addition to those outlined above that describe possible ways of organizing a system. Gouldner's equilibrium model and the oscillation model are dualistic in the sense that the organizational state of a system is fixed at any given time by the values of both parameters of the whole and parameters of the parts. On the other hand, in monistic systems, either parameters of the whole or parameters of the parts (but not both) determine the state of the system. Thus, collectivism exists where the interests and purposes of the whole are in continuous ascendance, and multarchy is the case where the interests and purposes of the parts are never balanced or are in serious tension with the interests and purposes of the whole because they permanently dominate action. There are, then, four possibilities in the classification scheme: balanced or oscillating dualistic systems and monistic systems that are either collectivistic or multarchic.

What is the heuristic value, if any, of this simple classification system in the context of the problematic of this paper, that is, broadening our understanding of the relationship between religion and power in societies? The claim argued below is that once a society has been classified it is possible to specify the general form of the relationship between religion and political expression and, furthermore, to gain some purchase on the understanding of stasis and change in the religion-power relationship. In what follows, then, the United States will be examined as an empirical case. The claim to be established and applied is that America is an oscillating dualistic system.

America and Structural Dualism

While the point will not be considered further here, it may be true that dualism, and especially oscillating dualism, can exist only where a polity is organized as a stable multiparty democratic system. In that case, conflict is institutionalized, and a victorious party in principle has no guaranteed long-term monopoly on the means of governance allowing it to fix the society permanently in a multarchic mode. Democracy, then, may be a necessary condition for oscillating dualism. In any case, the United States is a stable democracy, and its dualistic nature is indexed by certain shifts that have occurred from time to time in terms of the parts-wholes complex. Electoral change is a manifest indication of these shifts, but the changes to be described are not simply electoral victories. Rather what we are dealing with are emphases within the society that exist as latent possibilities and are given a manifest form by political processes.

While any electoral change has implications for shifts in policy, some elections so redefine the field of political action and symbolize such a clear break with the past that they constitute watersheds or divides marking a new direction in the exercise of power. Although they are, clearly, not the only watershed elections in American electoral history, Thomas Jefferson's presidential victory in 1800 was the first, and Ronald Reagan's successful 1980 campaign was probably the most recent, watershed election. Both elections signaled a movement away from an emphasis on the interests and purposes of the whole to the interests and purposes of the parts.

Viewed against the background of the preceding Federalist period, encompassing the presidencies of George Washington and John Adams and, in particular, the ascendance of the political theory and policies of Alexander Hamilton, the election of 1800 ensured the institutionalization of popular democracy in the life of the new American nation. Simply put, the difference before and after the 1800 election was the difference between Hamilton and Jefferson: "Hamilton wished to concentrate power: Jefferson to diffuse power" (Morison, 1965: 328).

It is difficult to decide whether Hamilton's centralizing tendencies were motivated more by his class interests or by a desire that the nation succeed and a distinct view regarding the path to success. In any event, he ensured the stability of the new government by putting it on a sound financial footing. Called upon by the House of Representatives to prepare a plan for the adequate support of public credit, Hamilton recommended that the war debts of the states be assumed by the federal government, that all federal debts be funded at par, that the price of government securities be supported, and that a Bank of the United States be established to serve the banking needs that would be created by his proposals. Revenue generated by duties and excise taxes were to pay the principal and interest on the federal debt.

Hamilton's plan was accepted and within a short period of time the credit worthiness of the United States was firmly established in the world's financial centers. "By August 1791 United States 6 per cents were selling above par in London and Amsterdam, and a wave of development and speculation had begun" (Morison, 1965: 325). Hamilton's success not only established the reputation of the fledgling nation as a responsible fiscal authority but also, as Hamilton deliberately intended, increased the "number of ligaments between the government and the interests of individuals" by linking the pecuniary fortunes of individuals and states to the federal government. In *that* regard, Hamilton provided a model for all subsequent national policies by demonstrating that the interests of individuals on which the ideological justification of the nation rested could be linked to fundamental collective needs and purposes.

There is no doubt, however, that Hamilton's definition of collective needs served the interests of "the old families, merchant-shipowners, public creditors, and financiers" who, in Hamilton's view, had to be made into a loyal governing class by a straightforward policy serving their interests. The debts of the states that Hamilton shifted to the federal government had originated during the Revolutionary War, when states issued securities to planters, farmers, soldiers, shopkeepers, and the like for services rendered or goods supplied. When hard times followed the war, the securities were sold at deeply discounted prices. "By 1789 the bulk of the public debt was in the hands of the 'right people' at Philadelphia, New York, Charleston, and Boston; and the nation was taxed to pay off at par, securities which they had purchased at a few cents on the dollar" (Morison, 1965: 326).

The price for securing the loyalty of a would-be governing class was the rising opposition of the Republicans and their champion, Thomas Jefferson, who had proclaimed that the proper role of government was the preservation of "life, liberty, and the pursuit of happiness" for all citizens. Jefferson, in fact, represented the interests of rural-agrarian America, which Hamilton's policies had discriminated against. Yet once in office, Jefferson did not destroy the structures put in place during the Federalist period. Officials, of course, were changed, but the machinery of government set up by Washington and Adams was continued. Frugality was encouraged, but the Federalist methods of financing the government's obligations remained intact.

The only Federalist creation Jefferson tried to destroy was the judiciary, which had been packed by Adams before he left office. When Jefferson's secretary of state, John Madison, refused to deliver the commission of William Marbury, a justice of the peace appointed by Adams, just before his term as president expired, Marbury sued in the Supreme Court, and Chief Justice John Marshall found in his favor, delivering at the same time his famous opinion in *Marbury v. Madison* that the Constitution is superior to Acts of Congress and must be so treated by the courts. In frustration, Jefferson tried to move against the federal judiciary by impeachment in the House of Representatives. This course of action ultimately failed when Justice Samuel Chase of the Supreme Court was found not guilty of abuse of office. The court remained intact under Marshall and proceeded to develop a "subtle (conservative) offensive of ideas—the supremacy of the nation, the rule of law, and the sanctity of property" (Morison, 1965: 363).

Given Jefferson's actions once in the presidential office, is it correct to label the election of 1800 a watershed? I think so, because although Jefferson continued to operate within the structures and means of government set up during the Federalist period, he did represent the presence in the highest office of the land of the interests of the rural-agrarian sector of the nation, which had a stake in the diffusion of power on behalf of a free rural yeomanry. At the same time, Jefferson's election institutionalized the ideology of the Declaration of Independence, which would, thereafter, be used in the struggle against centralizing tendencies. Furthermore, it is arguable that without Jeffersonian Republicanism, Jacksonian Democracy would not have been possible. Thus, when Andrew Jackson was elected president in 1826, he put into effect those principles that were firmly entrenched as part of the political culture twenty-six years earlier in the election of 1800.

One hundred and eighty years after Jefferson's election, Ronald Reagan became president of the United States. Whether Reagan's election marks the beginning of a stable new trend in American society remains to be seen, but it clearly represents, in any event, a definite break with the tradition of government inaugurated in 1933 by Franklin Delano Roosevelt. Ironically (for Roosevelt's Democratic Party was the putative heir of the Jefferson-Jackson tradition), Roosevelt institutionalized the American version of the welfare state with its centralizing tendencies although, in contrast to the centralization of the Federalist period, a national policy was pursued that favored the interests of "little persons"—labor, underindustrialized regions, white ethnics, and the economically less well-off. Without doubt, Lyndon Johnson's "Great Society" marked the apogee of the trends initiated by Roosevelt. In this regard, it should be noted that Eisenhower's two terms in the 1950s were, arguably, a period of consolidation of New Deal policies and structures rather than a radical departure from them (Simpson, 1985a).

In contrast to the situation in Hamilton's day, the web of the American political economy is now so complex that it is very difficult to disentangle its threads and see a clear, straight line from policy formation through policy implementation to known outcomes, although there are, of course, exceptions to this generalization. One such exception would appear to be the apparently unintended increase in the incidence of infant mortality in the United States after Reagan took office, an outcome that has been attributed to cutbacks in the welfare system (Miller, 1985). In any event, the rhetorical thrust of the Reagan regime clearly favors the freedom side of the equality/freedom dialectic. Thus, its wish and policy is to return power to the elements and interests in the system that think they were forgotten, inadvertently passed over, or systematically excluded from the benefits of centralizing America. At the same time, the Reagan administration was faced with the task of overseeing the recapitalization of American industry as it moved away from the age of smokestack industrialization. Whether less "big government," more local control, and the changing needs of the economy encompass a contradiction that requires more rather than less centralized action remains to be seen. In the meantime, Reagan's sociocultural *kampf* on behalf of the so-called social issues—abortion, homosexuality, school prayer, and so forth—paradoxically conjures up the specter of less rather than more freedom for the individual, although it is entirely consistent with the relocation of the focus of control away from "higher" units to "lower" units in the society.

Dualism and Religion in America

The major working hypothesis of this paper is that American society undergoes periodic alternations between an emphasis on the exercise of power on behalf of the interests and purposes of the whole and the use of power to serve the interests and purposes of the units or parts of the system. How do those alternations affect religion?

There are, of course a number of perspectives that encapsulate very general hypotheses specifying the form of the relationship between power and religion. A distinction can be drawn between those that contain the assumption that religion is, essentially, independent of the sources and forms of power, and those that assume that there is some kind of correspondence between religious forms and processes and the exercise of power. In general, sociological perspectives and theories fall into the correspondence camp, and they may be divided into three subcategories: (1) perspectives assuming that religion is determined by power, (2) perspectives that view religion as a determinate and/ or legitimizing force in societies, and (3) perspectives which assume that a dialectical relation exists between religion and power.

From an analytic standpoint, it should be noted that empirical evidence that a correspondence exists between religious forms and expressions and the exercise of power in a society has no bearing on the explanation of that correspondence. In short, evidence that a correspondence exists may be consistent with either a Marxist, Durkheimian, Weberian, or other model and, in fact, the usefulness of any explanatory approach may vary across societies and within a given society over time. In what follows, I will suggest that a correspondence can be detected between alternations in American society as described above and religious movements and expressions. The question of why such a tie exists is, however, bracketed and reserved for future exploration.

In the contemporary search by scholars and intellectuals for an understanding of America, no interpreter has received more notice than Tocqueville, and no single feature of Tocqueville's analysis has been emphasized more than his stress on the voluntaristic form of action which, it is assumed, went hand in hand with the development of democracy in America (Hammond, 1983; Caplow, 1985). Now, while it is true that the freedom of association has, for the most part, been respected in a nation that identifies itself as democratic, the voluntarism observed by Tocqueville was not being pursued in the name and for the sake of radical democracy. Rather, it was the organizational mode that was used to give form and substance to the ideals and yearnings of the theocratic reformists in post-Revolutionary America, whose political sympathies lay with the Federalists and Whigs. The voluntary associations and benevolent societies that were founded in the early part of the nineteenth century were specifically constructed to Christianize the nation through education, mission, and moral reform. They included the American Bible Society (1816), the American Tract Society (1824), the American Sunday School Union (1824), the American Temperance Society (1826), the American Sabbath Union (1828), and the American Home Missionary Society (1828). These organizations were founded for the most part by orthodox Calvinistic clergy, Congregational and Presbyterian, whose theological view of the common man (as immoral and depraved) neatly paralleled the assumption of the Federalists that ordinary citizens were not fit to govern. The reformists' attempt to Christianize America was designed to insure order and good government where, with power ultimately wielded by the people, it was thought that the destiny of the government was directly linked to the character of the people.

Among the religious notables of the day, two major figures opposed the theocratic reformists: the Unitarian William, Ellery Channing, and Alexander Campbell, the frontier preacher. Both rejected the Old Testament legalism of the theocrats, Channing because he espoused, essentially, a humanistic ethical perfectionism, and Campbell because he believed that humans could be perfected by the direct action of the Holy Spirit, which was not dependent upon human activity (hence the antimissionary stance of the Campbellites). Furthermore, Charles Finney, the most important preacher of the Second Great Awakening, stood outside the reformist camp, where his evangelistic devices—the anxious bench, the inquiry room, the protracted meeting—were deemed undignified and unseemly.

What Channing, Campbell, Finney, the Jeffersonian Republicans, and the Jacksonian Democrats all had in common was a belief in individualism. "They believed that the highest source of truth resided in the individual and that the liberty of the individual was the chief end of all political institutions. They held that the individual was the ultimate criterion in religion which made them reject all 'ecclesiasticism' so characteristic of the theocratic pattern" (Bodo, 1952: 26). This faith in individualism stood in marked contrast to the centralizing tendencies of the Federalists and the attempts by the theocratic reformists to make their version of the Christian God immanent in the collective life of the nation through education and moral reform. The evidence, then, seems to favor the conclusion that the dualism found within the polity as America moved through the Federalist, Republican, and Democratic eras had its counterpart in the religious sector in the period from 1789 to the end of the Second Great Awakening. Theocratic-reformist aspirations tracked Federalist/Whig sensibilities, while Jeffersonian Republicanism and Jacksonian Democracy were in correspondence with the individualistic perfectionism of the Second Great Awakening and the more secularized individualism of Deism and Unitarianism.

Turning to the present, there would appear to be a striking similarity between the reformist impulse in post-Revolutionary America and the politics of morality in contemporary America. Both reformists and Moral Majoritarians are concerned with conformity to codes of strict personal moral standards, both link such conformity to the health and vigor of the nation, and both strive to implement their goals through legislation. Yet there are two crucial differences that set the reformists and the Moral Majoritarians apart. Given the Calvinistic assessment of mankind as essentially depraved, and the absence in America of a governing class—that is, a nobility, a standing army, and an established church—the reformists were intent on underwriting propriety and order in the public arena which, in their view, was a fundamental resource upon which the survival and prosperity of the nation depended. In other words, the reformists were trying to capitalize the "characterological" base of the nation in order to guarantee what they considered to be the appropriate form of action in the public arena. This problematic is clearly evident in Samuel Fisher's attack on Congress from his Presbyterian pulpit in 1814:

> A view of our national Council must . . . convince every unprejudiced person that, as a nation, we are practically infidel. If we were to separate from the number of those, whom we have placed over us as rulers, the professed infidel, the openly vicious and impure, the Sabbath-breaker, the profane swearer, the gambler, the intemperate, the duellist, the murderer, and all those who uphold and countenance persons of this description, we have reason to fear that a small minority would be left behind.[1]

In a similar vein, Ezra Stiles Ely, pastor of the Third Presbyterian Church of Philadelphia, had firm views about the exercise of the franchise by Christians: Christians should "never wittingly . . . support for any public office" anyone possessing "a bad moral character," which includes not only "confirmed sots and persons judicially convicted of high crimes," but also "all profane swearers, notorious sabbath-breakers, seducers, slanderers, prodigals, and riotous persons, as well as the advocates of duelling."[2]

While Moral Majoritarians would, presumably, welcome the election of Christians who support their principles, unlike the reformists, the Moral Majority is not intent on either Christianizing America or on ensuring propriety in the public arena. Rather, the efforts of the New Christian Right are directed to achieving the regulation of private behavior and the creation of an effective public consensus on the range of private practices that, in its view, are morally acceptable.

It is true that Moral Majoritarians link private behavior to the vigor and health of an America defined in terms of a transcendental, mythical ideal. However, even in its desire to reinstate school prayer, certainly the most collectively oriented social issue, the New Christian Right is primarily concerned with restoring a "spiritual dimension" to American life by legislating behavioral conformity. Thus, the Moral Majority/New Christian Right directs its attention to the behavior of system parts (individuals) and is not in essence concerned, as the reformists were, with the foundation of acceptable collective action in the political/public arena.

A second difference between the agitation of the Calvinistic reformists in post-Revolutionary America and the activity of the Moral Majority/New Christian Right in the contemporary political arena is that the reformists represented an "established" but declining tradition under challenge from the revivalism of the Second Great Awakening, whereas the New Christian Right represents a challenge to the hegemony of the "established" mainline churches of America (cf. Roof, 1983). Reformist aspirations and actions, then, can be interpreted within the classic status politics framework, but it is difficult to put the Moral Majority/New Christian Right in that category unless the status politics argument is expanded to include groups on the rise as well as challenged or declining groups (Simpson, 1983, 1985b).

There is, then, a broad correspondence between the localism and rhetorical individualism of Reagan Republicanism and the campaign of the New Christian Right to regenerate the nation by insuring conformity to particular standards of personal conduct. Both emphasize the interests and behavior of system parts. That conclusion is consistent with the hypotheses of alternation and correspondence that I have been advancing and which now requires one more piece of evidence to attain rudimentary validity within the modest scope of this paper. Can it be argued that the centralizing collective emphasis of the period from 1933 to 1980 had its parallel in the religious sector? That the answer to the question is—yes—is underwritten by two well-known sociological analyses: Will Herberg's (1955) *Protestant-Catholic-Jew* and Robert Bellah's (1967) "Civil Religion in America." Herberg's book is a characterization of the nature of religiosity in America as it developed in the post–World War period. His conclusion that, despite formal differences, Protestants, Catholics, and Jews were celebrating the American way of life in their worship and observances has a clear collective orientation. Herberg, in effect, saw the parts united in collective celebrations of the whole.

Unlike Herberg, Bellah did not intend to characterize the religiosity of a period in the development of America. Rather, he isolated a tendency that he saw within the entire gamut of the nation's history: the celebration of America in a civil religion defined by the Puritan-theocratic theme of America as God's New Israel. Without doubting the essential validity of Bellah's argument, it can be asked why Bellah's essay seemed, at the time, to capture the essence of such a central feature of American culture. One reason, I submit, is that Bellah's essay is a good reflection of the dominant emphasis in the public arena from 1933 to the mid-1960s on America as a pluralistic yet symbolically unified collective entity, a reality that was being shattered as Bellah wrote.

Conclusion

In broad outline, the evidence suggests that the organization of power in American society conforms to the pattern of an oscillating dualistic system. Sometimes there is an emphasis on the needs of the whole, while at other times the society pays more attention to the demands and aspirations of its parts. Furthermore, it should be observed that the pattern of dualism exhibits great stability. The structural pattern that was established early in the nation's history with the transition from Federalism to Republicanism is echoed in the contemporary period by the transition from the New Deal "settlement" and its aftermath to Reagan Republicanism.[3] Finally, general trends in the religious sector of the society appear to be in correspondence with the dualistic nature of the system.

In the final analysis, the burden of this paper is methodological and programmatic. If we are to understand the relationship between religion and power, we must first classify societies in terms of the ways in which power is organized and then search for a correspondence between those ways and the structure and dynamics of religion. Empirically, a correspondence may not exist in a given case but, in any event, an explanation is needed for each observed pattern or absence of a pattern. The construction of explanations will, necessarily, lead us back to Marx, Durkheim, Weber, and Parsons, and to a consideration of the extent to which their arguments make sense of contemporary data. Where they do not, new interpretations are needed.

Notes

1. Samuel Fisher, *Two Sermons Delivered at Morris-town, New Jersey* (Morristown, 1814), 1–37, 41. Quoted in Bodo (1954: 35).
2. Ezra S. Ely, *The Duty of Christian Freemen to Elect Christian Rulers* (Philadelphia, 1827). Quoted in Bodo (1954: 46).
3. The structural elements underlying the dualism discussed in this chapter predate the Federalist and Republican (Jeffersonian) periods. Thus, in his exhaustive study of political parties during the period between the Declaration of Independence and the drafting of the Constitution, Main (1973) demonstrates that the roll-call votes of state legislators can be explained by a local-agrarian/cosmopolitan-mercantile dimension which is highly correlated with Federalism/Anti-federalism, measured in terms of support for or rejection of ratification of the Constitution. As regards religion, Garrett (1973) has argued persuasively that Puritanism defined the bounds of the arena of religious action in American society by spawning both religious individualism, and the revivals that support it, and religiously inspired social reformism, which has underwritten such collectively oriented movements as the Social Gospel and, more recently, the political activism of the "New Breed" clergy of the 1960s.

References

Bellah, Robert N. 1967. "Civil Religion in America." *Daedalus* (Winter): 1–21.

Bodo, John R. 1954. *The Protestant Clergy and Public Issues 1812–1848*. Princeton, NJ: Princeton University Press.

Caplow, Theodore. 1985. "Contrasting Trends in European and American Religion." *Sociological Analysis* 46: 101–8.

Garrett, William R. 1973. "Politicized Clergy: A Sociological Interpretation of the 'New Breed.' " *Journal for the Scientific Study of Religion* 12: 383–99.

Gouldner, Alvin W. 1959. "Reciprocity and Autonomy in Functional Theory." In *Symposium On Sociological Theory*, edited by Llewellyn Gross, 241–70. New York: Harper and Row.

Hammond, Phillip E. 1983. "Another Great Awakening?" In *The New Christian Right*, edited by Robert C. Liebman and Robert Wuthnow, 207–23. New York: Aldine.

Herberg, Will. 1955. *Protestant-Catholic-Jew: An Essay in American Religious Sociology*. New York: Doubleday.

Main, Jackson Turner. 1973. *Political Parties Before The Constitution*. Chapel Hill, NC: University of North Carolina Press.

Miller, C. Arden. 1985. "Infant Mortality in the U.S." *Scientific American* (July): 31–37.

Morison, Samuel Eliot. 1965. *The Oxford History of the American People*. New York: Oxford University Press.

Roof, Wade Clark. 1983. "America's Voluntary Establishment: Mainline Religion in Transition." In *Religion and America: Spiritual Life in a Secular Age*, edited by Mary Douglas and Steven Tipton, 130–49. Boston, MA: Beacon Press.

Simpson, John H. 1983. "Moral Issues and Status Politics." In *The New Christian Right*, edited by Robert C. Liebman and Robert Wuthnow, 188–205. New York: Aldine.

———. 1985a. "Status Inconsistency and Moral Issues." *Journal for the Scientific Study of Religion* 24: 155–62.

———. 1985b. Review of *The Sacred and the Subversive: Political Witch Hunts as National Rituals*, by Albert J. Bergesen. *Journal for the Scientific Study of Religion* 24: 443–44.

Stark, Rodney, and William Sims Bainbridge. 1985. *The Future of Religion*. Berkeley and Los Angeles: University of California Press.

6
Religion, Politics, and Life Worlds: Jurgen Habermas and Richard John Neuhaus

Thomas Walsh

ALTHOUGH MAX WEBER did grant to religion a catalytic role in the emergence of modernity, he nevertheless viewed religion as bound to abdicate to the force of rationality and, at length, to retreat to a private sphere set apart from science and politics. While religion may have been instrumental in the generation of various legal, political, and economic institutions that characterize modern Western society, it has been logically rejected by its progeny. The rationality originally generated by religious interests in making sense of the world comes to judge the foundations of religious belief and commitment to be inadequate rationally. As a result, there occurs an autonomization of various vocational ethics or logics, for example, economics, politics, aesthetics, and sexuality.[1] Autonomization, furthermore, entails secularization.

In the essay "Politics as a Vocation," Weber argues that political ethics and religious ethics are vastly different and incommensurable.[2] Whereas in politics consequences—whether intended or not—are of the utmost importance, in religion purity of intention is cherished. Within the realm of politics, Weber writes in another essay: "Our ultimate yardstick of values is 'reasons of state.' "[3] Weber's political realism leaves little room for the consideration of a fruitful interaction between religion and political order: neither are "cabs to be taken at will." Weber writes: "He who seeks the salvation of the soul, of his own and of others, should not seek it along the avenue of politics, for the quite

91

different tasks of politics can only be solved by violence. The genius or demon of politics lives in an inner tension with the god of love, as well as with the Christian God as expressed by the church. This tension at any time can lead to an irreconcilable conflict."[4] This political philosophy provides a model for understanding religion and politics as two irreconcilable and independent value-spheres. Thus, we have a Weberian call for the separation of church and state that parallels his call for a methodological distinction between fact and value.

Weber's politics, however, represent neither a pure value-free science nor a merely arbitrary value-laden exercise of power. Rather, it is best characterized by an "ethics of responsibility," which is attentive, on the one hand, to value preferences that admit to no rational foundation, and, on the other hand, to the systematic (scientific) monitorization of consequences policies produce. Weber's political ethics, in effect, represent a blend of decisionism in ethics and positivism in science.[5] Moreover, this model of politics serves as a kind of paradigm for Western liberal democracy.[6]

By contrast, a more classical model of politics, if we consider the work of Aristotle, links ethics and politics in a different way. The political sphere or *polis* is very much related, if not to religion, to a substantive *ethos*, such that reasons of state are not autonomous in the sense of having little to do with the values and virtues that are understood to be basic to the creation of a good society. Under the conditions of modernity, however, where heterogeneous visions of the good life conflict, political deliberation and policy formation have come to be guided by appeal to neutral and generalizably acceptable procedures. Such neutrality and generalizable acceptability invariably require a distanciation from the blatantly parochial perspective. Politics, in this sense, comes to have less to do with the practical wisdom of those who have internalized a particular *ethos* and who are, therefore, equipped to guide a community in accordance with and toward the "highest good"[7] than it has to do with either administrative efficiency or public virtues of civility, neutrality, and broad-mindedness. Politics then tends to become Weberian, that is, on the one hand, value-neutral as related to the multiplicity of irrational value forces, and, on the other hand, scientific as applied to various technological, administrative, and public relations skills.

Contemporary efforts to retrieve and revise a more classical model of politics, including both critical theorists such as Jurgen Habermas and neoconservatives such as Richard John Neuhaus, attempt in very different and opposed ways to overcome the alienation of politics from ethics. For Habermas, politics is in need of being rescued from the perils of both scientization—wherein elite cultures of experts manipulate information and public opinion and dictate policy over the heads of citizens—and decisionism.[8] More particularly, he defines his task as one of eliminating conditions that systematically distort communication; thereby he hopes to secure the possibility for a communicatively rationalized life world which impacts in some way on political processes and public policy formation. Neuhaus, whose position is anathema to Habermas's, nevertheless also holds that politics ought not to be alienated from ordinary forms of life; however, unlike Habermas, Neuhaus makes a much stronger claim in requiring both that the life world be unambiguously related to politics, and that the life world's religious dimension be understood as eminently relevant to processes of policy formation.

Habermas and Neuhaus have very different understandings of the character of the life world and of its relationship to the political sphere. Habermas sees the life world not only as a "finite province of meaning," in the Schutzian sense, but as a public sphere of communicative action threatened with reification due to encroachment by the noncommunicative media of money and power. Although the life world is characterized by a taken-for-granted stock of knowledge, its rational potential is realized insofar as formal processes of communicative action, that is, *discourses,* are institutionalized. Neuhaus, on the other hand, understands the life world as a reservoir of moral sentiments, virtues, and traditions which are to be integrally related to public discourses. In contrast to both Weber and Habermas, Neuhaus sees religion as not only instrumental (during early stages) in the *generation* of American democracy and universalism, but in its *maintenance* and *reproduction* as well.[9] Neuhaus holds that an American political process which disembeds itself from a narrative that includes religion insures a politics that is both sterile and authoritarian. In this way, he espouses what Habermas can only interpret as a rollback of certain Enlightenment achievements; at the same time, Neuhaus calls into question what he perceives as an unproductive neutralization of politics.

This attempt to relate perspectives so diametrically opposed as those of Habermas and Neuhaus yields more than the illumination of an impasse between one who seeks to serve the fulfillment of a developmentally conceived world historical process of Enlightenment and one who proposes a religiously musical public philosophy that defies the irreversibility of secularization processes. Both Habermas and Neuhaus provide illuminating analyses of pathologies that characterize our modern world, pathologies which, as both thinkers realize, cannot be adequately corrected by nostrums provided by conventional leftist or rightist ideologues. Solutions are to be sought which avoid excesses of the past. On the one hand, the current crisis that faces both Marxism and democratic socialist politics—evidenced in the ascension of both neoconservative and post-Nietzschean movements—indicates some need to recover or identify how post-Enlightenment perspectives relate to particular values, and not merely to formal universal principles that, as Neuhaus believes, may be made to serve centers of authoritarian power, in which case an authoritarian and unthematized civil religion keeps guard against theocracy. On the other hand, a responsible neoconservatism must avoid lapsing into the kind of obscurantism or mere traditionalism that can characterize a *Gemeinschaft* backlash, such as religious or nationalistic fundamentalism.

Habermas's own version of the more familiar *Gemeinschaft-Gesellschaft* distinction, that is, his distinction between *system* and *life world,* represents a promising proposal for the reconciliation of liberal democratic and neo-Marxist social theories. However, by providing a life world without religion and with only an ambiguous relationship to politics, Habermas's position is blunted of its practical import. Neuhaus, on the other hand, in a way that can serve to strengthen Habermas's position, develops a political theory which remains related to ethos, such that ethos guides and enables processes of public discourse.

Decoupling System and Life World

Habermas argues that the realization of a communicative life world requires an understanding of the dual structure of society. That is, society is comprised of both system and life world. The former represents autonomous spheres of economy and state administration—for example, spheres governed not by communicative action but by the control media of money and power. The life world, on the other hand, refers to an autonomous social sphere reproduced and normatively regulated according to processes of communicative action. Most importantly, the life world is a sphere of participatory social action where undistorted communication may flourish and where identity formation, socialization, and social emancipation may be realized without interference from control media that serve the self-maintenance of the system. Habermas conceptually "decouples" *system* and *life world* in an attempt to prevent the system's utter, pathological "colonization of the life world." In this sense, he seeks to preserve the life world as though it were an endangered species. At the same time, he seeks to thematize and bring to fruition the life world's fundamental communicative core, which is to serve the normative self-regulation of society.

The notion of "dialogue free from domination" constitutes the governing concern for Habermas. This image, which he considers to be immanent in speech itself, is understood to be a universal norm embedded in the structure of language and serving as the fundamental ground for the human interest in autonomy and responsibility. He writes:

> The human interest in autonomy and responsibility is not mere fancy, for it can be apprehended *a priori.* What raises us out of nature is the only thing whose nature we can know: *language.* Through its structure, autonomy and responsibility are posited for us. Our first sentence expresses unequivocally the intention of universal and unconstrained consensus. Taken together, autonomy and responsibility constitute the only idea that we possess *a priori* in the sense of the philosophical tradition.[10]

Like previous Frankfurt School theorists (Max Horkheimer and Theodor Adorno), Habermas seeks to overcome the reduction of practical reason to a form of technical reason. Reason, reduced to its role in technical employment, represents for him "the repression of ethics as such as a category of life."[11] A critical theory is developed in order that political and social existence might be spared the domination of technocratic manipulation. The uniqueness of Habermas's own contribution to the Frankfurt School's efforts to resist the reification of modern consciousness stands on the promise of the linguistic turn which he takes, that is, instead of speaking of the way in which capitalism reifies consciousness, he speaks of the system's colonization of the life world and "the impoverishment of expressive and communicative possibilities."[12]

The emancipation of the life world requires both a decoupling from the system and the institutionalization of universal pragmatic speech processes, that is, of the conditions which allow for the achievement of an intersubjectively valid consensus. For Habermas, validity claims of one kind or another— to the truth, rightness, sincerity, and comprehensibility of an utterance—are basic to speech acts. The rationality of a life world is made possible only if both social and psychic conditions allow for the undistorted raising and testing of validity claims; hence the need for fora, or discourses, reserved for such activity. Discourses are undistorted communicative processes devoted unconditionally to the goal of questioning and/or redeeming validity claims having to do with truth or rightness. Truth claims are to be redeemed or delegitimated by means of a process of theoretical discourse (science), whereas rightness claims are called into question and either redeemed or not through a practical discourse (ethics). Discourses are courts of communicative rationality guided purely by a desire for understanding, and set apart from strategic and manipulative forms of rhetoric, such as teleological and self-centered speech guided by a desire for success rather than understanding. It is Habermas's hope that the normative core of speech—which all who speak implicitly affirm—may be recognized and institutionalized in the life world; this requires the institutionalization of procedures that guarantee unconditional symmetry and reciprocity in regard to any and every speaker's opportunity to make claims or to call existing claims into question. Such would be the fulfillment of the Enlightenment project of securing an intersubjectively valid foundation for the realization of a rational and just society. He writes: "Communicative action provides the medium for the reproduction of life worlds."[13]

Habermas seeks to uncover the reason that is embedded within a particular practice of social reproduction, namely, communication, just as Marx had sought to explain reason, alienation, and emancipation in terms of the concrete practice of labor. The distinct pathology of modernity is then understood in terms of the commodification or reification of communication; the notion of alienated labor is replaced by the idea of the delinguistified life world. Habermas writes:

I explain the alienation phenomena specific to modern societies by the fact that spheres of the communicatively structured life world have increasingly been subjected to imperatives of adaptation to autonomous subsystems, which have

been differentiated out through media such as money and power, and which
represent fragments of norm-free sociality. That the life world remains dependent
on forms of social integration, and cannot be transferred over to mechanisms for
system integration without reification effects, calls for an explanation in terms of
communication theory.[14]

Habermas anticipates a "rationalization of the life world" insofar as discourses
are institutionalized. In this way, conflicts may be resolved and claims legitimately redeemed or rejected according to a process of communicative action.

Habermas departs sharply from neoconservatives who, in his assessment,
fail to recognize the unique pathology of modernity. According to Habermas,
for example, Daniel Bell unfortunately views the problem of modernity not as
the imperialism of systems of money and power, but as related to the "autonomous tendencies of Western culture." Habermas holds that Bell and other
neoconservatives have missed the mark in focusing on aesthetic and cultural
decay to the neglect of system factors which are destructive to the life world.
Habermas writes:

> I do not want to be misunderstood: the non-renewable resources of our natural
> environment and the symbolic structures of our life world—both the historically
> developed and the specifically modern life forms—need protection. But they can
> be protected only if we know *what* is threatening the life world. The neoconserva-
> tives confuse cause and effect. In the face of the economic and administrative
> imperatives . . . they focus on the specter of an expansive and subversive culture.[15]

Habermas charges neoconservatives—and this would include Neuhaus—of
being all too affirmative of social modernity, that is, of capitalism, while
attributing the problems of modernity to an adversarial culture, particularly
aesthetic modernism. Habermas describes the neoconservative line of argument as saying "that the bohemian life-styles with their hedonistic and unlim-
itedly subjective value orientations are spreading and eroding the discipline of
bourgeois everyday life." Habermas suggests furthermore that neoconservatives are seeking "the safe shores of post history, post-Enlightenment, and
postmodernism."[16]

In interpreting the pathology of modernity as essentially a "spiritual-moral
crisis," effect is confused with cause. This kind of counter-Enlightenment view
tied to a return to religion, in Habermas's assessment, requires a rollback of
the advances Habermas attributes to the Enlightenment, particularly the
emergence of universalistic morality and law. Habermas says that "a universalistic moral naturally recognizes no limits; it even subjects political action to
moral scrutiny. In contrast, the neoconservatives desire to minimize the burden of moral justification incumbent on the political system."[17] Habermas
wishes to protect the life world, but without abandoning the Enlightenment
project. In neoconservatism, he fears that the "rejection of cultural modernity

and the admiration for capitalist modernization will corroborate a general antimodernism ready to throw out the baby with the bathwater."[18] Andreas Huyssen writes:

> Habermas tries to salvage the emancipatory potential of enlightened reason which to him is the *sine qua non* of political democracy. Habermas defends a substantive notion of communicative rationality, especially against those who will collapse reason with domination, believing that by abandoning reason they free themselves from domination. Of course Habermas's whole project of a critical social theory revolves around a defense of enlightenment modernity, which is not identical with the aesthetic modernism of literary critics and art historians. It is directed simultaneously against political conservatism (neo or old) and against what he perceives, not unlike Adorno, as the cultural irrationality of a post-Nietzschean contemporary French theory. The defense of enlightenment in Germany is and remains an attempt to fend off the reaction from the right.[19]

Where Bell sees excess and erosion, Habermas sees social movements emerging at the seams of the system–life-world boundary. In the interstitial regions, these new grammars of variant forms of life—new social movements—challenge both system colonization and other noncommunicative forms of life-world regulation.

Within this framework, what may be called "countersecularization" processes, such as Bell's own call for a "return of the sacred," can only be interpreted as regressive.[20] In significant ways, Jurgen Habermas follows Weber's theory of the inevitability of rationalization and secularization, and, like Weber, he offers a "sacrifice of the intellect" theory of religion. Habermas's own sociology of religion is based on a theory of the "linguistification of the sacred," a developmental process whereby that which has been perceived as a referent set apart—God—comes to be known immanently as a communicative structure.[21] For Habermas, the emergence of undistorted communication is not only the fulfillment of an Enlightenment ideal, it also represents the ideal inchoately and insufficiently thematized in various religious worldviews. This ideal is to be realized in the emergence of life worlds which are normatively regulated according to the criteria of communicative action.

In this view, logos supersedes mythos through a series of "devaluative shifts." Mythical views of the world, according to Habermas, involve little or no differentiation between culture and nature, between language and world; there is no differentiation between "speech as the medium of communication and that about which understanding can be reached in linguistic communication." Habermas concludes that "a linguistically constituted worldview can be identified with the world order itself to such an extent that it cannot be perceived as an interpretation of the world that is subject to error and open to criticism. In this respect the confusion of nature and culture takes on the significance of a reification of worldview." Habermas charges that "mythical worldviews prevent us from categorically uncoupling nature and culture." He states: "To the degree that mythical worldviews hold sway over cognition and orientations for action, a clear demarcation of a domain of subjectivity is apparently not possible."[22] Stated differently, yet without distortion of Habermas's meaning, full communication is not possible under the conditions of religion. *Mundigkeit* requires secularization.

The question that emerges, however, is whether or not any forms of communicative action, even discourses, can avoid the taint not only of religion, but of a variety of historically conditioned interests, passions, and perspectives. While Habermas does seemingly hold that discourses allow that we *talk about* the truth and rightness of religion, religious energies are not to serve in any foundational or enabling way the exercise of emancipated communicative action. While he does not explicitly state this, it seems fair to conclude that Habermas sees religion as incompatible with communicative competence. For example, he states: "The achievement of cultural modernity consists in detaching the formal structures of reason from the semantic contents of traditional world-interpretation, that is, in letting reason come apart into its different moments." Such an achievement, Habermas admits, is not without its costs: "The reverse side of this *rendering autonomous* of science, morality, and art is, however, a *splitting off* from the streams of tradition that nourish the processes of reaching understanding in everyday life."[23] It is just this "splitting off" from sources of nourishment that concerns the neoconservatives.

Habermas's concern for the life world seems at first glance to signal a conservative concern, and indeed Habermas does seek to recover for the political left themes captured by the political right, such as community and tradition. Unlike standard conservatives, however, he characterizes the life world as *essentially* a community of discourse. Habermas's life world is less a community whose intersubjectivity is based on taken-for-granted values than one characterized by its capacity for discourse and distanciation, constituted by principles of criticism rather than by traditional values.

Habermas's communicative life world is much less an ecclesiological—and certainly less a sect—than it is a certain kind of post-Enlightenment political community, that is, a community which is also and most essentially rational. In this view, politics becomes the attempt to approximate the procedures of argumentation and discourse embedded within speech. Habermas, however, remains unclear as to whether or not the political life world has any bearing on the system. In seeking to avoid "colonization" through a decoupling of life world from system, Habermas does not indicate the way in which values and norms communicatively generated and reproduced in the life world might infuse the system; in other words, Habermas does not tell us how or if a political community or life world affects a political system. How are life world and system to relate nonpathologically? Is politics a function of system imperatives or a process restricted to the communicative action which is to characterize the life world?

Habermas decouples the life world from a scientized form of political administration (from "reasons of state" or the "logic of systems"), and he also decouples religion from the life world. In either case, it seems that, while preserving the autonomy of the life world, he differentiates the system from value orientations which might be provided by resources generated and reproduced in a life world. And even were Habermas to allow two-way traffic between life world and system, the life world conceived as Habermas describes it may be one which lacks the resources for the generation of energies needed in order to make an impact on the system. That is, passing through the gates of discursive redemption may so require the attenuation of nondiscursive powers and energies—some of which may be theocratic and others highly emancipatory—that they do not qualify as intersubjectively valid.

On the one hand, politics seems to be a communicative process guided by the regulative principle of the "ideal speech situation," that is, whenever systematically distorted communication has been eliminated. Politics, insofar as it is to be responsive to this ideal, involves the effort to institutionalize the "ideal speech situation" which all speech anticipates—that is, a realm where communication and particularly discourses, undistorted by power, wealth, or coercion, are attentive principally to the force of the better argument, that is, to the argument that most adequately represents generalizable interests. The life world and politics are to be so characterized. At the same time, Habermas also suggests that political administration is a system which is not to be understood as a life world. For this reason, Thomas McCarthy has expressed concern that Habermas's understanding of politics has surrendered too much to systems theory, thereby abdicating an earlier emphasis on an action theoretical understanding of political participation.[24] McCarthy argues that Habermas is disturbingly unclear about political theory, and leans toward a loss of a representative democracy model to a politics-as-administration systems model. He states: "If self-determination, political equality, and the participation of citizens in decision-making processes are the hallmarks of true democracy, then a democratic government could not be a political *system* in Habermas's sense—that is, a domain of action differentiated off from all other parts of society and preserving its autonomy in relation to them, while regulating its interchanges with them via delinguistified steering media like money and power."[25] In effect, McCarthy suggests that Habermas has been seduced by a systems theoretical analysis that undermines the link between communicative action, that is, between life world and politics.

Habermas is thus charged with providing a theory of the life world which is only vaguely related to politics, or a theory of politics so guided by systems theory that communicative life worlds are apolitical. It is not that Habermas has no politics to go with his ethics, it is that politics and ethics seem to be decoupled along the same line that divides system and life world. Moreover, Habermas's own understanding of the life world as guided fundamentally by the formal ideal of discourse produces a life world potentially devoid of substance (e.g., religion) and, it would seem, all the more prone to being colonized by the system. It is with these criticisms in mind that we turn to consider Richard J. Neuhaus's coupling of religion, life world, and politics.

Religion, Life World and the Public Square

Understanding modernity's problematic differently, Neuhaus represents an American version of the very kind of "reaction from the right" that Habermas seeks to fend off in Western Europe. In *The Naked Public Square,* Neuhaus argues that the differentiation of politics from religion—which is the most basic substance of the American life world—has reached a point of excess, such that politics seeks to operate "value-free," and has in the bargain lost its soul. Politics and, more importantly, law, have sought to achieve authority or legitimacy without "being suspected of committing religion."[26] But religion, Neuhaus contends, will make its way willy-nilly into the public square: "When recognizable religion is excluded, the vacuum will be filled by *ersatz* religion, by religion bootlegged into public space under other names."[27] He argues that absent the notion of transcendent value and transcendent authority the way is paved for totalitarianism and the state-sponsored subversion of the life world. Neuhaus contends that we require a public role for religion because politics involves something more than a series of neutral procedures to be applied equally to myriad interest groups. Rather, politics must be related to those mediating structures—family, neighborhood, church, voluntary association—where "the things that matter most happen."[28] Neuhaus takes a position that opposes Habermas's seeming affirmation of the parallelism of system and life world; in Habermas's view, Neuhaus represents a call for dedifferentiation of a regressive kind.

In relation to the issue of religion and political order, Habermas seems not only to exclude religion from the public square, but, to exclude religion from the communicatively rationalized private sphere; religion, insofar as it is to be public, is subordinated to and bound to comply with standards of truth and rightness derived through discourses. Habermas's political ideal affirms what Neuhaus calls "the naked public square." Neuhaus defines the "naked public square" as "the result of political doctrine and practice that would exclude religion and religiously grounded values from the conduct of public business. The doctrine is that America is a secular society. It finds dogmatic expression in the ideology of secularism. I will argue that the doctrine is demonstrably false and the dogma exceedingly dangerous."[29]

Neuhaus holds that the public square has been sterilized such that only a most residual and tamed religiosity has an opportunity for entry into a political sphere guarded by a cultural elite. As Neuhaus describes it, "matters of *public* significance must be sanitized of religious particularity."[30] In the concepts of Habermas, system and life world, decoupled from each other, are both to be decoupled from religion. However, the view that religious meanings generated in local life worlds have no bearing on public issues is being challenged by both the politically religious left and the politically religious right; they each "insist that they will not check their own beliefs in the cloakroom before entering" the public square.[31] Neuhaus sides with such efforts to "restore the role of religion in helping to give moral definition and direction to American public life and policy."[32] He also charges that within religion-neutral life worlds and systems, there emerges some form of civil religion lacking in resources for questioning its own theocratic aspiration.

Neuhaus, it seems, is amenable to *system/life world* differentiation. However, unlike Habermas, he wishes to allow for more interdependence, albeit under conditions of a division of labor. There is, for Neuhaus, an interdependence between government and culture affirmed in republican theories of government. He says, "the tradition of republican virtue recognizes the rule of culture and the fact that culture is composed not just of individuals but of communities. Those communities are the bearers of values and truth claims that impinge upon the political process."[33] Neuhaus adds: "In the tradition of republican virtue, politics is the cultivation of a community of morally responsible persons. In that view of politics, the churches would presumably have much to say."[34] Religion plays a role in "sustaining communities of virtue that could inform public discourse."[35] The life world is charged with the task of entering the system and challenging the state authority and its claim to legitimacy. Insofar as culture is generated and transmitted in the life world, and insofar as religion may be understood as the heart of culture, Neuhaus holds that "politics is a function of culture."[36] What Lincoln has referred to as "the mystic chords" of our common life, and what Adam Smith and other Scottish moral philosophers understood as the "moral sentiments," are central features of the life world, and thus of politics. When politics and the judiciary exclude the meanings and values generated and maintained in the life world, politics becomes decoupled from the life world and is more easily governed by the media of money and power.

In Neuhaus, one finds an argument that contrasts strikingly with Habermas's own theory of a rationalized life world which has only an ambivalent relationship to the state administrative system. For Neuhaus, politics unrelated to the life world loses its "vital center" and must resort to entertaining abstract notions of historyless persons and universal rights. Hence, he stresses the particularity of American politics and does not attempt to understand the political system apart from the consideration of the particular life world which forms its context.

Given Habermas's own interest in retrieving a classical notion of politics, it would seem that a fuller understanding of the life world is in order, that is, an understanding attentive not only to generic procedures but to moral and religious sentiments. His own, largely well-founded fear of the counter-Enlightenment tradition, however, seems to prevent his taking seriously the substantive character of values and the factor of virtue as it relates to politics.

Habermas, departing from Aristotle, writes his *Politics* without an Ethics, and fails to fully appreciate the relationship that exists, if not between character and knowing, then between character and speaking and understanding. Neuhaus, on the other hand, and this is one strength of the neoconservative turn, appreciates the role of tradition, virtues, and history in the constitution of political actors. He is also appreciative of religion's role, which, he says, bears the "moral meanings which form the matrix of the discourse in the public square."[37]

Neuhaus strikes certain "mystic chords" in his understanding of a substantive political life. At the same time, he develops his politics on the foundation of an ethics which has "internalized the contributions of the Enlightenment."[38] Thus, his is no espousal of a regressive dedifferentiation, no call for heteronomous theocracy, no idea of a Christian civilization which would exclude the Jew. Realizing that the history of religious wars has served as the concrete historical grounding for a secularization of public life as much as any totalitarian aspiration of an enlightened civil religion, he does not call for the rollback that Habermas rightly fears. He does ask, however, that "the current insurgency of the religious right" be recognized as something more than "a last gasp of the culturally backward, a futile defiance of the inevitable."[39]

Conclusion

In keeping with contemporary neoconservative trends, Habermas affirms the primacy of the life world and fears its further erosion. Habermas's "conservatism," however, is an Enlightenment conservativism. His task is one of protecting Enlightened culture—which he understands as being teleologically on the way to the communicative society—not only from colonization by the institutions of money and power, but also from a conservative rollback. Habermas fears that counter-Enlightenment conservativism seeks to "throw the baby out with the bathwater."

I have argued that Habermas remains unclear as to the location of the state, and its relation to either *system* or *life world*. On the one hand, he seems to suggest that the norms inherent in ordinary speech should not only govern the resolution of conflict within the life world, but that these universal norms ought to be approximated at the political level where power and strategic communication dominate. Habermas, however, seems to have abandoned this latter move. That is, he seems to hold that *communicative action* is restricted to the enclave or life world, set apart from the political administrative system. In this sense, Habermas seems strikingly Weberian. Apart from this unclarity, one must also question the centrality of universal communicative norms as the foundation of either the life world or the polis. Hegel's criticism of Kant's formalism applies equally to Habermas's own synthesis of Kant with George Herbert Mead. Habermas's life world remains abstract and historyless, lacking, for example, the kind of moral power that Dr. Martin Luther King, Jr.

had precisely because his concern with principle and law was inextricably related to "mystic chords," and to religious as well as moral passion.

Overall, Habermas seeks to create a life world based on a linguistic theory of justice that underestimates the generalizable need for meanings, which are most often, and even best, expressed in narratives, sacred symbols, and myths. Harvey Cox has commented, in his recent effort to map a postmodern theology, that he cannot subscribe to Habermas's nonreligiously mediated postmodernism. He writes:

> Habermas's idea that the moral and legal gains of modernity are genuine and must not be lost, that they help provide an essential opening through which we may be able to muster the resources to move on to the postmodern, is valid. I also agree with Habermas's concentration on human communication in community. But, perhaps on the basis of a more theological view of human nature, I do not share his confidence that reasonable conversation alone, removed from a moral and religious tradition, can accomplish what he hopes for. People need larger ethical and symbolic frames of reference in which to converse; these grander settings have to be communicated through scriptures, stories, rituals and traditions.[40]

At least in this regard, Cox's position is close to Neuhaus's. Cox, however, sees little promise in neoconservatism.

The relevance of the neoconservative recovery of a life world infused with symbols, stories, and myths derives from a fear not only that the life world is being colonized by media of money and power—though this is certainly true as well—but that the life world is also being sterilized and marginalized by the force of abstract universalistic moralities. Habermas may indeed be correct to point out that neoconservatives fail to recognize the colonizing potential of an administrative-monetary complex. He nevertheless fails to recognize that abstract universalism also subverts the substance of the life world, and impoverishes moral discourse. Furthermore, if we cannot guarantee that any discursively derived consensus is either true or right, then discourse may become only a mask for majoritarian or elitist—those most communicatively persuasive—domination.

Neuhaus makes an argument suggesting that the political system needs the moral resources which only the life world can provide. Unlike Habermas, Neuhaus asserts his particularity as a modern, Christian American; thus he speaks—with unabashed ethnocentrism—of *American* politics and of the *Judeo-Christian* life world. Politics thus takes on life in the context of particular characters, stories, and traditions. While he does not espouse theocracy—which may be understood as the utter and nonecumenical conflation of the religious life world with political order—he does call for interaction between theological reflection and politics.

Neuhaus advances a theory which does not call for the regressive dedifferentiation that Habermas fears, in other words, the counter-Enlightenment rollback. It does, however, call Habermas to reflect on the more substantive foundations of the life world, and to reconsider a recoupling, without collapse, of religion and the political order. Neuhaus's neoconservatism amounts to more than a rail against the subversive culture that Daniel Bell indicts, for Neuhaus rails at that which is, for Habermas, the solution to the problems of modernity: universalist norms which have no ground in particular traditions. He suspects that abstract universalism is prone to totalitarianism and, ironically, to a kind of "colonization of the life world." His is not a rejection of reason, but an affirmation of reason's historicity. In keeping with this perspective, he underscores the inescapably embedded character of politics. While Neuhaus may indeed overlook the distorting effects of money and power, he nevertheless understands politics as related to the life world, and he understands the life world absent a theological vision as impoverished.

Admittedly, in affirming either political theology or theological politics, Neuhaus also resurrects a grim history of religious wars and totalitarian religious communities, a history of noncommunicative dogmatic theocracies. He recognizes that if his position is to carry the force that he hopes it will—and that applies to political theologians on the left and the right, whether drawing inspiration from Aristotle or Marx—more attention needs to be paid to the grim historical record of countermodernization movements. In this regard, Habermas's concerns must be taken seriously. Habermas's understanding of communicative action as basic to the normative regulation and symbolic reproduction of the life world seems to be a very fruitful regulative ideal. That life worlds ought to be communities of discourse is a fully acceptable proposal and one that Neuhaus no doubt accepts. What Neuhaus cannot accept, however, is a theory of discourses which either excludes or excessively constrains meanings and energies which might only be theologically expressed and theologically understood. Furthermore, Neuhaus cannot accept the idea of a life world so decoupled from the system. For Neuhaus, Habermas's life world needs to be understood as both substantive and political.

What Neuhaus provides is not a regressive dedifferentiation, but rather a way of both distinguishing and relating spheres of morals, religion, and politics. He implies that a healthy political life is characterized by the tense interaction among what David Little has referred to as the "three basic disparities" of civic, moral, and religious responsibility.[41] In this sense, Habermas seems to be more guilty of the dedifferentiation charge—religion, morals, and politics reduce without remainder to communicative action.

If Neuhaus's concerns are at all legitimate, Habermas's theory of the life world is in need of some revision. That is, the essential character of the life world needs to be described not only in terms of theoretical and practical discourses, but also in terms of the fundamentally historical and often religious quality of human theories and practices. Furthermore, Habermas, as McCarthy suggests, is called to connect his promising theory of the life world to politics; otherwise he seems to have only emancipated the life world in a way hat also privatizes it. Hence, I would argue that the real promise of Habermas's perspective can be further advanced by taking seriously the neoconservative concerns of persons such as Neuhaus. Even though Habermas seeks to further an Enlightenment project which is generally associated with the political, economic, and theological left, the realization of his ideals will require a greater appreciation for those whose "critical theory" is directed at programs such as Habermas has set forth.

Notes

1. See Weber's "Religious Rejections of the World and Their Directions," in *From Max Weber*. edited by Hans Gerth and C. Wright Mills (Oxford: Oxford University Press, 1981), 323–59.
2. Weber, "Politics as a Vocation," in *From Max Weber*, 77–128.
3. Weber, "Inaugural Lecture at Freiburg," in *From Max Weber*, 35.
4. Weber, "Politics as a Vocation," in *From Max Weber*, 126.
5. The term "decisionism" refers to an ethics that does not claim a rational foundation, but appeals finally only to a basic choice or decision.
6. Not uncommonly, thinkers seeking to move beyond or away from modern political presuppositions take their departure by way of some criticism of Max Weber. For example, see Leo Strauss, *Natural Right and History*. (Chicago, IL: University of Chicago, 1953); Karl-Otto Apel, *Toward a Transformation of Philosophy*. (London: Routledge and Kegan Paul, 1980); and Alasdair MacIntyre, *After Virtue*. (Notre Dame, IN: University of Notre Dame, 1981).
7. At the outset of the *Politics,* Aristotle says that "the state or political community," being the highest form of community, aims at the highest good. *Politics* 1252a5.
8. Jurgen Habermas, "The Scientization of Politics and Public Opinion," in *Toward a Rational Society*. (Boston, MA: Beacon, 1970), 62–80.
9. Neuhaus focuses not on the consideration of politics as such or humanity as such—as Habermas does—but rather develops a political ethics that he conceives as appropriate to an American ethos.
10. Habermas, *Knowledge and Human Interests*. (Boston, MA: Beacon Press, 1971), 314.
11. Habermas, *Toward a Rational Society,* 112.
12. Habermas, Introduction to *Observations on "The Spiritual Situation of the Age."* (Cambridge, MA: M.I.T. Press, 1985), 20.
13. Habermas, *The Theory of Communicative Action: Reason and the Rationalization of Society*. trans. Thomas McCarthy (Boston, MA: Beacon Press, 1984) 337. The concern with the fragility of the life world resembles Hegel's concern with the erosion of civil society and Marx's concern with the "commodification" of labor and all human relationships. One thinks also of Lukacs's concern with the "reification of consciousness," and George Simmel's understanding of the way in which money dominates social relationships.

14. Habermas, "A Reply to My Critics," in *Habermas: Critical Debates.* Edited by John B. Thompson and David Held (Cambridge, MA: M.I.T. Press, 1982), 226.
15. Habermas, "Neoconservative Culture Criticism in the United States and West Germany: An Intellectual Movement in Two Political Cultures," *Telos* 56 (Summer 1983): 88.
16. Ibid., 79–83.
17. Ibid., 86.
18. Ibid., 89.
19. Andreas Huyssen, "Mapping the Postmodern," *New German Critique.* 33 (Fall 1984): 31.
20. Daniel Bell, "The Return of the Sacred," in *The Winding Passage.* (Cambridge, MA: A.B.T. Books, 1980), 324–54. Peter Berger discusses "counter secularity" in "From the Crisis of Religion to the Crisis of Secularity," in *Religion and America: Spirituality in a Secular Age.* Edited by Mary Douglas and Steven Tipton (Boston, MA.: Beacon Press, 1985), 14–24.
21. Habermas, *Theorie des communikativen Handelns: Zur Kritik der funktionalistischen Vernunft.* (Frankfurt: Suhrkamp, 1985), 118–70.
22. Habermas, *Theory of Communicative Action,* 49–52.
23. Habermas, "A Reply to My Critics," 251.
24. Thomas McCarthy, "Complexity and Democracy or the Seducements of Systems Theory," *New German Critique* 35 (Spring–Summer 1985): 27–54.
25. Ibid., 44.
26. Richard John Neuhaus, *The Naked Public Square: Religion and Democracy in America.* (Grand Rapids, MI: Eerdmans, 1984), 81.
27. Ibid., 80.
28. Ibid., 28.
29. Ibid., vii.
30. Ibid., 98.
31. Ibid., 36.
32. Ibid., 59.
33. Ibid., 136.
34. Ibid., 138.
35. Ibid., 142.
36. Ibid., 190.
37. Neuhaus, "Religion, Secularism and the American Experiment," *This World* 11 (Spring–Summer 1985): 45.
38. Neuhaus, *Public Square,* 254.
39. Ibid., 164.
40. Harvey Cox, *Religion in the Secular City: Toward a Postmodern Theology.* (New York: Simon and Schuster, 1984), 219–20.
41. David Little, "The Origins of Perplexity: Civil Religion and Moral Belief in the Thought of Thomas Jefferson," in *American Civil Religion.* Edited by Russell E. Richey and Donald G. Jones (New York: Harper and Row, 1974), 185–210.

PART II
FUNDAMENTALISM
RECONSIDERED

7

Is There Such a Thing as Global Fundamentalism?

Anson Shupe
and
Jeffrey K. Hadden

A WORLDWIDE WAVE of political movements—some violent and revolutionary, others nonviolently contained within democratic structures—are basing their claims to legitimacy on religious orthodoxy. Shi'ite Moslems, Malaysian Dukwah proponents, Christian "Moral Majoritarians," Jewish Haredim and Japanese Soka Gakkai Buddhists are all finding their justifications and directions for social change in particular religious traditions (cf. Hadden and Shupe, 1986). Each of these movements, and others as well, claim that its quest is grounded in the *fundamentals* of a religious traditions. And it is these perceived fundamental values that proponents seek to reassert.

Fundamentalism is a term most commonly associated with a type of conservative Christianity that developed out of a liberal-conservative split in American Protestant evangelicalism during the early years of the twentieth century (Frank, 1986; Marsden, 1980). The movement took its name from a series of twelve paperback volumes issued between 1910 and 1915, which were privately financed by two businessmen brothers. The volumes consisted of edited articles by leading conservative evangelicals who defended biblical inerrancy and attacked the evils of secular "modernism." The very existence of these volumes revealed a rearguard attempt underway by conservative Christians to reassert truths and doctrines which they perceived as having eroded and to be endangered. Eventually the articles became, as Marsden (1980) indicates, "a symbolic point of reference for identifying a 'fundamentalist' movement" (119).

Historically speaking, therefore, fundamentalism is a new concept, applied to a particular religious development in the early part of this century. As far as we have been able to determine, the concept fundamentalist was not applied to any non-Christian group until the Islamic revolution in Iran in 1979. The mass media quickly settled on the concept of "Islamic fundamentalists" to characterize the Shi'ite followers of the Ayatollah Khomeini.

Iranian Shi'ites regarded the concept as just one more piece of evidence of the Western world imposing its concepts and history on the Muslim world. Islamic scholars and political leaders similarly decried the concept, expressing preference for most value-neutral concepts such as "re-Islamization." Fundamentalist leaders in the United States were likewise infuriated with the application of the concept to Muslims, for it suggested that the Ayatollah Khomeini and New Christian Right leaders like Jerry Falwell were fanatical "brothers under the skin." Notwithstanding widespread objections at home and abroad, the concept of fundamentalism was quickly applied to radical Muslim groups throughout the Middle East.

As our societal consciousness of the religious foundations of political protest has heightened over the past decade, the concept of fundamentalism has increasingly come to be used to characterize right-wing religious groups. Thus, in Israel, the ultra-orthodox Haredim, the Faithful of the Temple Mount, the Gush Emunin, and the Kach party (followers of Rabbi Meir Kahane) are increasingly referred to as Jewish fundamentalists. And in India, militant Sikhs are sometimes referred to as fundamentalists.

The emerging popular use of the concept of fundamentalism has largely gone undefined, but carries the implicit meaning of "militant" and "reactionary." Also implicit is the notion that fundamentalism is "antimodern" and, thus, necessarily "dangerous."

In sharp contrast, liberation theology, which has spawned widespread "base communities" and political organization throughout Third World Catholic countries and which supported a violent political revolution in Nicaragua, is never associated with the concept of fundamentalism. Neither are the religious leaders of South Africa who work to break down the walls of apartheid, or the militant Catholics who helped overthrow Duvalier in Haiti and Marcos in the Philippines in 1986.

On the face of it, the criterion for inclusion/exclusion in the category of fundamentalism seems rather obvious. The aforementioned are right-wing militants, while the latter are motivated by liberal ideology. This characterization is true as far as it goes, but it may camouflage features about all religiously grounded movements that are more alike than different. At least it is worth entertaining the proposition that such similarities may be so. Even if our hunch that there exist greater similarities than differences proves incorrect, entertaining the proposition of hidden likenesses may serve to help clarify and refine a concept.

While the notion that fundamentalism is a universal phenomenon, found in virtually all religious traditions, has gained widespread media currency, a small group of scholars has more cautiously approached the question of whether it is useful to consider fundamentalism a universal phenomenon. Following Roland Robertson, we prefer to refer to the apparent universal phenomenon as *global fundamentalism*.

By *global fundamentalism,* we do not mean a simple emerging form of fundamentalism equivalent in some way to conservative Protestantism or a homogeneous religious reaction to social change. Nor do we mean simply those rigid doctrinaire movements which, in the name of some revitalized religious orthodoxy, seek (at least rhetorically) world hegemony.

Rather, global fundamentalism in our view represents a pattern of many contemporary sociopolitical movements that share certain characteristics in their responses to a common *globalization process.*

In the broadest sense, this process may be characterized as *secularization,* wherein (1) religion becomes increasingly compartmentalized from and defined as irrelevant to other institutional spheres, and (2) the world is increasingly characterized by economic interdependency among nations.

What is most common to the infrastructures of movements we characterize as fundamentalist is resistance to the institutional differentiation process (secularization) which progressively renders religious institutions and belief systems irrelevant and marginal to culture. Resistance to global economic interdependence is a secondary reaction, grounded in the perceived threat to their religious beliefs and is not necessarily a nascent nationalism—although it may exhibit attributes of nationalism.

In simplest terms, we define fundamentalism as a proclamation of reclaimed authority over a sacred tradition which is to be reinstated as an antidote for a society that has strayed from its cultural moorings. Sociologically speaking, fundamentalism involves (1) a refutation of the radical *differentiation* of the sacred and secular that has evolved with modernization and (2) a plan to *dedifferentiate* this institutional bifurcation and thus bring religion back to center stage as an important factor or interest in public policy decisions.

The manner and process by which religious authority is proclaimed may be radically different depending upon the level of economic development and modernization, ethnic traditions, disparate theologies, and geopolitics. Nevertheless, we propose that all fundamentalist movements possess underlying similarities which warrant the use of the concept global fundamentalism to refer to the underlying process.

The common underlying processes present in global fundamentalism become more apparent with an exegesis of the definition here proposed. We identify three general but critical components. Two are explicit in the definition; a third is implicit.

First, while the notion of *proclamation* is critical to our definition, we will skip over it for the moment, beginning with the notion of reclaimed authority over a sacred tradition. Unlike the utopian call to create a social order heretofore only imagined by visionaries, the fundamentalist prophet calls the people to return to a tradition lost. This tradition is the carrier of values fundamental to a good and just moral order. It is a cry to reclaim the values of some earlier, allegedly finer and more pristine era so as to reorient society and culture toward more desirable trajectories. The clarion call to return is replete with symbols of good.

Second, if there existed, once upon a time, a good society, there must necessarily be an accounting of how the social order went astray. Fundamentalist ideology, thus, must identify symbols of evil. This will necessarily involve the identification and condemnation of individuals, ideologies, social trends, and perhaps even conspiracies that presumably steered or corrupted the society away from the romanticized ideal. Concepts such as "moral breakdown" and "corruption of values" proliferate, relying on the metaphor of an Edenic human fall from grace regardless of whether or not such movements are biblically Christian.

Third, there must be clear, discernible continuities between the fundamentalist movement and the faith tradition it professes to restore. Movement leaders must create enough links with the past to allow followers to perceive the modern movement as the credible guardian of the romanticized past. But fundamentalism as a social phenomenon will be significantly misunderstood in each variant of it is seen only as a sort of atavistic retreat from modernity.

Whereas the proclamation of restoration along with creditable evidence that the movement is grounded in the sacred tradition are essential requisites for a successful sociopolitical movement, fundamentalist movements present *new* solutions to the perceived problem.

Fundamentalism is a truly modern phenomenon—modern in the sense that the movement is always seeking original solutions to new, pressing problems. Leaders are not merely constructing more rigid orthodoxies in the name of defending old mythical orthodoxies. In the process of undertaking "restoration" within contemporary demographic/technological centers, *new* social orders are actually being promulgated.

For example, as Daniel Pipes argues in his essay in this volume, the "Islamic Revolution" of the Ayatollah Khomeini is not modeled on any actual, workable theocratic system once operating in ancient Persia or anywhere else. However viewed from the outside world, the programs and policies of the Khomeini regime are modern creations for modern times.

Likewise, the phenomenon of American televangelism does not simply package traditional evangelical Christianity for the electronic medium. In the name of the "old-time gospel," new theologies and a moral political movement are being formed to represent a variety of social-issue concerns that are unmistakably urban and twentieth century, from abortion to the conflict between individual liberties and the growing welfare state (Hadden and Shupe, 1988).

Fundamentalism is a vigorous attempt to use aspects of a religious tradition for both coping with and reshaping the changing world. What common processes make up the most important of those changes has become known among macrosociologists and economists as *globalization*. The current wave of religious responses to the metaprocess, in turn form what we call global fundamentalism. That this religious ferment is occurring at this point in the history of world economics and international relations is no coincidence. The dynamics of globalization, in brief, have prompted the dynamics of fundamentalism in a dialectical fashion.

The Dynamics of Global Fundamentalism

Our basic thesis is that on a global level a multitude of adherents of religious traditions are reacting to a common process of secularizing social change. We believe that this common secularization process, dominant theories to the contrary, has no inevitable end point at which religion will wither into obscurity. Indeed, we argue that this secularization process, or *thesis,* is part of a dialectic that eventually set in motion its *antithesis.* To put it simply: the economic and secular forces of so-called "modernization" contain the very seeds of a reaction that brings religion back into the heart of concerns about public policy. The secular, in other words, is also the cause of *resacralization* in a cyclical—not linear—process (Stark and Bainbridge, 1985: 2). And often, although by no means exclusively, this resacralization process takes fundamentalistic forms.

That events predicted by the secularization model have not worked out so neatly can be attributed to at least two sets of consequences: (1) the secularizing limits of the globalization process, and (2) the dysfunctional consequences of global mass communications.

The Secularizing Limits of Globalization. Not so long ago, many observers of religion forecast its demise as an important independent variable in political, economic, and sociological equations. Secularization, industrialization, and scientific advancement had presumably dealt religion a mortal blow from which it was not expected to recover. For example, Anthony F. C. Wallace, esteemed anthropologist and former president of the American Anthropological Association, wrote in 1966 (*not* 1866, when early anthropologists were naive Social Darwinists):

> [T]he evolutionary future of religion is extinction. Belief in supernatural forces that affect nature without obeying nature's laws will erode and become only an interesting historical memory. To be sure, this event is not likely to occur in the next generation; the process will very likely take several hundred years, and there will always remain individuals or even occasional small cult groups who respond to hallucination, trance, and obsession with a supernaturalist interpretation. But as a cultural trait, belief in supernatural powers is doomed to die out, all over the

world, as a result of the increasing adequacy and diffusion of scientific knowledge. . . . [T]he process is inevitable. (Wallace, 1966: 264–65)

Wallace's statement may seem extreme, but it is not so different from those
of other observers once similarly pessimistic about the future of traditional
religion.

For instance, Harvey Cox is a noted Harvard theologian who has traveled
many intellectual and spiritual highways. In 1965, in his celebrated treatise,
The Secular City, Cox wrote in a mood that closely paralleled the "death of
God" theologians:

> The rise of urban civilization and the collapse of traditional religion are the two
> main hallmarks of our era and are closely related movements. . . . What is secular-
> ization? . . . It is the loosening of the world from religion and quasi-religious
> understandings of itself. . . . The gods of traditional religions live on as private
> fetishes or the patrons of congenial groups, but they play no role whatever in the
> public life of the secular metropolis. . . . It will do no good to cling to our religions
> and metaphysical version of Christianity in the hope that one day religion or
> metaphysics will once again be back. They are disappearing *forever* [emphasis
> added] and that means we can now let go and immerse ourselves in the new world
> of the secular city. (Cox, 1965: 1–4).

Ironically, the premature announcements of a fatal decline in religion's
importance once seemed solidly grounded in mainstream social science. The
demystification of society and the world inherent in the classic secularization
paradigm posited a gradual, unilinear, unbroken erosion of religious influence
in urban industrial societies.

It was the grand assumption, as Hammond (1985) has summarized it, "that
society moves from some sacred condition to successively secular conditions in
which the sacred evermore recedes" (1).

Nineteenth-century theorists such as Comte, Durkheim, Toennies, Weber,
and Marx all prepared the West for this expectation. Thus, many contemporary social scientists have assumed that as "modernization" swept across the
globe traditional religion (in its myriad forms) would, conversely, lose its grip
on culture. Any sway it might continue to hold over individuals would
eventually be transformed into forms of *privatized* belief where religion would
become merely a personal matter anchored in individual consciousness rather
than remaining a collective force with mobilizing potential for social change.

Likewise, attempts to defend the secularization model in the face of mount-
ing contradictory evidence have interpreted the burgeoning religiosity as the
root of many contemporary political events to mean that we are witnessing
merely an anti-modernist backlash against science, industrialization, and liberal Western values. Jeffrey K. Hadden, in chapter 1 of this volume
("Desacralizing Secularization Theory"), criticized such attempts to "reduce"

or explain away the key role of religion in what the model suggests should be largely secular struggles:

> In many tension-ridden areas, there is the tendency to reduce religious conflict to "ethnic hostilities." . . . Sikhs assassinate Hindu leaders, Hindus do battle with Muslims, Buddhists oppress Tamils, and Tamils strike back with guerrilla warfare tactics; all of these are seen as part of a complex mosaic of ethnic conflict.
>
> Such simplistic explanation by labeling reduces our need to come to grips with one of the most important developments of the second half of the twentieth century. But the extent of political entanglement around the globe is simply too great to be ignored. Each episode cries out for explanation, not as an isolated event, but as part of a global phenomenon. The present data base for comparative analysis consists mostly of case studies. We do not yet have a very good conceptual model, much less a theory, to account for the tumultuous entanglement of religion in politics all around the globe. The one thing that is clear is that the classical imagery of secularization theory is not very helpful.

During the 1970s and 1980s, a perspective developed out of comparative historical and economic theories that took for granted the assumptions of the secularization model. This perspective is generally referred to as *globalization* theory. It postulates the consolidation of earth's nations and societies into an integrated, evolving *world system* of economic-political relations (see, e.g., Wallerstein, 1983, 1974a, 1974b). This new conceptualization can be described as a series of "processes by which the world becomes a single place, both with respect to recognition of a very high degree of interdependence between spheres and locales of social activity across the entire globe *and* the growth of consciousness pertaining to the globe as such" (Robertson, 1984: 348).

Globalization theory is heavily informed by Marxist and neo-Marxist economic deterministic assumptions. Thus, it also comfortably adopts the "strong version" of the secularization model—and a faith in the ultimate extinction of organized religion as a significant social force—as a *fait accompli*. Other than in occasional manifestations of cultic or doomed revitalization fervor, religion is assumed to be a spent, ephemeral force in the global arena.

But the calculus of the presumed globalization process is flawed. It is now apparent that there are opposing trends to globalization, as Robertson (1984) has observed, that its original theorists did not anticipate. In particular, as nation-states expand their "spheres of operation under the guise of enhancing the quality of life," among other things, they cross over institutional boundary lines into religious (and metaphysical) realms (Robertson, 1984: 348).

Governments become embroiled, wittingly or otherwise, in disputes over values which sociologist Talcott Parsons (1978: 352–443) referred to as "telic matters." These are the perennial concerns of destiny, meaning, and justice that arise for all thoughtful persons and which religions purport to resolve. Only the gods can tell human beings where they go when they die, Stark

(1981) reminds us. And as the economic conflicts and contests created in the international arena multiply, there is a sense that local gods may have something to say about such matters as well.

Robertson and Chirico (1985) argue that "the modern state 'invites' religious encroachment, precisely but not wholly because it is increasingly concerned with matters traditionally associated with the religious domain" (225). Moreover, in their view, "The globalization process itself raises religious and quasi-religious questions" (239).

The result is that any secularization trajectory accompanying globalization, because it necessarily involves culture conflict and challenges to the truth claims of various traditional religions, is self-limiting. There is, in short, a ceiling effect on secularization that eventually triggers reactions against it.

At some point, which further research may more precisely reveal, globalization sets in motion the dynamic for searches for ultimate meaning, values, and *resacralization* of social institutions. This resacralization is most logically accomplished by reaching deep into the culture's dominant religious traditions and proclaiming authority over its fundamental truths. Thus secularization turns in on itself and generates the very conditions for a resurgence of religious influence closely modeled along traditional or fundamentalistic lines.

Sociologist Roland Robertson has emerged as the most persistent critic of economic deterministic globalization theory. As his essay in this volume cogently argues, secularization is actually part of a dialectic unfolding in which pressures for universality and globality vie with the continuous resurfacing of pressures for sectarian, nationalistic particularism. The question often boils down to one of identity, with increasing *Gesellschaft* trends stimulating calls back to—or, in the case of innovative fundamentalist groups, forward to—religious tradition and nonrelative values. Religion reasserts itself as an important anchor in such identity struggles.

Stark and Bainbridge (1985) have concluded much the same thing in a series of analyses of cult formation and growth in the United States, Canada, and Europe. Innovative religious movements (cults) thrive in regions where traditional religion has been eroded and weakened by secularization. In contrast, cults do uniformly poorly where traditional churches and sectarian groups have hegemony. Secularization, in other words, does not push out the religious factor for very long, however much it may weaken any given tradition. Its pattern in the long run clearly seems more cyclical than linear.

The Dysfunctions of Mass Communications. The promise of mass communications, which in the current era is not limited to print media, radio, and television, but also includes satellite/laser technology, initially led many observers (e.g., McLuhan and Firore, 1967: 11) to suggest that as citizens of a planet now inextricably linked by electronics we would become members of a truly global community.

The logic of the "global village" seemed to be that rapid communications would facilitate instantaneous awareness of events occurring on all points of the globe and make them part of our daily reality. Walls of misunderstanding and misperception would be wondrously dismantled. Our appreciation for other peoples and their situations would be enriched. At least, that's the way global communication would work in theory.

The macroeconomic picture seems to support the thesis of an emerging global market, but it is not clear that global communication with instantaneous awareness of events from halfway around the world is leading to enhanced understanding and empathy. If anything, mass media communications seem to have exacerbated, not dampened, the sorts of intergroup/interfaith sensitivities that lead to tension.

So long as we are oblivious to, or only vaguely aware of, for example, conflict between Protestants and Catholics in Northern Ireland, we can go about our daily lives without having to deal with the legitimacy of the claims of the warring factions. But once we are aware of the conflict, there is a subtle cognitive need "to know" who is right.

The images the media present to us play a very powerful role in "locating" these groups in our own cognitive experience. But the very nature of mass media dictates that we *know about* a great deal that is going on in the world, but we *know of* (in the sense of understanding in some depth) very little. Hence, there is a tendency to "lock onto" images that are supported by our already-existing knowledge and experience. In this context, prejudice (prejudgment) and stereotypes are easily reinforced, even exacerbated.

Take, for example, the near simultaneous emergence of the New Christian Right in the United States and the Iranian Revolution. The negative stereotype of fundamentalists in America served to place the followers of Khomeini in a negative context. So labeled, the revolution didn't need to be understood. But as the Iranian Revolution became progressively militant, including the taking of American hostages, the imagery of "Islamic fundamentalists" loops back and reinforces the stereotype of American Protestant fundamentalists as militant and dangerous.

The mass media, particularly television, are adept at two-dimensional images and swift, slick, superficial coverage of issues. The pace of news coverage discourages analysis of complexities. Television deals more easily with caricatures, stereotypes, and particularistic details that are more likely to fuel hostilities. Electronic images of American flags being torched by jeering Iranian demonstrators or of Israeli soldiers shooting down teenage Palestinian protesters do nothing to bring the brotherhood of man closer to realization. Television in general encourages simplistic reduction of issues into a dichotomy of black and white, with villains and heroes rather than just actors in a complex drama. Some of the distortion is inherent in the medium (e.g., Altheide, 1976; Bagdikian, 1971); part is also due to the inevitable "sanitizing" of news to fit corporate and political interests affected by or sponsoring it (Parenti, 1986).

Media professionals who deal with news and information are themselves often aware of this problem. Eleanor Randolph (1987), feature writer for the *Washington Post,* comments: "Today's television writers are close to being caption writers. They are told to 'write to the pictures,' advice that sounds good, given the nature of the medium, but that can vastly limit their opportunity to explain and educate."

James T. Wooten, ABC correspondent formerly with the *New York Times,* likewise notes: "There is the danger that you give the viewer the illusion that he or she is well informed, when you keep shortening and shortening and abbreviating until appearance of information is merely that and that alone" (cited in Randolph, 1987).

Thus, despite all the theoretically sensible reasons for interdependence, mutual self-interest, and better understanding, the mass media if anything have become an accelerator of religious tension. Religion, as it is typically portrayed, is seen as a belligerent reassertion of particularistic identity, an unwelcome intrusion into a world in search of universalistic indicators of peace and harmony.[1]

If the mass media are unlikely to produce a homogeneous mass culture in which we develop the capability to be more empathetic and understanding of others, their potential for mobilizing social-movement adherents has been, as yet, only little explored and appreciated (Hadden and Swann, 1981; Hadden and Shupe, 1988). While it is still too early to assess the political impact of North American televangelists, we have at least glimpsed how the media might be utilized to forge a powerful fundamentalist movement.

Conservative Christianity virtually monopolizes religious broadcasting in the United States. Some of the reasons concern the profitability of religious broadcasting and televangelists' stellar abilities to raise the high revenues for such costs. In addition, conservative Christianity's themes are particularly suited to television: emotionalism and drama to attract audiences, myths of good and evil that help simplify "appropriate" stances on complex social issues, and the creation of identity labels for in-groups and out-groups that build movement solidarity. Cynics have dismissed religious broadcasting as sheer entertainment for the unsophisticated and gullible. That televangelist Pat Robertson's first bid for the presidency was unsuccessful invites premature, and, we think, misguided cloture on the potential of the airwaves to mobilize dissident and alienated Christians to political action. Meanwhile, the potential of television and radio to crystallize conservative religious sentiments on public policy and to mobilize political movements out of moral concerns is now being established in Central and South America by both North American and indigenous evangelists. In much of the Third World, the state has a monopoly or near monopoly on the means of mass communication. But as electronic technology advances at a blistering speed, the prospects for continued monopoly are reduced.

The audio cassette, for example, can be reproduced in great quantities at minimal cost. And audio cassettes may havè a much more profound impact on Third World countries than in developed nations. Still a fairly scarce commodity, cassette tapes may be played over and over in small groups that afterward talk about how they can act upon the content of the message. Indeed, some analysts assert that the Ayatollah Khomeini's exporting of large quantities of audio cassette tapes from his exile in suburban Paris to Iran was the decisive factor in his successful revolution.

Many religious groups, not just Christians, will see the potential and find ways to gain access to the airwaves and other forms of mass communication where they can proclaim authority over sacred faith traditions and send forth the cry to restore the faith.

Toward an Agenda of "Global Fundamentalism" Research

The concept of fundamentalism, as it has been popularly applied to contemporary situations in the non-Christian world, is little more than a variant on the concept as it has been popularly understood in the American experience. From our perspective, restricting the meaning of global fundamentalism to some variant of a worldwide conservative Christian awakening, or as a purely antimodernity backlash, leaves us with a concept of questionable utility. Such a limited concept should be rejected outright, not only because of its past association with a particular brand of Christianity, but also because it too narrowly limits the prospects for a comparative sociology of religion.

The more generic conception of global fundamentalism, along the lines we have outlined and for the reasons we have presented, offers the promise of comparative data and analysis. Implicit, but unstated, the conceptual model we are attempting to develop here falls into the broader analytical framework of social movement theory.

The social sciences do not have a well-developed vocabulary for typologizing social movements. The only term resembling the kind of concept we are proposing here is a "revitalization movement," taken from anthropology. But revitalization movements are generally localized reactions to colonial rule, from the cargo cults of Melanesia to the Ghost Dance uprisings of the nineteenth-century Plains Indians.

The study of the politics of religion and social change urgently requires some generic concept to deal with the conditions of modern religious responses to globalization. Without elaborating details here, our own thinking about religion and social movements has been significantly informed by "resource mobilization theory" (Zald and McCarthy, 1987), and elsewhere we have identified critical resources which religious institutions can bring to problem-solving social movements (Hadden, 1980). In order to refine the concept of global fundamentalism and better assess its analytical utility, we propose a set of questions as a modest beginning to a research agenda:

(1) Do the various movements which have been characterized popularly as "fundamentalist" movements, satisfy the definitional criteria here identified? If not, does this suggest a faulty conceptualization, or the presence of analytically discrete movement phenomena?

(2) Whereas our conceptualization of global fundamentalism incorporates the idea of reaction to modernization and secularization, need that reaction necessarily be characterized as "right-wing?" In particular, what is the case for considering some or all movements that are grounded in liberation theology as fundamentalist?

(3) Is there some "natural" life cycle to fundamentalist movements with measurable indicators? What are the determinants or antecedents of fundamentalist movements' extremism, accommodation, and so forth?

(4) On a global scale, what do fundamentalist movements of the current generation portend for global economic and political processes? Is heightened conflict through, say, repression of religion a probable or even inevitable outcome? How can secular globalization pressures deal with religious resurgence in nondestructive ways?

(5) Are there "styles" or strategies of manipulating values, symbols, and so forth which mobilize populations more or less successfully? Can we rank the fortunes or outcomes and correlate these with mobilization dimensions?

Something similar to the globalization process as it has been developed theoretically is happening on this planet; something similar to a global wave of fundamentalist movements is occurring in response to it. To interpret this conflict, social scientists can no longer afford the luxury of area specialists who narrowly focus on the historic minutiae that explain local social change. Comparative analysis means sacrificing idiosyncratic particulars in the quest for broader integrating concepts. We propose global fundamentalism as one such worthy candidate and invite a critique and elaboration of the comparative evidence. The questions posed here point the way to the macro-issues in need of comparative analysis so that critique and assessment of the utility of the concept is possible.

Notes

1. It is worth noting that the false assumption of an emerging media-promulgated mass global identity and its erosion of particularistic allegiances is actually the analogue of the older "convergence/modernization" school of writings in vogue among social scientists during the 1950s and 1960s. The logic of industrialization was seen as relentless, its impacts ranging from increased comparable rates of occupational mobility in industrialized societies (Lipset and Bendix, 1959) to personal values and life-styles wherein would develop "a consensus which relates

individuals and groups to each other" and which would provide "an integrated body of ideas, beliefs, and value judgments" (Kerr et al., 1969: 30). This *Gemeinschaft* juggernaut, Clark Kerr and his colleagues (1969) proclaimed, would produce a world of industrialized nations resembling the picture of affairs offered by globalization theory: "Each industrialized society is more like each other industrialized society—however great the differences among them may be—than any industrial society is like any pre-industrial society" (32).

References

Altheide, David L. 1976. *Creating Reality*. Beverly Hills, CA: Sage.

Bagdikian, Ben H. 1971. *The Information Machines*. New York: Harper and Row.

Cox, Harvey. 1965. *The Secular City*. New York: Macmillan.

Frank, Douglas W. 1986. *Less Than Conquerors*. Grand Rapids, MI: Eerdmans.

Hadden, Jeffrey K. 1980. "Religion and the Construction of Social Problems." *Sociological Analysis* 41 (Summer): 99–108.

Hadden, Jeffrey K., and Anson Shupe, eds. 1986. *Prophetic Religions and Politics*. New York: Paragon House.

———. 1988. *Televangelism: Power and Politics on God's Frontier*. New York: Henry Holt.

Hadden, Jeffrey K., and Charles E. Swann. 1981. *Prime Time Preachers: The Rising Power of Televangelism*. Reading, MA: Addision-Wesley.

Hammond, Phillip E., ed. 1985. *The Sacred in a Secular Age*. Berkeley and Los Angeles: University of California Press.

Kerr, Clark, John T. Dunlop, Frederick Harbison, and Charles A. Myers. 1969. "Industrialization and the Nature of Industrial Society." In *Comparative Perspectives on Industrial Society*, edited by William A. Faunce and William H. Form. Boston: Little, Brown.

Lipset, Seymour Martin, and Reinhard Bendix. 1959. *Social Mobility in Industrial Society*. Berkeley and Los Angeles: University of California Press.

Marsden, George M. 1980. *Fundamentalism and American Culture*. New York: Oxford University Press.

McLuhan, Marshall, and Quentin Fiore. 1967. *The Medium is the Message*. New York: Bantam Books.

Parenti, Michael. 1986. *Inventing Reality*. New York: St. Martin's.

Parsons, Talcott. 1978. *Action Theory and the Human Condition*. New York: Free Press.

Randolph, Eleanor. 1987. "Network News Confronts Era of Limits." *Washington Post*, 9 February.

Robertson, Roland. 1984. "The Sacred and the World System." In *The Sacred in A Secular Age*, edited by Phillip E. Hammond, 347–58. Berkeley and Los Angeles: University of California Press.

Robertson, Roland, and JoAnn Chirico. 1985. "Humanity, Globalization, and World-wide Religious Resurgence: A Theoretical Explanation." *Sociological Analysis* 46 (Fall): 219–42.

Stark, Rodney. 1981. "Must All Religions Be Supernatural?" In *The Social Impact of*

New Religious Movements, edited by Brian Wilson, 159–71. New York: Rose of Sharon Press.

Stark, Rodney, and William Sims Brainbridge. 1985. *The Future of Religion.* Berkeley and Los Angeles: University of California Press.

Wallace, Anthony F. C. 1966. *Religion: An Anthropological View.* New York: Random House.

———. 1974a. *The Modern World System.* New York: Academic Press.

———. 1974b. "The Rise and Future Demise of the World Capitalist System: Concepts for Comparative Analysis." *Comparative Studies in Society and History* 16: 387–415.

Wallerstein, Immanuel. 1983. "Crisis: The World Economy, the Movements, and the Ideologies." In *Crisis in the World System,* edited by Albert Bergesen. Beverly Hills, CA: Sage.

Zald, Mayer N., and John D. McCarthy. 1987. *Social Movements.* New Brunswick, NJ: Transaction Books.

8
Fundamentalist Muslims in World Politics

Daniel Pipes

FUNDAMENTALIST MUSLIMS have emerged in recent years as a major political force in the Middle East, Africa, and Asia. They, for example, overthrew the pro-Western regime of the Shah in Iran, attacked the Grand Mosque in Mecca, assassinated Sadat, blew up the U.S. Marine barracks in Beirut, and drove the Israeli army out of southern Lebanon. The prominence and power of fundamentalist Muslims compel an understanding of their place in world politics. This essay concentrates on their attitudes toward the two great powers, the United States and the Soviet Union.

Objectives of Fundamentalist Muslims

Fundamentalist Muslims pursue a political program that derives from their understanding of Islamic law, the Sharia. For them, the regulations contained in this divine code are the key to politics.

The Sharia is a massive body of regulations based on precepts found in the Koran and the other Islamic writings. It covers both the most intimate aspects of life (such as personal hygiene and sexual relations) and the most public (such as taxation and warfare). The law of Islam has changed very little during the past thousand years; it represents the permanent goals incumbent on believers.

In the public sphere, however, the Sharia sets out goals so lofty that Muslims have never been able to achieve them fully. The ban on warfare between fellow believers, for example, has been breached repeatedly, while judicial procedures have almost never been followed and criminal punishments have not been applied. Because its demands exceed human capacity, full implementation of the Sharia has always eluded Muslims.

123

In centuries past, pious Muslims coped with the problem of not attaining their religion's goals by lowering their sights. They postulated that full application of the law would occur only some day in the distant future. For the meantime, they agreed, it had to be adjusted to meet the needs of daily life; this they did by applying only those regulations that made practical sense. Those that did not they circumvented; religious leaders found ingenious methods to fulfill the letter of the law while getting around its spirit. For example, by devising ways to ignore the prohibition on usury, they enabled pious Muslims to charge interest on loans legally. This pragmatic approach to religion, which predominated for hundreds of years, is known as traditionalist Islam.

Traditionalist Islam began to lose its hold in the late eighteenth century, as the success of the West began to cause a steep fall in the power and wealth of the Muslim world. Many Muslims responded to this decline by looking to Europe for new ideas and methods. In the process, they forsook well-established practices. The traditionalist approach to Islam lost support as Muslims increasingly experimented with Western-influenced interpretations of the sacred law. Their efforts resulted in three new approaches to Islam: the secularist, reformist, and fundamentalist.

Secularist Muslims believe that success in the modern world requires the discarding of anything that stands in the way of emulating the West; they therefore argue for the complete withdrawal of religion from the public sphere. Rejecting the commands of the Sharia, for example, they do not allow a man to marry more than one wife, nor do they object to interest on loans. The government of Turkey subscribes fully to secularist principles; a few others, such as those of Syria and Iraq, do so with reservations.

If secularists push away the Sharia entirely and embrace Western civilization, reformist Muslims incorporate parts of both. They interpret the Sharia in such a way that its precepts become compatible with Western ways, facilitating the acceptance of whichever Western practices they wish to see adopted. Reformists transform Islam after their own fashion into a religion that forbids polygamy, encourages science, and requires democracy. The flexibility of their approach appeals to many Muslim leaders, so the great majority of them endorse reformism. (The Libyan ruler, Muammar al-Qaddafi, is a reformist who pursues a unique, personal notion of Islam.)

Fundamentalists, in contrast to both these groups and to traditionalist Muslims as well, believe that the law of Islam must be implemented in its every detail.[1] They point to the exact fulfillment of God's commands in the Sharia as the duty incumbent on all Muslims as well as their principal source of strength. The law is as valid today, they insist, as in the past. For fundamentalists, the challenge of modernity centers on the issue of how to apply the Islamic law in changed circumstances. Secularists and reformists accept Western civilization in varying degrees, but fundamentalists overwhelmingly reject the West; and some reject it in its totality. Fundamentalists make Islam into something larger and more influential than anyone had previously understood. In the memorable words of Hasan al-Banna, founder of the Muslim Brethren, "Islam is a faith and a ritual, a nation and a nationality, a religion and a state, spirit and deed, holy text and sword."[2]

Although aiming to recreate what they think of as an ancient way of life, fundamentalists in fact espouse a radical program that has never been implemented. They claim that their goal is to return to traditional ways, but their program differs from that of the traditionalists in many respects. Where traditionalist Islam is pragmatic, the fundamentalist version is doctrinaire. The former allows for human frailty; the latter demands perfection. Traditionalist Islam achieved a way of life so successful that it lasted for hundreds of years without major changes; fundamentalist Islam requires so much, it has yet to be achieved. (A fundamentalist like Ruholla Khomeini is often called "medieval"; in fact, he is unlike anyone who lived in past centuries and is very much a creature of his time, responding to the challenges of the twentieth century. To view Khomeini as medieval is to misunderstand all that he represents.)

The appeal of fundamentalism grows most when Muslim societies intensely experience modernization. The leaders who are typically the first Muslims to encounter the modern West—government officials, military officers, aristocrats, merchants—tend to experiment with secularism and reformism. But as the masses get caught up in modernizing, they try hard to preserve their accustomed ways. Fundamentalism attracts them precisely because it promises a method to fend off Western influences and practices. Fundamentalist organizations grow in strength as Muslim masses seek solutions to modern dilemmas.

Differences in sect and location have hardly any effect on their viewpoint. Communal disagreements aside, fundamentalists who are Shi'ite hardly differ from fundamentalists who are Sunni in goals or methods. Though they live in different parts of the Muslim world—West Africa, the Middle East, Central Asia, and Southeast Asia—Islamic fundamentalists everywhere pursue the same objectives. These include: a penal code based on corporal punishment; schools stressing Islamic subjects; taxes in accordance with levies; second-class citizenship for non-Muslims; separation of the sexes; warfare against non-Muslims only;[3] harmonious relations between Muslim governments; and ultimately, a union of all Muslims living in peace under one ruler.

The differences that do exist between fundamentalists are primarily due to the intensity of their commitment. Some of them live normal lives and promote their ideals in peaceable ways. But others are so consumed by the vision of a society ordered along Islamic principles that they can no longer tolerate the failings of their governments. These fervent fundamentalists reject the existing political system in its entirety. If a few retreat peaceably from society, most declare war on the rulers. They attack the authorities for pursuing policies not in accordance with the Sharia; whatever failures a government experiences—poverty, military defeat, injustice, inequity, moral laxness— they blame on its divergence from the sacred law. Acting with the self-assuredness and determination that accompany the certainty of knowing God's will, they feel justified in using any means to achieve power and often adopt extreme tactics. Convinced of the righteousness, as well as the urgency, of their cause, fundamentalists readily adopt violent methods, and not infrequently resort to terrorism.

Should they reach power, fundamentalists attempt to implement a program deriving from the Sharia. Because this inevitably arouses widespread resistance (among non-Muslims, secularist and reformist Muslims, and even rival groups of fundamentalist Muslims), they soon find it necessary to exercise coercive control. Fundamentalist Muslims are a minority in the Muslim world; their views are hotly disputed by other Muslims. As Islamic laws are applied, government rule becomes increasingly arbitrary and dictatorial. In the effort to build an order unlike anything now in existence, fundamentalists are prepared to impose their views on all opponents.

In sum, fundamentalists believe that Islamic law holds the answers to modern problems and that they alone are sincere about implementing the law. They disdain nonfundamentalist Muslims, and are hostile toward non-Muslims. They harbor a deep and abiding hatred of Western civilization, which they see as the supreme obstacle to the successful application of Islamic law.

The Pro-Soviet Bias of Fundamentalist Muslims

From the fundamentalist point of view, the United States and the Soviet Union appear more alike than dissimilar. Though political enemies, the two countries share much that fundamentalists reject. The men wear neckties, the women wear skirts, classical music appeals to the cultured, and many social and sexual mores are similar. Americans and Russians are historically both Christian peoples whose culture derives from Western civilization. They share a scientific methodolgy, humanistic idealism, and secularism. Their similarities extend even to ideology, the area where they differ the most, for Marxism is a strain of Western thought, and Marxists never dispute the primacy of Western civilization. In the light of all this, political differences between the two countries look relatively minor to fundamentalist Muslims.

Of the two, however, the United States poses greater problems. This is apparent in three domains: culture, ideology, and international relations. American culture is the more threatening, its ideology the more alien, its power the more feared. The result is a slight but consistent bias among fundamentalists in favor of the Soviet Union and against the United States.

The Western Cultural Challenge. Soviet influence derives almost exclusively from its military prowess: its dreary state culture and moribund economy have virtually no impact on the Muslim world. Who learns Russian, listens to Radio Moscow, watches Soviet films, buys Czech watches, or invests in the

Ukraine? It is the United States and Western Europe, rather, that influence Muslims everywhere. Their pop music, movies, video games, comics, text-books, literature, and art reach throughout the Muslim world. Their clothing, foods, household items, and machines are found in towns and villages. Their universities, banks, and oil companies beckon ambitious Muslims. Customs relating to the sexes—contraception, abortion, dancing, dating, nightclubs, pornography, mixed social drinking, tight clothing, scant swimming suits, mixed bathing, beauty pageants, female athletics, coeducation, and female employment—are most influential and break down divisions required by Islamic law.

The wide appeal of American and Western European culture deeply disturbs fundamentalists. Some fear the erosion of Islamic customs and laws; others worry about the very survival of Islam itself. In answer, they counter-attack. They condemn Western culture as aesthetically loathsome and morally decadent; they spread conspiracy theories to inspire fears in Muslims of American motives; and they warn of disasters befalling those who abandon the Sharia.

Fundamentalists also strongly discourage instruction in European languages and attendance at American schools. In the words of the Ayatollah Khomeini: "We are not afraid of economic sanctions or military intervention. What we are afraid of is Western universities."[4] This sentiment goes far to explain why fundamentalists assaulted two successive presidents of the American University in Beirut. David Dodge was kidnapped in July 1982 and held for a year; Malcolm Kerr was assassinated in January 1984. Although both were prominent sympathizers with the Arabs and of Islam in the United States, their politics mattered less to the fundamentalists than that they both headed the American University of Beirut, the outstanding bastion of United States culture in the Middle East. Few things upset fundamentalists more than Muslim youth absorbing American customs, precisely what happens when they attend a Western-style university.

Further, Christian missionaries are seen as directing a frontal assault on Islam, and they come only from the West. Although no longer a prominent force in the West itself, missionaries remain a central concern to fundamentalist Muslims. In the words of Hasan al-Banna, founder of the Muslim Brethren, "It was natural that there should be a clash between the two [the Brethren and missionaries] in view of the fact that one of them defends Islam and the other attacks it."[5] The involvement of so many missionaries in education only makes their presence that much more threatening.

What Americans see with pride—the unselfish spread of advanced methods—appears to fundamentalist Muslims as a mortal danger. They stop at nothing to eliminate the offending cultural presence. Just before Malcolm Kerr's assassination, the former leader of the group that occupied the United States embassy in Tehran declared that the main objective of the Islamic revolution was to "root out" American culture in Muslim countries.[6]

Fundamentalists view the culture of the United States and Western Europe as the main threat because its influence so greatly exceeds that of the Soviet bloc.

Between Liberalism and Marxism. At the level of ideology, fundamentalists find American political ideals more alien and more challenging than Soviet ones.

Liberalism, socialism, nationalism, and the other systematic political programs developed in the West offer Muslims goals unrelated, and often contrary, to the Sharia. For example, whereas Islam calls for ultimate loyalty to the whole community of Muslims, nationalism directs loyalty to the nation-state, and these two units cannot be reconciled. Ideologies present a major danger to fundamentalists; from the nineteenth century on, as increasing numbers of Muslims have been attracted to Western ideologies, these have inexorably alienated them from Islamic aspirations.

As Muslims fall under the influence of Western ideologies, winning them back to the Islamic law and keeping others from straying becomes a preoccupation of fundamentalists. To achieve this, they turn Islam into an ideology, transforming its theology and law into a system of economic, political, and social theories. In the process, it must be emphasized, fundamentalists endow Islam with an unprecedented political role. They contend that Islam contains a political program comparable to, but better than, those originating in the West. They find grievous fault with all Western ideologies—anarchy in liberalism, brutality in Marxism, heartlessness in capitalism, poverty in socialism— and argue that Muslims should ignore all these in favor of an Islamic ideology. In the words of a Malaysian leader: "We are not socialist, we are not capitalist, we are Islamic."[7]

Fundamentalist Muslims live, however, on a globe dominated by two Western superpowers, each promoting its own ideology. Which of them does the fundamentalist Muslim vision resemble more closely, liberalism (meaning here, the classic tradition of Locke and Mill) or Marxism? Which do fundamentalists find less obnoxious? Overall, Marxism appears to them to be the lesser evil. In some ways, liberalism is the preferable of the two, for, like Islam, it respects religious faith, the family unit, and private property. In contrast, of course, Marxism abolishes each of these and replaces them with dialectical materialism, the state, and communal ownership.

But there exists a compatibility of spirit between fundamentalist Islam and Marxism that more than makes up for these differences. Their compatibility has several aspects. Both fundamentalist Islam and Marxism lay claim to the whole truth, both entail all-embracing systems, and both have founding scriptures giving guidance on all variety of matters, private and public, great and small. Their specific regulations differ greatly, of course, but details matter less than the fact that each of them aspires to regulate all of life.

Fundamentalists and Marxists alike see government as an instrument for molding society in conformity with highly elaborated written theories. Unlike liberalism, which has no overriding purpose but which allows each citizen the freedom to choose his or her own path, these two have precise visions of righteousness. If Islam begins with the private sphere and then extends to control the public, and Marxism moves in the other direction, in the end both touch on nearly every aspect of life. Even such activities as drinking wine or painting abstract canvases have political implications and therefore involve government control. Both systems discourage dissent; anyone who insists on proceeding his own way is severely punished. And both rely on the power of the state to enforce norms.

As this implies, fundamentalist Muslims and Marxists also differ from liberals in the ambition of their programs. In contrast to liberalism's mundane aspirations, Islam calls for a society in harmony with God's laws, while Marxism envisages a society in accord with "scientific" principles. Each system requires an impossible transformation in human behavior—on their own, humans do not live according to divine or scientific standards. The religious bonds of Islam lead to a prohibition of war between Muslims; the class solidarity of Marxism leads to demands for total allegiance to one's class. Neither of these goals are fulfilled, however, as Muslims and proletarians invariably do clash among themselves. Similarly, Islam outlaws the charging of interest on money and Marxism prohibits private profit; but interest and personal gain are economic necessities, which can never be eliminated, only disguised. For both fundamentalists and Marxists, the unsuccessful effort to achieve lofty goals brings on a sense of inadequacy; this can prompt a redoubling of efforts and a turn toward extremism.

Two other features of liberalism challenge fundamentalist Muslims and Marxists alike. Liberalism is closely associated with the development of the nation-state, while fundamentalist Islam and Marxism are both universalist affiliations for which national divisions are artificial and deplorable. In addition, liberalism allows an open way of life that challenges the highly structured patterns required by fundamentalists and Marxists. Though in no way inherent in liberalism, the self-indulgent and individualistic features of contemporary Western life appear to them both as damaging by-products that invariably follow from relaxing state control.

These shared traits do not mean that fundamentalist Muslims approve of Marxists or resemble them, only that they have as much in common with Marxists as with liberals. Other factors being equal, when forced to choose between the two, their radicalism causes them to understand Marxists better and usually to cooperate with them more.

The United States and the Soviet Union. International relations is the third factor that biases fundamentalist Muslims in favor of the Soviet Union. As with culture and ideology, they distrust both powers and want nothing better than to stay out of the Soviet-American conflict. Fundamentalists have little stake in its outcome and wish both sides to be exhausted in their struggle. They want no part of the battle: "Capitalism and communism are not our concern; let the Christians fight these matters out on their own."[8] Fundamentalists everywhere resist superpower involvement: in Turkey they press for disengagement from NATO, and in Syria they terrorize Soviet technicians.

Cooperation with a superpower is tactical only: the fundamentalists' long-range goals differ too profoundly for common purpose with the Christian rulers of America or the atheists of Russia. The issues contested by these two countries are irrelevant to the fundamentalists' goal of applying Islamic sacred law. Their alignment with a particular superpower is like Americans cooperating with Communist China against the Soviet regime. Both these coalitions are forged reluctantly and for specific goals, without expectations of friendship.

This inclination toward disengagement notwithstanding, fundamentalist Muslims usually see themselves more threatened on the international level by the United States. In their eyes, Washington more often appears to stand in the way of Muslim independence. Ironically, for it was instrumental in the post–World War Two decolonization by Great Britain and France, the United States has inherited their imperial mantle. Despite Soviet rule over fifty million Muslims in Central Asia, the Soviet invasion of Afghanistan, Soviet control of South Yemen, and the evident Soviet interest in controlling Iran and the Persian Gulf, fundamentalists see the United States as the greater threat.[9]

Iran is a case in point. Although the leaders of Iran align with neither great power (as their slogan "Neither East nor West" indicates), they maintain somewhat better relations with the Soviet Union. Despite the much greater threat to Iran posed by the Soviet Union along their long common border, Khomeini and his followers vent their fury less against it than against the United States. In Khomeini's words: "America has created disasters for mankind. It has appointed its agents in both the Muslim and non-Muslim countries to deprive everyone who lives under their domination of his freedom." "Everything in our treasury has to be emptied into the pockets of America." "The danger that America poses is so great that if you commit the smallest oversight, you will be destroyed." "Iran is effectively at war with America." "America plans to destroy us, all of us."[10]

Blaming almost every problem in Iran on America, from traffic jams to the Shah's death, from drug addiction to Iraq's decision to go to war, leaves little attention for the Soviet Union Khomeni does, to be sure, address the Soviet danger as well, but almost always as an addition to that posed by America. "We are at war with international communism no less than we are struggling against the global plunderers of the West . . . the danger represented by the communist powers is no less than that of America." "Before, it was the British that brought us misfortune, now it is the Soviets on the one hand, and the Americans on the other."[11] Almost always, the Americans are blamed more.

"Those who are creating disturbances on the streets or in the universities . . . are followers of the West or the East. In my opinion, they are mostly followers of the West."[12]

In the fundamentalists' view, the Russian record of aggression against Iran over the past two hundred fifty years pales in comparison with what they see as the United States' role in the twenty-five years before the Islamic revolution. According to Khomeini, the United States put the Shah in power in 1953 and kept him there; during those years, he was an agent or puppet of the American government. In effect, Khomeini argues, the United States occupied Iran in that period. The Soviets may loom across a long border, but many in Iran believe the Americans were already inside and want to return. Khomeini sees it as his duty to lead Iran away from American (not Soviet) occupation and back to Islam.

Together, these three reasons explain why the fundamentalists are more anti-American than anti-Soviet and why they are among the most profound enemies of the United States. The United States and its friends almost always lose when fundamentalist Muslims gain power. Fundamentalist Muslims share with the United States a hostility toward Marxism and the Soviet Union. This tends, however, to be more than canceled out by an even greater hostility toward liberalism and the United States.

Notes

1. Fundamentalist Muslims, not traditionalists, secularists, or reformists, are discussed in the following pages. Fundamentalists alone have the deep and consistent hostility toward the United States described here; other Muslims have a great diversity of views, including ones favorable to the United States.
2. Hasan al-Banna, *al-Mu'tamar al-Khamis,* 10. Quoted in Richard P. Mitchell, *The Society of the Muslim Brethren* (London: Oxford University Press, 1969), 233.
3. Despite their intent to battle only unbelievers, militant fundamentalist Muslims often view nonfundamentalists as non-Muslims. Thus, the leaders of Khomeini's Iran see the leaders of Iraq as outside the faith because of their actions, which makes them fair game.
4. Quoted in Shaul Bakhash, *The Reign of the Ayatollahs* (New York: Basic Books, 1984), 122.
5. Hasan al-Banna, *Mudhakkarat ad-Da'wa wa'd-Da'iya* (Cairo, ca. 1951), 157. Quoted in Mitchell, *Society of Muslim Brethren,* 231.
6. *New York Times,* 29 January 1984.
7. *New York Times,* 28 March 1980.
8. Private communication, Cairo, June 1972.
9. This is due in part to the legacy of decolonization. At a time when Muslim countries sought independence from their West European masters, the Soviet menace had great utility. Sayyid Qutb, a leading Muslim Brethren thinker, wrote:

132

DANIEL PIPES

"We are in temporary need of the communist power" to pressure the colonial powers to make changes. Sayyid Qutb, *as-Salam al-ʿAlami waʾl-Islam* (Cairo, 1951). Quoted in Mitchell, *Society of Muslim Brethren,* 271.

10. Ruholla Khomeini, *Islam and Revolution,* trans. Hamid Algar (Berkeley, CA: Mizan Press, 1981), 214, 221, 286, 305, 306.

11. Ibid., 221, 286.

12. Ibid., 297.

9
Organizational Conflict in the Southern Baptist Convention

Nancy T. Ammerman

OVER THE PAST DECADE, the nation's largest Protestant denomination has been in the throes of conflict between the *moderate* (to adopt the terminology commonly used) leaders, who have controlled church agencies for the last generation and *fundamentalists,* who wish to establish a closer doctrinal uniformity and a more single-minded attention to evangelism.[1]

The leaders of this insurgency have strong links to the New Christian Right. At stake here is not only control of the denomination's vast resources, but the possible use of those resources for various causes of the political right. The New Christian Right has been both helped and hindered by its reliance on a network of independent, mostly Baptist, churches as its organizing base (see Liebman, 1983). The addition of a large major denomination to that base of support would be a political plum of considerable consequence. Whether that will be possible, however, is still very much in contention.

By June 1985, when the Southern Baptist Convention (SBC) met in Dallas, the battle had become open and heated enough to command the attention of the nation's press (even if only momentarily). Charles Stanley's success in protecting his second term as President of the convention—and his appointments—from the challenges brought by moderates tipped the scales in the conflict in the direction of long-term denominational control by the fundamentalists.[2]

What is not yet clear is the implication of this victory. The central question everyone asks is "Will the denomination split?" To that question, there cannot as yet be an answer. The larger project I am now directing is aimed at shedding

133

FIGURE 1
Structure of Authority in the Southern Baptist Convention

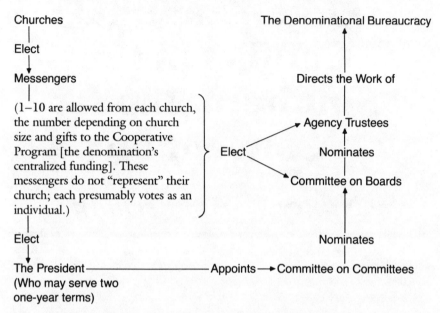

some sociological light on that question and following the dynamics of the struggle as it unfolds. This paper reports one small aspect of that larger whole.[3]

Among the many issues over which Southern Baptists are now divided is the issue of abortion.[4] The ways in which the various groups within the convention—fundamentalist dissidents, moderate activists, and establishment leaders—respond to this issue can provide a case study of the dynamics of the larger conflict in the denomination. This paper will focus on the organization of conflict in a divided denomination facing a divisive issue. But first, we must place this battle in its larger context.

Theoretical and Historical Background

When we attempt to answer questions about why religious groups fight and divide, we are drawn almost immediately to the long tradition that has come to be known as church-sect theory. Since the beginning of sociological time, and more specifically since H. Richard Niebuhr (1929), social scientists have known that the way in which people organize themselves into religious groups reflects at least as much the social boundaries they recognize as the theological ideas to which they are willing to give their lives. What Niebuhr, following Troeltsch, theorized was that when new religious bodies form, they are usually drawn from among those whose disadvantaged life-situation places them at odds with the more comfortable experience of their religious leaders.

Certainly Niebuhr and all his followers have been right in arguing that we cannot understand why religious groups divide unless we understand the social worlds that keep them apart. In attempting to account for these social differences, I have identified three broad, interrelated categories: economic differences, differences in degree of modernization, and political differences.[5]

Economic Differences. Economic differences, of course, are the most familiar to sociologists. Though class divisions are rarely a perfect predictor of religious schism, they often play an important role, as Niebuhr so convincingly argued. More recently, Dean Hoge's (1976) study *Division in the Protestant House* has demonstrated that the class base for current divisions is not so much in objective differences in income, occupation, or region as in the degree to which individuals perceive middle-class values to be threatened by change.[6] He documents an incipient schism across American Protestantism that pits the traditional conservatism of the upper class and of the lower middle class against the innovation of those in the upper middle class who are neither so entrenched nor so insecure as to feel threatened by change. Among Southern Baptists, it appears that the moderate leadership is coming disproportionately from precisely this change-oriented upper middle class, with the fundamentalists coming both from the lower classes and from newly arrived middle-class folk.[7] It is ironic that it is not "dispossessed" Southern Baptists who may be forced into a "sectarian" movement but rather the relatively less privileged who may very well take the reins of the denomination and leave the more privileged no alternative but departure.

Differences in Degree of Modernization. Though differences in degree of modernization have not much interested students of religious conflict in advanced capitalist societies, it may be that our lack of interest is not well-advised. Those in the postindustrial Northeast often forget that there are large sections of this country where a whole range of "modern conveniences" (from electricity to paved roads) have been ushered in only within the last generation. When either ordinary folk or elites in such changing cultures find themselves in a new economic and technological context, displaced from old loyalties and living in a world that operates by different rules, religious revolutions are possible. Such modernization has had a clear impact on the South in the last generation, and is probably crucial to understanding this Southern Baptist conflict.

Modernization not only produces dislocation and change, it also creates a situation of genuine diversity. Among the many aspects of modernity with which today's Southern Baptists are dealing, pluralism is probably the most important. The denomination's constituency is no longer just Southern, and even the Southern part of it is no longer the homogeneous, white, mostly lower middle class, rural, and minimally educated group of a generation ago. It is possible that a major component in the present conflict is a reaction against the pluralism of belief and life-style that has always been associated with "modernism."

Political Differences. Finally, religious conflict also occurs because religious life cannot be separated from the political circumstances in which people exist. The prejudices and divisions of everyday life are more often reflected in religious separation than overcome by religious unity. When a nation becomes independent, the churches in it are also likely to declare their independence. When immigrants travel to a new land, their ethnic churches often reflect the particular political concerns that drove them from their homeland (see Fahey and Vrga, 1971, for an example). I think we would be making a mistake to discount the impact of Yankee immigration into the South[8] and the impact of Southern Baptist expansion outside its traditional southeastern boundaries. Both these movements have been accomplished in the last generation and affect the current identity struggle in the denomination.

When believers fight and divide, then, their division makes sense only as a part of the lives of people in a given time, place, and social position. When social change occurs, people's understanding of the religious life changes as well. Conflict occurs not only because people come to hold incompatible views about salvation but also because those views are born of differences in life worlds.

Though these social sources are the most familiar to us, they are rarely the most visible dimensions of religious conflict. Theological and ecclesiological differences most commonly dominate that stage. Though these raucous theological actors should not be taken as the authors of their scripts, neither should they be dismissed as puppets of hidden economic or social forces. Ideological differences are real differences (as W. I. Thomas would have wanted us to remember) that often create the breaches between persons and groups that result in schism.

When religious people divide, differences in belief and practice are almost always at stake. The ultimate values of most groups are vague enough to allow for differences in practical interpretation. In religious groups, those practical differences can create divergent paths to salvation and opposing definitions of good and evil, with each side nevertheless justifying its beliefs in terms of the same core of sacred values. In this controversy, for example, both sides claim the Bible as their ultimate source of authority. But one side means by this a hermeneutic shaped by dispensational premillenialism and "proof texting," while the other reads scripture through the lens of historical critical interpretation. Not surprisingly, the two come up with very different understandings of who God is and how people should relate to God and to others.

Once having developed differing ideas about core values, divided groups are also likely to develop differing goals for the organization and differing evaluations of the current organizational leadership. Leaders of religious organizations are not just subject to charges of inefficiency and poor administration but to charges of violating a sacred trust. When dissidents seek to reform a religious organization, they often charge that those in power have corrupted the true ideals of the group.

The Necessity of Organizational Explanations

All of the theological, cultural, economic, and political factors that give rise to conflict are necessary, not sufficient, causes. Niebuhr, for instance, was able to support his thesis with snatches of historical evidence, but neither the evidence nor the theory tells us very much about the *process* by which the dispossessed (or any other group) come to recognize themselves as different from their leaders and to mobilize their resources in opposition to that leadership. If we think of differences in culture, politics, and social class as the antecedent variables, and schism as the dependent variable, Niebuhr leaves us without a satisfactory set of intervening variables. He leaves us asking why some religious bodies are able to continue for generations with significant social differences held in check, while others, with seemingly less-crucial divisions, break apart so easily. The intervening organizational variables are simply missing in his model.

The people who supply us with some of the theory to complement Niebuhr's are the social movement theorists. They are interested in the question of *how* movements occur and have developed a variety of models to explain why one group succeeds and another fails. Foremost among these models is Resource Mobilization theory and its variants. Zald (1982) has suggested that social movements within religious organizations can be studied profitably within this framework. Briefly, the success of a movement can be analyzed in terms of the rewards it has to offer, the resources of time, money, facilities, and knowledge it can mobilize, and its effectiveness in minimizing costs to the participants. For churches and denominations, he suggests, these resources are shaped by polity, the relative autonomy of various agencies, communal and ideological loyalties, and relations with the environment (see also Zald and Berger, 1978). He notes, however, that very little empirical work has been done to test this model, with the notable exceptions of that of his students Wood (1970; Wood and Zald, 1966) and Takayama (1980). The result is that we are just beginning to understand the organizational dynamics of religious divisions.

This look at Southern Baptist conflict over abortion, then, is set against a larger effort to study both the internal and external sources of division. The hypothesis is that division in a religious body—in this case, the Southern Baptist Convention—can be understood as a product of external "social sources" that have led to ideological differences, which in turn take concrete form in mobilized organizational resources. Having identified the likely social

sources, the paper will then systematically examine the ideological and organizational results in the Southern Baptist abortion controversy.

Southern Baptists and Abortion

Traditional Southern Baptists have probably always found abortion repug-
nant. Nevertheless, in 1972, the convention adopted a resolution written by
its Christian Life Commission that largely left the matter open to individual
moral choice as sometimes the least among evils. But when abortion became a
national issue in the 1970s, Southern Baptists were natural constituents.
Many began to have their "consciousness raised" by various arms of the Right-
to-Life movement. Today, 11 percent of Southern Baptist clergy and laity
think abortion should be prohibited under all circumstances; 29 percent
would be willing to allow abortion to save the life of the mother; 50 percent
would take into account such circumstances as rape and incest; and 10 percent would leave such a decision entirely in the hands of the individual (see
Table 1).

TABLE 1
Clergy and Laity Positions on Abortion by Theological Self-Identification

| | Do you believe abortion should be prohibited? | | | | | | |
| | Clergy | | | Laity | | | |
Position	Fundamen-talist	Conser-vative	Moderate/Liberal	Fundamen-talist	Conser-vative	Moderate/Liberal	Grand Totals
In all cases	27.0%	7.4%	1.5%	17.6%	12.9%	3.5%	10.5%
Except to save mother's life	38.1	40.4	14.1	29.4	25.9	17.5	29.4
Except for rape or incest	33.3	48.2	62.5	45.1	53.5	51.7	50.0
Rarely; it's the in-dividual's choice	1.6	3.9	21.9	7.8	7.7	27.3	10.1
Totals	100.0%	100.0%	100.0%	99.9%	100.0%	100.0%	100.0%
	N = 63	N = 282	N = 64	N = 102	N = 286	N = 143	N = 940

The goal of a constitutional amendment to outlaw abortion is supported by
65 percent of the Baptists surveyed, though that number masks an enormous
polarization in the convention (see Table 2). Clergy who choose the label
fundamentalist favor such an'amendment almost unanimously, while only 26
percent of clergy who choose the moderate label are supporters. Likewise,
clergy support of an anti-abortion amendment exceeds lay support by 10
percentage points (70 percent compared to 60 percent). The fact that Baptists
still do not like abortion is reflected in the 80 percent who think Southern

Baptist churches should be actively involved in opposing it (see Table 3). Here again, though, the laity are less conservative and there is considerable distance between fundamentalists and moderates. Because of the very different positions taken by different groups on when to allow abortion, it is not at all clear just what each means by "active involvement"; and that is at the heart of the organizational debate.

TABLE 2
Clergy and Laity Supporting a Constitutional Amendment to Outlaw
Abortion by Theological Self-Identification

	Fundamen-talist	Conser-vative	Moderate/Liberal
Clergy	96.8%	74.7%	26.2%
Laity	78.2	67.9	34.1
Total (All Categories) = 65.1% (N = 918)			

TABLE 3
Clergy and Laity Supporting Churches Being
"Active Against Abortion"

	Fundamen-talist	Conser-vative	Moderate/Liberal
Clergy	98.4%	90.3%	54.8%
Laity	89.2	80.8	56.2
Total (All Categories) = 80.4% (N = 928)			

In 1980, the Southern Baptist Convention, meeting in St. Louis, passed a resolution condemning abortion except to save the physical life of the mother.[9] That resolution has essentially been reaffirmed several times since. Resolutions, however, have no binding authority on anyone—persons, agencies, or churches. They merely state the opinion of the "messengers" (non-representatively elected delegates) meeting at that time (see Figure 1). Autonomous churches that were so inclined became actively involved in the Right-to-Life struggle, other churches sympathized inactively, and still others (though few in number) took pro-choice positions. The national agency that could have been expected to provide support for political action, the Christian Life Commission, was noticeably invisible, encouraging the churches to go their own ways.

In 1984, however, a change in this organizational response to the issue was initiated when David M. Blackney of North Carolina made a motion from the floor of the convention that the Denominational Calendar Committee be instructed to investigate the possibility of a Sanctity of Human Life Sunday to be observed in January in Southern Baptist churches, a practice already gain-ing momentum in the Right-to-Life movement. A leader of the fundamental-ist movement observed later that the man was shrewd in choosing this course of action. If he had directed something to the Christian Life Commission or to the Executive Committee of the convention, it likely would have died there. But the Calendar Committee is chaired by a loyal member of the fundamental-ist leadership and controlled by a majority from that side.

In January 1985, the committee met to consider the proposal, and the Christian Life Commission presented it with a counterproposal. The execu-tive of that agency, Foy Valentine, proposed that the convention observe a Concern for Life Sunday in April, rather than on the January date that would coincide with the annual protests against *Roe v. Wade*. He was defeated in committee, 3 to 2, but the Christian Life Commission chose to take the counterproposal to the floor of the convention as an amendment to the Calendar Committee's report. The elected chair of the Christian Life Commis-sion's board presented the amendment, but it was soundly defeated. As of January 1986, Southern Baptist churches found on their calendar of emphases a Sanctity of Human Life Sunday. Though no church is obligated to do anything, Southern Baptist churches that choose to participate in the Right-to-Life protest on that day will do so with the implied approval of the denomination. Whether the messengers in Dallas intended it or not, the Southern Baptist Convention is now, in effect, a cosponsor of those protests.

In addition, this decision implies an obligation by denominational agen-cies—the Christian Life Commission in particular—to produce materials to support observance of a Sunday the agency opposed creating. For both the agency and the churches, this action poses dilemmas that highlight the com-peting ideologies in the convention and the disputed resources necessary for implementing those ideas.

The Sanctity of Human Life Sunday

To maintain its viability, an organization in conflict must be able to marshal more resources than are available to those who would take it over. These resources, I suggest, are of three sorts. First, the organization's ideas and goals must receive support from its constituency. Second, it must have the material and organizational resources to put those goals into action. And third, it must have the political resources to enforce its right to set the agenda and imple-ment the goals.[10]

Ideological Resources. Perhaps the most potent resource the fundamentalists have on their side in this fight is the very moral clarity with which they approach the issue. They are quite sure of the evils of abortion, its threat to the very fabric of the nation, and the mandate for all people who claim to be

Christian to fight against it. Theirs is a very single-minded vision, unclouded by doubts or qualifications.

Closely related is the resource fundamentalists have in their charismatic leadership. These are men (there are no women in real leadership roles on the right) who are recognized evangelists and honored speakers, some with a wide television following. When former SBC President Adrian Rogers stepped to the microphone in Dallas to speak on behalf of "millions of unborn babies who are being slaughtered every year," the Sanctity of Human Life Sunday received powerful ideological support.

On the other side, the moderates, represented by the Christian Life Commission, argued with neither clarity nor charisma. They argued first that the denomination should be "careful of its alliances," but without ever speaking openly or strongly against the Moral Majority or the Catholic Right-to-Life Movement. Second, they argued that concern for human life should be more broadly based than just the concern for unborn life. Without a specific object of that broader concern, however, it could hardly compete with "slaughtered unborn babies" for sympathy. Though they may summon great moral fervor in private, moderates were unwilling to state those arguments publicly in this case. One agency staffer spoke with passion, in private, of the convention caving in to the New Christian Right which, he said, is but a new variation on the old economic and political right. He and other moderates, however, are afraid to attack that political right head-on and unwilling to come out as clearly pro-choice. Fearing that a clearly pro-choice, anti–Moral Majority position would alienate them from the majority of Southern Baptists, they opt for a cautious middle ground, thereby losing the moral clarity that might give their cause greater strength.

On this, as on other issues, moderates refuse to see issues in black and white. Their view of the world prevents the single-mindedness that allows fundamentalists to state the issue so clearly. As inhabitants of a "modern" world, they accept both diversity and the "gray areas" that go with it.

The ideas themselves, however, mean little in an organizational battle, without control of the means of communication. In this case, both the moderates and the fundamentalists have widely read national news magazines serving their respective constituencies (*SBC Today* for the moderates and the Southern Baptist *Advocate* for the fundamentalists), in addition to the official channels of the Baptist Press. On this specific issue, however, both partisan publications were silent. Neither ran stories prior to the convention alerting their readers to the proposed addition to the denominational calendar. As a result, both sides came to the convention relatively ignorant about the specific calendar proposal.

But that does not mean that communication resources were evenly distributed. One side had the benefit of extensive previous communication about the issue of abortion. The *Advocate* regularly runs stories on abortion and on the

Right-to-Life movement, while *SBC Today* has said nothing one way or the other. The fundamentalists came with a ready set of ideas embodied in familiar words and phrases. Their leaders could call on rhetoric already well rehearsed in the pages of the *Advocate*,[11] as well as in the speeches and pamphlets of the entire Right-to-Life movement.

At the convention itself, the fundamentalists were also able to control the structure of the debate through several means at their disposal. First, the Committee on Order of Business (controlled by presidentially appointed fundamentalists) scheduled the Calendar Committee report for the very last session, when the fewest people would be present and the pressure of time would likely limit debate. In addition, the Calendar Committee rarely presents anything very interesting or controversial, increasing the likelihood that the report might just slide through unnoticed. Second, the courtesy period of presiding extended to Don Wideman, the moderate second vice president, was terminated before this report, placing Charles Stanley back at the podium to guide the debate. Third, the platform was virtually closed off, though a long line of potential speakers waited at the bottom of the steps. Except for the official presentation of the amendment from the Christian Life Commission, all statements opposing the Sanctity of Human Life Sunday came from unprepared, unofficial people, speaking from floor microphones, where they could be heard, but only poorly seen. All statements supporting the Sunday came from well-known people, well versed in the rhetoric, who spoke from the main microphone on the platform. The visual impact of this contrast should not be ignored, since everything was being shown on three huge closed-circuit TV screens. Those on the platform looked "official," while those on the floor looked "unrehearsed." The result was a kind of visual legitimation of platform speakers. These and most of the rest of the communication resources were clearly in the hands of the fundamentalists during the Dallas convention.[12]

Material and Organizational Resources. Having shaped the ideas and goals of the organization through their moral clarity, powerful rhetoric from charismatic leaders, and control of the means of communication, what remained was implementation of these goals: But for that, the fundamentalists would need the cooperation of the moderate establishment. As much as they would like to see the entire budget of the Christian Life Commission devoted to conservative causes such as fighting abortion, they did not yet control that budget nor the staff and expertise of the agency. To achieve that, they would have to gain control of the agency's board of directors (an event that did not occur until 1987).

Those on the right would like to see the Christian Life Commission respond to this new addition to the denominational calendar with a full complement of resources for the churches—bulletin inserts, posters, suggestions for Bible study, sermon suggestions, Sunday School lessons, film and book lists, and so forth.[13] They would, of course, hope that the content of all that material would urge involvement in the annual January protests and strong opposition to abortion. Such strong support from a denominational agency would greatly increase the tangible effects of a Southern Baptist Sanctity of Human Life Sunday.

What the Commission actually planned to do largely consisted of wider distribution of the materials they already had produced, materials that present abortion as a difficult moral choice but that do not counsel political action against it. They developed a bulletin insert, but they did not hurry to have it done in time for January 1986. They will cooperate with another denominational agency in four regional conferences on alternatives to abortion.[14] In short, the agency used some of its resources to respond to this new demand, but it shaped the use of those resources to fit its goals, not those of the Right-to-Life movement.

Even if the fundamentalists could not count on either the Sunday School Board or the Christian Life Commission to meet their demands, however, they were not without material resources. There are alternative organizational structures at their disposal in fighting abortion. Most prominent, of course, is the entire Right-to-Life movement; but more recently, a branch of that movement has been formed just for Southern Baptists. It is called Southern Baptists for Life and is receiving strong support from former convention president Jimmy Draper. Such a group exists totally outside the regular structures of the denomination, but indirectly challenges the legitimacy of those structures and competes with them for resources. The implication of its existence is that no forum exists for expressing Southern Baptist opposition to abortion, and that one must be created outside the usual channels.[15] Thus, if the Christian Life Commission fails to produce the desired materials, churches can turn to this other organization for inspiration and support. In fact, for the first observance of the Sanctity of Human Life Sunday, Southern Baptists for Life mailed materials to all Southern Baptist pastors.

Political Resources. In order to maintain control of these material and organizational resources and the goals they support, establishment Southern Baptists were required to mobilize the resources of legitimacy and power. The power to use the organization's resources in unpopular ways rests directly on the ability of that organization to minimize its vulnerability to sanction.

Here it may be instructive to contrast the reactions of the Christian Life Commission with its Nashville neighbor, the giant Sunday School Board, the denomination's publishing house. The Commission has two points of vulnerability: its board and its budget. Both are voted on by messengers like those in Dallas and could be radically altered. That possibility is made less likely by the fact that the Commission also does politically popular things, such as encouraging opposition to legalized gambling, preaching the evils of alcohol, and so forth. Even its strong emphasis on world hunger is seen by most fundamentalists as a worthy activity. Many in the convention would simply hate to see the Commission disappear. Until 1985, fundamentalists had not systematically nominated sympathizers to the Commission board. So long as there was a friendly board and a budget for doing the work, the Commission could continue to do unpopular things along with the popular.

The Sunday School Board also has a board of directors elected by the convention, but it receives no budgetary support from the convention. It is a profit-generating institution and actually contributes those enormous profits (13.2 million dollars in 1983) to the convention budget. For that reason, ironically, it is much more sensitive to the direct wishes of people like the messengers in Dallas. If this giant publishing house were to take an opposi-tional stance, it would immediately lose revenue—a much more powerful sanction than any censure from convention messengers.

The results of this sensitivity to the market are already being seen. In 1986, a Sunday School lesson was apologized for and its writer removed from the list for future assignments. Also, the editor of the *Baptist Student* magazine was removed from his post for producing issues supportive of women in ministry and uncomplimentary of the New Christian Right. The Sunday School lesson uproar is especially noteworthy, since it was precipitated by the receipt of less than two hundred letters of protest from among the more than 700,000 users of adult Sunday School quarterlies. Not surprisingly, it appears that a large profit-making bureaucracy is responding in ways to protect its existence and institutional viability, even if it means significant shifts in the content of what is produced. By 1988, plans were underway for including a lesson oñ Sanctity of Human Life Sunday in the Sunday School curriculum for all ages, from six through adult.

Just as vulnerability to sanctions can predict the parent organization's responses, so the ability of challengers to pursue a course of opposition also depends on that ability to avoid sanctions. In part, SBC fundamentalists have been able to avoid punishment because of the congregational polity of the denomination. No bishop can officially declare them deviant. But such official polity masks the power of the unofficial hierarchy of local (roughly county-level) "associations," which cooperate with "state conventions," which, in turn, cooperate with the national body. The Southern Baptist Convention has always had a very well-developed career system for its clergy. Those who go to approved schools, make friends with approved people, promote approved programs, and otherwise demonstrate their loyalty to the denomination can expect to be recommended by denominational staff people to good churches, recognized by election to state and national offices and boards, and possibly hired for a denominational staff job. Likewise, those who do not acknowledge their debts to the system are unlikely to be rewarded by it. Nor does the system reward those who "make waves." News about pastors who are "uncoopera-tive" or "troublemakers" travels the grapevine from local associations on up, and those pastors have traditionally been excluded from systems of decision making and reward.

Those who are leading the dissenting fundamentalists have never done well in this traditional, "old-boy" network. Despite building big churches, they were both too conservative and too contentious. One leader described himself as a "troublemaker from way back" (an assessment of his role shared, in just those words, by two moderate pastors from his home state). Fundamentalists have had to develop alternative ways to get rewards and to avoid sanctions, in addition to devaluing the rewards available through conventional means.

Conventional rewards have been devalued by holding the denomination and its programs at arm's length. Fundamentalists have made notoriously small financial commitments to the denomination and have historically invested their money and commitment in a variety of nondenominational efforts. Many have effectively belonged to the network of independent institutions of which American fundamentalism is comprised. However, not until recently did these independents begin to identify themselves as having something in common as Southern Baptist fundamentalists and begin to develop a distinct branch of institutionalized fundamentalism with that label.

Among the results of this new identity are increased opportunities to lead and to be recognized. People who are not invited to speak at official denominational gatherings get invitations from fellow fundamentalists instead. Those who never felt at home in local denominational affairs nevertheless serve as local liaisons for the dissidents. It is a common complaint among moderates these days that the people being appointed to SBC boards are "unknown" or "known as uncooperative in their local associations." The people who are now getting to lead the convention were previously excluded and are thus "unknown" by the older establishment. Such leadership opportunities are a powerful reward being offered by the dissidents.

Likewise, the growing network of fundamentalist/Southern Baptist institutions offers additional career opportunities. From Southern Baptists for Life to Mid-America Baptist Seminary, these alternative organizations form a parallel quasi-denomination, ready for incorporation into the whole, whenever the whole is firmly in the hands of fundamentalists. Along with a newly self-conscious network of fundamentalist churches, these offer an additional cushion against the sanctions of the denomination.

Evidence of the extent to which the fundamentalists have established nontraditional reward structures could be seen in the proceedings of the convention meeting itself. Those who head the various agencies and institutions of the convention—moderates to a person and outspoken at that—were by custom seated in a reserved section near the steps to the platform. These *staff leaders* proceeded on and off of the platform to make their official reports, but were otherwise almost completely disconnected from those who routinely occupied center stage—the *elected leaders*—fundamentalists to a person. These latter have their loyalties with the dissidents led by Paige Patterson (President of Criswell Center for Biblical Studies in Dallas) and Paul Pressler (a Houston judge). In earlier days, friendship and loyalty networks would have dictated extensive interaction between the denominational bigwigs and the people who occupied the platform during the convention. That is simply no longer the case. Fundamentalists were much more likely to proceed from the platform to the back of the press section to greet Paul Pressler than to the agency table to greet any official person.

Not all the organizational resources are so clearly in the fundamentalists' hands, however. Legitimate authority is now a quantity very much in dispute. When the convention meets, *both* the denominational bigwigs and the elected leadership present reports and recommendations. These people represent those who make the day-to-day decisions when the convention is not in session, and who are usually presumed to know what is best for the convention. There is a strong tendency, especially in a meeting of 45,000 voting messengers, to ratify whatever report or recommendation is brought by a duly elected or duly hired official. Partly this is a respect for legitimate authority. Partly it is practicality. And partly it is an extension of the Southern tradition of "niceness." It is simply not "nice" to challenge and debate each other.

This tendency to ratify official recommendations currently aids both sides in the controversy, since there are essentially two groups of leaders in the convention, each "official" in its own way. Most *staff* authority is still in the hands of moderates. Had Foy Valentine spoken on behalf of the Christian Life Commission he heads, respect for his authority might have swayed some. In this case, however, even Valentine would have had the disadvantage of speaking against the report of a duly elected committee. And virtually all *elected* positions (including boards of trustees) have been filled by fundamentalists since 1979. Having the Sanctity of Human Life Sunday come from an official committee gave it legitimacy that probably quieted the doubts of some who might otherwise have opposed the entry of Southern Baptists into the Right-to-Life movement.

But the issue of legitimacy extends beyond the shaping of debate in convention meetings. At stake in the present controversy is the legitimate authority to give direction to the agencies and institutions of the convention. Here the crucial resource is the *constitutional structure* of the denomination, which dictates that the gathered messengers have almost no direct authority over any agency. Agencies are governed by their boards of directors, not by the messengers. Even if the messengers "instructed" an agency to do something, that agency's board could decide to ignore or reinterpret that instruction. The messengers' only recourse, then, is censure *and* to elect new people to the board. The power to elect boards of trustees is the infamous "jugular" of the convention for which Paul Pressler is reputedly grasping. Of this power, Stanley said in Dallas, "If they take that away, we've lost everything." The moderates did not succeed in any maneuvers aimed at separating Stanley from that power, and by the time the last of his appointees nominates trustees, virtually all convention boards will be controlled by fundamentalist majorities.

In this battle for legitimate authority, then, some bring "bureaucratic" credentials, while others bring the authority of popular election; but both must work under a constitutional authority that makes the boards of trustees the final arbiters.

One final political resource, this one still in the hands of the establishment, must not be ignored: tradition and loyalty. Southern Baptists have the denomination in their blood, it seems. They even refer to it as their mother, their family. This loyalty is more than a generalized sense of familylike identity, however. Today's church leaders grew up with some of the most effective programs of denominational socialization ever devised. The missions education program of Sunbeams, Girl's Auxiliary, and Royal Ambassadors, along with the church training programs offered by the Sunday School Board in the 1930s, 1940s, and 1950s, were ingenious at attaching youth not only to their distinctives as Baptists but to the very organizations and personnel of the denomination. Young people memorized the names and locations and chief executives of the boards and commissions and had lessons on the work each did. Now that those youths are adults, abolishing an agency or firing its head is a little like banishing a relative.

Those youths also learned that the convention and its Cooperative Program method of funding exist to carry on the largest denominational mission effort in the world. And now, as adults, they are loath to do anything that would jeopardize the flow of those funds. There are enormous pressures toward reconciliation that have resulted in the formation of the much-heralded "Peace Committee." Whether that committee represents a step toward reconciliation, however, is doubtful (see note 10).

The pressures toward loyalty, tradition, and peace are strong, but so are the intense divisions that now crisscross the convention. Whether loyalty to the denomination will overcome ideological division remains to be seen. How that battle is settled will in large measure be determined by the resources each side is able to bring to the fight. The analysis contained here suggests where many of those resources now lie, but both the battle and the analysis are far from over.

Notes

1. Funding for the study described in this paper has been provided by the Center for Religious Research, Candler School of Theology, and by the Society for the Scientific Study of Religion.
2. The distribution of power in the convention is rather complicated. See Figure 1 for an explanation.
3. This study of the Southern Baptist Convention is proceeding on a number of levels. A questionnaire has been developed to provide quantitative data on social, ideological, and organizational dimensions of the conflict. That questionnaire has

been distributed to randomly selected samples of Southern Baptist clergy (1200) and lay leaders (900 men and 900 women). In addition, a variety of publications is being analyzed, including the national magazines serving both sides in the controversy, those representing the traditional "establishment," and a small nonrandom sampling of local church newsletters. Interviews are being conducted with leaders among the fundamentalist dissidents, the moderate activists, and establishment agency and institutional leaders. In addition, a team of observers spent a week in Dallas, listening to the sermons and debates and talking to the participants. The data reported here come primarily from that participant observation (as well as from a review of the videotapes of the sessions) and from interviewing leaders.

4. That abortion is among the most divisive issues facing Southern Baptists is also supported by James Guth's (1985) study of Southern Baptist pastors and the New Chrisitan Right. Supporters of the Moral Majority almost unanimously claimed to have addressed the issue of abortion often or very often, while less than half the Moral Majority opponents had done so.

5. It was Weber (1958), of course, who theorized that the social bases of power rest on status (style of life) and party (political alignments), as well as on class (economic position). Changes in the configuration of these elements would be expected to disturb the "elective affinity" between any set of religious ideas and the way of life in which it makes sense.

6. This distinction between purely economic concerns and "value" or "life-style" concerns has become an important one. Schwartz (1970) argues that the Adventists and Pentecostals he studied adopted their religions more out of a *status* deprivation than out of an economic one. Glock (1973) has theorized that the roots of religious movements can be in the soil of various kinds of deprivation, from psychic to social. More recently, Lorentzen (1980) and Moore and Whitt (1985) have again offered evidence that the impulse for conservative religion and new right politics comes not from the absolutely deprived, but from those whose sense of what is right pits them against a society that they see as threatening their way of life.

7. All of these summary statements about the probable social and cultural dynamics of the current struggle should be read as hypotheses. They are being tested with the data currently being gathered and are thus subject to empirical disconfirmation. They are presented here to provide a framework in which to set the analysis of the abortion controversy.

8. Stump (1985) has demonstrated that in the core areas of the South, the increased presence of non-Southerners is associated with lower church membership rates, increased denominational diversity, and decreased dominance of "Southern" denominations. Where the population is no longer homogeneous and stable, Southern norms about churchgoing are weakening.

9. It should be noted that only 40 percent of our sample (36 percent of the laity) support this restrictive view of abortion. At least 60 percent would be willing to allow abortion at least in the cases of rape and incest.

10. Harrison (1959), especially in chapters 4 and 5, provides a similar organizational analysis of the American Baptist Churches. Though the issue in that case is not overt conflict, his analysis is most useful. He points to the sources of strain in a denomination with an official polity based on congregations, but an everyday

practice based on bureaucratic authority. If anything, the bureaucracy of the Southern Baptist Convention is *more* centralized, both officially and unofficially.

11. In the ten issues prior to the 1985 convention, the *Advocate* printed at least ten articles and/or news notes on abortion.

12. Another aspect of fundamentalist control of communication appears to be their use of the newly formed "Peace Committee" and its call for a moratorium on "divisive" debate. Everyone is trying hard to "be nice," but being nice means different things to each side. Because the spokespeople for the moderate side are so visible in their institutional roles, they have effectively been silenced. Their nearly successful challenge to Charles Stanley could not have been carried out if the Peace Committee guidelines had been in effect last year. For the fundamentalists, however, the first loyalty is to the truth as they see it. Being nice is not interpreted to mean that they cannot make accusations of heresy, nor that they should cease appointing only fundamentalists to committees and boards.

13. The recommendation adopted at the October 1985 meeting of the Christian Life Commission Board reads: "(1) That the Christian Life Commission distribute widely its educational materials on abortion, (2) that the Commission actively cooperate with the Home Mission Board in four regional conferences on alternatives to abortion, (3) that the Commission expand its program of responsible sex education through the distribution of Christian Life Commission pamphlets, guest editorials, articles in *Light,* and speeches, as a way to deal with the issue of problem pregnancies and abortion, (4) that the Commission expand its service as a resource for other agencies as these agencies seek to deal with matters related to abortion, (5) that the Commission produce a bulletin insert on the issue of abortion, and (6) that the Commission seek to help Southern Baptists make maximum use of the newly established date on the Denominational Calendar to deal with this grave moral issue." In the January 1986 issue of the Commission's publication *Light,* the back page was devoted to "The Sanctity of Human Life: A Prayer." Though it warned against casual abortions, it also urged prayer and improved quality of life for mothers and fathers, children already born, and the elderly. It urged rejection of the "tragic epidemic of abortions," but provision of "clear counsel" regarding decisions surrounding sexuality.

14. Before the Sunday was even officially adopted, the man who proposed it, Blackney of North Carolina, offered a motion charging the Christian Life Commission with "promoting the observance of The Sanctity of Human Life Sunday as a day to voice in strongest terms our opposition to all forms of induced abortions for whatever reasons, except in cases to save the physical life of the mother, and that such promotion take the form of biblically based and carefully prepared themes, topics, art work, and other support materials for use in state Baptist papers, in denominational magazines, and in Southern Baptist churches for the observance of this special emphasis day on the denominational calendar; and that such promotion be a number one budget resource priority of the Christian Life Commission beginning in 1986" (Southern Baptist Convention *Annual* 1985: 67–68). Following convention practice, since this referred directly to the work of a convention agency, it was referred to the Commission for consideration and not debated on the floor.

15. The Executive Director of Southern Baptists for Life cites the following as reasons

for forming the organization: "(1) No single SBC agency is doing much in the pro-life area; (2) The observation that many Southern Baptists will not find acceptable anything that doesn't have an SBC label on it; (3) Many of our churches desire qualified pro-life speakers but are reluctant to contact predominantly Catholic pro-life groups; (4) The belief that the vast majority of Southern Baptists take a strong pro-life position; and (5) The conviction that we, as a convention with 14 million members, can effect major change in this nation" (Southern Baptist *Advocate* 5(7): 13).

References

Ammerman, Nancy T. 1987. "Schism." Vol. 13, 99–102 in *The Encyclopedia f Religion*, edited by Mircca Eliade. New York: MacMillan.

Fahey, Frank J., and Djuro J. Vrga. 1971. "The Anomic Character of Schism." *Review of Religious Research* 12(3): 177–88.

Glock, Charles Y. 1973. "On the Origin and Evolution of Religious Groups." In *Religion in Sociological Perspective*, edited by Charles Y. Glock. Belmont, CA: Wadsworth.

Guth, James L. 1985. "Political Activism Among a Religious Elite: The Case of the Southern Baptist Clergy." Paper presented to the Society for the Scientific Study of Religion meeting in Savannah, Georgia.

Harrison, Paul M. 1959. *Authority and Power in the Free Church Tradition*. Princeton, NJ: Princeton University Press.

Hoge, Dean R. 1976. *Division in the Protestant House*. Philadelphia, PA: Westminster.

Liebman, Robert. 1983. "Mobilizing the Moral Majority." In *The New Christian Right*, edited by R. Liebman and R. Wuthnow, 50–72. New York: Aldine.

Lorentzen, Louise J. 1980. "Evangelical Life Style Concerns Expressed in Political Action." *Sociological Analysis* 41: 144–54.

Moore, Helen A., and Hugh P. Whitt. 1985. "The New Religious Right: A Test of the Value Dislocation Hypothesis." Paper presented to the Association for the Sociology of Religion meeting in Washington, D.C.

Niebuhr, H. Richard. 1929. *The Social Sources of Denominationalism*. New York: World (1957).

Schwartz, Gary. 1970. *Sect Ideologies and Social Status*. Chicago, IL: University of Chicago Press.

Stump, Roger W. 1985. "Regional Migration and Religious Patterns in the American South." Paper presented to the Society for the Scientific Study of Religion meeting in Savannah, Georgia.

Takayama, K. Peter. 1980. "Strains, Conflicts and Schisms in Protestant Denominations." In *American Denominational Organization: A Sociological View*, edited by Ross P. Scherer, 298–329. Pasadena, CA: William Carey.

Weber, Max. 1958. "Class, Status, Party." In *From Max Weber*, edited by H. H. Gerth and C. Wright Mills, 180–95. New York: Oxford University Press.

Wood, James R. 1970. "Authority and Controversial Policy: The Churches and Civil Rights." *American Sociological Review* 35: 1057–69.

Wood, James R., and Mayer N. Zald. 1966. "Aspects of Racial Integration in the

Methodist Church: Sources of Resistance to Organizational Policy." *Social Forces* 45: 155–65.

Zald, Mayer N. 1982. "Theological Crucibles: Social Movements in and of Religion." *Review of Religious Research* 23: 317–36.

Zald, Mayer N., and Michael Berger. 1978. "Social Movements in Organizations: Coup d'Etat, Insurgency and Mass Movements." *American Journal of Sociology* 83: 823–61.

10
The Quixotic Quest for Civility: Patterns of Interaction Between the New Christian Right and Secular Humanists

W. Barnett Pearce, Stephen W. Littlejohn, and Alison Alexander

SIMPLY PAIRING the term "civility" with the interaction between the New Christian Right and secular humanists denotes a dramatic shift in the rapidly evolving conversation about the nature and place of religion in contemporary society.[1]

In the 1960s, proponents of religion were on the defensive. The primary agenda seemed to be that of finding some way of accommodating a thoroughly secular society, or of finding some sacerdotal meaning in secularism itself. By the late 1970s, many conservative Christians perceived themselves as

152

spurned by the institutions which shape national laws, morals, and symbols. They lamented the progressive deconstruction of the godly heritage from the Founding Fathers which, in their judgment, was directly responsible for the prosperity of the United States.

For some conservative Christians, being rejected by the cultural mainstream was neither surprising nor particularly distressing. Ensconcing themselves in a rhetoric of personal victimage and social criticism, they thrived in the role of unheeded prophets.

Others found themselves caught in a dilemma between "spiritual" and "political" obligations. Their ideology led them to distain active participation in politics in favor of personal evangelism. Justice, like salvation, was in the hands of God, and would be accomplished by a triumphant Divine intervention in history, not by the efforts of fallible human beings. Their mandate was to facilitate individuals' preparation for the next life, not to eradicate the sources of evil in this life. On the other hand, they became increasingly convinced that the social and political agenda of the 1960s and 1970s were subverting precisely those characteristics of the nation which facilitated their evangelistic activities. A small band of strategically placed "secular humanists" was using the new technologies of communication and politics to undermine social and political institutions based on the Judeo-Christian heritage.[2]

The dilemma was solved by wedding a new sense of nationalism to evangelical purpose in a blazing vision of apocalyptic drama. Commanded to preach the gospel to the entire world before the second coming of Christ, the "New Christian Right" interpreted recent political history and the technological revolution as God's way of providing it the means for an unparalleled ministry. Rather than the result of democratic and humanistic policy, communications and transportation technologies, civil liberties, and economic prosperity were seen as the latest phase of the Divine plan for human history. In a stunning display of hermeneutical virtuosity, the New Christian Right succeeded in baptizing a jingoistic reading of history and an entrepreneurial participation in the economy. For the sake of evangelism, it has a vested interest in continued economic prosperity, military belligerence, and at least certain civil liberties.

Some fundamentalists quickly learned the social technologies of political activism. They organized political lobbying groups and launched a crusade against the election of designated "liberal" politicians and against "moral insanity" as it manifests itself in sexually explicit films, public acceptance of homosexuality, government-sanctioned abortion, erosion of the family, and weak national defense. These and other departures from the reconstructed biblical/historical image of "Christian America" were seen as immoral because they imperil the mission of evangelism by eroding the economic and social system which enable a "high-tech" worldwide campaign.

Jerry Falwell exemplifies this development of a "New" Christian Right. In the mid-1970s, he preached against his colleagues who became involved with politics, citing evangelism as the primary duty. However, in 1979, he

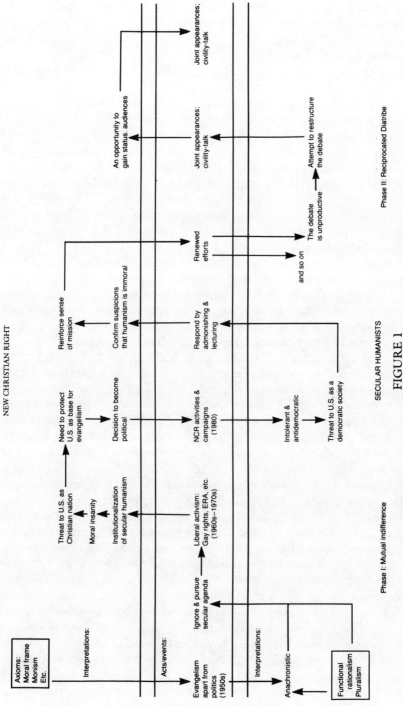

FIGURE 1

Analysis of the Interaction Between the New Christian Right and "Secular Humanists"

established the Moral Majority, Inc., which has subsequently become the most audible voice of the New Christian Right and, for many, its primary symbol.[3]

Three Periods in the Interaction

Figure 1 depicts an analysis of the interaction between the New Christian Right and those who opposed it or were opposed by it. According to this analysis, there have been three major periods in this interaction. In the first, the New Christian Right was dismissed as ineffectual, anachronistic, and politically unimportant.

This phase came to an abrupt end with the elections of 1980 and 1982. The New Christian Right claimed, and many observers agreed, that it had exercised significant "clout." The widespread belief in the political potency of the New Christian Right inaugurated a new period in the interaction, which we characterize as "reciprocated diatribe." Opponents accused the New Christian Right of being antidemocratic and a threat to the American way of life, and lectured it about the proper role of religion and politics. Not surprisingly, the leaders of the New Christian Right found this form of discourse offensive, and responded by polemics and apologetics.

The "reciprocated diatribe" has not ended, but an additional form of discourse was introduced by Senator Edward Kennedy's address at Liberty Baptist College in 1983 and continued with joint appearances between Senator Kennedy and the Reverend Falwell at the National Religious Broadcasters' annual convention in 1985. Following the vocabulary of the participants, we call this form of discourse period the "quest for civility."

The specific purpose of this paper is to assess the prospects for converting the "reciprocated diatribe" into "civil discourse." However, an answer to this specific problem requires an understanding of the structure of the interaction between the New Christian Right and those it calls the secular humanists. We conclude that the quest for civility between the New Christian Right and the secular humanists is precluded by the structure of the pattern of agreements and disagreements which locks them into adversarial roles. We term the quest "quixotic," and spend some time analyzing the reasons why this interaction and others with comparable structures are intractable even to goodwilled efforts to "improve" the quality of argumentation.

The Reciprocated Diatribe

By the early 1980s, the New Christian Right had established itself as a successful rhetor in contemporary social life. The public agenda contained the issues raised by its attacks on abortion, secular education, feminism, homosexuality, and pornography. The leaders of the New Christian Right had regular access to the citadels of power—the White House, Congress, network television news—as well as owning their own television networks, colleges, and publishing houses. A number of prominent liberal political leaders, like George McGovern, Birch Bayh, and the late Frank Church, offered the most sincere testimonies to the political clout possessed by the New Christian Right: They attributed their electoral defeats to the activities of this group and the (overlapping) National Conservative Political Action Committee.

Once taken seriously, the New Christian Right provoked surprisingly intemperate responses from the mainstream of American society. The self-appointed guide to Shakespeare, science, the Bible, and more, Isaac Asimov characterized the leaders of the New Christian Right as "ignorant people, the most uneducated, the most unimaginative, the most unthinking among us, who would make of themselves the guides and leaders of us all; who would force their feeble and childish beliefs on us. . . ."[4] Yale President Giamatti echoed this view: "[The positions of the Moral Majority are] dangerous, malicious nonsense!"[5] Cal Thomas printed letters addressed to him by journalists which far from exemplify the highest standards of objectivity.[6] One was a response to his protest about "slanted" coverage of a Moral Majority rally which appeared in the *Omaha World-Herald*. The reporter replied:

First and foremost, you should know that I feel the fundamentalists are the most single-minded, self-righteous, tunnel-visioned fools I have ever met. . . . I don't care if what I wrote disturbs you. I don't write for fundamentalist fools. I write for the 99.5 percent of the population that faces reality, rather than hiding behind a book that you say has all the answers.

Another was provided by the distribution of a news release.

I request that you remove the [Marshall, North Carolina] *News Record* from your mailing list. As editor, I do not wish to receive any information from your organization. It is my opinion that your organization is a threat to the freedom enjoyed by Americans for the past 200 years. So long as I am editor, and I intend to be editor for many years to come, your organization will not receive coverage in our paper. We will cover the Moral Majority when it butts out of politics, until then, don't call us and we won't call you.

Finally, the American Civil Liberties Union took out a full-page advertisement in the *New York Times* with the headline: "If the Moral Majority Has Its Way You'd Better Start Praying."

The rhetoric of the New Christian Right was similarly strident. A full-page advertisement in the 23 March 1981 *New York Times* included this apologia: "Moral Majority, Inc., is made up of millions of Americans . . . who are deeply concerned about the moral decline of our nation, and who are sick and tired of the way many amoral and secular humanists and liberals are destroying the traditional family and moral values on which our nation was built."

Another member of the New Christian Right, Richard A. Viguerie, described the "liberals" who held political offices in the 1960s and 1970s as "a gang of Don Quixotes gone berserk, not only tilting at windmills but trying to build them everywhere too."[7] Similarly, Tim LaHay bemoaned the fact that: "Most people today do not realize what humanism really is and how it is destroying our culture, families, country, and, one day, the entire world. Most of the evils in the world today can be traced to humanism, which has taken over our government, the United Nations, education, television, and most of the other influential things of life."[8]

The *Moral Majority Report* of 18 May 1981 (16) contains a full-page advertisement opposing abortion with the statement "Last year, 1.5 million unborn babies were killed by abortion" and the preachment "We must not stand by and allow the slaughter of millions of infants to continue."

As the instances cited above amply show, harsh things are being said by individuals about other individuals or groups. But the public discourse presents itself not as a number of isolated individuals but as a conflict between groups. Identifying these groups, however, is not as easy as many of the participants assume.

The Moral Majority can best be seen as an intentionally constructed public *persona* for Falwell, permitting him to speak with a voice greater than his own. The Moral Majority is a media creation: It has a membership, newsletter, officers, headquarters, and other trappings of being a grassroots organization. The leadership, however, is neither elected nor reviewed by the membership, and there are no national or state meetings for members.

Among other implications, this curious structure of the Moral Majority makes it inappropriate to analyze the public discourse by describing what the "typical" Moral Majoritarian thinks or does, or to interpret surveys about the membership as explanations of why the leadership did or did not act in particular ways, or even to cite statistics about membership or audience as estimates of the movement's strength. This analysis does *not* necessarily imply that Falwell is out of touch with those who identify with him; rather, it suggests that the Moral Majority must be understood in a particular way.

The Moral Majority is better understood as a culture than as an organization, and Falwell is better understood as a charismatic leader and a native informant of that culture rather than as its chief executive officer. The Moral Majority is a cluster of people who recognize each other as being one of "us" and who apply a similar set of rules to interpret and evaluate their own and others' actions. Falwell did not invent that set of rules, nor did he convince the others to employ them. Rather, he provided a well-publicized label with organizational trappings and a demonstrated ability to be politically effective. He "speaks for" those "millions of Americans" to whom he frequently refers because he is a part of their culture and does not go beyond it so far that they repudiate him. They do not necessarily agree with him on all of the issues, and often embarrass him by being more adamant than he. (For example, he has had to distance himself from the self-styled Moral Majoritarian who called for the death penalty for homosexuals, and the Baptist minister who declared that God does not hear the prayers of Jews.)

Secular humanists are even harder to identify as a group, since they do not self-identify as a group and have no common self-ascriptive term. There is no headquarters and no membership roster of secular humanism. (Perhaps only Tim LaHay could identify all 275,000 of them!)

However, they, too, may be understood as a culture. They recognize each other (particularly in contrast with the New Christian Right), and they employ a similar set of rules to interpret and evaluate their actions. Again, it is a mistake to assume that all secular humanists think or act alike. Rather, their commonality derives from a common set of standards which they use as a model for their behavior and as the basis for criticizing themselves and others. This model is articulated in the "Humanist Manifesto" (both I and II), and is perhaps best revealed by what is taken for granted in the oratory of Senator Kennedy and in the various documents produced by the "People for the American Way."

It takes no special expertise to discern that the interaction between these groups fell considerably short of the best traditions of either rational debate or Christian love. In fact, the discourse *between* the groups seemed to bring out the worst sides of each group.

When addressed to proponents of creationism rather than to other evolutionists, arguments for evolutionary theory lose the careful qualifications and open-endedness that characterize science at its best. Shrill attacks on creationism seem to oppose indisputable "facts" known by scientists with unsupported "faith" exercised by creationists, as if scientists made no assumptions beyond their data and as if creationists had no empirical ground on which to build a rational argument. Among other things, this way of casting the argument misrepresents science and makes it vulnerable to the creationists' criticism that "science" is just another "religion."

The arguments against homosexuality, on the other hand, bore little evidence of Christian compassion. Among other things, a historical, literal exegesis of scriptures calling for the death penalty for homosexuals and facile interpretations of the statistics about sexually transmitted diseases portrayed the proponents of the New Christian Right in an unnecessarily unfavorable light and made them vulnerable to the accusation of being uncaring bigots.

At least these summary propositions may be made about the reciprocated diatribe in the early 1980s.

(1) Each side felt threatened by the other. Each perceived the other as differing from their own positions on political issues, but more importantly, as differing about the ways in which people should come to decisions about those issues. Both sides could live with the fact that others disagree with them (e.g., on nuclear disarmament), but each is impelled into political conflict when they perceive that the other does not share their way of making decisions about policy. To the secular humanists, the New Christian Right practices

foolishness; to the New Christian Right, the secular humanists practice "moral insanity."

Disagreements about ways of adjudicating differences threaten and motivate them into action due to a common feature of their heritage. Both cultures share a tradition which, particularly in the United States, seeks clarity and precision ("univocality") rather than ambiguity in dealing with the political agenda. Levine noted that "the American way of life . . . affords little room for the cultivation of ambiguity. The dominant American temper calls for clear and direct communication. It expresses itself in such common injunctions as 'Say what you mean,' 'Don't beat around the bush,' and 'get to the point'." This moral code of communicative clarity derives, he writes, from the influences of both the ascetic Puritan tradition and the practices of scientific method.[9]

Given this morality of clarity, a fundamental value is threatened by those who obstinately use a means of decision making other than one's own: the ability to believe that there is a knowable, "right" position on the issues.

(2) The arguments between them did not "engage." That is, the issues raised in a claim were not those addressed in a rebuttal or in a subsequent extension of the argument. This, too, results from the fact that they used different forms of argument: A response which represented the most cherished ideal of argumentation by one side was perceived by the other as foolish or insane. This quickly led to perceptions of the other side as either deficient or perverse.

(3) The discourse produced *within* each group was significantly richer than that produced *between* groups. Each side told a coherent story which located itself in sociohistorical context, which presented its motives as pure and its methods as well considered, and which showed the other side to be contemptible. When the two sides began talking to each other, the contempt was soon expressed.

The asymmetry between the two sides and the interaction between them is not surprising. There are plenty of examples of patterns of interaction that underrepresent the rationality and the compassion of the participants.[10] The question is, what is it about the interaction between these two groups which produced such an unsatisfying interaction?

The Incivility of the Reciprocated Diatribe

There are three possible explanations for the incivility of the interaction between the New Christian Right and the secular humanists.

The first may be quickly dismissed. An incivil discourse is to be expected between incivil people. If it were the case that the participants in the interaction were coarse, brutish, and unskilled in argumentation, we might attribute the form of the interaction to just that, and have a shorter paper. However, one reason the problematic of this paper is so interesting is the discrepancy between the discourse the protagonists produce when confronting each other and that produced when speaking to their own supporters. Apparently, something in the interaction itself has made it so incivil.

A second possibility is that the context of this particular encounter violates fundamental norms of contemporary society, and thus stands outside the bounds of convention. This is the interpretation suggested by Hunter—and the one apparently accepted by at least two of the major protagonists in the interaction, Falwell and Kennedy. Hunter argued that the evangelical politics of the New Christian Right violated the norms of civility as understood in contemporary society. In a civil society, there are two "innovations." First, "humanity itself is split into public and private realms," in which "religion is relegated to the private." The separation of church and state has come to entail the isolation of religion from politics. It may be good for politicians to be privately religious, but this should not affect their public performance except, one supposes, to reinforce general attention to morality and dependability. Second, citizens are required to be "tolerant of others" and to be "tolerable to others." Hunter further states:

> The ethic of civility is an ethic of gentility and studied moderation. It speaks of a code of social discourse whereby religious beliefs and political convictions are to be expressed discretely and tactfully and in most cases, privately. Convictions are to be tempered by good taste and sensibility. . . . The greatest breach of these norms is belligerence and divisiveness; the greatest atrocity is to be offensive and thus, intolerable. . . .
>   . . . For a religion to attempt to reclaim authority for itself in the public sphere is a coarse and tactless act of incivility. From this perspective it becomes clear that the commotion over the New Christian Right largely centers around the fact that the New Christian Right (as institutions and individuals) has violated the moral structure of civility. It has crossed over the barriers separating public and private spheres by attempting to infuse the public sphere with its own distinct version of religious orthodoxy. With the sudden and forceful reintroduction into the public realm of conservative Protestant symbols . . . political decorum has been violated.[11]

The third explanation is that the conflict is between two incommensurate worldviews.

In the present sense, the concept of incommensurateness originates in contemporary philosophy of science, particularly in the work of Thomas Kuhn and Paul Feyerabend.[12] "Normal science," so the argument goes, always occurs in the context of fundamental assumptions about what is true, what is good, and how to determine what is true and good. Kuhn called these clusters of assumptions and the "research exemplars" associated with them "paradigms." From time to time, paradigms change, and so do the meanings and evaluations of data, theories, and the means for producing data and theories. The studies that seemed good and true in one paradigm may seem wrongheaded in another, and vice versa.

In a provocative discussion of this problem, Bernstein differentiates three potential relationships among paradigms. They are *incompatible* if they lead to different conclusions—that is, if one says yes and the other says no to the same question. They are *incommensurate* if they offer answers to different questions or if they disagree about the meaning of events and objects. In a comparison between incommensurate paradigms, there may be no means of adjudicating their differences that is acceptable to both. Paradigms are *incomparable* if they differ so substantially that it is impossible even to explain the ways in which they disagree.

The interaction between the New Christian Right and secular humanists should be seen as the current manifestation of an enduring issue in Western society, traceable at least to the trial of Socrates (accused of atheism and of corrupting the young) and the seventh-century B.C. Hebrew prophets. In the first century A.D., it was expressed in Tertullian's question "What has Jerusalem [the symbol of religious faith] to do with Athens [the symbol of humanistic reason]?" Later, the same issues appeared in the debates about the relative role of science and faith in the writings of Voltaire, in the debates between Julian Huxley and the anti-evolutionists, and in the trials of Galileo and of John Scopes.

From a historical perspective, then, the contemporary conflict between the New Christian Right and secular humanism possesses a significance which transcends the outcome of any of the controversial issues which provide the content of that conflict. The current manifestation of an unresolved dialectic between fundamentally incommensurate worldviews has given shape to contemporary society and will, no matter how the specific issues are resolved, continue as a major formative force in our culture. There have been other times when the conflict between these worldviews has been open and heated, and more times when one side or the other has successfully muted the other, but there has been no clear "victory." Just as one worldview seems triumphant, the other makes an unexpected comeback.

At least one reason for the continuation of this conflict can be seen in the implications of each worldview for ways of deciding what is true, good, and practical. For secular humanists, we are all involved in a process of discovering how it is best to think and act; for the New Christian Right, there are clear directions which have only to be followed. The moral issues are quite different, then, for the two sides, and to act virtuously means something quite different. The unsatisfactory interaction is so durable because it is *in principle* interminable: There is no criterion by which both sides will agree to let it stop. If the relationship between the New Christian Right and the secular humanists is incommensurate, then attempts to make it civil are not likely to succeed.

This interpretation subsumes rather than contradicts Hunter's "civility" hypothesis. The first step in its explication is to show that, despite public endorsement by the principals, civility has not been established by well-published joint appearances and cordial relations between the opposing principals.

The Attempt to Make the Interaction Civil

In the middle third of the decade of the 1980s, Falwell and Kennedy have become, as Cal Thomas put it, the "traveling odd couple" in a quest for civility.

It all began with a mistake in the Moral Majority's sophisticated computerized direct-mail program. Kennedy was sent a card identifying him as a member of the Moral Majority, along with a letter urging him (and others) to help combat "ultraliberals such as Ted Kennedy." In the subsequent embarrassment and good humor, an invitation was issued and accepted for Kennedy to speak at Liberty Baptist College. Subsequently, Falwell and Kennedy presented a debate before the forty-second annual convention of the National Religious Broadcasters held in Washington, D.C., in February 1985.

The debate constitutes a recognition by mainstream liberals that the New Christian Right has become institutionalized and warrants formal attention, but unlike many of the early responses of liberals, Kennedy now appears to be taking the Falwell group seriously and attempting to deal with their position in a more thoughtful way than have others in the past.

Despite its explicit goal of civility, however, this debate maintains the basic split between incompatible worldviews. By prearrangement, the debate dealt primarily with the issues of church and state, South Africa, and the famine in eastern Africa. Kennedy, who spoke first, began by discussing his personal relationship with Falwell. He noted how the two men have become acquainted and have developed a warm respect for each other. Ironically, however, this talk of friendship itself reinforces humanist values of tolerance and civility:

> We continue to have our disagreements, and I'm sure we always will. I do not expect to find him supporting any candidacy of mine for public office, at least not any time soon, or to find myself endorsing many of his positions on public policy. Yet we have come to see each other not merely as opponents, but as fellow human beings who know the hopes, tears, and laughter of life. I believe something even more important has happened in the public arena. We have had a genuine exchange of ideas, a continuing debate about truth and tolerance in American society.

Falwell, too, began with friendship talk, but did not emphasize pluralism and dialogue. Instead, he focused on a rare and somewhat precarious ideological agreement: "I agree, I concur, with what the Senator said here this morning, that we have one very basic common denominator that equates every one of us, and that is: we are free born Americans, and we are charged with the responsibility of keeping this the bastion of freedom at any price for our children's and children's children's sake."

This is a somewhat surprising summary of Kennedy's presentation, and the differences deepen as the meaning of phrases which both use are unpacked. For Kennedy, America is great because it is the product of and a place for civility; for Falwell, America is great because it is God's chosen nation. If each speaker's position were extended, each would see the other as a clear and present danger to their own notion of the nation and of the requisites of national security.

Significantly, Kennedy emphasized functional means for handling conflict, while Falwell dealt with desired end states. In his conclusion, Kennedy spoke of an obligation for human beings "to work together . . . for peace and justice," while Falwell's final words spoke of "a God in heaven who loves us more than we love ourselves and who rules in the affairs of men." These differences in worldviews go far beyond disagreements about specific topics. Kennedy spoke throughout of the need to keep religious and political concerns appropriately separate: "I believe that religious witness should not mobilize public authority to impose a view where a decision is inherently private in nature or where people are deeply divided about whether it is." In keeping with the contemporary liberal concept of civility, he lectured Falwell for not doing likewise:

> Frankly, I also suggest that on the other side there has not been a similar effort to set a coherent standard for the relation between church and state. Depth of feeling or clarity of scriptural command cannot be the determining contract. No matter how much any of us may revere them, simply because the New Testament or the Pope say something does not mean they can be written into the law of a free and pluralistic nation, where tens of millions of people do not accept the authority of the Pope or follow only the Old Testament or believe in no Bible at all.

This statement exemplifies the difficulty confirmed humanists have in understanding the New Christian Right. Kennedy took as self-evident a secular perspective and "framed" the New Christian Right within it. From this perspective, the arguments and acts of the New Christian Right appear to be incompetent or unconscionable.

Falwell, on the other hand, emphasized the need to let religious beliefs guide moral positions, even when they involve public issues. In a style typical of the New Christian Right, he cited the immorality of secular society as the cause of all national problems and as the first priority:

> And then we're facing moral and social issues, which in my opinion as a Bible-believing and born-again Christian holds even greater danger for our beloved homeland than the deficit, the nuclear arms race, or the Central American prob-

lem. It is my conviction that we have far more as a nation to fear from the wrath of an almighty God, who's angry with us for the destruction of 15 million innocent, unborn children during the last twelve years than we have to fear from the Soviet Union.

Especially revealing are the ways in which the two speakers dealt with the South African issue. Kennedy, of course, spoke out vigorously against apartheid, emphasizing repression and human rights, If, as is the case with the humanist worldview, pluralism and rational decision making are important values, then any society that perpetuates racism or denies all its citizens the right to participate democratically is to be condemned. As right-minded people, we should pressure the governments of such nations to change. The answer, according to Kennedy, is human concern and action:

> The people in every American city who care about this issue are proving by their protests that the 1980s need not be a decade of disinterest, a time of lonely hopes and narrow horizons. They're demonstrating, as so many have in South Africa, that individuals are still ready to respond when they are challenged, to stand up not only for themselves, but for others, not only for their interests, but for their ideals.

Falwell's position was, predictably, quite different. While he condemned apartheid, his main concern was the need to maintain friendship with the South African government as a bulwark against Marxism in Africa. He faulted liberals for demonstrating against repression in South Africa, while they ignore repression in the Soviet Union. He noted the advance of communism in Africa and other "losses" throughout the world. In sharp contrast to Kennedy's remedy, Falwell's answer comes through commitment to Jesus Christ: "In summary, the world is in turmoil, and we who believe in the gospel of our Lord and Savior Jesus Christ and who have accepted the claims of his death, burial, and resurrection as the full atonement for our salvation, we have an obligation. We are our brother's keeper."

It is interesting to speculate at this point on how each side in this debate would interpret the other. If our hypothesis is correct, Kennedy would see in Falwell's statement a continued intransigence and inability or unwillingness to consider the complexity of the issues and to consider perspectives other than that of the Christian Right. From his humanist structure, he would question Falwell's ability to be a good humanist. For example, he would question how Falwell's moral position could remain so oblivious to the fact that the American public consists of such a diversity of moral beliefs. Falwell, on the other hand, would take Kennedy's position as blind to moral standards and as misguidedly relativistic. He would, for example, wonder how someone could suggest that the state should not be called upon to dictate matters of personal morality like abortion, and then turn around and suggest that apartheid demands American public outrage. Falwell would take such a position as a double standard divorced from moral principle.

The Interaction Between Incommensurate Worldviews

To make the case that the interaction between the New Christian Right and the secular humanists is a conflict among incommensurate social realities, we followed a three-step procedure.

First, we did an interpretive study of each of the agents in the interaction. This required the ability to hear, at different times, both the New Christian Right and the "secular humanists" speaking in their own voice and within their own social reality. Such interpretive work, in our judgment, requires suspending—at least for the moment—whatever evaluative judgments the researcher might want to make, and learning to "hear" (if not "speak") like a native. This is not easy; it requires moving back and forth between incommensurate paradigms, constantly interpreting what we see from *within* each perspective. One reviewer chastised us for "whitewashing" one group and vilifying the other. If we have done our job well, *both* groups will feel that *in this phase of the project* we have presented them sympathetically and shown the weaknesses of the other group. This asymmetrical perception occurs because terms such as "simplism" take different evaluative and denotative meanings in each worldview; what is for one an insult is for the other an accurate description of a virtue.

Second, at another phase of the project, we had to be able to focus on the forms of talk that occur when these agents confront each other. This required moving back and forth between the social realities of the interacting groups, understanding how particular messages are interpreted by the group who produces them and by the group who responds to them. If we do this phase of the project well, both groups will become suspicious of us, because each will hear us saying about them what the other group says.

Third, we framed the interaction among the groups as a whole. This required moving both within the social realities of the participants of the interaction and stepping outside them in order to characterize the way they "fit" each other. This last step is vitally important to an interpretive study of communication because the form of the interaction as a whole may be, and in this case certainly turned out to be, different from the intentions or perceptions of any of the participants.

The New Christian Right. The worldview of the New Christian Right is surprisingly well captured in Lipset and Raab's six (highly interconnected) terms for describing extremist conservative politics: simplism, moralism, monism, conspiracy, preservationism, and activism.[13] These terms are not incompatible with Medhurst's axioms of classical conservative thought, including theocentricism, the imperfection of human action, the emphasis on moral virtue, and veneration of tradition.[14] While Medhurst warns against equating mainline conservative philosophy with the kind of thinking described by Lipset and Raab, several similarities are apparent and illustrate well how the New Christian Right is both radical and conservative.

Simplism is "the unambiguous description of single cause and remedies for multifactored phenomena."[15] The New Christian Right believes that all issues are moral issues, and that moral issues are by their very nature *not* complex. Tim LaHaye claimed that "most of the evil in the world today can be traced to humanism" and that simple solutions are possible.[16] Falwell repeatedly calls for a "return" to the principles upon which America was built as a solution to contemporary problems.[17] In a fundraising letter, he asks his followers to "cast your vote to 'clean up America.' "[18] The issues are portrayed as clearcut and simple, calling for similarly straightforward solutions.

Simplism leads to a focus on the *reason for* rather than the *effects of* moral action. In a manner reminiscent of Einstein's dictum "while the ways of the Lord may be subtle, they are not perverse," members of the New Christian Right perceive the world as reflecting an underlying moral *order*.

They do not anticipate ironic consequences of moral actions, or expect to find themselves in true moral dilemmas. In fact, one of the attractions of the ideology of the New Christian Right is the explicit assumption of "certainty" in moral decisions.[19]

Moralism is the use of morality as the single criterion for dividing the world of events. Reality is literally defined in terms of "moral sanity" and "moral insanity." Therefore, in the Moral Majoritarian discourse, nothing is amoral. This clear and highly stable criterion provides a sense of unity and clarity to any issue: When in doubt, the Christian activist knows that moral constructs are relevant and will provide sufficient guidance. Purely speculative intellectual play or unbounded curiosity is outside the system and poorly understood from within it, usually being relegated to the subconstruct "evil."[20]

"Moral sanity" is not just a list of preferred positions on the issues; it is a way of conceptualizing the world in which persons subordinate their own thinking to divinely ordained principles. The morality of one's acts derives from the fact that they were done in submission to God's will. LaHaye said: "We believe that it is impossible to maintain a morally sane society without some basic framework for moral decency, some standards that we live by. . . . I have noticed that humanists talk a lot about moral values, but haven't been able to define them. We Christians, however, have easily defined moral values."[21]

Franky Schaeffer expressed the New Christian Right's antipathy to a "man-made" morality: "[Secular humanism] is a philosophy which holds that god is nonexistent or irrelevant to human affairs, and that man must choose or invent his own ethics; secular humanism makes man the measure of all things. This philosophy always seeks to exclude God from the discussion of moral issues, and to do so . . . puts it at loggerheads with Christianity."[22]

Moralism accounts for the frequent use of aphorism and anecdote in "romantic" discourse, which enables participants to see themselves as part of a vision of life. The success of romantic discourse depends upon three qualities:

First, a romance must differentiate a pure and complete idyllic world which is wholly "pious" from a demonic world which is not. The second criterion is verisimilitude, the degree to which the worlds that are described in the romance are congruent with an auditor's reconstructions of his or her past experiences. . . . The truth of romance also depends [third] on the rhetor's ability to adopt an acceptable language. In this language of romance, words about society and human relationships express spiritual truths. In an idyllic society, every sociopolitical term also is a supernatural term, the sociopolitical and spiritual realms are merged.[23]

One of the reasons that scripture is so often used as proof by Moral Majoritarians is that it combines history and divine authority in a form that makes the morality principle live for its adherents. Michael McGee calls the use of biblical texts to criticize contemporary morality "radical reflection": "The Bible is a collection of stories about the 'sameness' of humanity. If Falwell is right, one can find some story in the Bible structured narratively in the same way the story of contemporary political and moral condition would be structured."[24]

The third element of the New Christian Right's worldview is *monism*. In a pluralistic society, politics is "the constant process of negotiation through which conflicting interests come to live with each other. It is not a body of knowledge of truth, but a regulated contest whose purpose . . . is to construct agreements" or to make possible compromise as a substitute for harsher remedies.[25] Monism, on the other hand, is the substitution of a particular doctrine or position as right. Such a doctrine may be grounded on an appeal either to revealed truth or to populism. The New Christian Right combines both by using an appeal to the will of the people while using its religious traditions as proof that what the majority believe is right. Lou Barnes, head of the California Moral Majority, put it crisply: "We have a mandate to return to broad principles of biblical law, to restore order to our society."[26]

Monism leads to intellectual practices which are at variance with standards applied by secular humanists. Sharp differentiation among levels of meaning or among different contexts or topics is considered inappropriate, and speakers often link issues that for other people seem to have no connection, such as abortion, homosexuality, prayer in the schools, women's rights, and the defense budget. In an article about abortion, Cal Thomas linked his argument not only to the general notion of sacrifice but to the politics of the 1960s, McGovern, civil rights, Vietnam, and the relationship between Jews and Hitler. Following is a brief excerpt:

Should slaves have been content with a Cabinet post in the Lincoln Administration if slavery was allowed to continue? Would Jews have been satisfied with a post

in the Hitler "administration" while the gas chambers continued to operate? . . .
What are YOU willing to give up to save the lives of unborn babies who, someday,
will thank you for what you did?[27]

Monism also makes the politics of compromise and accommodation seem
immoral. Because so many issues and positions are collapsed together under a
single moral frame, one cannot give up on one issue without giving up on all
of them. As a result, the communication patterns of the Moral Majority are
not characterized by an examination of nuances between the polar choices of
these issues; any middle ground is summarily dismissed as an illegitimate
betrayal of the larger moral position. For example, the Moral Majority was
incensed by President Reagan's decision to make economic policy his first
priority after being elected in 1980. To them, this betrayed their monistic
concept of the social agenda. Thomas explained: "[Even] if Reagan cleans up
the economy, and lots of babies go on being killed, I think we will go down the
tube. I think we'll forfeit the right to exist as a nation."[28] Since the New
Christian Right perceives ruin as inevitable if moral issues are compromised, it
is entirely reasonable for them to take "extreme" positions, and, ask along with
Thomas: "[Is] there nothing on which we will stand as absolute truth and say,
'here I stand'?"[29]

The fourth element of the New Christian Right's worldview is the *conspiracy
theory*. History is consistently interpreted in terms of a conspiracy. The conspiracy is comprehensive, extending throughout time and space, and is effi-
cacious in manipulating the majority of the people by the malicious, cunning
acts of the few. The conspiracy is linked to political monism, and the effect is
to legitimate closing down the marketplace of ideas. In the summer of 1981
LaHaye warned that although they number only 275,000, humanists control
the means of producing our cultural symbols, and that "most of the evil in the
world today can be traced to humanism."[30] As Conrad puts it:

> Moral Majority rhetoric depicts a demonic world which is so complete in its
> depravity that its members are blind to its intrinsic evil. Its citizens have adopted a
> language which makes the good seem bad and the wrong seem right. Its leaders
> have built impenetrable walls between themselves and the voices of righteousness,
> creating a condition in which their actions are influenced only by agents of evil. Its
> educational, political, and legal institutions strengthened the forces of evil.[31]

The conspiracy theory makes it easy for the Moral Majority to make use of a
rhetoric of victimage. It describes itself as distrusted, feared, and unfairly
treated by its opponents, especially by the media. The response of its critics
reinforces this notion.

The fifth element of the worldview is *preservationism*, an orientation in
which a greater symbolic investment is placed in the past than in progress and
change. This past may be real or imagined, corporate or individual. This
attitude "becomes operative when [the person] seizes upon some aspect of the

past with which to identify and express dissatisfaction with the changing present. And in either case, there are variably involved his power, his prestige, his self-esteem, his sense of connectedness, his sense of privilege, his sense of social comfort: in brief, his status."[32] The New Christian Right takes its reconstruction of American history as the ideal for the future.

Finally, the worldview of the New Christian Right includes *activism* as an important part. Activism is here defined as the absence of democratic restraint, which produces extremist positions. Dean Wycoff's comparison of homosexuality to murder, and his call for the capital punishment of gays, though later denounced by Falwell, is a good example.[33] Activism further implies a collective assumption of responsibility for individuals: The enlightened "we," stipulated to be the majority, must protect the vulnerable "them" from the predations of "our enemies."

It is no wonder, then, that the New Christian Right created the social drama of moral war. Paul Weyrich drew parallels between the mission of the New right and the military philosophy attributed to General Douglas MacArthur: "There is no substitute for victory." Weyrich argued: "It is a war of ideology, it's a war of ideas; it's a war about our way of life. And it has to be fought with the same intensity, I think, and dedication as you would fight a shooting war."[34] Howard Phillips described the war plan in these terms: "Conservatives must establish ourselves first as the opposition, then the alternative, finally the government."[35]

Consequently, the New Christian Right's approach to communication is one of confrontation and a rhetoric of salvation. The metaphor of "saving" its order from its enemies provides a transcendent theme around which the New Christian Right may interpret its own activities as messianic and thus worth any sacrifice. It also provides a ready account sufficient to disregard the arguments made by opponents of the group. Such was the case, for example, in the *Moral Majority Report*'s statement about the nuclear freeze initiative: "The Nuclear Freeze Movement, which is attempting to gather momentum around the U.S., is simply another ploy by the radical left to strip America, weaken her defenses, and make the nation vulnerable to foreign attack."[36]

Secular Humanists. Those who oppose the New Christian Right have no collective label for themselves. Some call themselves liberals, others humanists, and still others are not happy with—or at least not given to using—either of these labels. Still, the label "secular humanism" is descriptive of the worldview commonly held by those who espouse academic freedom, liberal education, free press, scientific and technical commitments, and other pluralistic, relativistic positions in our society.[37] Hunter summarizes the humanistic world view in these terms:

[I]t assumes that the universe is material in its nature and origin; that all social reality, including ethical prescriptions and normative codes, is exclusively a human construction and therefore relatively defined; and that reason and the empirical method in conjunction with an opaque conception of the human good is the crucible that determines what is right and wrong, legitimate and illegitimate—and ultimately what is good and evil. [The human good is subject to multiple definitions, varying with interest and circumstance.] It is a world view that is open-ended and malleable.[38]

This worldview celebrates functional rationalism, the infusion of rational controls in to all spheres of human experience: "Reason and intelligence are the most effective instruments that humankind possesses. There is no substitute: neither faith nor passion suffices in itself. The controlled use of scientific methods, which have transformed the natural and social sciences since the Renaissance, must be extended further in the solution of human problems."[39]

This orientation is expressed in a thoroughgoing skepticism toward all dogma, "pragmatic" willingness to adapt innovations, a belief in progress, and a willingness to measure progress by human standards. Humanism is the belief that there are no values independent of humankind, and a willing dependence on human capabilities in addressing questions of knowledge and action:

If the starting point of humanism is the preservation and enhancement of all things human, then what more worthwhile goal than the realization of the human potentiality of each individual and of humanity as a whole? What more pressing need than to recognize in this critical age of modern science and technology that, if no deity will save us, we must save ourselves?[40]

Pluralism is a way of thinking which presupposes the existence of incommensurate groups within society and thus makes tolerance and means of communication more important virtues than faith and evangelical zeal. The authors of the *Humanist Manifesto II* wrote: "We believe in cultural diversity and encourage racial and ethnic pride, we reject separations which promote alienation and set people and groups against each other; we envision an integrated community where people have a maximum opportunity for free and voluntary association."[41]

Pluralism also presupposes a distinction among domains of life, particularly between secular, public activities and matters of individual taste, which may be religious.

Kennedy's speech "Tolerance and Truth in America" was a landmark statement of humanistic ideals.[42] He began and ended by expressing his faith in a pluralistic society in which people who disagree live peaceably in mutual tolerance. His major theme was the relation between church and state, which, he felt compelled to note, is not a simplistic principle. The danger he envisioned is that those of "deep religious faith . . . may be tempted to misuse government in order to impose a value which they cannot persuade others to accept." He suggested a differentiation between public and private issues, claiming that religion should appeal directly—not through government—to individuals about private matters, and that religious leaders should "bear witness" but not seek to impose their views on public issues. There are, he said, four "tests" which define the difference between "imposed will and essential witness," and that if all adhere to them "we keep church and state separate— and at the same time, we recognize that the City of God should speak to the civic duties of men and women."

This worldview constructs a schema for handling social and moral questions. Each issue is to be handled separately, on its own merits. Rival opinions are to be expected, their expressions encouraged, and the matter adjudicated on the basis of empirical facts, and the rivals should accept the result because they are persuaded by those facts that the decision is correct. All participants are to exhibit a high degree of tolerance toward others and be ready to sacrifice their own position as the data demand: "We are committed to an open and democratic society. . . . decision making must be decentralized to include widespread involvement of people at all levels—social, political, and economic."[43]

Secular humanists do not see themselves as partisan, one group among many, who have come into recent and perhaps temporary ascendancy. Rather, they see their policies as the ultimate triumph of reason, emerging from a historical confrontation with powers of ignorance and superstition: "Science and economic change have disrupted the old beliefs. . . . In every field of human activity, the vital movement is now in the direction of a candid and explicit humanism."[44]

Their forms of communication stress the process of posing a variety of options and selecting among them on the basis of the probability that they will lead to desired consequences. This process is always subject to review, and those who use it are expected to be willing to abandon their most cherished principles and theories in the face of tangible evidence. The enemies to be constantly fought are the dead hands of tradition, ignorance, and unreason.

This pattern of talk carries with it a myth of ultimate openness, that all opinions are accepted and subjected to the same criteria of evaluation.[45] These criteria are stipulated as relentless, and in practice they are capable of deconstructing and thus devaluing any basis for epistemic or moral certainty. Unlike the New Christian Right, secular humanists do amuse themselves with stories of moral and intellectual perplexity, and honor those with sufficient courage to throw away previously acceptable standards in favor of the new information generated by successive iterations of the process. An apparently inevitable concomitant of secular humanism is a persistent pattern of change in standards and practices.

The one thing that secular humanists cannot tolerate, or treat as a viable alternative, is just that procedure for making policy decisions which the New Christian Right describes as "moral sanity": the subordination of all judgment to divine principle. For secular humanists, this is not an option to be evaluated like all others, but a threat to the process of evaluating options on the basis of their effects. This attitude has led to the intemperate attacks on the New Christian Right cited earlier in this paper.

The Interaction. Charles Conrad accurately noted: "It is, of course, not surprising that the Moral Majority's actions tend to provoke intense reactions. However, while the more vitriolic of these responses may express adequately the moral indignation of their authors, they do little to illuminate either the Moral Majority or its rhetoric."[46] Given the ontological and epistemological gap between the worldviews of the New Christian Right and the secular humanists, what can be made of the communication between these groups? We can dismiss the view that the conflict is merely disagreement on issues. Each side is offended by and denies the validity of precisely those forms of discourse in which the other places the most confidence.

For secular humanists, the willingness to subordinate oneself to dogma is precisely the mindset that they consider that they have painfully overcome, and to be urged to adopt such a stance is frightful. For members of the New Christian Right, the willingness to entrust oneself to the products of human reason is a guarantee not only of adopting an erroneous life-style, but of having no basis for certainty in moral questions.

For example, at issue in the campaign for the Equal Rights Amendment is not only whether the amendment itself should be passed, but the larger question of how the issue should be conceptualized and the language with which it should be discussed. On this, and on all other issues under contention, neither side is willing to lose gracefully, because it must avoid the very way of thinking and talking adopted by the other. Even worse, neither side seems to understand the true nature of the conflict. The interaction is therefore like an iterating and often escalating cycle, and the consequences are grave.

The interaction between the New Christian Right and the secular humanists is snarled in a particularly frustrating pattern of reciprocated diatribe. The frustration results in part because the pattern of interaction is so much simpler and more barren than the social realities of either of the groups participating in it, and in part because this contemporary instance of the dialectic between the sacred and the secular seems unlikely to enrich the longer, historical conversation. Previous instances of this debate—particularly in the hands of Voltaire and the *philosophes*—seem much richer than the contemporary version.[47]

Further, the contemporary interaction perpetuates deep misunderstandings by each side of the other. Although the New Christian Right often exchanges messages with individuals and groups with whom it disagrees, its worldview channels it into patterns of action which practically preclude the possibility of mutual understanding or eventual agreement. The secular humanists, on the other hand, either dismiss the New Christian Right with thoughtless invective or lectures it on how to fit more effectively into the humanist worldview. Neither of these approaches strikes a particularly resonant note with the New Christian Right.

Secular humanists, for the most part, have been unable to focus on the worldview of the New Christian Right. Instead, they treat the New Christian Right as if it were trying to act within the secular framework and doing poorly at it.

On the other hand, the New Christian Right interprets the liberals' response as confirming their judgment that the mythology of "secular humanism" has become so deeply entrenched in the contemporary social and political institutions that the liberals no longer see it as a "perspective." The content of liberalism is "tolerance" and "pluralism," and this, ironically, makes liberals particularly blind to the possibility of a view which does *not* celebrate tolerance and pluralism. As a result, the New Christian Right accuses the liberals either of arguing in "bad faith" or of being deluded by their own ideology.

The interaction between the New Christian Right and its critics, then, is marked by varying rules for interpreting and acting on the communication of the other. Figure 1 summarized our interpretation of the interaction, showing that it has the basic structure of an ideological conflict. This illustration should be read in three parts:

(1) The middle row describes the sequence of events in the interaction. Reading it from left to right produces something like a narrative description of who said/did what.

(2) The information above the sequence of events depicts the rules for meaning and action of the New Christian Right as it interprets its actions and those of its opponents. The information below the sequence of events depicts the rules for meaning and action of the secular humanists as they interpret the various aspects of the interaction. To identify the way the logic of the interaction emerged from the particular sequence of events, the figure is read in a serpentine manner, from upper left downward to lower left, one space to the right, then from lower to upper, one space to the right, and so on.

(3) The pattern of interaction is seen by combining the sequence of events with the social reality of each group, and framing the whole as a single entity. In this reading, the whole figure is read at once. Of special importance in this regard is the most interesting and significant aspect of the figure, the circular loop pictured on the right. Once the interaction became entrenched, it creates the repetitive pattern which has been described in some detail in this section.

Conclusion

The thesis of this paper is thoroughly pessimistic. We began by noting a new element in the until-now vitriolic interaction between the New Christian Right and the secular humanists. At least some of the primary figures in that interaction are taking concerted efforts to make it "civil." We conclude, however, that the quest for civility is quixotic. The worldviews of the groups are profoundly incommensurate. To the extent that they understand each other and have to intermesh their actions regarding such issues as abortion, balanced budgets, and military spending, the conflict will continue. We argued that the interaction is looped; it cannot terminate by finding some mutually acceptable criterion for adjudicating conflicting claims. The issue is not really *what* to think but *how*; not so much what specific *acts* are right or wrong but how *morality* is to be determined. This feature of the interaction creates the "strange bedfellows" phenomenon, such as the Moral Majority joining with the National Organization for Women to oppose—for strikingly different reasons—pornography.

If our analysis of this interaction is right, the relationship between the New Christian Right and the secular humanists exemplifies a kind of conflict which numerous critics have cited as an ominous aspect of contemporary society. We call it "ideological conflict."

The problem manifests itself as a series of prolonged conflicts in which participants disagree not only about specific issues, but about the moral rationale for resolving those issues. Whatever the surface structure of the controversy, the significant differences stem from the fundamental concepts of reality embraced by the protagonists, including their understanding of what is real, what is good, and the means by which the real and the good can be known and acted upon.

Ideological conflicts pose vexing problems for critics as well as for protagonists and the society in which they occur. A conventional analysis of the quality of the argumentation is precluded by the fact that the standards for argument differ depending on which worldview one embraces, and these differences themselves are at issue in the conflict. Further, the contradictory worldviews make the exigencies of the rhetorical situation inherently problematic. The means by which the rhetors may be true to their own cause may be incompatible with the requisites for effective engagement with the other group.[48]

But while we are pessimistic about the prospects for making the interaction between the New Christian Right and the secular humanists civil, we are not content to let the discourse revert to and remain at the level of reciprocated diatribe. Historically, when discourse is not used as a way of achieving coordination among conflicting groups, one side or the other is silenced—but not refuted—by the ballot box, terrorists' bombs, military or police action, the inquisition, or social/economic exploitation.

There are more powerful means of intervening in ideological conflict than by imposing the rules of civility. One such intervention is for those not so embroiled in the controversy to seek to implement what Habermas called "undistorted communication" about the issues.[49] An appropriate means by which this can be accomplished is to call into question the assumptions behind the assertions made by the most vocal partisans on both sides, using the tools of interpretive and critical research.[50] The effect is to refocus the interaction from charge and countercharge about particular issues to the underlying worldviews from which they emerge. This is not likely to make the New Christian Right and the secular humanists "compatible" nor even "commensurate," but it will show them to be "comparable"; and with comparability, discourse, rather than its dehumanizing surrogates, can continue.

Notes

1. Robert J. Branham graciously shared with us the results of his critiques of Kennedy's and Falwell's public discourse. Sheryl Perlmutter-Bowen and Brian Duke participated in the research upon which this paper is based when they were graduate students in the Department of Communications at the University of Massachusetts, Amherst.

2. The term "secular humanism" is itself a part of the public discourse produced by the interaction which is the problematic of this paper. As noted later, it is *not* self-ascriptive: most of those identified as exemplars either do not recognize the term or object to it.

    The rejection of the term by most of those whom it is supposed to identify poses a problem for interpretive researchers like ourselves. Since the term is used in the interaction (albeit more by one side than the other), it must become part of our vocabulary, but we must decide in what manner we shall use it.

    Most "secular humanists" argue that the term is inherently vague, used as a bludgeon with which the New Christian Right attacks its opponents. On the other hand, spokespersons for the New Christian Right argue that it denotes a pattern of thought and action which is one among many of the subcultures of contemporary society. Further, they explain that secular humanists reject the term because they think that they are "right," and thus do not comprise only *one* of many "religions."

    The sensitive reader may see in this quarrel the major outlines of the reciprocated diatribe which has characterized so much of the recent public discourse about values, religion, and policies.

    In this paper, we follow the New Christian Right's usage, but without their pejorative connotations. The secular humanists' distaste for this—or any other label—seems to grow organically from their worldview described at length later in this paper, and is reminiscent of the existential philosophers of the 1950s, all of whom rejected the label "existentialist."

    However, the public discourse with which we are concerned has been seriously impaired by this refusal to see secular humanism as a cluster of values and institutionalized practices which is—at one level of abstraction—parallel to those of the New Christian Right. Among other reasons, this refusal has necessitated a certain blindness by the secular humanists. For example, William Safire's etymology of the term in the *New York Times Magazine* (26 January 1986, 6, 8) cites legal texts and sociological essays back to 1933, but ignores contemporary conservative theologians such as Francis Shaeffer. Cal Thomas bitterly describes such systematic ignorance of conservative Christian literatures as a blatant form of censorship.

3. Jerry Falwell's name is frequently mentioned when alluding to the New Christian Right, and the Moral Majority, Inc., is often cited as a synecdoche for the New

Christian Right. Like "secular humanism," the term "moral majority" has inflamed passions as well as provided convenient labels. For whatever reasons, in January 1986, Jerry Falwell announced that the Moral Majority will hereafter be known as the "Liberty Federation," explaining that this change reflects the new emphasis on international policies.

4. Isaac Asimov, "The Blind Who Would Lead," *MacLeans* 2 February 1981, 6.

5. A. Bartlett Giamatti, "The Moral Majority Is a Threat to the Freedom of Americans," *Pittsburgh Post-Gazette*, 5 September 1981, 8.

6. Cal Thomas, *Book Burning* (Westchester, IL: Crossway Books, 1983), 116–18.

7. Richard A. Viguerie, *The New Right: We're Ready to Lead* (Falls Church, VA: Viguerie Company, 1980).

8. Dr. Tim LaHay, quoted by Corlis Lament, "Answering the Moral Majority," *The Humanist* 19 (1981): 19.

9. Donald N. Levine, *The Flight From Ambiguity: Essays in Social and Cultural Theory* (Chicago, IL: University of Chicago Press, 1985), 29.

10. See W. Barnett Pearce and Vernon E. Cronen, *Communication, Action and Meaning* (NY: Praeger, 1980), chapter 5.

11. James Davison Hunter, "Religion and Political Civility: The Coming Generation of American Evangelists," *Journal for the Scientific Study of Religion* 23 (1984): 365–66.

12. See Richard Bernstein, *Beyond Objectivism and Relativity* (Philadelphia, PA: University of Pennsylvania Press, 1984).

13. Seymour M. Lipset and Earl Raab, *The Politics of Unreason* (NY: Harper and Row, 1970).

14. Martin Medhurst, "Resistance, Conservatism, and Theory Building: A Cautionary Note," *Western Journal of Speech Communication* 49 (1985): 103–15.

15. Lipset and Raab, *Politics*, 7.

16. Tim LaHaye, *The Battle for the Mind: A Subtle Warfare* (Old Tappan, NJ: Fleming H. Revell, 1980).

17. Jerry Falwell, *Moral Majority Report* (18 May 1981): 8.

18. Undated letter received 25 March 1981.

19. See, for example, Franky Shaeffer, *A Time for Anger: The Myth of Neutrality* (Westchester, IL: Crossway Books, 1982), 15–25.

20. See, for example, Jerry Falwell, *Listen America!* (Garden City, NY: Doubleday, 1980), 206–7.

21. Frederick Edwards, "The LaHaye-LaRue Dialogue," *The Humanist* (August 1981): 13.

22. Schaeffer, *A Time for Anger*.

23. Charles Conrad, "The Rhetoric of the Moral Majority: An Analysis of Romantic Form," *The Quarterly Journal of Speech* 69 (1983): 161–2.

24. Michael McGee, "Secular Humanism: A Radical Reading of 'Culture Industry' Productions," *Critical Studies in Mass Communication* 1 (1984): 6.

25. Lipset and Raab, *Politics*, 19.

26. *U.S. News and World Report* (8 June 1981): 45.

27. *Moral Majority Report* (24 September 1981): 10.

28. *Christianity Today* (5 February 1981): 52.

29. *Moral Majority Report* (21 September 1981): 10.

30. LaHaye, *Battle for the Mind*, 9.

31. Conrad, "Rhetoric," 169.
32. Lipset and Raab, *Politics,* 504.
33. *Maclean's,* 4 May 1981, 13.
34. Quoted by Viguerie, *New Right,* 58.
35. Quoted by Viguerie, *New Right,* 63.
36. *Moral Majority Report* (April 1982): 6.
37. Some current exemplars of humanism include the American Humanist Society, the American Humanist Asociation, Norman Lear and the People for the American Way, and the American Civil Liberties Union.
38. James D. Hunter, "The Liberal Reaction," in *The New Christian Right,* edited by Robert C. Liebman and Robert Wuthnow (New York: Aldine, 1983), 161.
39. Paul Kurtz, ed., *Humanist Manifestos I and II* (Buffalo, NY: Prometheus Books, 1973), 17.
40. Kurtz, Preface to *Humanist Manifestos,* 3.
41. Kurtz, *Humanist Manifestos,* 20.
42. Reprinted in *Church and State* (November 1983): 18–21.
43. Kurtz, *Humanist Manifestos,* 19.
44. Kurtz, *Humanist Manifestos,* 7.
45. "To be modern, I said, is to experience personal and social life as a maelstrom, to find one's world and oneself in perpetual disintegration and renewal, trouble and anguish, ambiguity and contradiction: to be a part of a universe in which all that is solid melts into air. To be a moder*nist* is to make oneself somehow at home in the maelstrom, to make its rhythms one's own, to move within its currents in search of the forms of reality, of beauty, of freedom, of justice, that its fervid and perilous flow allows." (Marshall Berman, *All That Is Solid Melts into Air: The Experience of Modernity* [New York: Simon and Schuster, 1982], 345–6).
46. Conrad, "Rhetoric," 159.
47. Alasdair MacIntyre, *After Virtue: A Study in Moral Theory* (Notre Dame, IN: University of Notre Dame Press, 1981).
48. This idea is developed by Robert J. Branham and W. Barnett Pearce, "Text and Context: Toward a Rhetoric of Contextual Reconstruction," *Quarterly Journal of Speech* 71 (1985): 19–36.
49. Juergen Habermas, "Toward a Theory of Communicative Competence," in *Recent Sociology # 2,* ed. Hans Peter Dreitzel (London: Collier-MacMillan, 1970), 114–48; "On Systematically Distorted Communication," *Inquiry* 13 (Autumn 1970): 205–19.
50. Brian Fay, *Social Theory and Political Practice* (London: George Allen and Unwin, 1975), 92–110.

11
How New Is the New Christian Right? A Study of Three Presidential Elections

Benton Johnson
and
Mark A. Shibley

THE RECENT EMERGENCE of a politically militant conservatism among America's evangelical Protestants caught most students of religion and politics by surprise. They knew that studies had repeatedly shown that Protestants as a whole were more likely than any of the other major religious communities to identify themselves as Republicans (Lipset, 1964; Knoke, 1974). They also knew that among the clergy theological belief was related to political ideology, party identification, voting behavior, and attitudes on a wide range of social and economic issues. They were therefore aware that among Protestant ministers fundamentalists and evangelicals were less politically liberal than the "new breed" of theological radicals who were so prominent in the civil rights and antiwar movements of the 1960s (B. Johnson, 1966, 1967; Hadden, 1969; Quinley, 1974). Even so, they were unprepared for the upsurge of conservative activism on Protestantism's theological right wing a decade later.

There are at least three reasons why most scholars were not prepared for the upsurge. One reason is that in recent decades conservative Protestant leaders had tended to maintain a low political profile. They were not actively involved

178

on either side of the political campaign that led to the passage of the Civil Rights Act. During the controversy over the Vietnam War they were less likely than their theologically liberal colleagues to preach about or take a public stand on the war. Observers were correct to point out that the eschatology of premillennial dispensationalism widely subscribed to by fundamentalist and evangelical leaders made the saving of souls far more important than any matters of public policy. After all, if Jesus could return tomorrow, why concern oneself with politics? This was Jerry Falwell's position when he was a young pastor. Two decades ago he wrote: "Believing the Bible as I do, I would find it impossible to stop preaching the pure saving gospel of Jesus Christ and begin doing anything else, including fighting communism, or participating in civil rights reforms. Preachers are not called on to be politicians but to be soul winners. Nowhere are we commissioned to reform the externals" (*New York Times*, 2 September 1984, 1:1).

The second reason social scientists were unprepared for the rise of a militant political conservatism among evangelicals is that studies of the Protestant laity had produced no clear-cut or consistent evidence that evangelicals were any more likely than other Protestants to be politically conservative. David Knoke (1974), for example, in an analysis of national postelection survey data from the 1960s, found Episcopalians and Presbyterians more likely than Baptists and fundamentalists to identify themselves as Republicans. He reported, in fact, that Baptists were almost as likely as Catholics to consider themselves Democrats.

It is no wonder, then, that most research and commentary on the New Christian Right (NCR) has focused on the elements of novelty and change that are associated with it. Arthur H. Miller and Martin P. Wattenberg (1984), for example, in an analysis of 1980 postelection data, have shown that white fundamentalists were more likely than nonfundamentalists to have voted in 1980, and Corwin Smidt (1983a), using the same data, has shown that white evangelicals voted in greater numbers than in previous presidential elections. Miller and Wattenberg also reported that 85 percent of white respondents with the highest scores on an index of fundamentalism voted for Reagan, a percentage higher than that of any other category on their six-point scale.[1] In a 1980 study of Southern Baptist ministers, James L. Guth reported that these "traditionally apolitical" respondents "had matched the political activism of the 'New Breed' liberal Protestant mainline clergymen of the 1960s" (Guth, 1985: 13–14). A follow-up study four years later showed a marked tendency for Southern Baptist clergy to abandon their traditional Democratic party affiliation and to identify themselves as Republicans. By early 1985, fully three-quarters of Southern Baptist clergy residing in the Deep South thought of themselves as Republicans (Guth, 1985: 16). Although it is now generally agreed that the actual contribution of the New Christian Right to the outcome of the 1980 election—especially the presidential election—was either nonexistent or very slight (Lipset and Raab, 1981;

Johnson and Tamney, 1982) many expect to find that its impact was more substantial in 1984 (Miller and Wattenberg, 1984; Smidt, 1983b). In short, the focus of studies of the New Christian Right has been on recent developments and prospects for the future. In Miller and Wattenberg's (1984) words, the New Christian Right is "a small but solid voting bloc" that "is being formed," a community "for whom religious beliefs have become politicized" (315).

Is There an Old Christian Right?

But is the New Christian Right entirely new? Has a community of politically conservative evangelicals been in existence for decades? Did it, prior to its recent highly visible mobilization, exert a quiet but persistent influence on some aspects of political life? This is the question we shall explore here.

Why should anyone suppose that such a community antedated the efforts of Falwell and others to politicize evangelicals? The first reason for supposing that it did is a historical one. Most students of the relation between religion and politics in American history now believe that a close alliance existed between the Republican party, including its antebellum antecedents in the North, and a broad coalition of Protestant denominations made up primarily of persons of British stock, denominations such as the Presbyterians, the Congregationalists, the Methodists, and the Baptists (Hammond, 1979; P. Johnson, 1978; Lipset, 1964). These denominations not only had a spiritual and moral program for individuals, they also had a moral and political agenda for America. These older evangelicals, both clergy and laity, were periodically active in campaigns that had a clear political dimension, such as campaigns against slavery and alcoholic beverages.

The issues that tore this Protestant coalition apart in the first decade of the present century were largely theological in nature, but the theological disputes were paralleled by disagreements on political issues. Those theological liberals who supported the Social Gospel broke with traditional Republican ideology and embraced a progressive politics that eventually led many of their descendants into the modern Democratic party. Fundamentalists, on the other hand, made no such political shift. Although great numbers of them espoused a form of premillennial theology that discouraged direct intervention in political affairs, this theology taught nothing that altered traditional moral or political values, such as a preference for free enterprise and the Republican party, and an opposition to gambling and drinking. Moreover, premillennialism never taught that political affairs had no religious significance. In fact, it was highly sensitive to the flow of national and world events and encouraged their continuous monitoring for signs of the fulfillment of biblical prophecy.

Another reason for supposing that a community of politically conservative evangelicals existed before the late 1970s is the series of surveys of the relation between theology and political preference among the Protestant clergy to which we have already referred. On many issues, the differences in political outlook were astonishingly sharp. For example, data from a 1968 survey of California clergy revealed that 76 percent of fundamentalists, as opposed to only 8 percent of theological liberals, advocated increased U.S. military effort in the Vietnam War (Quinley, 1970: 46). A survey of the Baptist and Methodist clergy of Oregon, conducted six years earlier by the senior author of this paper, showed that 88 percent of the respondents affiliated with the premillennialist Conservative Baptist Association of America, the largest Baptist body in Oregon, had tended to favor Republican candidates for office over the preceding five years. By way of contrast, only 39 percent of those Methodist respondents who described their theology as liberal or neo-orthodox had preferred Republican candidates (B. Johnson, 1966: 203, 205).

The only question that remains is whether this community of politically conservative evangelicals has recently been swollen by an influx of newly mobilized lay supporters or whether it has had a substantial support base among the laity all along. On balance, previous research would suggest that it has not had such a support base. It seems clear, for example, that in the United States, religious conservatism, or traditionalism, does not by itself produce or reinforce a posture of political conservatism. For decades devout Irish Catholics supported the Democratic party and its economically liberal policies. Black evangelicals, whose theology is very close to that of white evangelicals, have in recent years been even more solidly Democratic than Catholics. But we are not concerned here with religious conservatism in the abstract or with theology as a formal system of thought divorced from the experience and accumulated memory of concrete communities. We are concerned with the political culture of a specific community, or set of communities, of Protestant Christians that in this century coalesced as the right-wing remnant of the old evangelical coalition.

How are the members of this community to be identified? First, very few of them are black. Despite many points of similarity between white and black evangelicals, the two communities overlap very little and have developed cultures that are distinctive in style and substance. The evangelical right is overwhelmingly white. Second, the cultures of white Northern and Southern evangelicals are not identical, owing largely to the unique historical experience and traditions of the South, including its tradition of loyalty to the Democratic party. For this reason, analyses of the political attitudes and behavior of white evangelicals should be performed separately for Southerners and non-Southerners. Lumping whites and blacks, Northerners and Southerners all together, as Knoke (1974) did in examining the political makeup of Protestant denominations, is an exercise in obfuscation.

The third point to bear in mind in identifying the evangelical right wing is that it is an interdenominational community. Some denominations, e.g., the Conservative Baptists and the Orthodox Presbyterian Church, are uniformly evangelical in culture, but most of the larger denominations contain a mix of liberal, moderate, and evangelical elements. The Southern Baptist Convention, for example, which is often considered the largest evangelical body in the United States, contains many ministers and lay people who are not biblical literalists and who are put off by the program of the Moral Majority. On the other hand, the United Methodist Church, whose leadership is markedly liberal, contains enclaves of evangelical sentiment. Denominational membership is therefore a poor way of identifying evangelicals. A far better way of identifying them in social surveys is through a set of items tapping specifically evangelical beliefs, experience, and practice. In 1978 the Gallup organization was the first to make use of such items in a nationwide survey conducted for the evangelical magazine, *Christianity Today*. In 1980 the Center for Political Studies at the University of Michigan, which had conducted presidential election surveys for many years, incorporated a number of items of this kind for the first time. Much of what we now know about the political attitudes and behavior of white evangelicals in the 1980 election, and their recollections of the 1976 election, is based on indexes which make use of these items (Miller and Wattenberg, 1984; Smidt, 1983a, 1983b). Such indexes should make it easy to keep track of the evangelical right in the years to come.

The New Christian Right Index

Because our interest is in tracking the evangelical right in the years before 1980, we have had to rely on an indirect measure of evangelicalism. Our search for an appropriate index of this kind was guided by two considerations. First, we were determined not to base the index on denominational affiliation. Second, the index had to be constructed from items that were repeated in a series of national surveys covering the 1980 election, the 1976 election, and at least one earlier election. Only by comparing the political position of evangelicals in the 1980 election with their position in previous elections could a test be made of the thesis that an evangelical right existed before the rise of groups like the Moral Majority.

The data for this study are from the National Opinion Research Center's (NORC) *General Social Surveys* (1972–1984).[2] The cumulative file contains a variety of attitudinal items on issues that figure prominently on the agenda of the New Christian Right as well as items concerning political attitudes and behavior. The principal advantage of this data lies in the continuity of relevant questions, which will permit an examination of the relation between evangelical sentiment and political attitudes and behavior over a period spanning three presidential elections. For information about presidential voting in the 1976 election we have used the NORC survey of 1977. Because NORC conducted no survey in 1981, we have used its 1982 survey for information about the 1980 election, and because some of the items we considered essential for an index of New Christian Right attitudes did not appear on the 1973 survey, we have relied on the 1974 survey for information about the 1972 election.

As a first step in developing an index to identify potential supporters of the evangelical right we selected eight attitudinal items that reflect positions articulated by the leaders of the New Christian Right on a number of key social and economic issues.[3] The attitudinal index consists of two questions dealing with sexual morality, one question on the proper role of women in society, two questions on abortion, one question gauging support for prayer in the public schools, and two questions on ideological intolerance, one regarding atheism and the other communism.[4] The values of each item were recoded for directional consistency, with a score of 0 indicating positions opposing the Christian right, a score of 1 indicating neutral or "don't know" positions, and a score of 2 indicating positions favoring the Christian right. The recoded values on the eight items were then summed for each respondent, creating an index with scores ranging from 0 to 16 that measures attitudinal consistency with Christian right values. The reliability alphas for the attitudinal index are .737 (1974 survey), .738 (1977 survey), and .743 (1982 survey).

Although the attitudinal index consists of issues of concern to the New Christian Right, these issues are of equal concern to civil libertarians. It is therefore not clear whether it should be referred to as a civil liberties index or as an index of Christian right opinion. To be sure, we would expect supporters of the Christian right to score very high on the index and civil libertarians to score very low, but the absence of a specifically religious component in the index makes it impossible to distinguish high scorers who are religiously motivated from those whose motivations are secular. Clearly, a religious component needs to be added if the index is to serve as a measure of Christian right opinion. In the absence of appropriate theological items, we have chosen to weight the attitudinal index by a measure of religiosity based on frequency of church attendance, thereby weeding out from the high end of the scale those respondents who do not actively participate in organized religious life. Frequency of church attendance, measured on a nine-point scale with 0 at the low extreme and 8 indicating attendance more than once a week, is utilized for this purpose. Church attendance and the attitudinal index are positively correlated (r=.334 in 1974, r=.363 in 1977, r=.412 in 1982). This finding is in accord with Yinger and Cutler's report (1982), also based on NORC data, that church attendance is consistently the best predictor of Moral Majority attitudes.

To construct what we shall refer to as the New Christian Right (NCR) Index, we recoded individual items to eliminate values of zero and simply multiplied the attitudinal index scores by church attendance for each respondent. The NCR Index has a range of scores from 8 to 216. For purposes of bivariate analysis we have grouped Index scores into four categories. Respondents with scores ranging from 8 to 60 are considered strong opponents of the New Christian Right, those with scores from 60.01 to 112 are considered moderate opponents, those with scores from 112.01 to 164 are considered moderate supporters, and those with scores from 164.01 to 216 are considered strong supporters. Table 1 shows the percentage of respondents in each of the four Index categories for all three surveys. It is worth noting that opponents of the New Christian Right outnumber supporters by almost three to one and that strong opponents outnumber strong supporters by almost six to one. This pattern resembles Miller and Wattenberg's (1984) finding that those scoring in the lowest category on their seven-point scale were far more numerous than those scoring in the highest category. It should also be pointed out that the proportion of the white population scoring highest on the NCR Index has varied less than one percentage point over the three surveys, which suggests that potential sympathizers with the Moral Majority are not a growing presence on the national scene.

TABLE 1
Percentage Frequency Distribution for the NCR Index

NCR Categories	1974	1977	1982
Strong opposition (8–60)	45.5%	47.4%	49.8%
Moderate opposition (60.01–112)	26.7	26.7	25.2
Moderate support (112.01–164)	19.7	17.1	17.0
Strong support (164.01–216)	8.2	8.8	8.0
Totals	100.1%	100.0%	100.0%
N =	1302	1333	1312
Index Mean	80.43	79.42	76.61
Index Standard Deviation	53.95	55.13	54.90
Min = 8 Max = 216	Range = 209		

The data in Table 2 permit a comparison of the percentage of strong NCR supporters and all other respondents within a variety of demographic categories. Before noting the highlights of the table we must explain what some of these categories stand for. First, the South consists of the regions coded on the NORC surveys as South Atlantic, East South Central, and West South Central. These three regions include the states of the old Confederacy plus Delaware, Maryland, the District of Columbia, West Virginia, Kentucky, and Oklahoma. This is a rather broad definition of the South, but no narrower definition is possible without omitting some states that are unambiguously Southern. Second, the category labeled Miscellaneous Evangelical was constructed from the list of specific religious bodies in the NORC codebook that make up the general code category of "other Protestant denomination." Miscellaneous Evangelical consists of denominations generally considered evangelical, e.g., the Assemblies of God and the Churches of Christ, as well as other less familiar religious bodies which respondents identified with one or more key words, e.g., "sanctified," "Wesleyan," or "full gospel." A list of these denominations and key words appears in Box 1 at the end of the chapter.

TABLE 2
Percentage of Strong NCR Supporters Within Demographic Subgroups

Demographic Groups		1974	1977	1982
Region	South	13.5%	12.8%	12.9%
	Non-South	5.8	7.1	5.8
Age	18–35	5.0	3.8	3.7
	36–60)	8.5	8.9	8.7
	61+	13.5	17.3	13.8
Sex	Male	7.4	7.4	6.3
	Female	8.9	9.9	9.3
Class	Petit Bourgeois	7.5	11.5	5.8
	Professional/Managerial	5.9	7.2	2.5
	Routine White-Collar	6.3	8.1	6.0
	Blue-Collar	10.8	8.2	9.7
Education	Less Than High School	12.1	13.1	14.9
(Diploma)	High School	7.3	6.5	6.3
	College (2- and 4-year)	3.6	6.6	2.4
Religion	None	0.0	1.3	0.0
	Jewish	0.0	2.9	0.0
	Episcopalian	0.0	3.0	0.0
	Presbyterian	2.8	1.6	2.9
	Methodist	5.3	3.5	3.4
	Catholic	6.9	9.8	6.9
	Lutheran	9.7	2.9	0.8
	Baptist	13.6	12.9	17.7
	Misc. Evangelical	27.1	32.6	28.4
	Other	9.8	7.5	10.8

The findings in Table 2 strengthen our confidence that the NCR Index is an acceptable surrogate for a more direct measure of evangelical right sentiment. Although strong supporters of the New Christian Right are a minority in all the religious categories in the table, they are proportionately more numerous among Baptists than among the more liberal Protestant denominations, and they are most numerous of all among the miscellaneous evangelical bodies. Other demographic differences parallel the findings of nationwide surveys using different measures of evangelicalism. Strong New Christian Right supporters are most likely to live in the South, to be more than sixty years old, to be female, to be blue collar, and to have failed to complete high school. They are least likely to be young adults, to have professional or managerial occupations, and to have completed college. However, as Miller and Wattenberg (1984) have pointed out regarding similar findings of their own, it is important not to exaggerate these differences. For the most part, they are fairly small. Evangelicals are much more nearly a cross section of the population than many people suppose. For example, our data (not shown here) also reveal that about half of all strong New Christian Right supporters live outside the South, about a third hold professional, managerial, and white-collar jobs, three-fifths are under the age of sixty-one, half have completed high school or college, and more than a third are men.

Finally, just as Table 1 showed that strong New Christian Right supporters are not a growing proportion of the white population, Table 2 shows that variations over time in the proportions of strong New Christian Right supporters within virtually all demographic categories are small and show no clear pattern.

Findings

If we find that the relationship between the NCR Index and various measures of political attitudes and behavior is stronger in NORC's 1982 survey than in the two earlier surveys, then we will have good evidence that support within the evangelical community for conservative causes is a very recent phenomenon. If, however, a different pattern emerges, the recency of this support will be called into question.

TABLE 3

Political Ideology of Strong New Christian Right Supporters and All Others, by Region (by percentage)

Region	Political Ideology	Strong NCR Supporters			Others		
		1974	1977	1982	1974	1977	1982
Whole Country	Liberal	8.4%	5.6%	6.2%	14.7%	13.6%	10.8%
	Conservative	26.0	23.4	33.0	12.9	14.2	17.3
	N =	96	107	97	1155	1172	1159
South	Liberal	12.3	8.5	6.1	12.9	12.8	9.7
	Conservative	24.5	27.7	36.7	15.3	17.0	22.3
	N =	49	47	49	334	328	331
Non-South	Liberal	4.3	3.3	6.3	15.3	14.0	11.2
	Conservative	27.6	20.0	29.2	11.9	13.2	15.3
	N =	47	60	48	821	844	828

Table 3 allows us to compare the political ideology of those scoring highest on the NCR Index with the political ideology of the other respondents. The

terms liberal and conservative in the table designate the two extreme categories on each end of a seven-point scale of political ideology. Because the
political traditions of white Protestants in the South have differed from those
of white Protestants elsewhere, the table includes a control for region. The
table shows that in 1982 there was a fairly marked relationship between
political ideology and score on the NCR Index. In both regions of the
country, a 14 percentage-point difference separates those with high Index
scores from the other respondents. But there was also a discernible relationship between NCR Index scores and political conservatism in the two earlier
surveys. In 1974, for example, there was a 16 percentage-point difference
among non-Southerners between those scoring high and those scoring lower.
Moreover, non-Southerners with high Index scores were only slightly more
conservative in 1982 than they were in 1974. Only in the South do high
scorers show a clear trend toward greater ideological conservatism over time
and only there does this trend appear more pronounced than the trend toward
conservatism that has also taken place during this period among the rest of the
population.

TABLE 4

Political Party Affiliation of Strong New Christian Right Supporters and All
Others, by Region (by percentage)

	Political Party	Strong NCR Supporters			Others		
		1974	1977	1982	1974	1977	1982
Whole Country	Democrat	44.8%	42.4%	46.2%	40.8%	41.7%	35.6%
	Republican	28.6	34.5	28.8	24.4	22.9	24.9
	N =	105	116	104	1130	1203	1196
South	Democrat	47.3	51.0	55.8	43.7	41.1	40.2
	Republican	23.6	27.5	25.0	25.9	22.7	24.7
	N =	55	51	52	332	348	348
Non-South	Democrat	42.0	35.4	36.5	39.6	42.0	33.7
	Republican	34.0	40.0	32.7	25.4	23.0	25.0
	N =	50	65	52	798	855	848

Table 4 presents the relationship between political party affiliation and score
on the NCR Index. For ease of presentation, NORC's seven-point index of
party affiliation has been collapsed into two categories, with the category of
Independent, the midpoint of the scale, omitted. The table shows no clear
increase over time in the proportion of Republicans among any category of
respondent. Southern supporters of the Christian right may be becoming

more conservative ideologically, but in 1982 they were only slightly more Republican than in 1974, and were actually a bit less Republican than in 1976. Nor was there a surge of Republican identification among high Index scorers living outside the South. The most striking pattern in the table, however, is that in all three surveys traditional regional differences in party affiliation persist more markedly among those with high Index scores than among other respondents.[5] Over the entire eight-year span, the largest proportions of Democratic identifiers in the table are high scorers who live in the South and the largest proportion of Republican identifiers are their counterparts who live in the North and West. Moreover, there is no sign that these differences have been decreasing. In fact, the only clear-cut trend in the table is an *increase* in proportion of high scorers in the South who consider themselves Democrats.

TABLE 5

Percentage of Strong New Christian Right Supporters and All Others Who Voted in Presidential Elections, by Region

Region	Strong NCR Supporters			Others		
	1972	1976	1980	1972	1976	1980
Whole Country	70.9%	74.3%	70.6%	72.7%	67.3%	68.8%
N =	103	113	102	1152	1167	1149
South	69.8	72.5	72.0	67.2	62.4	66.4
N =	53	51	50	332	338	327
Non-South	72.0	75.8	69.2	75.0	69.2	69.8
N =	50	62	52	820	829	822

Table 5 compares the voting turnout of those scoring high on the NCR Index with others in the presidential elections of 1972, 1976, and 1980. The table shows that in the nation as a whole high scorers were slightly less likely to vote in 1972 than were other respondents, but that their level of voting increased in 1976, whereas that of other respondents declined. The turnout of high scores fell in 1980 to the level of 1972 but remained proportionately greater than the turnout of those who scored lower. In short, the data support the findings and inferences of other studies that a mobilization of Christian right supporters has taken place, but it does not support the contention that the mobilization took place in 1980 in response to the appeals of the Moral Majority and other Christian right activists. The mobilization appears to have been in response to the excitement caused by Jimmy Carter's candidacy in 1976. Despite the fact that Ronald Reagan was a conservative, a Republican, and a backer of the objectives of the Moral Majority, voting turnout among non-Southerners with high Index scores sagged in 1980 to a level lower than their turnout of 1972. Only in the South did the supporters of Christian right issues maintain in 1980 the level of voting they attained in 1976.

TABLE 6

Presidential Voting of Strong New Christian Right Supporters and All Others, by Region (by percentage)

Region	Presidential Voting	Strong NCR Supporters			Others		
		1972	1976	1980	1972	1976	1980
Whole Country	Democrat	25.4%	47.5%	45.8%	34.4%	50.9%	40.3%
	Republican	69.0	52.5	52.8	61.8	47.9	51.4
	N =	71	80	72	808	772	764
South	Democrat	27.0	47.2	52.8	23.7	49.0	48.6
	Republican	67.6	52.8	47.2	72.6	50.0	49.0
	N =	37	36	36	215	206	208
Non-South	Democrat	23.5	47.7	38.9	38.3	51.6	37.2
	Republican	70.6	52.3	58.3	57.8	47.2	52.3
	N =	34	44	35	593	566	556

In Table 6 we examine the presidential voting behavior of high scorers on the NCR Index and others in the three presidential elections. It will be well to bear in mind that these data, like virtually all other national data on individual voting, represent the reports respondents gave to interviewers after the elections were over and are therefore more error-ridden than respondents' reports of their current opinions and activities. Table 6 reveals that in the nation as a whole the increase in Republican presidential voting in 1980 over 1976 was actually less among high NCR-Index scorers than it was among other respondents. Outside the South, high scorers were slightly more likely than others to increase their Republican voting, but in the South high scorers were somewhat less likely than others to do so. There was no surge of Republican presidential voting in 1980 on the religious right. The most striking patterns in the table involve the persistence of traditional partisan alignments involving region and religion. In all three elections, high scorers who reside in the North and West were more likely than other respondents in those regions to have voted Republican. The difference was greater by far in 1972 than in the two later elections, but it has not disappeared. Moreover, among high scorers, regional differences, which disappeared in the election of 1976, were even more pronounced in 1980 than they had been in 1972. Finally, in the South high scorers were slightly more likely than others to have voted Democratic in 1972 and 1980.

TABLE 7

Summary of Regression Analysis of Political Ideology, by Region

| | South | | | | | |
| | 1974 | | 1977 | | 1982 | |
Predictor	Beta Weights	Sign. Level	Beta Weights	Sign. Level	Beta Weights	Sign. Level
NCR Index	.180	.003	.186	.002	.215	.0001
Party affiliation	.123	.04	.178	.002	.319	.0000
Education	.089	ns*	−.002	ns	.020	ns
Age	.062	ns	.122	.05	.066	ns
Sex	−.056	ns	.087	ns	−.073	ns
Social status	−.052	ns	−.050	ns	.007	ns
Income	.049	ns	.135	.04	.043	ns
N =	295		293		315	
Multiple R_2 =	.243		.332		.407	
R =	.059		.110		.116	

| | Non-South | | | | | |
| | 1974 | | 1977 | | 1982 | |
Predictor	Beta Weights	Sign. Level	Beta Weights	Sign. Level	Beta Weights	Sign. Level
Party affiliation	.224	.0000	.265	.0000	.184	.0000
NCR Index	.199	.0000	.160	.0000	.152	.0000
Age	.125	.0009	.142	.0001	.149	.0001
Social status	−.094	.02	.037	ns	.053	ns
Education	−.070	ns	−.023	ns	−.076	.05
Income	−.067	ns	−.037	ns	.030	ns
Sex	−.044	ns	−.093	.006	−.076	.03
N =	719		792		770	
Multiple R_2 =	.378		.376		.322	
R =	.143		.141		.103	

* ns refers to beta weights not significant at least at the .05 level.

Regression analysis will enable us to assess the magnitude of the independent contribution of New Christian Right attitudes to political ideology and party identification in relation to that of other independent variables. Table 7 summarizes the regression analyses for political ideology in each region. An inspection of the beta weights and significance levels shows that in all three surveys and in both regions New Christian Right attitudes have a highly significant, independent influence on political ideology that is rivaled only by party identification and that is consistently greater than that of education, income, or social status. Only in the South, however, does the relative contribution of New Christian Right views to political conservatism increase over the period covered by the three surveys. Outside the South, there is a steady decrease in their relative contribution over the same period. In the North and

West, the NCR Index was a better predictor of political conservatism in 1974 than it was eight years later.

Table 8 shows that the NCR Index has a relatively low and statistically nonsignificant independent contribution to political party affiliation in all the surveys and in both regions. Of all the variables, only political ideology shows a consistent and statistically significant relation to party affiliation. There is no indication of an increase in the independent contribution of New Christian Right views to Republican affiliation over time. In fact, in both regions scores on the NCR Index are associated with a slight movement away from Republicanism after the 1974 survey. In any event, 1974 was the only year in which the Index showed a positive relationship to affiliation with the Republican party.

TABLE 8

Summary of Regression Analysis of Political Party Affiliation, by Region

	South					
	1974		**1977**		**1982**	
Predictor	Beta Weights	Sign. Level	Beta Weights	Sign. Level	Beta Weights	Sign. Level
Political ideology	.126	.05	.193	.002	.331	.0000
Social status	.079	ns*	−.024	ns	.051	ns
NCR Index	.069	ns	−.083	ns	−.072	ns
Sex	.063	ns	−.065	ns	.032	ns
Income	.017	ns	−.041	ns	.060	ns
Education	.015	ns	.099	ns	.081	ns
Age	.006	ns	.011	ns	=.027	ns
N =	295		293		315	
Multiple R_2 =	.189		.213		.366	
R =	.036		.045		.134	

	Non-South					
	1974		**1977**		**1982**	
Predictor	Beta Weights	Sign. Level	Beta Weights	Sign. Level	Beta Weights	Sign. Level
Political ideology	.234	.0000	.279	.0000	.193	.0000
Social status	.161	.0001	.024	ns	−.027	ns
Sex	.080	.03	.079	ns	−.010	ns
Income	.071	ns	.081	.03	.087	.03
NCR Index	.048	ns	−.025	ns	−.030	ns
Age	.032	ns	.026	ns	.002	ns
Education	.016	ns	.088	.02	.125	.002
N =	719		792		770	
Multiple R_2 =	.319		.311		.244	
R =	.102		.097		.060	

* *ns* refers to beta weights not significant at least at the .05 level.

In order to assess the contribution of New Christian Right views to voting behavior, we have used discriminant analysis, which produces coefficients that are roughly equivalent to those of regression analysis. No significance tests, however, are available for discriminant analysis. Table 9 reveals that the NCR Index is a relatively unimportant factor in predicting votes in any of the three presidential elections. In both regions, party affiliation far outweighs the influence of New Christian Right views, or indeed of virtually all the other predictors, on presidential voting. Outside the South, the NCR Index is associated with Republican voting in all three elections. The association is strongest in 1980 and weakest in 1976. In the South, the Index is associated with Democratic voting in 1972 and 1980, and with Republican voting in 1976. In view of the smallness of all the coefficients in Tables 8 and 9, these variations should be interpreted with caution.[6]

TABLE 9

Summary of Discriminant Analysis of Presidential Voting, by Region

	South		
	Standardized Discriminant Coefficients		
Predictor	1972	1976	1980
Party affiliation	.775	.992	.955
Political ideology	.600	.073	.103
Age	.405	−.015	.226
Education	−.206	.003	−.334
Social status	.166	−.011	−.118
Income	.132	−.022	.314
Sex	.115	−.034	.018
NCR Index	−.042	.070	−.042
N =	191	188	206
Percentage classified correctly by this model:	83.8%	81.4%	81.6%

	Non-South		
	Standardized Discriminant Coefficients		
Predictor	1972	1976	1980
Party affiliation	.911	.931	.857
Political ideology	.200	.181	.323
Income	.187	.063	.189
NCR Index	.085	.040	.127
Social status	−.065	.172	.095
Age	.042	−.103	.108
Sex	.036	.105	−.036
Education	−.019	−.001	−.033
N =	512	540	471
Percentage classified correctly by this model:	77.0%	83.1%	77.3%

Discussion

Neither the bivariate nor multivariate analyses provide clear support for the view that evangelicals have recently become a conservative force on the American political scene. It is true that there was a discernible trend toward greater conservatism between 1974 and 1982 among Southerners with high NCR Index scores, but outside the South Index scores were weaker predictors of conservative ideology in 1982 than they were in 1974. It is also true that high scorers voted in smaller numbers in 1972 than they did in later elections, but their greatest voting turnout was in 1976 rather than in 1980. Moreover, there was a modest decline in Republican party affiliation between 1977 and 1982 among high scorers in both regions of the country, and in the South this decline was paralleled by a slight increase in Democratic voting in the 1980 election. Only in the North and West was there a clear increase in Republican voting in 1980.

On the other hand, the analyses are consistent with the view that a tradition of political conservatism has existed for many years among a segment of the evangelical laity. The most compelling evidence for this view is the fact that in all three surveys the NCR Index is a good predictor of conservative political ideology. The persistence of tradition is also suggested by the fact that in all the surveys high NCR-Index scorers who live in the North and West were more likely than their neighbors to identify themselves as Republicans and to vote for Republican presidential candidates. With only one exception, namely presidential voting in 1976, their counterparts in the South were more likely to identify themselves as Democrats and vote for Democratic candidates. And with only one exception, these high-scoring Southerners were also more likely than other Southerners to identify themselves as Democrats and vote for Democrats. Nor, with the exception already noted, is there any steady pattern of change over the eight-year period. A comparison of multivariate coefficients across the three surveys shows that the NCR Index was a stronger predictor of political conservatism in the South in 1982 than it was in 1974 or 1977. Similarly, it was a stronger predictor of Republican voting outside the South in 1980 than in 1972 or 1976. On the other hand, longitudinal comparisons of the coefficients also show that the Index was a stronger predictor of Republican voting in the South in 1976 than in 1972 or 1980, and that it was a stronger predictor of political conservatism and Republican party affiliation outside the South in 1974 than in 1977 or 1980.

Still, there appear to be some interpretable variations within the larger pattern of the persistence of traditional political orientations on the Christian right. In 1976, Carter's candidacy seems not only to have increased the voting turnout of high NCR-Index scorers, it also seems to have pulled a disproportionate number of high scorers in the North and West away from their traditional Republican voting habits. In 1980, with a self-proclaimed conser-

TABLE 10
Distribution of Responses to NCR Attitudinal Items

Summary of Question	Percentage by Year		
	1974	1977	1982
Allow antireligious book in library, favor removal or not:			
0–not favor	61.3	59.8	61.7
1–don't know	2.3	1.4	2.4
2–favor	36.4	38.8	35.9
N =	1304	1337	1323
Allow communist's book in library, favor removal or not:			
0–not favor	59.4	56.4	58.4
1–don't know	2.9	2.2	3.5
2–favor	37.6	41.4	38.1
N =	1299	1334	1316
Support availability of legal abortion in the case of pregnancy due to rape:			
0–yes	84.4	83.1	84.9
1–don't know	3.9	3.2	3.7
2–no	11.7	13.7	11.4
N =	1302	1332	1317
Support availability of legal abortion if a woman is married and does not want any more children:			
0–yes	45.8	44.9	47.2
1–don't know	4.9	4.3	4.6
2–no	49.3	50.9	48.2
N =	1304	1333	1320
Feelings about sex before marriage:			
0–not always and sometimes wrong	51.3	57.2	59.3
1–don't know	3.2	2.3	3.1
2–almost and always wrong	45.5	40.5	37.6
N =	1297	1330	1318
Feelings about homosexual relations:			
0–not always and sometimes wrong	20.7	22.0	21.5
1–don't know	4.8	4.6	4.1
2–almost and always wrong	74.5	73.4	74.4
N =	1257	1332	1314

TABLE 10 (*Continued*)

Summary of Question	Percentage by Year		
	1974	1977	1982
Women should take care of home not country:			
0–disagree	63.7	61.3	72.1
1–not sure	3.1	2.3	2.6
2–agree	33.2	36.4	25.3
N =	1304	1337	1323
Court ruling disallowing Bible prayer in public schools:			
0–approve	29.4	35.0	39.4
1–no opinion	3.7	2.5	2.5
2–disapprove	66.8	62.5	58.1
N =	907*	1336	1320

* In the 1974 survey, a split ballot with two slightly different questions was used to measure the same issue of school prayer. One half is the same form used in the 1977 and 1982 surveys. The other question had different response categories, only some of which could be recoded in a useful manner. The two questions on school prayer in the 1974 survey were combined to attain the greatest possible number of valid cases; however, 397 cases are missing for this question in 1974.

BOX 1
Recoding Evangelicals

A "pure" group of evangelical Christians was sorted out of the "other" category of the Protestant variable using two criteria: (1) denomination, and (2) a term or terms typically associated with one or another wing of conservative Protestantism.

DENOMINATION

Church of God	Church of Christ
Christian and Missionary Alliance	Missionary Baptist
Assembly of God	Four Square Gospel
Free Methodist	Mennonite
Free Will Baptist	Nazarene
Open Bible	Salvation Army
Christian Reformed	Seventh Day Adventist

KEY TERMS

Advent	Holiness
Apostolic Faith	Holy Roller
Bible	New Testament
Brethren	Pentecostal
Calvary	Prophecy
Covenant	Sanctified
Evangelical	Wesleyan
Full Gospel	Zion
Fundamentalist	

vative and friend of the Moral Majority on the Republican ticket, many of them returned to their traditional ways. In the South, the fact that in two of the three presidential elections high Index scorers gave more than 50 percent of their votes to the Republican candidate indicates that the general pattern of presidential Republicanism that has been emerging in that region for more than thirty years has made deep inroads in the evangelical community. This fact, together with the increasing ideological conservatism of Southerners with high Index scores suggests that their Democratic loyalties will not withstand a vigorous appeal by a conservative Republican, especially if the Democratic candidate is neither an evangelical nor a conservative. As late as 1982, however, Southern evangelicals remained, in the words of one research team, "the most doggedly Democratic white group" in their region (Perkins et al., 1983: 80).

The thesis that the New Christian Right has been built on the foundation of a distinctive, regionally differentiated, evangelical political culture of long standing will require further empirical support before it can be fully accepted. All we have done here is to establish its plausibility by showing that one index of evangelicalism suggests that political culture existed as early as 1972 and that the Moral Majority and Reagan's first campaign had virtually nothing to do either with shaping it or mobilizing it. The next step in testing the thesis will be to identify items on nationwide surveys conducted prior to 1972 from which approximate indexes of evangelicalism can be constructed so that the profile of continuity and change in the recent history of popular evangelical political culture in America may begin to be sketched.

We conclude this chapter with Table 10, which provides more detailed information on the question wording and distribution for each item used in this study, and with Box 1, which concerns the recoding of evangelicals by denomination and by key terms associated with conservative Protestantism.

Notes

1. Miller and Wattenberg (1984) use the term fundamentalism as if it were synonymous with evangelicalism. In the parlance of the Protestant right, however, the terms refer to different perspectives and subcultures which are at odds on certain issues. (The Protestant right contains a number of other subcultures and emerging tendencies as well. For treatments of some of these see Quebedeaux, 1974; Wells, 1981; Webber, 1981; Hunter, 1981; Ammerman, 1982). There is, however, a growing trend among scholars to employ the term evangelical in a sense broad enough to encompass both the fundamentalists and all who comprise the more doctrinally diverse community linked to the National Association of Evangelicals. We use the term in this broader sense.

2. Each National Opinion Research Center (NORC) survey is an independently drawn sample of English-speaking persons eighteen years of age or over, living in noninstitutional arrangements in the United States. Block quota sampling was used in 1974. Full probability sampling was employed in the 1977 and 1982 surveys. Our analysis is restricted to white respondents (1974 N = 1304, 1977 N = 1339, 1982 N = 1323).
3. The model for this index is based on a technique used by J. Milton Yinger and Stephen Cutler (1982) to measure attitudinal support for the Moral Majority.
4. See Table 10 at the end of the chapter for detailed information on the question wording and distribution of responses for each item.
5. The same pattern appears in Corwin Smidt's (1983b) data on the political orientations and behavior of white evangelicals.
6. In interpreting the beta weights in Tables 7 and 8 and the standardized coefficients in Table 9, it should be kept in mind that political ideology, party affiliation, and presidential voting have been coded to make high scores represent conservative and Republican preferences, respectively.

References

Ammerman, Nancy T. 1982. "Operationalizing Evangelicalism: An Amendment." *Sociological Analysis* 43 (Summer): 170–1.

Guth, James L. 1985. "The Christian Right Revisited: Partisan Realignment Among Southern Baptist Ministers." Paper presented to the 1985 annual meeting of the Midwest Political Science Association.

Hadden, Jeffrey K. 1969. *The Gathering Storm in the Churches.* Garden City, NY: Doubleday.

Hammond, John L. 1979. *The Politics of Benevolence. Revival Religion and American Voting Behavior.* Norwood, NJ: Ablex.

Hunter, James Davison. 1981. "Operationalizing Evangelicalism: A Review, Critique, and Proposal." *Sociological Analysis* 42 (Winter): 363–72.

Johnson, Benton. 1966. "Theology and Party Preference Among Protestant Clergymen." *American Sociological Review* 31 (April): 200–8.

———. 1967. "Theology and the Position of Pastors on Public Issues." *American Sociological Review* 32 (June): 433–42.

Johnson, Paul E. 1978. *A Shopkeeper's Millennium: Society and Revivals in Rochester, New York, 1815-1837.* New York: Hill and Wang.

Johnson, Stephen D., and Joseph B. Tamney. 1982. "The Christian Right and the 1980 Presidential Election." *Journal for the Scientific Study of Religion* 21 (June): 123–31.

Knoke, David. 1974. "Religion, Stratification and Politics: America in the 1960s." *American Journal of Political Science* 18 (May): 331–45.

Lipset, Seymour Martin. 1964. "The Sources of the 'Radical Right,'" in Daniel Bell (ed), *The Radical Right.* Garden City, NY: Anchor Doubleday. 307–1.

Lipset, Seymour Martin, and Earl Raab. 1981. "The Election and the Evangelicals." *Commentary* (March): 25–31.

Miller, Arthur H., and Martin P. Wattenberg. 1984. "Politics From the Pulpit: Religiosity and the 1980 Elections." *Public Opinion Quarterly* 48 (Spring): 301–7.

Perkins, Jerry, Donald Fairchild, and Murray Havens. 1983. "The Effects of Evangelicalism on Southern Black and White Political Attitudes and Voting Behavior." In *Religion and Politics in the South: Mass and Elite Perspectives,* edited by Tod A. Baker, Robert P. Steed, and Laurence W. Moreland, 55–83. New York: Praeger.

Quebedeaux, Richard. 1974. *The Young Evangelicals.* New York: Harper and Row.

Quinley, Harold E. 1970. "The Protestant Clergy and the War in Vietnam." *Public Opinion Quarterly* 34 (Spring): 43–52.

———. 1974. *The Prophetic Clergy: Social Activism Among Protestant Ministers.* New York: Wiley.

Smidt, Corwin. 1983a. "The Mobilization of Evangelical Voters in 1980: An Initial Test of Several Hypotheses." Paper presented to the 1983 annual meeting of the American Political Science Association.

———. 1983b. "Born-Again Politics: The Political Behavior of Evangelical Christians in the South and non-South." In *Religion and Politics in the South. Mass and Elite Perspectives,* edited by Tod A. Baker, Robert P. Steed, and Laurence W. Moreland, 27–56. New York: Praeger.

Webber, Robert E. 1981. *The Moral Majority: Right or Wrong?* Westchester, IL: Crossway.

Wells, David F., and John D. Woodbridge, eds. 1981. *The Evangelicals.* Grand Rapids, MI: Baker.

Yinger, J. Milton, and Stephen J. Cutler. 1982. "The Moral Majority Viewed Sociologically." *Sociological Focus* 15 (October): 289–306.

PART III
NEW
PERSPECTIVES ON
RELIGION AND
THE MODERN
WORLD

12
God and Caesar in Conflict in the American Polity

Richard L. Rubenstein

THE RELATIONSHIP between religion and the capitalist rationalization of the economy and society has always been highly problematic. On 10 November 1984, a new chapter in the continuing national debate unfolded when the U.S. Bishops' Ad Hoc Committee on Catholic Social Teaching and the U. S. Economy made public the first draft of a proposed pastoral letter on the economy. Although the draft was a tentative statement subject to revision, it did indicate that in their final letter the majority of the bishops were likely to express profoundly ambivalent opinions about the American capitalist system.

The bishops' draft letter was in keeping with an admonition expressed in the bishops' 1980 letter on Marxist communism in which they cautioned against identifying Christian social principles "with our own social-economic structure." In that same letter, the bishops observed that consumerism and America's failure to deal seriously with the sources of global injustice "weaken our credibility" and heighten the attraction of communism to the less-developed countries of the world.[1] The bishops asserted that the extreme economic inequality to be found in contemporary America and the world at large is "morally unacceptable." To remedy the situation, the bishops proposed the following:

(1) A national commitment to reduce the unemployment rate to 3 to 4 percent, partly implemented by federally sponsored job-creation programs targeted at the structurally unemployed. The bishops also urged the funding of public and private job-training programs.

(2) Proposals for a drastic overhaul of the welfare system including: (a) uniform national eligibility standards, (b) a uniform minimum benefit level, (c) welfare programs restructured to encourage rather than discourage gainful

employment, (d) annual cost of living adjustments, (e) participation by welfare recipients in the design of public assistance programs, and (f) programs
designed to strengthen rather than weaken the family.

(3) Curtailment of the arms race, which diverts energy and resources away
from the economic problems besetting the nation and the world.

(4) New labor laws designed to help workers organize unions, to prevent
worker intimidation, and to defend workers expeditiously against unfair labor
practices.

(5) A changed U. S. foreign policy that would reemphasize human needs
rather than military programs. The bishops were especially critical about the
militarization of the U.S. economy and American arms sales and arms grants
to developing nations.[2]

Coming so soon after the president's reelection on an unabashedly pro-
capitalist platform, the bishops' critical attitude toward free-enterprise capitalism undoubtedly surprised many Americans. Nevertheless, the bishops' views
were consistent with traditional Catholic attitudes toward capitalism. Joseph
Califano, Secretary of the Department of Health, Education, and Welfare
from 1977 to 1979, tells of a private audience he had with Pope John Paul II
on 11 November 1978 in which the Pontiff declared that both capitalism and
communism had serious moral flaws—in the case of capitalism, its mal-
distribution of material wealth; in the case of communism, its repression of the
human spirit.[3]

The Church has traditionally been suspicious of ethically unregulated market economies. There is little in Catholic ethical doctrine that could concur
with Adam Smith's faith in an economic system in which the sum total of self-
regarding economic actors yields the greatest good for society as a whole.
Historically, the Church has tended to view society in organic terms and to
reject the self-aggrandizing economic individualism of free-enterprise capitalism.

Long before Pope John Paul II expressed his dissatisfaction with contemporary capitalism, Max Weber outlined some of the reasons the Church and
many other religious traditions have had a tradition of deep distrust of capitalism. Writing of the antipathy between Catholic religious institutions and
capitalism, Weber observed:

> The reasons for this mutual antipathy must be sought in the fact that the
> domination of capital is the only one that cannot be ethically regulated, because of
> its impersonal character. Most of the time this domination appears in such an
> indirect form that one cannot identify any concrete master and hence cannot make
> any ethical demands upon him. . . . Decisive are the need for competitive survival
> and the conditions of labor, money, and commodity markets; hence matter-of-fact
> considerations that are simply non-ethical determine individual behavior and
> interpose impersonal forces between the persons involved. The penalty for non-
> compliance is extinction, and this would not be helpful in any way. More impor-

tant is the fact that such economic behavior has the quality of a *service* toward an *impersonal* purpose.[4]

The extreme anonymity, moral neutrality, and depersonalization characteristic of the contemporary economic order is a consequence of a market economy. Again Weber can instruct us:

> The market community as such is the most impersonal relationship of practical life into which human beings can enter with one another. . . . The reason for the impersonality of the market is its matter-of-factness, its orientation to the market and only to that. When the market is allowed to follow its own autonomous tendencies, its participants do not look toward the persons of each other . . . there are no obligations of brotherliness or reverence, and none of spontaneous human relations that are sustained by personal unions. They all would just obstruct the free development of the bare market relationship. . . . Market behavior is influenced by rational, purposeful pursuit of interests.

Having described the market system, Weber offers the following comment:

> Such absolute depersonalization is contrary to all the elementary forms of human relationship. . . . The "free" market, that is, the market which is not bound by ethical norms . . . is an abomination to every system of fraternal ethics. In contrast to all other groups which always presuppose some measure of fraternal relationship or even blood kinship, the market is fundamentally alien to any type of fraternal relationship.[5]

It is therefore hardly surprising that a highly influential group of Roman Catholic bishops found themselves in fundamental opposition to the Reagan economic philosophy in spite of agreement on such issues as abortion, school prayer, and economic relief for parents of children attending nonpublic schools. No administration in recent history has been as committed to free-enterprise capitalism as President Reagan's. In spite of the president's assurances, undoubtedly made in good faith, that a "safety net" would be maintained for the poor, the logic of free-enterprise capitalism *must* lead to a progressive diminution of such support. The poor have failed the ultimate test of the system, namely, the ability to prosper in the marketplace. When their failure is given a religious interpretation as a sign of divine rejection, there is even less incentive to be concerned with their fate. This does not mean that there will be no "safety net." Historically, a principal motive for state support of programs of relief for the poor has been the control and bureaucratic policing of potentially disruptive elements within society.[6] Such motives are, however, very far removed from Christian charity and compassion as understood by the bishops.

While capitalism has yielded an extraordinary advance in material wealth, no system is as inherently destabilizing of fixed economic relationships. A major consequence of this tendency has been the misery experienced by the millions of human beings who have been unable to adjust to the technological and social revolution engendered by so dynamic a system. Those religious leaders, whose traditions are rooted in an era of relatively greater stability, are likely to find much that is wanting in American capitalism, especially if they focus their attention, as did the bishops, on the millions who have been unable to adjust to the system. Moreover, in addition to the ethical and doctrinal sources of the bishops' criticism, there is a demographic and socioeconomic reason for the bishops' emphasis on the poor: The native-born, non-Hispanic whites of the South and the West, the regions that have prospered most in the past decade, are predominantly Protestant. By contrast, large Roman Catholic working-class populations are to be found in those Northeast and Midwestern states that have been injured most seriously by the decline of America's "smokestack" industries.

In spite of the fact that the bishops' reservations concerning free enterprise capitalism are largely grounded in traditional Catholic views, a number of prominent Catholics have taken issue with the bishops' draft letter. Edward L. Hennesy, Jr., Chairman of the Board of the Allied Corporation and a Roman Catholic layman, has commented: "As a Catholic, I listen carefully and sympathetically when the bishops describe the plight of the poor as a special concern of the church. As a businessman responsible for managing an enterprise with 117,000 employees, I worry that the bishops' remedies, while giving a larger handout to the poor, might injure the economy on which all of us depend."[7]

Hennesy argues that the bishops ignore the fact that, as a country, we are living beyond our means. Thus, while the bishops go into considerable detail to propose measures that would increase government assistance to the poor, they offer no serious counsel concerning how to attain the kind of economic growth that would materially diminish poverty.

The failure of the bishops to offer a realistic program of implementation was noted by Father Andrew Greeley, who has commented that the bishops' politics were decidedly dated: "[T]he bishops . . . have produced a document that is little more than a rehash of the party-line conventional wisdom of five to fifteen years ago, with a touch of class conflict ideology (the poor against the powerful) that hints vaguely at pop-Marxism. They have, in other words, provided religious underpinning for the latter day New Deal of the 1980 Democratic party platform."[8]

The bishops have not been the only religious leaders to evaluate contemporary America in the light of their religious commitments. Of all the developments in recent American politics, none has been as significant as the rise of the New Right to a position of influence and power in American politics. Until the end of the 1960s, those intellectuals and social scientists whose opinions influenced public-policy decision makers included few conservatives and fewer right-wing intellectuals. Since then, conservative and right-wing academics and intellectuals have become increasingly influential in the shaping of the national political agenda. Similarly, conservative Protestant evangelical and fundamentalist leaders have moved from a posture of relative political quiescence to one of extreme political activism. Indeed, it is impossible to imagine that the political New Right would have achieved its spectacular gains absent the political activities of the New Christian Right.[9]

According to Jerome Himmelstein, it would appear that the political program of both the political and religious right is characterized by three distinct concerns: economic libertarianism, social traditionalism, and militant anticommunism.[10] We have already noted the underlying assumption of the New Right's economic libertarianism, faith in the power of the self-regulating marketplace to transmute the economic egoism into the common good. A corollary of this view has been the tendency of the right to blame economic crises either on direct government interference in the marketplace or on indirect intervention through programs which transfer resources from the economically productive classes to the dependent and unproductive. According to the right, another source of economic distortion has been needless government regulation. The New Right would, if it could, dismantle almost all of the liberal New Deal and Fair Deal programs of the last half century. As President Reagan has reiterated, the least government is the best government.

Implicit in the New Right's economic libertarianism is a commitment to individualism and personal freedom. As noted, this position is profoundly at odds with the predominant Roman Catholic view of the way human existence is structured politically, socially, and religiously. Paul of Tarsus's view that Christians, though many, are members of one body in Christ provided the basis for the classical definition of the relation of the individual to the community in Catholicism. It also provided a theological foundation for the Church's understanding of the obligations of fortunately situated Christians to their less-fortunate brethren:

> For as the body is one, and hath many members, and all members of that one body, being many, are one body; so also is Christ. For by one Spirit are we all baptized into one body, whether Jews or Gentiles, whether bond or free. . . . And the eye cannot say unto the hand I have no need of thee; nor again the head to the feet, I have no need of you. Nay, much more those members of the body, which seem to be more feeble, are necessary. . . .[11]

Such a view is hardly conducive to the predominantly individualistic values of contemporary American capitalism.[12] By contrast, the pursuit of individual economic self-interest is not regarded by the right as disruptive but as the basis for the social bond. Although most New Right thinkers would accept Weber's description of the market community as essentially accurate, they would vehemently reject his social and cultural pessimism.

One of the least understood aspects of the right's position is the relation between its optimism concerning economic libertarianism on the one hand

and its commitment to social traditionalism on the other. Far from contradicting each other, these two aspects of the right's position complement each
other. Absolutely fundamental to the right's program is a reversal of what they
regard as the breakdown of the family, religion, and traditional morality. We
need not dwell on the forms this program has taken on such issues as abortion,
school prayer, women's rights, school busing, pornography, and the general
secularization of culture. The right's social traditionalism stresses the themes
of community and behavioral restraint in which society is regarded as a
network of shared values and integrating institutions. The New Christian
Right holds that it is society's function to bind individuals together, placing
limits on their egoism, destructiveness, and self-indulgence. It is hardly surprising that the morals revolution of the 1960s and 1970s brought in its train
a negative response on the part of conservative Americans. From the perspective of the New Christian Right, religious people have at least as much right to
restore moral and religious values to American society as secular relativists,
often identified as secular humanists, have had in vitiating them. One astute
observer has commented that what is at stake is the "struggle to define
America."[13]

The third New Right concern is militant anticommunism. Communism is
the political and cultural antithesis of the New Right's economic libertarianism. To the extent that right-wing thinkers regard the free-enterprise system
as divinely ordained, its polar opposite must be viewed as satanic or, at the
very least, "an evil empire." A practical consequence of anticommunism has
been strong support for increased military expenditures and an active anticommunist foreign policy. This, in turn, has helped to create the unprecedented
budget deficits of the Reagan Administration. Although conservatives have
traditionally sought a balanced federal budget, the current deficits go a long
way to assure that, no matter which party comes to power in the decade after
Reagan, the Federal government will be compelled to continue to reduce its
support of social and welfare programs. The future has been so effectively
mortgaged to military expenditures that, absent large and unpalatable tax
increases, the federal government has come close to reaching the limits of its
capacity in nonmilitary expenditures. Moreover, there exists the suspicion that
this strategy was clearly understood by the Reagan Administration and one of
the many Republican initiatives for which the Democrats were wholly
unprepared.

The Christian Right has set about to transform America. It regards liberalism, which it sees as a bipartisan phenomenon, as responsible for the monumental failures in the American system which became evident in the 1960s and
1970s, namely, the rise of a class of unemployed individuals wholly dependent
upon a bloated welfare system, the collapse of personal morality and acceptance of religiously taboo life-styles, decline of religious faith especially among
established elites, the turning away from continuity with historic American
cultural and social traditions (which are perceived to have had their origins in

evangelical Protestantism), rampant inflation, a punitive and dishonest tax system, the defeat in Vietnam, and the contempt heaped upon America by the seizure of American hostages in Iran and by Third World beneficiaries of American largesse in the United Nations.

Above all, it would be unwise to underestimate the importance of the Vietnamese defeat and the Khomeini hostage seizure in the formation of the new pro-military posture of the American right or of the long-term bitterness caused by liberal opposition to the war. The right is convinced that the war was lost at home, a defeat for which they hold liberal academics and media professionals largely responsible.

As noted above, there would appear to be a contradiction between the economic libertarianism and the social traditionalism of the New Right. By itself, untrammeled economic individualism has little interest in the constraints of social traditionalism. It knows no value more important than the "cash nexus." Recently, American society has witnessed all too many examples of unprincipled behavior in the service of the "cash nexus": illegal overcharges and deliberate cost overruns by defense contractors; the conviction of a former assistant secretary of defense on charges of perjury in connection with his admitted misuse of insider knowledge to gain stock-market profits for his mistress; the failure of a number of banks and dealers in federal securities as a consequence of the misconduct of their senior corporate executives. Indeed, the very decline in morals and religion that the New Right has decried may have been a direct consequence of a society whose commitment to unadulterated economic freedom knows few restraints. Such freedom can easily end in the very materialism, self-indulgence, and selfishness which the New Right has opposed so vigorously.

Moreover, social traditionalism normally entails a view of life which tends to encourage conservative constraints not only on individual behavior and morals but on economic growth and development as well. Such pessimism has not been a predominant element in mainstream American culture. It goes counter to the optimism concerning the power of human inventiveness, which is so much a part of the New Right's values and which has very deep roots in American experience. By themselves, neither economic libertarianism nor social traditionalism would be capable of generating the kind of political and social dynamism the Christian right has exhibited in the last decade. However, when the two concerns are linked, they generate an enormous motivating force which is rooted in the Protestant ethic and which, according to Max Weber, facilitated the growth of modern Western capitalism in the first place.

Traditionally, the most potent legitimations for material success in America have been those which endowed this striving with religious meaning. The Protestant tradition of serving God through one's calling gave to a career in business a status and a dignity it had never attained in precapitalist society. The conviction that one's business or profession was a means of serving God transformed what could have been unvarnished economic individualism into the basis of a world of stable social relationships.

As Himmelstein has observed, the religious right has flourished *because* of its combination of social traditionalism and economic libertarianism.[14] The American religious right captures the libertarian emphasis on material progress and individual success but transforms it into a calling, thereby placing it within the context of divine providence. At the same time, it adopts a traditional concern for social stability and spiritual values but without other-worldliness or pessimism about progress and human nature. The New Right is thus able to affirm both God and capitalism, social stability and economic and technological dynamism, thereby encouraging the individual to maximize his/her economic and professional potential without appearing to destablize the traditional order.

One of the criticisms most frequently leveled by liberals at the New Christian Right is that its injection of religious issues into the national political agenda is inherently divisive and distracts attention from pressing national problems, such as the declining ability of America's older industries to compete in the world market, mass structural unemployment, and the long-term dangers inherent in the massive federal deficit.[15] Those liberals who criticize the New Christian Right are convinced that in a multireligious, multiethnic community like the United States, government must be neutral in religious matters and that no religious group has the right to impose its views on others.[16]

Regretably, liberal critics seldom appear to understand that the right's insistence on the political significance of religious issues involves far more than blind dogmatism. Given the right's non-negotiable commitment to free-enterprise capitalism, its insistence upon the political significance of religious values becomes an absolute necessity. By diminishing government's capacity to restrain the moral abuses and the human desolation a free market economy can visit upon the losers in the battle for economic survival, the only remaining constraint is religion. At the outset of this study, we noted Max Weber's pessimistic observations concerning the destruction of all "obligations of brotherliness or reverence" entailed in a depersonalized, self-regulating market economy. Weber was opposed to socialism and saw capitalism as by far the better system. Nevertheless, he spoke of the future under capitalism as an "iron cage," for he could foresee no force capable of restraining the amoral and dehumanizing characteristics of the system. At some level, the New Christian Right seems to have had a comparable insight and would create a godly, if not a Christian, commonwealth to counter the worst excesses of a pure market economy. Moreover, its vision of a godly commonwealth can hardly be said to be without indigenous roots in American history.

If this analysis has merit, it would follow that a politically active Christian right can be expected to remain a permanent and highly influential aspect of the American political landscape. In part, its rise reflects the shift away from the old Northeastern and Midwestern centers of financial, intellectual, and old-style industrial power to the newer centers in the South and the Southwest. That this power shift has been accompanied by a shift from the Democratic to the Republican party is hardly surprising. The rise of the Christian right also reflects something of both an evangelical-Catholic and an evangelical–mainline Protestant power shift, in both cases favoring the evangelicals and fundamentalists. While the financial and corporate elites of the Northeast and the Midwest have remained predominantly Protestant and Anglo-Saxon, Catholic influence has traditionally been far stronger in the Democratic party than in the Republican party, save for the South, where the inclusion of conservative, white Southern Protestants in the Democratic party was largely a legacy of the Civil War and the Reconstruction period.[17] While many conservative Southern Democrats identify with the Christian right, the Republican party, especially under President Reagan, has been the Christian right's party of choice. Moreover, in spite of attempts to win a permanent national majority, the party remains more fundamentally white Protestant in its leadership and ethos than the Democratic party.

A number of social theorists have used the hypothesis of "status politics" to understand right-wing American religious and political movements.[18] According to this hypothesis, these movements cannot be explained solely in terms of economic or class conflict but as responses to challenges to their values, life-styles, and traditions. Thus, the 1919 ratification of the Eighteenth Amendment to the Constitution, which resulted in Prohibition, has been interpreted as the high point of middle-class Protestantism's ability to enforce its definition of social reality on the entire country. Prohibition was thus a "status triumph" for conservative Protestantism and a "status degradation" for Catholics and Jews who (a) did not share fundamentalism's ethic of abstinence, (b) were more likely to be urbanized and concentrated in the Northeast and the Midwest than evangelical and fundamentalist Protestants, and (c) were far more likely to be immigrants or the offspring of immigrants, and hence less "American," than the Protestants. It is not irrelevant to this hypothesis that the era of Prohibition coincided with the enactment of the Johnson Immigration Act of 1924, which drastically curtailed immigration from Eastern and Southern Europe, while favoring immigration from the Protestant nations of Northern Europe. At the time, conservative Protestants tended to be far more hostile to Catholics and Jews than are their contemporary counterparts. In 1924, the Ku Klux Klan's membership reached an all-time high and numbered in the millions.

Fundamentalism's "status triumph" proved to be short-lived. The 1933 Repeal of the Eighteenth Amendment represented a repudiation of the values of indigenous conservative Protestantism. However, this "status degradation" could never have been achieved solely by a Catholic-Jewish coalition. The active participation of the Eastern Protestant establishment and the mainline Protestant denominations was indispensable. These denominations were modernist, and tended to regard the fundamentalists in a patronizing manner, as provincial, culturally backward, poorly educated, and "fanatic." On issues regarded by the fundamentalists as non-negotiable, such as the literal truth of scripture and a triumphalist religious self-interpretation, the modernist position can best be described as compromising and relativizing. The patronizing attitude of the Protestant mainstream was reinforced by the fact that all of America's most prestigious academic and theological institutions were affiliated, in fact if no longer in name, with the mainstream, modernizing denominations.

The situation of the fundamentalists began to change in the 1960s. According to John H. Simpson: "Increasingly, Fundamentalist, Evangelical, and Conservative Christians realized that the real enemy was not the Roman Catholic or Jew but the smiling, flexible, civil Protestant modernist who wrote them off as 'religious fanatics' unwilling to take the rough edges off their beliefs and practices and glide along smoothly with others in the prosperity of post-war America."[19]

According to Simpson, it was not the challenge of modernity but "the failures of modernity in its guise as establishment America that provided the Protestant religious right with the opportunity to go public once more."[20] The fundamentalists had always been convinced that their conception of a Christian life-style is divinely sanctioned. By contrast, the modernists had difficulty identifying any behavioral norm as either literally sanctioned or prohibited by God. On one issue after another, such as birth control, premarital sex, abortion, homosexuality, and even extramarital sex, the modernists tended to take relativizing and compromising positions. Absent a belief in the inerrancy of scripture or an alternative source of moral and religious authority, it was impossible for them to do otherwise. Faced with the multiple crises besetting America in the 1960s and 1970s, mainstream denominations have had little that was indubitably Christian to contribute. As noted above, without a sense of divinely sanctioned laws, modern capitalism can easily become little more than economic egoism. After Vietnam, Watergate, the morals revolution, and the Iranian hostage crisis, the Christian right no longer appeared to be or felt themselves to be outmoded fanatics.

If the Protestant right has experienced great status enhancement, the same cannot be said for the liberal wing of America's Roman Catholic Church. The bishops' letter is clearly a product of that sector of Church leadership which is politically and economically, if not theologically, liberal. Catholic liberalism can be seen as having experienced considerable status degradation recently. Within the Church, the appointment of conservatives such as John Cardinal O'Connor of New York and Bernard Cardinal Law to positions of preeminent leadership have been widely taken as signifying a trend. Indeed, it is difficult to imagine a committee led by either cardinal as producing the bishops' draft letter. Moreover, the growing strength of the conservative wing must be seen as a parallel to the rise of the New Christian Right and the relative decline of the mainline Protestant denominations.

The liberal origins of the bishops' draft letter are all too obvious. As such, they reveal the letter's principal weakness. The bishops assign the "highest priority" to the fulfillment of "the basic needs of the poor." The document calls for the "evaluation of decisions, policies, and institutions in the light of their impact on the poor." The bishops take their stand on the side of those favoring income redistribution rather than income incentives. Both the Reagan administration and the New Christian Right strongly favor the latter and would under no circumstances accord "highest priority" to the problems of the poor. As noted above, even Catholic conservatives argue that to do so would seriously injure the economy's prospects of genuine economic growth and, hence, its long-term capacity to alleviate poverty. It is this author's opinion that the bishops would have strengthened their case had they acknowledged more fully that there is serious debate on their proposals and had they spelled out the economic as well as the theological rationale for their own position. Instead, they have used the very great moral authority of their office to take sides on some of the most complex economic issues facing the republic, while seldom acknowledging that many experienced and reputable economists, who are as committed as the bishops to alleviating poverty, regard their proposals as both unworkable and counterproductive.

When one compares the position of the draft letter with that of the New Christian Right, it would appear that the bishops manifest far greater concern for the poor than does the New Christian Right. Nevertheless, it is by no means certain that the bishops' program would yield greater long-term bene-fits for the poor. The Christian right has addressed, perhaps intuitively, a question which is absolutely fundamental to the American future, namely, "What is required to give capitalism an ethical valence?" Their answer is, as noted above, religious. Its obvious difficulty is that what fundamentalism means by religion cannot easily be reconciled with American pluralism. A less obvious but perhaps equally important problem is the triumphalism of the Christian right vis-à-vis mainline Protestant denominations, Catholics, Jews, and America's increasingly numerous adherents to other traditions. Given that triumphalism, the Christian right's insistence on the place of religion in the public realm cannot be divorced from its status politics. As such, it is not a unifying insight but an element in a struggle for power. In that struggle, it must be noted that the vast majority of the poor are not middle-class, white Protestants. Because the New Christian Right is more closely identified with America's original religious and cultural tradition, it undoubtedly has the capacity to fare exceedingly well in any long-term status struggle. While it is not likely to win a total victory—indeed few victories are total—it may be able to create a cultural and political climate which is increasingly conservative in religious matters for all traditions.

The New Christian Right's victory could, however, prove to be Pyrrhic. In their justifiable concentration on the challenge of the Soviet military strength and communist ideology to American interests, the Christian right has all but ignored a challenge which may ultimately prove more serious than that of communism. The Christian right gives no evidence of having taken seriously the long-range challenge of Japan to America's economy and society. In fairness, it must be noted that the bishops' letter is equally negligent in considering the impact of the Japanese challenge on American labor and industry. Regarding the least government as the best government, the Christian Right has had little, if anything, to say concerning the challenge to American interests of a society in which government and industry cooperate intimately and effectively in long-range planning that has as its objective the economic debilitation, if not destruction, of one American industry after another.

The Christian right would relegate the problems of unemployment and poverty to the workings of the marketplace and private charity. The bishops propose to alleviate the problems by greater government expenditures on welfare and public works. By contrast, Japan has largely solved the problem of unemployment by an extraordinarily successful combination of planned industrial development, high finance, and trade. Obviously, the decline of America's older industries cannot be attributed solely to Japanese competition. For our purposes, however, it is important to note that Japan has utilized the kind of political and economic strategy that the New Right emphatically rejects to devise a practical, long-range program for keeping unemployment and poverty at a minimum in that country.

Undoubtedly, the small-town and rural roots of the predominantly middle-class Christian right have played a part in its inability to consider seriously the Japanese challenge. Nor has the Christian right's religious triumphalism served that movement well with regard to the Japanese challenge. Its contacts with the Orient have been largely mediated by its own missionaries, who have tended to emphasize what the Christian world can teach non-Christians more than what can be learned from them. Nevertheless, if evangelical and fundamentalist Protestantism are to take the leading role in American life to which they aspire, they will be unable to ignore the long-term challenge posed by Japan, especially the intimate connection between Japanese industrial and trade policy and the problems of unemployment, poverty, and economic justice in both Japan and the United States.

Moreover, there is yet another reason both the Christian right and the bishops would do well to consider the utter seriousness of the Japanese challenge. On 29 May 1985, Mr. Kenichi Yamamoto, President of the Mazda Motor Corporation, participated in ground-breaking ceremonies for the new Mazda plant in Flint Rock, Michigan. The governor of Michigan was present and took part in the ceremonies which included a two-hour dedicatory service conducted by a Shinto priest. Unlike the United States, sacred and public realms are intertwined in Japan. One can never speak of any significant Japanese activity as being purely secular. On the contrary, as the Shinto ceremony in Michigan demonstrates, there is no such thing as a purely economic activity for the Japanese.

A number of students of Japanese business and management have observed that religion has played a very significant role in the success of Japanese capitalism.[21] In the West, the advent of capitalism was accompanied by secularization and the desacralization of public life. In contrast, Japanese modernization at the time of the Meiji restoration was facilitated by the intensified sacralization of the political order. This was accomplished through the establishment of State Shinto and the adoration of the Emperor as a living *kami* (divine spirit). Animistic, polytheistic Shinto, with its doctrine of divine kingship, is the very antithesis of biblical religion, the religion of the New Christian Right, with its persistent tendency to desacralize both the natural and the political orders, a tendency identified by Weber as "disenchantment of the World" (*Entzauberung der Welt*). Japanese civilization presents the image of a thoroughly modern, high-technology civilization, whose ethical and political foundations rest upon religious traditions that biblical religion rejects as archaic, primitive, and even idolatrous. Moreover, unlike most allegedly "primitive" religions, Shinto has demonstrated its power to undergird a civilization capable of successfully competing with the West economically, technologically, and culturally. At stake in the long-term Japanese-American competition is the question of which spiritual universe, the Shinto or the Christian, can produce the better society for all of its people.[22] If the New Christian Right is successfully and effectively to assume a predominant position of leadership in American life, it will have to recognize the extraordinarily comprehensive character of the Japanese challenge. Having recognized the challenge, it will have to provide the nation with the leadership with which that challenge can be met. It remains to be seen whether the New Right's spiritual and cultural resources are adequate to that task.

Notes

1. See *Origins: NC Documentary Service,* 15 November 1984, 338.
2. The text of the bishops' draft letter is to be found in *Origins: NC Documentary Service,* 15 November 1984. See also Kenneth Briggs, "Catholic Bishops Ask Vast Changes in Economy of U. S." in the *New York Times,* 12 November 1984, pp. 1, 15.
3. See Joseph A. Califano, "The Prophets and the Profiteers," *America* (5–12 January 1985): 5–7.
4. Max Weber, *Economy and Society: An Outline of Interpretive Sociology,* edited by Guenther Roth and Claus Wittich (New York: Bedminster Press, 1968), vol. 3, 1186–87.

5. Weber, *Economy and Society,* vol. 2, 636–37.
6. See Richard L. Rubenstein, *The Age of Triage,* (Boston: Beacon, 1983), 60 ff.
7. Edward L. Hennesy, Jr., "A Pastoral for the Poor, Not for the Economy,"*America* (5–12 January 1985).
8. Andrew M. Greeley, "The Bishops and the Economy: A 'Radical' Dissent," *America* (5–12 January 1985).
9. For an overview of this development, see Thomas Byrne Edsall, *The New Politics of Inequality* (New York: Norton, 1984).
10. See Jerome L. Himmelstein, "The New Right." In *The New Christian Right,* edited by Robert C. Liebman and Robert Wuthnow (New York: Aldine, 1983), 15–27, for the analysis of these concerns.
11. 1 Cor. 12: 12–22.
12. On American individualism, see Robert N. Bellah, Richard Madsen, William M. Sullivan, Ann Swidler, and Steven M. Tipton, eds., *Habits of the Heart: Individualism and Commitment in American Life* (Berkeley and Los Angeles: University of California Press, 1985).
13. See Donald Heinz, "The Struggle to Define America." In *The New Christian Right,* edited by Liebman and Wuthnow, 133–49.
14. See Himmelstein, 23.
15. For a particularly harsh criticism of the New Christian Right, see Walt Michalsky, "The Masquerade of Fundamentalism." *The Humanist* (July–August 1941), 15–51.
16. See Kenneth Connors, "Public Issues and Private Morality," *The Christian Century* (22 October 1980).
17. See Edsall, 26–28, 68–70.
18. See Joseph R. Gusfield, *Symbolic Crusade: Status Politics and the American Temperance Movement* (Urbana, II: 1963); Richard G. Hofstadter, *Anti-Intellectualism in American Life* (New York: Random House, 1962).
19. John H. Simpson, "Moral Issues and Status Politics." In *The New Christian Right,* edited by Liebman and Wuthnow, 201.
20. Ibid., 202.
21. See, for example, Richard Tanner Pascale and Anthony Athos, *The Art of Japanese Management: Applications for American Executives* (New York: Simon and Schuster), 21.
22. See Richard L. Rubenstein, "Marxism, America, and the Challenge of Asian Capitalism," *International Journal of World Peace* 2 (1) (Winter 1985).

13
Religion and the New Mandarins

Barbara Hargrove

WHILE IT IS TRUE that history never repeats itself in detail, it is also true that there is nothing entirely new under the sun. With that frame of reference, it seems appropriate to explore parallels and differences between the ruling mandarin class of the old China and our own rising class of educated professionals, with particular emphasis on the consequences for religion of this type of dominant class. This paper will rely heavily on what Max Weber has said of the "old mandarins" and their consequences for the religion of China. Most of the discussion of what I consider their contemporary parallel will rely on work that has been done on the so-called "New Class." This class, still amorphous in its boundaries, consists of those whose source of power is expertise and the control of information, whose institutional source of identity is generally that of higher education, and whose primary loyalties may be to professional colleagues or scientific truths rather than to the nation-state. (For further descriptions of this class, see Bell, 1973; Gouldner, 1979; and Hargrove, 1986.)

Mandarins as a Comparative Concept

A number of parallels have been noted between the dominant Chinese mandarin class and groups in other societies. For example, the term has often been applied to the corps of upper-level civil servants in England, who have tended to be educated in the same schools, to have formed a distinct social set, and to have provided their nation with distinguished and stable governmental leadership. To quote a Canadian observer: "In England there is a mystique about public service. It has a romantic aura composed of power, associations with empire, and first-class intellects singularly devoted to the service of Britain's permanent national interests, whatever they might be. Politicians come and go, the occupants of 10 Downing Street change their party labels, but the national interest endures. And the mandarins are its keepers" (Granatstein, 1982: 1).

215

Granatstein (1982) also finds a period in Canadian history where a similar tradition held:

> From the 1930s to the 1950s Canada's civil-service mandarins—like those of Whitehall—had many things in common. They were a coherent group, united not only by their work but by their friendships and those of their wives and children. They operated almost anonymously within a tight and private little world—offices moments away from each other, homes nearby, clubs close at hand. Yet this mandarinate was not a closed circle. It was remarkable open to new men throughout its ascendancy; its members were constantly on the alert for able recruits who would fit in. (2)

While it is appropriate to use the term "mandarins" for such an elite of civil servants, Weber (1951) offers a description of the Chinese mandarins that gives them a much broader role in the society. A more modern use that is reflective of this has been the application of the term to a class of intellectuals, in which Weber himself has been included, who dominated German cultural life in the period between the turn of the twentieth century and the rise of Hitler. It is not difficult to find direct linkages between these "German mandarins" and the contemporary New Class. F. K. Ringer (1969) has written: "I would define 'mandarins' simply as a social and cultural elite which owes its status primarily to educational qualifications, rather than to hereditary rights or wealth" (5–6). Ringer focused particularly on the intellectual leadership of the German mandarins among the university scholars in the areas of the humanities and the social sciences. The status of German scientists in the "harder" fields was somewhat less clear. For example, Paul (1984) has described many of the conflicts between the more romanticist and humanistic elites and the scientists. However, this seems more an argument within a particular elite than a true division. The status of both humanistic and scientific intellectuals was high in Germany during that period, and their influence extended far beyond the university walls to the society at large. In a way, they became the definers of German culture.

There is a growing awareness in modern—and modernizing—societies of a new stratum that is attaining cultural dominance. Members of this stratum hold power not in the main through election, nor through the possession of great economic resources, but because of specific expertise which they have gained, usually, through higher education and often through certification by some professional board as well. They are the advisers and consultants, the managers and civil servants, and the social service professionals who provide the information on which basic decisions are made, and who often organize the very processes of decision making. Gouldner (1979) has defined them as a "cultural bourgeoisie" whose capital is not money but the control over valuable cultures (21). To call members of such a stratum "mandarins" would not seem improper. It behooves us, then, to see if there are enough parallels between the original carriers of the title and the contemporary "mandarins" to give insight into some of the processes occurring in modern society.

Weber used the mandarins as one aspect of his concept of different styles of leadership, as an early case of the kind of legal-rational authority he saw replacing charismatic or traditional authority in societies where bureaucracy was becoming a dominant form of organization. Because the Chinese mandarins emerged before the development of a world society in which bureaucracy is so important, their case may have led to a different conclusion from what we may expect today. Yet we may learn something from the comparison as we look at contemporary phenomena.

The "old mandarins" of China rose to power in spite of latent, and sometimes overt, opposition from two other segments of Chinese culture and social structure, the traditional power of the extended family as embodied in the clan or sib, and the specific political power of appointed imperial favorites. Their dominance over the latter is more understandable to the modern mind. As Weber (1951) put it, in discussing their rise to power at the beginning of the Han Dynasty: "In the end, however, success fell to the literati whose rational administrative and economic policies were again decisive in restoring imperial authority. Also they were technically superior to the administration of favorites and eunuchs, who were constantly opposed, and, above all, they had on their side the tremendous prestige associated with knowledge of precedent, ritual, and scripture—at that time something of a secret art" (45).

The end of that quotation points toward the method by which the mandarins were also able to dominate traditional power. They achieved their position by passing examinations to prove their ability to cite precedent, ritual, and scripture, thus becoming certified to handle administrative detail in their culture. At the same time, as Weber (1951) wrote: "If the technique and substance of the examinations were purely mundane in nature and represented a sort of 'cultural examination for the literati,' the popular view of them was very different: it gave them a magical-charismatic meaning. In the eyes of the Chinese masses, a successfully examined candidate and official was by no means a mere applicant for office qualified by knowledge. He was a proved holder of magical qualities" (128)

Ringer (1969), in his discussion of the German mandarins, also points to this paradoxical mixture of the practical bureaucratic certification and function and a broader and more value-laden definition of their place in the social order. As they rise to power, he says, mandarins, and particularly their intellectual leaders, move beyond the narrow ideology that has justified their position on rational grounds to an ideal of learning as an end in itself, as the kind of value that can substitute for nobility of birth. This, then, gives them a kind of cultural dominance beyond their immediate social usefulness (Ringer, 1969: 9).

Today it is possible to see an international trend toward cultural, political, and economic dominance in a stratum that shares many of the characteristics of the older mandarinate, tied to the processes of modernization and development. Increasing complexity in the industrialized nations of East and West has brought to power the managers and bureaucrats who are trained to organize and utilize complex systems. In areas only beginning to modernize, great influence is exercised by those whose training allows them to deal with the new elites of the more powerful nations. Networks of communication and common expectations of rationality and expertise serve to pull members of this stratum into self-conscious identification with one another. Such identification can be interpreted as the beginning of class consciousness in an emerging international social class, though not the international proletariat envisioned by Marx.

This New Class appears to share many elements with the old mandarin tradition. There are, for example, strong parallels between the qualification by examination necessary for mandarin status in the traditional sense and today's demand for certification through certain programs of education and/or through examination by which persons qualify for today's New Class. It is rare for a person to enter this stratum without some graduate training, some degree beyond the bachelor's. In addition, further professional certification is often required. One evidence of the cultural dominance of this class is the striving for professional status of those who have not previously been so classified—social workers, librarians, nurses, accountants, and the like—with accompanying demands that persons be required to have advanced degrees and, perhaps, to subject themselves as well to examining boards for proper certification to bear their title. While it is assumed that modern people do not equate degrees or certification with magical powers, the very language used both in support and in criticism of the holders of advanced degrees indicates an inordinate amount of faith placed in their competency.

We expect of doctors, lawyers, consultants, and the like forms of arcane knowledge not really in the public realm, and there are many persons who look upon the holder of a Ph.D. as someone set apart by great knowledge. This attitude may be changing with the increase in the numbers of holders of professional titles, and with the imperfections of many of them, but there still remains enough of this attitude to give social power to the New Class.

Knowledge is power in our society as it was in the old China. For this reason, the institution of education in modern society is held to be almost sacred. Controversies surrounding educational methods and ends are among the most virulent, a testimony in itself to the importance of the subject.

Another consideration is the direct inheritance of the American graduate school from the universities of Germany that produced and were ruled by the German mandarins. While many American universities may have responded to cultural pragmatism by reflecting more closely the educational system at Halle than other German universities, the elite institutions of this country, and in particular its graduate schools, have directly copied their programs and form of organization from the more dominant German universities. In the process, they have learned many of the attitudes and values of what Ringer (1969) has called the "mandarin intellectuals," who, as he put it, "are concerned with the educational diet of the elite. They uphold the standard of qualification for membership in the group, and they act as its spokesmen in cultural questions" (5–6). The exportation of this form of educational institution throughout the world has been one aspect of the process we have called modernization, as has the training of cultural elites of Third World countries in the universities of Britain, Europe, America, and the Soviet Union.

Ringer (1969) sees the political conditions for the rise of a mandarin elite as the "gradual transformation of an essentially feudal state into a heavily bureaucratic monarchy" (7). Here a monarch is involved in trying to overthrow the power of a traditional aristocracy, and finds the mandarins useful in doing so because of their efficiency in government and social service. It is tempting, at least, to move beyond Ringer's analysis to consider the proposition that the real condition of the rise of a mandarin elite may not be a transition out of feudalism, but rather any widespread social transformation where tradition is questioned, the future is unclear, and anyone who appears to have certain kinds of knowledge is likely to be sought out for leadership.

The rise of the New Class in post-World War Two communist countries as documented by Djilas (1957) may fit the feudal-to-modern pattern rather well, as may the rise of educated elites in some Third World countries. It is possible, however, that the transition from traditional capitalism to a post-modern corporate international structure is also likely to awaken a desire for leadership by those who are both specialists in the complexities of the new order and who are able to deal in abstractions that transcend the chaos of the present situation. Such experts are useful to those who hope to supplant political power holders who rely on the support of the society's traditional cultural system, whatever that may be. Yet one can expect them also to begin to assert their own power independently of those whom they serve, particularly through the articulation of an ideology that makes their learning a cultural value in itself. But in the meantime, they tend to be under attack by the forces of tradition, by those presently in power and also by the older forms that current power structures may have replaced.

The Mandarin Ideology

Any new class that gains ascendency in a society must contend with at least two opposing forces, the traditional claims of kinship and the power held by those currently in office. Kinship patterns themselves work against new elites in two ways. First, to become part of a new stratum is to deny the given social status of one's family or clan. This was particularly problematic in tradition-ridden China, where, as Weber (1951) said: "The strongest counterweight to officials educated in literature was a-literate old age *per se*. No matter how many examinations the official had passed, he still had to obey unconditionally the completely uneducated sib elder in the traditionally fixed affairs of the sib" (95). In modern society, the family holds far less power over its members, but there are still important resistances to be encountered when one moves away from family tradition and the life-styles of old friends. Only as the New Class becomes established does its way of life perhaps become that of one's family.

The second problem created by family traditions is that rising elites are likely to be perceived as upstarts seeking to replace status groups whose societal leadership has long been legitimized by tradition. They are not considered proper material for leadership, not having come from the "right families." This was a common problem for the old mandarins and is somewhat likely to plague the new ones as well, though family connections are not taken as seriously in much of the modern world as they were in the old China. In the contemporary world, these considerations often emerge as evidence of racism or ethnic prejudice.

In most cases, the opposition of current power holders is more obvious. Persons in a "knowledge class" usually rise to power as servants of the reigning elites. To replace those elites is all too clearly an act of insubordination. Thus, the Chinese mandarins frequently found themselves ousted by royal favorites, and contemporary civil servants escape sacking by new administrations only if they serve at levels protected by law. It becomes a matter not only of class interest but often of survival for such groups to develop an ideology that challenges the legitimacy of current power holders as well as the traditions that would hold them to given family patterns or ethnic roots.

The primary focus of the mandarin ideology is, unsurprisingly, the value of knowledge. As noted above, Weber traced the development of mandarin ideology from its beginnings in simply demonstrating the usefulness of the educated person to the administrators of the society to a point where the mandarins' education took on value in and of itself. Admission to mandarin ranks was through examination, and it was the mandarins who controlled the content of those examinations. While family background made it easier for some persons to gain the requisite knowledge, anyone who was able to learn what was necessary could be accepted as a candidate. The mandarinate was— and is—a meritocracy, in which knowledge is the basis of all merit.

While we generally think of the Chinese mandarins as civil servants exercising their power through the political structures, their influence was far broader. In order to maintain and legitimate their political power, they needed to make their way of life and style of thinking culturally dominant. They functioned with a style of rationality derived from principles found in the classical literature they studied. As Weber (1951) put it: "The examinations of China tested whether or not the candidate's mind was thoroughly steeped in literature and whether or not he possessed the *ways of thought* suitable to a cultured man and resulting from cultivation in literature" (121).

The rise of a mandarin class is not instantaneous, nor does its ideology develop all at once. It may be, also, that the idea of a mandarin stratum as a distinct social class is something fairly new. Modern society is based on *class* distinctions much more than on traditional status groups, when compared with much of the historical past. In addition, Weber (1951) does not see the Chinese mandarins as an independent status group of scholars such as the Brahmans in India, but that has more to do with the openness of the group to bright young men from any stratum than with some incompleteness of identifiability of them as a specific social group (122). One of the constant concerns of modern students of the New Class is whether or not it can constitute a class in the traditional sense for exactly that reason—the openness to new candidates who do not come from New Class families. Yet one may question whether it is necessary for a class to continue kinship lines in modern society. One may also note that, for most persons, a family background steeped in New Class activities is much more likely to result in graduate training and, hence, admission to the New Class for the next generation.

In comparing the development of the mandarin ideology in other cultures to that of China, it seems evident that the British mandarinate has, for the most part, retained the early position—an ideology of public servants whose learning is a tool rather than an end in itself. Ringer (1969), however, makes it clear that the German mandarins moved beyond that point. They contested the power of the state by articulating a set of abstract laws and principles to which any state should conform and which, of course, they understood best:

> The demand that the state should embody a fixed and rational law derives especially from the strong bureaucratic wing of the elite and could be reconciled with a relatively humble civil servant's notion of practical learning. The doctrine of cultural content, on the other hand, enlarges the elite's more advanced claim upon a broader cultural leadership. It argues that the state derives its legitimacy not from divine right, for that would stress the prince's whim, nor from the interests of the subjects, for that would suggest a voting procedure, but exclusively for its services to the intellectual and spiritual life of the nation. (11)

Unlike the Chinese mandarins, this more modern stratum in Germany had to contest not only the state and certain remaining kinship rights, but also the rising importance of the economic sector under capitalism. The German manderins did this by helping to spread the fear of social disruption created by industrialization, as well as by charging that the factory system and economic rationalization threatened the development and self-expression of individual persons (Ringer, 1969: 158).

The ideology of today's emerging New Class seems similar in many ways, though considerably broadened. New Class teaching points not only to rational principles on which the state should rest, but also to a similar set of laws or principles that govern social life in all its manifestations. While Ringer (1969) found that the German mandarins opposed the interference of the rational state in activities of the private sphere (10), today's new mandarins, particularly those in state agencies, propose principles upon which family life and other activities in the private sphere may be rationalized and supported by the state. They also propose systematic methods of counseling and self-development, are called in as expert witnesses concerning issues of child custody, family welfare, religious practices, and a host of other subjects once considered to be the realm of human affection and personal decision rather than that of scientific axioms. When anything goes wrong, personally or socially, we are taught to seek professional help.

It is through the cultivation of this widespread demand for their services that today's new mandarins have risen to the status of an emerging dominant class. Yet their legitimacy is still questioned on many fronts, particularly because their ideology, while aimed at utilizing general principles to meet desired ends, is itself poorly equipped to articulate those goals. It is a rationality of means, not of ends. It is, in the broadest sense, secular, deliberately detached from the wellsprings of "collective effervescence," from the nonrational communal traditions and practices of humankind.

On the other hand, like the German mandarins, the New Class has undermined confidence in the older economic and political systems, once again casting doubt on the system of industrialization because of the dehumanization that occurs in much of modern production, as well as the pollution and degradation of the environment that has accompanied it. One basic pillar of the ideology of the new class is the importance of individual development, which should not be restricted by either the economic order or the state. Nor should the upward thrust of personal development be constrained by the forces of tradition or religion.

In this way, then, bureaucratic rationalism as a form of leadership has been exerted in society as a substitute for the leadership of traditional elites. In the past, mandarin groups have met with severe repression when populist movements under charismatic leaders have sought redress from the constraints of a society dominated by bureaucratic rationality. The Chinese mandarins met competition from the more specialized experts of Western training, but the tradition was violently uprooted after the Communists under Mao Tse Tung took over the country, and especially during the cultural revolution of the 1960s. The German mandarins suffered uprooting and often far worse fates under the reign of Hitler. Each of these movements was a form of secular religion. The charismatic leader, according to Weber, can be understood to be a prophet, leading religion at times to move from legitimating traditional forms of leadership to instigating social change. It is less likely to be a violent change if the charismatic impulse is found within the religion already celebrated in the society, though even then it is likely to create serious disturbances. If there is to be a genuine change in the leadership structure of modern society from the more kinship- or production-based forms of tradition we have known, religious forms may be the site of the legitimation of that change.

The problem for the new mandarins, as for the old, is whether a stratum opposed to charismatic activity has the power to mobilize popular support for social changes that would afford it full legitimation.

The Mandarinate and Religion

Religion traditionally has been problematic for the mandarinate. Much of the basis of religion, ancient or modern, has been tribal or ethnic, celebrating kinship identity and enforcing traditions of behavior and responsibility to the kin group. In this way, religion has increased social solidarity and in return limited social mobility. The mandarinate, as a class based on mobility, has always had to struggle with the constraints of religious tradition in this context.

In addition, while the mandarins in China were often in charge of state rituals, they controlled these in their own way: "The state cult was deliberately sober and plain; it consisted of sacrifice, ritualist prayer, music, and dance. Obviously all orgiastic elements were strictly and intentionally eliminated. . . . In the official cult almost all ecstasy and asceticism, as well as contemplation, were absent and were considered elements of disorder and irrational excitement. This, bureaucratic rationalism could not stand" (145). For Weber, then, the mandarins stood as a prime example of the rationalization of charisma and the link to bureaucracy of that process.

The case of the German mandarins makes that idea particularly applicable to the modern situation, for the elite of that group, whom Ringer called the "mandarin intellectuals," included theologians who remain influential in modern Christianity. It was this group which developed modern biblical criticism, which has had the effect of undermining elements of the tradition that had constrained Christians through orthodox interpretation of the scriptures. Like the Chinese mandarins, these German scholars and their successors can claim to have possession of the correct interpretation of the traditional scriptures, and so call into question the power of other potential interpreters of the religious tradition. Theologians who were members of Germany's mandarin elite developed a rational theology based on philosophical methods rather than ritual, piety, or charismatic impulse. And modern churches, reflecting the bureaucratic structure of the rest of the society, have organized along rational lines, demanding of their clerical leadership advanced education that is highly imbued with the patterns of the German model. Weber's description of the Chinese state cult is not far from the patterns of the typical contemporary mainline church.

Insofar as the mainline churches of the West are understood to be the dominant religious expression of society and are structured organizationally and ritually along New Class lines, it would seem that the religious tradition has come to a position where it legitimates the New Class, moving not only its ideology but also its membership into full dominance. However, much of what we have been observing in the contemporary sociology of religion has given evidence of strong resistance to that kind of cultural and social dominance by the New Class. A question we may need to be considering is whether the outcome of current movements is likely to be a further consolidation of New Class power or the regulation of the new manderinate to a more traditional position as public and social servants.

One of the first indicators that the New Class was not on a clear path toward societal and cultural dominance came with the rise of new religious movements, primarily among young persons being trained for New Class positions. Many of the first religious movements to appear demonstrated some weakness in the mandarin ideology as promulgated in modern society. On the one hand, the development of the individual has been a plank in mandarin ideology from the beginning, if one is to believe Weber (1951): "The individual best served Heaven by developing his true nature, for in this way the good within every man would unfailingly appear. Thus, everything was an educational problem and the educational aim was the development of the self from one's natural endowment" (153).

At the same time, the sober rationalism of the bureaucratic mind which has also been a part of the mandarin ideology has tended to repress the more ecstatic elements of human behavior and consciousness. Many of the religious movements in the early 1970s were aimed at the development of the expressive side of human nature. Religion was sought for its charismatic elements, whether in charismatic movements within traditional religions or in more ecstatic practices borrowed from other cultures or made up on the spot. Even the drug culture was a religious movement in this sense, seeking ecstasy through chemical means. (See, e.g., Huxley, 1954; Leary et al., 1964.)

Many of these new movements also sought to reestablish some kind of communal structure to take the place of kinship ties long weakened by the mobility patterns of modern society and particularly missing from the lives of young persons pursuing higher education in impersonal institutions far removed from family and local structures. These groups experimented with forms of social organization, and often found that the effort to have total communal decision making was entirely too cumbersome. For some, the response was a return to authoritarian patterns more rigid than the bureaucratic structures against which they had rebelled. This new authority, however, was based not in the rationality of the bureaucracy but in the emotional ties of a celebrative community, and more and more in the recovery of ancient scriptures and traditions.

While most of the study of these phenomena has been undertaken in America and Europe, the same process may be seen in such countries as Iran, where the rise of militant traditional Islam has been the source of political revolution against a modernizing elite with strong elements of New Class ideology. In the United States, the new religious right is a similar rebellion against bureaucratic rationalism and the usurpation of power in the political order of which they accuse the New Class. This movement would reassert the older traditions of a literal interpretation of scripture and a morality that does not take the development and expression of the self as the primary goal of human life.

Unlike the bureaucratic ethos of the mandarins, the background of these groups is quite conducive to an appreciation of charismatic leadership. Thus it has been easy for nativistic movements to arise in opposition to the influence of the mandarinate, and to make full use of modern facilitators of charismatic influence such as the mass media. Movements against the mandarinate in the name of older, more emotional religious forms are easy to organize, and indeed have proliferated around the world.

The New Mandarins and the Political Order

In this way, we see a double process going on. The mandarinate has been fairly successful in calling into question the legitimacy of many of the ruling elites of modern society, primarily on the basis of counterproductive aspects of modern industrialization. While this would point to the New Class as the successors of previous elites to political and cultural dominance, some of the conservative rebellions against the mandarinate have been undertaken with the understanding that New Class "experts" function at the will of the older elites, the capitalists or the socialist revolutionaries. The new mandarins are in some ways the carriers of modernization, but their ideology blames the older elites for the discomforts it has brought. Insofar as it is the older elites who are identified with forms of modernization against which new movements are rebelling, these nativistic movements could, ironically, open new vistas of influence for the highly trained mandarins. What may be in the wings are not just movements in opposition to the forms that modern society has been taking, but also revitalization movements that herald a new era of human civilization. The place of the new mandarins in any such movements is at present ambiguous but temptingly open. Most new movements, if they are to succeed at all, need ideologues who can articulate a rationale for their rise, and it is the intellectuals of any society who have been the ones to do this. In most cases, this has meant a coalition, however temporary, of intellectuals with some rising class. For those New Class members whose training has been as intellectuals, it may put them in a position to find allies who could assist the new mandarins to become truly dominant, though these allies may instead hope to make of the mandarins once again the servants of this coming elite. Those whose style and training are mostly technological, dealing with advanced forms of modernization and industrialization, may be pushed into obscurity along with those they once served.

Given the size of today's New Class, it may be hard to relegate it into the servant role, regardless of the nature of the elite it might support. Yet for this class itself to become a dominant elite, it must meet the criticism of those who say that it has no moral base from which to guide the society. Attachment to some revitalization movement may be essential for this class to gain legitimacy and identity if it is to rise to power.

One place where this appears to be happening is in the southern half of the Western Hemisphere. (Africa is also experiencing a similar process, but movements there are not as well known in the West, and perhaps not quite as well developed.) In South and Central America there seems to be coalescing a number of movements which could possibly become the seeds of a new religious reformation that would also be a cultural revolution of the magnitude of that which initiated modern commercial-industrial society.

Until recently, the majority of the people in many of these nations have been captive to a traditional religion that has not encouraged change, mobility, or question. But in recent decades much of the leadership of that religion, even at the local level, has come to reflect a New Class background. Priests and nuns from North America and northern Europe, where they have been trained as New Class professionals, have come to serve in this part of the world, and have been outraged by what they see as the oppression of the people by church, state, and economic conditions. They have helped to organize small local groups similar to the Protestant sects that Weber (1946) and Tocqueville (1969) found so empowering of the settlers on the North American frontier. These "Christian base communities" meet for worship, study, and community organizing. They find in their newly raised sense of solidarity the power to face the large organizations that have oppressed them, and they seek to wrest from these structures rights and privileges long denied. They make use of Marxist analysis without accepting the dependence upon a central state that has characterized most previous Marxist activity. They make use of Christian viewpoints without accepting the devotion to capitalism that has characterized Western Christianity for the past three centuries.

With these communities as a power base, ideologues from the contemporary mandarinate have been able to articulate a new theological vision that moves beyond that of the old German mandarins. This vision, labeled "liberation theology," takes as the basis of its theological reflection not the literal scriptural traditions of the more conservative Christian bodies, nor the philosophical presuppositions of previous mandarin theology, but the sociology of knowledge. That is, the assumption is that theological reflection must arise out of the direct experience of the people rather than from some previous tradition. As Harvey Cox (1984) has put it, theology is now beginning to come not from the core of the academic enterprise, but from the margins and the bottom, from those previously ignored.

Some of this new theological reflection may be a product of worldwide economic and political change that is still in its initial stages. For example, many students of "the modern world system" are beginning to talk of the decline in power of the core, primarily the economic power of Europe and the

United States in that portion of the world dominated by Western capitalism (see, e.g., Bergeson, 1985). If indeed world power is moving out into the former periphery, the rise of a theology that is not entirely indebted to the traditions of Europe and North America may both indicate some of the ferment attached to such change and also offer it direction.

This leaves open and problematic the place of the contemporary mandarins, the New Class. In these southern movements, elites from this group seem to be falling into the usual pattern of serving as ideologues for rising social movements, the pattern articulated by Karl Mannheim (1936). But given the size and importance of this class, we may find that they are using the populism of the underclasses to provide a legitimation for the new mandarins that will allow them to assume mastery over the political order and the culture as well.

Indeed, there are developments within the New Class itself that appear to be seeking out this kind of legitimacy. An interesting parallel to the Christian base communities among poor and Third World peoples is the rise of small support groups, often in or loosely connected with mainline churches, where persons of New Class provenance attempt to work out problems of identity, meaning, and purpose within a religious framework. Many of these groups are inward-turning, never moving beyond personal problems and life in the private sphere. Others, however, often as an extension of personal quests for meaning, are moving out into the public arena in the name of a code of ethics appropriate to the New Class. They fight for justice, which they define as the provision of resources and environments which will allow all persons to reach self-fulfillment, through structures of education, politics, and the economy. Like the German mandarins before them, they seek public support for the extension of aesthetically pleasing art and activity to all within the society.

The development of an ethic for the New Class is, of course, conditioned by the prevalent worldview in any society in which it is located. In the case of the United States, Robert Bellah and his associates (1985) have provided a good description of the basic self-understanding of what they call the modern middle class, but which I would define as the New Class, in noting a movement from the utilitarian individualism of the earlier bourgeois ethic to an *expressive* individualism. This demand for individual expression allows them to move beyond the pragmatism and rationalism of the earlier ethic into an appreciation of the more affective side of life, which then opens the possibility of harnessing expressive religion to their hope of becoming part of the moral order. However, as Bellah and his associates observe, they must move beyond expressivity to some kind of public sense of responsibility for this to become a reality.

Daniel Yankelovich (1981) reports that an increasing percentage of Americans are expressing "an ethic of commitment," a desire to be involved in meaningful public work, that may come out of an earlier quest for the self and a growing perception that the self is never complete unless expressed in social settings of some significance. Such an ethic, arising out of inner compulsion rather than external pressure, could indicate the development of a highly positive approach that might indeed make of the New Class a positive leadership stratum for the future.

Less is known about such dynamics among members of the New Class in areas of the world that are not yet fully modernized in the economic sense. It is likely that some of this ethical approach is a luxury only fully applicable in societies where the meeting of basic needs can be taken for granted. In less economically privileged areas, the desire for self-aggrandizement may more often be checked by traditional loyalties and responsibilities to the kin group. It is possible that in the hands of the new elite of those societies this newer, more expressive ethic may be combined with those older forms of connectedness in ways that are more creative than the ethic now emerging in more "advanced" nations.

However, at the moment, the situation is far more uncertain. In modern societies, and also in those undergoing modernization, we have a stratum of highly educated persons who are so important to the functioning of the society that they are often perceived as the holders of real power, but who are also often resented as having no right to that power. Like the mandarins of old, they are in a position to influence the culture in which they are embedded, including its religious viewpoints. There are forces which would push them back into the more circumscribed role of the mandarins as servants of legitimate power holders, or who would seek to make them servants of a new rising elite. However, this mandarin stratum is so large and is growing so fast that it may be impossible to contain it in such a subsidiary position. In that case, religion may be used, not to put them in their place, but rather to define a legitimate place of leadership for them. Some of the new religious movements, some of the renewal movements in mainline churches, local base communities among the oppressed, and new theologies arising out of the experience of people in these groups, may provide the organization and ideology for a restructuring of society that will herald a major cultural shift, one in which the new mandarinate may have a significant role. The Chinese mandarinate may prove to have been, in the long run, the harbinger of a postmodern age where a much larger segment of the society shares the ideal of an educated and specialized elite, but finds ways to avoid the pitfalls of over-rationalization, bureaucratic rigidity, and lack of public responsibility that have led to the downfall of earlier forms of the mandarinate.

References

Bell, Daniel. 1973. *The Coming of Post-Industrial Society*. New York: Basic Books.

Bellah, Robert N., Richard Madsen, William M. Sullivan, Ann Swidler, and Steven Tipton. 1985. *Habits of the Heart: Individualism and Commitment in American Life*. Berkeley and Los Angeles: University of California Press.

Bergeson, Alfred. 1985. "Religious Studies and World-System Theory." Paper presented to a joint session of the Association for the Sociology of Religion and the American Sociological Association, Washington, D.C., 26 August.

Cox, Harvey. 1984. *Religion in the Secular City: Toward a Postmodern Theology.* New York: Simon and Schuster.

Djilas, Milovan. 1957. *The New Class: An Analysis of the Communist System.* New York: Praeger.

Granatstein, J. L. 1982. *The Ottawa Men: The Civil Service Mandarinate, 1935–1957.* Toronto: Oxford University Press.

Gouldner, Alvin. 1979. *The Future of Intellectuals and the Rise of the New Class.* New York: Seabury.

Hargrove, Barbara. 1986. *The Emerging New Class: Implications for Church and Society.* New York: Pilgrim Press.

Huxley, Aldous. 1954. *The Doors of Perception.* New York: Harper and Row.

Leary, Timothy, Ralph Metzner, and Richard Alpert, eds. 1964. *The Psychedelic Experience.* New York: University Books.

Mannheim, Karl. 1936. *Ideology and Utopia.* Translated by Louis Wirth and Edward Shils. New York: Harcourt, Brace and World.

Paul, Robert. 1984. "German Academic Science and the Mandarin Ethos, 1850–1880." *British Journal of the History of Science.* 17: 1–29.

Ringer, Fritz K. 1969. *The Decline of the German Mandarins: The German Academic Community, 1890–1933.* Cambridge, MA: Harvard University Press.

Tocqueville, Alexis de. 1969. *Democracy in America.* Translated by George Lawrence, edited by F. P. Mayer. New York: Doubleday Anchor Books.

Weber, Max. 1946. "Protestant Sects in America." In *From Max Weber.* Translated by Hans Gerth and C. Wright Mills. New York: Oxford University Press.

———.1951. *The Religion of China,* Translated by Hans Gerth. New York: Free Press.

Yankelovich, Daniel. 1981. *New Rules: Searching for Self-fulfillment in a World Turned Upside Down.* New York: Random House.

14
Religious Broadcasting and the Mobilization of the New Christian Right

Jeffrey K. Hadden

Introduction

Evangelical religious broadcasters are amassing a power base which has the potential of changing American society in ways that are revolutionary in character.[1] This paper seeks to shed light on how this has happened. The argument which will be pursued can be succinctly summarized as follows:

(1) The charismatic leaders of religious broadcasting are principal actors in a social movement of monumental importance in the late-twentieth century.

(2) The ideological origins of this social movement are deeply grounded in the long-held view of America as a "New Israel," a land providentially endowed by God with a special mission in world history.

(3) The organizational resources and managerial techniques of modern televangelism grew out of nineteenth-century urban revivalism, and they are now being applied to fuel a social movement.

(4) By stereotyping fundamentalism as a backwater, anti-intellectual reaction to the modern world, scholars and the mass media alike have seriously misunderstood the complexity, diversity, and strength of evangelical faith in America.

230

(5) The collapse of the liberal vision now provides the opportunity for evangelical Christians to reassert their influence and reshape American culture.

This task is informed by two important theoretical considerations. The first is the author's critique of secularization theory (see "Desacralizing Secularization Theory" in this volume). Second, the "resource mobilization theory" of social movements is taken as a point of departure for analyzing the religious/ social movement that has reemerged in the late-twentieth century.[2] This theoretical approach is seen as holding greater promise for understanding the buoyant quality of religion in the modern world than does secularization theory (Hadden, 1980a).

Traditionally, the concept of social movement has been subsumed under the broader concept of collective behavior. Deeply felt and broadly held grievances coupled with an ideological rationale for change have been viewed as necessary conditions for the emergence of social movements. The research mobilization approach to the study of social movements has shifted the focus of inquiry away from grievances and ideology to look at the structure of movements and how resources are mobilized and managed to achieve goals. Social movements may take the form of reform, rebellion, or revolution. Religion is a resource which will be used both to legitimize and to repress social movements.

The major thesis of this inquiry is that what we are today experiencing, with the emergence of the New Christian Right, is another cycle of a centuries-old social movement. This centuries-old social movement has no formal name because its existence has not been recognized as such. Its manifestation corresponds in a rough, but by no means precise, way to what historians have identified as "great awakenings."

The Roots of a Social Movement

The Crisis of Dominion. If a single concept can describe what the problem and what the social movement is all about, I would say that it is a reoccuring crisis of dominion. It is undergirded by a creation myth of America and is periodically fueled when Christians perceive God's dominion over this land to be threatened. Such is the case today. The creation myth can roughly be recounted as follows:

> After God had created the heavens and the earth, he made Adam and Eve and told them to multiply and have dominion over the earth. They sinned and fell short of the glory of God's commandments, as did subsequent generations, but each time man fell, God provided a pathway for repentence and redemption. And in the course of time, God showed man this promised land and taught him his unalienable rights. And when man stumbled, God raised up a great leader who stood in

the bloodstained battlefield of Gettysburg and renewed our pledge that this nation, under God, shall not perish from the earth.

While there are many variations on this creation myth it is the central motif in the New Christian Right's image of contemporary America. At the heart of its proponents' anguish is the belief that America, this special place in God's divine plan, has stumbled again. Their rhetoric resonates with an imagery of God's dominion, humanity's unfaithfulness to stewardship, the call of repentance, and the promise of redemption.

Their sermons intertwine the Old and New Testaments with American history and the contemporary malaise as if they were all one continuous experience. They proclaim that "Righteousness exalteth a nation, but sin is a reproach to any people" (Proverbs 14: 34). We have "forgotten God," wrote Abraham Lincoln in the anguish of our Civil War. "It behooves us, then," he wrote in proclaiming a National Day of Humiliation, Prayer, and Repentance, "to humble ourselves before the offended Power, to confess our national sins, and to pray for clemency and forgiveness."

A call for renewed repentance was sounded at the Washington for Jesus rally on the Mall April 29, 1980, before a quarter of a million faithful: "If my people, which are called by my name, shall humble themselves, and pray, and seek my face, and turn from their wicked ways; then will I hear from heaven, and will forgive their sin, and will heal their land" (II Chronicles 7: 14).

Some of the particulars of this creation myth are unique to fundamentalism, but the broad contours have been a part of American history from very early. From the days of the earliest settlers in North America through the mid–twentieth century, the idea that this land and its people had a very special relationship to God was never very far from center stage. "Throughout their history," wrote Conrad Cherry (1971), "Americans have been possessed by an acute sense of divine election. They have fancied themselves a New Israel, a people chosen for the awesome responsibility of serving as a light to the nations, a city set upon a hill" (vii). Each generation has embellished the theme with particulars which gave special meaning to the events of their time—the birth of the nation, westward expansion, the Civil War, the industrial revolution, and the journeys to Europe and Asia to defend freedom. Each epoch was interpreted as having a special meaning and purpose in God's divine plan.

Urban Revivalism and the New Christian Right. So pervasive and persistent is this dominion theme that one could tell the story of the rise of the New Christian Right from the first permanent settlement in Jamestown in 1607. Indeed, M. G. "Pat" Robertson finds providential meaning in the location of his Christian Broadcasting Network.[3]

If locating the roots of this social movement is somewhat arbitrary, I think that we appropriately set the stage if we look back to the early-nineteenth century. In 1800, the United States was still a small nation of a mere five million people, and approximately ninety-five percent of them lived in rural areas. In 1820, even as great numbers were packing their wagons and moving westward to explore and settle the vast territory on the other side of the Allegheny and Blue Ridge Mountains, the number of new immigrants to the nation was still at a trickle of about seven hundred per month.

But then this changed. At first, it was like opening a valve just a little. Then the trickle became a steady stream, and the stream became a flood. By the 1880s, the flow of immigrants was approaching half a million a year. By the end of the century, there were seventy-six million Americans, a fifteen-fold increase. And while the westward settlement increased throughout the century, most newcomers took up residence in cities. And those cities, which by our present standards were only towns in the early 1800s, grew into industrial metropolitan areas.

Between westward resettlement and the millions of urban newcomers, America was fast becoming an unchurched nation. The vast population increase included millions who were not Protestants, and this threatened the hegemony that had characterized this land from its beginning.

The revival emerged as a response to the migration flows which had left whole new settlements unchurched. The agents of revival were itinerant Baptist and Methodist preachers. They were, literally, socializing agents taming the violent frontier (Hofstadter, 1963). But the great waves of immigrants were also making frontiers of the cities. So revival found its way to the city as well. By midcentury, "the cutting edge of American Christianity . . . was the revival, adopted and promoted in one form or another by major segments of all denominations" (Smith, 1957: 45).

We face here a question of what to call this revival phenomenon. Sociologists of religion have differentiated between religious movements, which are aimed at changing religious beliefs, values, or practices, and social movements which aim to change some broader aspect of society (Stark and Bainbridge, 1979: 124). While revivalism clearly sought to change religious practice, I think that its broader objective was to change society. The intolerable social problem was unbelief and its concomitant "uncivilized" behavior. Perhaps we can think of the religious problem as an inadequate number of churches and preachers to launch an adequate assault on the social problem. Revivalism, thus, is partly a religious movement, but those who fueled the movement were fundamentally committed to changing society through changing religious behavior. If more people were religious, then society would be more civilized and tolerable.

When the revival went to the city, its social movement character, in contrast to its religious movement character, became more pronounced. The goal of the urban revivalists was not simply to make Christians of the unwashed masses. Rather, they had in mind a more or less explicit image of how Christianizing people transformed their social character. Salvation was viewed as a solution to the problem of urban poverty. Save souls and people will lift themselves out of poverty. Some revivalists argued that the way to win souls was first to care for physical needs so that people might then be better prepared to understand their spiritual condition. But that view did not prevail for long among the big-time urban revivalists. For them, salvation begat motivation to work—it was straight out of Andrew Carnegie's (1949) "gospel of wealth."

The most important thing that happened in the life of urban revivals is that revivalism became a discrete institutional form. The process by which urban revivalism became differentiated as an institution apart from the denominational structures of American Protestantism has been analyzed by Razelle Frankl (1984).[4] Frankl shows how these autonomous structures provide, in both form and content, the organizational model for the contemporary electronic church. Others have traced the roots of modern televangelism to urban revivalism, but the importance of this observation is not clear until one notes the significance of revivalism as an autonomous institutional form.

With no obligation to answer to any Protestant denomination or ecclesiastical authority, urban revivalism took on a life and form all its own. Out of this autonomous structure emerged other detached structures that contributed to private or parachurch structures, most notably Bible institutes and conferences, and independent missionary societies.

These structures, in turn, provided environments which encouraged and fostered much of the rich variety of religious activity in the late-nineteenth and early-twentieth century. Pentecostalism, the holiness movement, and fundamentalism were all nourished within the broad tenets of urban revivalism.

Frankl (1984; 1985) singles out three figures who made marked contributions to the development of urban evangelism as an institutional form: Charles G. Finney, Dwight L. Moody, and Billy Sunday. I shall briefly identify the contributions of each, although it is perhaps best to think of this as a cumulative process, with each building upon his predecessors.

Charles G. Finney (1792–1875), widely acclaimed as "the father of modern revivalism," stands as a transitional figure between the agrarian camp meeting, which characterized the Second Great Awakening in the West, and the urban revival. Finney established the principles of modern evangelism. Well ahead of Frederick Winslow Taylor's (1911) development of the "principles of scientific management," Finney pioneered the development of principles of scientific revivalism. Systematic and comprehensive planning, creation of a proper environment, development of rational arguments, playing on emotions, and utilization of theatrics were all critical elements of Finney's approach to evangelism.

Undergirding Finney's innovative techniques, which he called "New Measures," were important transformations in theological thought which were popularized by the spread of Methodism. John Wesley's doctrines of "salvation by grace through faith" and "individual perfection" cut a deep rift with the Calvinist doctrine of predestination. Responsibility for salvation was shifted from the whims of a God of wrath to the individual who had only to reach out and accept a merciful and loving God's grace. Finney believed that it was the responsibility of the evangelist to do everything he could to confront the individual with that choice. Here, too, the process of revival was turned on its head; man is responsible for producing revivals rather than waiting for God to send a revival.

It was Dwight L. Moody (1837–1899) who advanced urban revivalism from emerging principles to established and routinized techniques. Moody's legacy is the institutionalization of revivalism and the autonomously standing religious institutions which it spawned. Moody was a businessman merchandising salvation. His was a simple business proposition—eternal life in exchange for accepting Christ. Most importantly, Moody rationalized the organization of revivals, creating a complex division of labor with specialized roles and expertise to assure the smooth execution of every detail in the planning and execution of a revival (Frankl, 1984).

Of particular interest is the manner in which he was able simultaneously to engage local ministers in very elaborate planning and participation while keeping some considerable social distance from denominational and other institutionalized religious authorities. This he achieved, in considerable measure, by the utilization of the business community to raise money for the revivals. With their leading laity enthusiastic about the impending revival, local pastors were in no position to be indifferent, but neither were they in a position to control the organization of the revival.

Moody thus developed the autonomous institution of religious revival not by schism, as had been the pattern since the Reformation, but by innovation. There was, to be sure, plenty of antagonism toward this autonomous parachurch structure, but neither denominational nor local ecclesiastical authorities were in a position to block the development of this new institutional form. Moody's revivals provided surplus resources for creating Moody Bible Institute, which, in turn, became a model for other autonomous Bible schools and institutes. It was, to be sure, an institution formed solely on the principles of free enterprise (Marsden, 1980: 34). This was a lesson contemporary televangelists learned well.

Moody also left an important theological legacy. In some ways the principal progenitor of fundamentalism, Moody "lacked the one trait that was essential to a 'fundamentalist'—he was unalterably opposed to controversy" (Marsden, 1980: 33). He wasn't interested in theology and, in fact, claimed not to have a theology (Hudson, 1973: 233). Still, his theological views were not hard to discern. He was a premillennialist and accepted biblical infallibility (Marsden, 1980: 33). His reluctance to publicly pursue theological issues no doubt contributed to opening even wider the door of privatized faith. Thus, Moody may be seen as a key progenitor of fundamentalism, while also tacitly endorsing the proliferation of privatized faith.

If Moody was not openly political, the underlying political implications of his preaching were clear; "a closer reading of the sermons showed that he was a thoroughgoing conservative" (Weisberger, 1958: 224). One of the reasons he got on so well with businessmen was because he believed and preached a doctrine that was in total accord with their worldview.

Billy Sunday (1862–1935) built upon and refined Moody's organizational skills, but he also added the roles of entertainer and celebrity to the evangelist's repertoire. Both would prove to be important components of the recipe for success when revivalism found a new form of expression in television. At the organizational level, McLoughlin notes some twenty specialized roles, and cites an economics professor who claimed that Sunday's organization was one of the five most efficient businesses in the country (McLoughlin, cited in Frankl, 1987: 52). Weisberger (1958) notes that "there was never a machine better designed for publicizing 'the Lord's work' " (251). Entertainment had been creeping into evangelism for a while, but Sunday greatly magnified that trend. Wrote Weisberger (1958): "He synthesized and magnified to the hundredth degree the tendencies towards big-time religious showmanship begun by those before him" (231).

No preacher before or since has commanded as much media attention and celebrity status as did Sunday. His flamboyant antics were criticized as vulgar and as an abomination of religious leadership. But Sunday also had many supporters. After his New York crusade in 1918, which claimed nearly 100,000 souls for the Lord, Sunday's supercharged evangelistic career began to wind down. The New York crusade was not only his last great hurrah, but the last hurrah for revivalism for three decades to come (Weisberger, 1958: 267). If ever the revivals had brought in the unwashed masses in need of being snatched from the grasp of satan, increasingly the audiences were there for a peculiar kind of amusement and entertainment. The revival, in the end, writes Weisberger (1958) "was not even so much . . . a ritual as a spectator sport with religious overtones" (272).

In the later years of his ministry, Sunday became a transition figure to a new role that would become important to televangelism. Sunday was long a staunch supporter of the laissez-faire capitalists he golfed with, but when the United States belatedly entered World War One, Sunday became a super-patriot.

Fundamentalism as a Social Movement. Among the several religious movements spawned by urban revivalism, fundamentalism no doubt grew the strongest. The term fundamentalism derives from a series of paperback volumes published between 1910 and 1915 called the "Fundamentals." Conceived as a testimony to biblical literalism, in contraposition to "higher criticism," they served the cause of pulling together a diverse coalition of similarly minded conservative Christians. The "Fundamentals" were clearly an important resource in a religious movement. The free distribution of three million copies of the booklets went a long way toward creating a communications infrastructure.

Fundamentalism as a critique of culture and, hence, a social movement, did not appear until later. When it did appear, its life as a social movement was short-lived and stormy. Sunday was an important figure. Initially, fundamentalists stood in staunch opposition to America's becoming involved in the war effort, in clear opposition to the support lent by the "modernists" (Marsden, 1980: 141–53). The transition to superpatriots resulted, in part, because the modernists accused them of being sympathetic to Germany. But fundamentalists associated Germany with Nietzsche's "might makes right" philosophy, which in turn they associated with "the survival of the fittest" and "evolutionism." They came to view the war effort, thus, as a struggle between civilization and barbarism.

Marsden (1980) notes Sunday's role in whipping up fundamentalist patriotism: "As the war effort accelerated [Sunday] used the rhetoric of Christian nativism to fan the fires of anti-German furor and was famous for sermons that ended with his jumping on the pulpit waving the flag. "If you turn hell upside down," he said, "you will find 'Made in Germany' stamped on the bottom" (142).

This step into the political arena, once taken, gave fundamentalism a much more decided political character. But as a nascent social movement it was not well focused. The enemy was omnipresent in the form of "barbarism," "Bolshevism," "religious modernism," "evolutionism," and a dozen other "isms." As fundamentalist leaders came to see themselves as locked in a struggle for the survival of God's dominion over the affairs of man, their premillennialist view of the futility of involvement in this world, which had earlier kept them at arm's length from worldly affairs, was overshadowed. They had to get involved.

Diffuse, poorly organized, and inexperienced in politics, the fundamentalists enlisted William Jennings Bryan to lead the movement. Fighting the sinister evolutionists became their main crusade. When John Scopes decided to challenge a Tennessee statute against the teaching of evolution in 1925, Bryan decided that this was an opportune time to square off and do battle. Scopes was found guilty of teaching evolution, but Bryan's knowledge of the Bible was no match for the sharp cross-examination of Clarence Darrow. Victorious, but humiliated, Bryan took ill and died five days later in Dayton, Tennessee. And with the passing of Bryan the burgeoning social movement collapsed. What remained became more and more like the stereotyped image the media had delighted in portraying during the eleven-day trial—a backwater remnant of fools comically battling the inexorable forces of modernity.

The "Monkey Trial" became an epoch-ending event from which fundamentalism might never regain respectability or power. The demise of urban revivalism parallels this devastating blow to conservative religion in America. After Sunday, there were no more great evangelists until Billy Graham. After William Jennings Bryan, there was Billy James Hargis, Carl McIntire, Dr. Frederick Schwarz, Edgar Bundy, and a whole host of lesser luminaries, who probably contributed more to reinforcing the stereotypes of Sinclair Lewis and H. L Mencken than they did to saving America from communism and other evils. Each of these persons attracted followings, but none ever managed to develop sufficient resources to challenge seriously any aspect of American life. Thus, while they represent surviving residuals of the movement, we can conclude that the fundamentalist social movement, which had gained considerable strength during the first half of the 1920s, lost its momentum and then fizzled after 1925.

In retrospect, it is fairly obvious that the fundamentalist social movement was not well defined, nor was its attention well focused. Also with the benefit of hindsight, the movement was probably doomed when it picked Williams Jennings Bryan to be its leader. Three times the Democratic party's standard-bearer for the presidency, Bryan had never won any office for which he was nominated. His oratory skills were not matched with organizational acumen.

When Jerry Falwell came upon the national political scene in 1980, proud to be a fundamentalist and professing to speak for millions who were going to reclaim America in the name of God, few political analysts were prepared to take him seriously. Contemporary political analysts had come to see fundamentalism through the eyes of secularization theorists—as intermittent residual noise from an archaic religious form.

The Reemergence of a Social Movement

To understand how and why fundamentalism eventually reappeared as a social movement in the late 1970s, and why it is destined to become the major social movement in America during the last quarter of the twentieth century, we need to pull together four separate threads or developments. The first is the link of televangelism to urban revivalism. This is important because religious broadcasting is the critical resource in mobilizing the social movement.

The second thread involves the process by which the religious airwaves became the nearly exclusive domain of evangelical and fundamentalist Christians. This dominance was not always the case. In fact, for a long time in the history of radio, and during the first major phase of television, the liberal church tradition had a near monopoly on the airwaves. Without this very considerable media access, the New Christian Right would be a much less formidable social movement.

The third thread involves the role of fundamentalism in preserving the dominion creation myth as the central motif in interpreting American history. As the liberal dream seemed to be collapsing during the 1960s and 1970s, fundamentalists had an alternative vision of a better America, along with the motivation to press their grievances against what they saw as the causes of a failing social order.

A final thread involves the restoration of the Christian worldview of dominion. Dispensational premillennialism, with its pessimistic view of this world, was just plain bad luck for evangelicals. A critical step in the transformation of the New Christian Right into a world-transforming social movement is the junking of premillennialism and the restoration of a post-millennial world-view. Restoration of postmillennialism can provide the social movement with the conceptual, or theoretical, rationale for resuming the historic quest for dominion. This process has already begun.

The Link to Urban Revivalism. Urban revivalism as an important cultural form never completely disappeared, but it achieved a high profile once again in 1949 when William Randolph Hearst delivered his celebrated two-word command, "Puff Graham," to his newspaper empire. The following year, after an incredible flurry of media attention, Billy Graham decided to do a weekly radio program, "Hour of Decision." That decision firmly linked nineteenth-century urban revivalism to modern religious broadcasting.

Graham's decision to go on radio was even more momentus to his career and to the future of religious broadcasting than was the great boost he got from Hearst's patronage. About a year after going on radio, Graham made another important decision. In 1951, the Billy Graham Evangelistic Association began packaging his crusades for television. This gave Graham even greater visibility and success.

Like Moody and Sunday before him, Graham relished rubbing shoulders with the rich and powerful. He particularly liked presidents, until he got soiled by the carnage of Watergate. His role as the "preacher of presidents" no doubt rendered legitimacy to the political status quo. Graham's sermons have always had a ring of patriotism, but never the bellicose "100 percent Americanism" of Sunday in his later days. Still, while Graham would eventually repudiate his own involvement in politics, he set the stage for others to become more deeply involved than he.

Excluding Graham, the early days of televangelism could be characterized as apolitical. At about the same time Graham decided to go on television, two itinerant evangelists from Oklahoma and Arkansas also recognized the potential of television for saving souls. Oral Roberts brought the television cameras into his revival tent, and Rex Humbard sold his tent and built a cathedral especially equipped for broadcasting. A new era was born.

These three men play roles in the development of the electronic church that parallel those of Finney, Moody, and Sunday in the development of urban evangelism. Building on the organizational principles which resulted in the institutionalization of urban revivalism, Graham, Roberts, and Humbard created yet another institution—the electronic church.

The Billy Graham Evangelistic Association modeled its crusades after the methods of Finney, Moody, and Sunday: the engagement of local pastors and churches before the decision to conduct a crusade, advanced planning activities to arouse interest, topflight entertainment—albeit in a much more subdued form than Sunday's vaudeville antics—guest celebrity appearances, appeals to the emotions, and the expressing of the urgency of a decision for Christ. The great boost Graham received from Hearst gave him a competitive edge in access to evening prime-time television, which Roberts and Humbard were never able to overcome. Roberts and Humbard became innovators in the structure of programming and the development of communication feedback loops with their audiences.

Of the two, Roberts has been much more innovative. He hired topflight secular entertainers to appear on his programs as a way of hooking audiences. Through rather crude studies of audience response, he guaged audience size and aggressively bought the best time slots. He learned early that people will give for bricks and mortar while they don't get excited about paying for airtime. With this knowledge, he built a university. That he eventually overextended himself with his hospital doesn't detract from the principle he established, which almost every successful televangelist has copied: Major projects excite audience response.

Humbard has been most successful in mastering the art of parapersonal communication. When he looked into the camera, people thought he was talking directly to them. From the beginning, there were participants in the program, and audiences came to feel that they too were members of the Humbard family, or vice versa. Humbard developed audience loyalty rarely achieved in television, and his audience stuck with him for a very long while.

What all of these ministries have in common, which would in time revolutionize religious broadcasting, is their relationship to their audience. Whereas commercial broadcasting sells advertising to support programming, the electronic church sells itself and its projects. Televangelists solicit support for general and specific projects from their audiences and offer premiums in exchange for donations. Over time, their solicitation tactics have become extremely sophisticated.

All but one of the major televangelists have used their broadcasting to build substantial off-camera empires. The limits of growth potential for existing operations is still unknown. With increased competition, airtime has become very expensive. There can be no question that it is a precarious operation. Humbard's empire collapsed in 1985, and Roberts's has appeared to be on the brink of disaster since the raising of the medical complex. If Roberts survives, the implication of the Humbard fate is that the dangers of failing to build a bricks-and-mortar empire are more hazardous than trying to sustain a broadcasting enterprise without projects.

If one can use a television ministry to build colleges, cathedrals, hospitals, and spiritual Disneylands, it seems likely that it can also be used to pursue projects that are not necessarily direct derivatives of the religious broadcasting. Falwell's decision to create the Moral Majority was the first bold attempt to test this proposition.

In a more subtle, and in the long run more effective way, Pat Robertson, too, has used his religious television role to demonstrate to the world his political acumen and to build a following for his political views. His bid for the Republican presidential election in 1988 aside, Robertson's blending of religion, politics, and economic analysis on "The 700 Club" has elevated his personal status as a respected conservative spokeperson. His potential to capitalize upon this status is considerable.

Other televangelists, such as Jimmy Swaggart and D. James Kennedy, are well positioned to channel their audiences toward explicit political projects. So long as the Federal Communications Commission, the Congress, and the courts do not change broadcasting rules, the potential for using religious broadcasting as a base for building social movements and political organizations seems quite likely.

In summary, the institution of urban revivalism has been resurrected in the form of the electronic church. Like revivalism, the electronic church functions autonomously from other religious institutions. Two unique qualities are (a) the potential to generate surplus resources and (b) the capability of directing those surplus resources to other projects. Other projects may include building colleges, hospitals, and cathedrals. What has happened over the past decade, with increasing velocity, is that resources have been directed toward social-movement activities. Resources are here understood to include exposure (advertisement of the social-movement cause), recruitment of constituents, and transfer of fiscal and leadership resources from "conventional" electronic-church activities to social-movement activities.

Control of Airwaves. A second important thread for understanding how the New Christian Right has become an important social movement is the process whereby religious broadcasting in America came almost exclusively into the hands of evangelicals and fundamentalists. From the beginning of broadcasting, the liberal church traditions associated with the Federal Council of Churches (which became the National Council of Churches in the 1950s) held a privileged position in access to network airtime. This advantage increased over time, so that by the early 1940s evangelical and fundamentalist broadcasters were virtually squeezed off the air.

How the transition from liberal dominance to virtual monopoly by the conservatives occurred is a fascinating and basically untold story—and, regrettably, beyond the scope of this paper. It is possible only to identify the most critical variables that brought about this revolution.

The Communications Act of 1934 authorized the FCC to license individual stations. The granting of a license in effect constitutes a monopoly to use a scarce commodity, namely a specific airwave, to transmit messages. Without specifying precise details, it has always been presumed that stations "owe" some proportion of their broadcast time to general "public interest" in exchange for this monopoly right. From the beginning, religious broadcasting has been designated as public-interest broadcasting. Both network and local broadcasters preferred to allocate this time to the "mainline" religious traditions on a "sustaining" (free) basis. Among the networks, only the Mutual Broadcasting System offered commercial airtime, and eventually they severely restricted the amount of time and the conditions for access.

In 1960, the FCC released a policy directive specifying that no important public interest was served by differentiating between gratis airtime and commercially sponsored programming. The implication of this ruling was that local stations could sell airtime for religious programs and still get "public-interest credit" in the eyes of the FCC overseers.

Several important developments followed. First, the evangelical and fundamentalist syndicators rushed in to compete with one another for the airtime. Their competition enhanced the value of the time slots. As a result, many local stations that had previously followed network policies of not selling airtime for broadcasting decided to cash in on the new demand.

The implications of this process for sustaining-time programs was devastating. Local stations dropped sustaining-time programs produced both by their network and individual denominations. This effect was dramatically demonstrated in a report by the Communications Committee of the U.S. Catholic Conference to the FCC in 1979 (Horsfield, 1984: 89). In 1959, 53 percent of all religious broadcasting in America was paid-time programming. Following the FCC ruling, that proportion increased to 92 percent in 1977. Thus, for all intents and purposes, religious broadcasting has become a commercial enterprise in America on both radio and television. The de facto implication of this is that the "mainline" or liberal denominations of Protestantism, as well as Catholics and Jews, have been virtually squeezed off the air.

Mainline denominations have not been able to compete in commercial religious broadcasting for a variety of reasons (for details, see Hadden, 1980b). Among other things, liberal church traditions are less comfortable in asking people to give money or to give their souls to Jesus. By contrast, the confluence of evangelical proselytizing zeal and the commercial free-enterprise system go together well. And the oligarchically structured bureaucracies of the electronic church permit rapid adaptation and prompt execution of decisions in response to perceived opportunities.

Other FCC policies have had a significant bearing on the preponderance of commercial-time religious broadcasting. It is conceivable that these policies might be altered significantly. But it is also unlikely that this will happen without confrontation. The National Religious Broadcasters (NRB) have proved themselves effective lobbyists in Washington. Their chief legal counsel is a former chairman of the FCC. At the annual meetings of the NRB, they hold a luncheon to honor the commissioners of the FCC.

Whereas the founding of the National Religious Broadcasters is grounded in a religious conflict between evangelicals and "modernists," it has become an important resource for the New Christian Right social movement. NRB retains top legal counsel to lobby for the group's interests and to protect against any attempt to assault the favored position it occupies. It has more than 1,100 member radio and television stations.

The Dominion Creation Myth. A third thread that provides insight into why a fundamentalist social movement of the first quarter of the twentieth century has reappeared during the last quarter involves the peculiar and ironic circumstances by which the fundamentalists became the custodians of the dominion creation myth.

There was also, of course, a certain irony to the political engagement of fundamentalists in the first quarter of the century. The irony results from the fact that premillennialism is an eschatology of defeat and despair. Things are getting so bad, the doctrine holds, that only Christ's return can stay the tide against Satan. It invites retreat from the world, not hand-to-hand combat with the minions of Satan.

However one may view the inconsistency, the fundamentalists of the 1920s, perceiving Christian civilization to be crumbling around them, could not content themselves with waiting for Christ's return. At least some of them were not able to disengage from the world. The reason this was so in the 1920s and again in the 1970s is that premillennialism runs in sharp contradiction to the dominion creation myth.

For nearly the whole of American history, its people have believed that God had special providential plans for this land. However compelling the premillennialist doctrine may be for those who see the modern world as sinful and corrupt beyond redemption, premillennialism has never completely defeated the dominion doctrine. The latter was reinforced throughout the nineteenth century by the doctrine of free will. If the individual is compelled to choose between good and evil and if God has a plan for America, then the choice is to join in the struggle.

The premillennialist doctrine focuses attention on saving as many souls as possible before it is too late. The doctrine of dominion, in sharp contrast, would transform society. The tension between engagement and disengagement is a struggle that goes on not only between groups within the fundamentalist and evangelical sectors, but also involves personal struggle to discern God's will.

In 1965, Jerry Falwell preached that he could not imagine ever turning his attention from preaching the "pure saving gospel . . . [which] . . . does not clean up the outside but rather regenerates the inside" (Hadden and Swann, 1981: 160). That was premillennialist Falwell. A decade later, as America prepared its bicentennial, Falwell was feeling the tension of the "broken covenant" as he organized "I Love America" rallies. In 1980, after he had organized the Moral Majority, he wrote: "If Americans will face the truth, our nation can be turned around and can be saved from the evils and the destruction that have fallen upon every other nation that has turned its back on God"

(Falwell, 1980: 18). Falwell is still preaching premillennialist theology, but the dominion covenant is tugging at his soul.

The dominion creation myth, with its recurring cycles of sin, repentance, and redemption, is an inextricable part of the American conscience. About the same time Falwell began sounding the trumpet for America to repent, sociologist Robert Bellah (1975) wrote: "Once in each of the last three centuries America has faced a time of trial, a time of testing so severe that not only the form but even the existence of our nation have been called in question" (1). Bellah's understanding of why the covenant has been broken and what must be done to repent is at odds with Falwell's. The important observation is that two persons, so different in their intellectual understanding of America, agree that America is broken and in need of fixing.

This consensus is the result of the survival of the dominion creation myth, and it is widely shared in sacred and secular form across American culture. Harvey Cox's (1984) scenario for the return of the sacred to the secular city is a liberal church vision of repentence and redemption. Neoconservative Richard John Neuhaus (1984) would return God to the "naked public square" as a first step in restoration of the covenant, and even Catholic atheist Michael Harrington (1983) agonizes about "the politics at God's funeral" and pleads for a rational recreation of something like the creation myth.

Secularization fosters pluralism which, in turn, demonopolizes religious dogma (Berger, 1967: 134). This is true of both formal theological doctrine and religious mythology. The dominion creation myth has survived in America, but the tremendously diverse array of variations on the theme cited above bear testimony to the reality of cultural pluralism. If there is a general sense that America needs to mend her ways so that she can be healed and once again return to greatness, how that is to be achieved is a matter of deep division.

The critical question from the perspective of resource mobilization analysis is whether any group or coalition of groups possesses resources sufficient to generate a major social movement. To address this question, we have to move from the generalized perception that the society faces serious problems to more precise identification of those problems.

This is not the occasion to analyze the conservative mood in America today vis-à-vis the more liberal mood of previous decades. But the liberal social-problems agendas of the previous two decades do have important implications regarding the options for working through a crisis of dominion. Two factors are of particular importance.

First, social movements are not easily sustained for long periods of time. Maintaining momentum requires more and more resources. The capacity of social structures (public and private) to respond is not without limits. Movements tend to become bureaucratized and, with this, they develop survival imperatives independent of the movements. In brief, movements have cycles. Over time, they lose momentum, and they must either be regenerated or they fade.

Second, movements do not necessarily give way to countermovements, but it is not unusual for new problems to be identified as a consequence of solving other problems. Thus, addressing the problems of inequality and human rights during the 1960s and 1970s is now seen as a source of some of the problems of the 1980s. Whereas most movement leaders would not wish their movements to be judged in terms of the goals and activities of the most extreme elements of the movement, there is a tendency to do so. Counter-movements will seek to highlight fringe groups and characterize them as exemplary of the entire movement. Thus did a violent element of the black community in America hasten the conclusion of a formal civil rights movement. And radical feminists and gays have provided highly visible targets for those who seek to organize countermovements against them.

These more or less natural movement tendencies have important implications for understanding (and misunderstanding) the present conservative tendencies in America. First, a variety of liberal social-movement activities dominated American politics for over two decades. Whatever the empirical links may be between the liberal social-movement agendas and the current array of intolerable social issues, there is an appearance of causal relationship—an appearance that the New Christian Right (NCR) has not hesitated to exploit.

Viewed as a countermovement to the liberal social agenda of the 1960s, the New Christian Right bears many similarities to the fundamentalist movement of the 1920s. And viewed from this assumptive framework, it is easy to dismiss it as yet another backlash by persons who have been left behind and who are out of step with the mainstream of American culture. From this perspective, it seems terribly significant that "creationism" should reappear as a serious issue on the NCR agenda.

One cannot escape an element of backlash in the NCR agenda. My quarrel with much of the analysis about the NCR to date is (a) it fails to understand the importance of playing on the old themes as an instrument for mobilizing previously passive adherents, and (b) it does not see new elements which have the potential for mobilizing much broader followings.

First, some comments on the value of playing on old themes. To an outsider, the "creationism" issue has the appearance of a case of déjà vu of William Jennings Bryan on the witness stand being cross-examined by Clarence Darrow. To fundamentalists, there is a redemptive vindication. The new creationism is not going to put evolution to rest, but it is a far more sophisticated scrutiny of the theory of evolution than the first round of Bible thumping. Meticulous rational scrutiny of the theoretical aspects of the science of evolution has laid bare the "faith" assumptions of secular scientists. Further, the fact that secular scientists are generally not prepared to deal with fundamentalists at this level of analysis has provided a tremendous moral victory and, from their perspective, vindication against the stereotypes of "antievolutions" as "dummies."

But more importantly, the evolution issue provides a springboard for a more general critique of contemporary public education. If evolution can be demonstrated to be a theory, with some gaps in empirical evidence, and if secular education refuses to teach the alternative biblical "theory" of creation, then public education must certainly be guilty of committing "secular humanism," as charged.

In this context, creationism becomes a very important issue because it symbolizes a critique of public education in America, which has dismissed God and morality. For one hundred and fifty years, the constitutional issue of the relation between church and state was essentially moot. With few notable exceptions, there were no cases in the courts. Not only was God's place in the classroom firmly established, socializing "barbarians" to godly and moral principles was an important basis for public education (Collins, 1979: 95–118). After a long history of congenial accommodation of God in public places, the last twenty years have seen the court dockets filled with challenges to the entanglement of religion in public life. An extraordinary number of cases have dealt with religion and public education. And, on balance, the large number of cases points toward exclusion of God from the classroom.

As a springboard to a more general critique of what has happened to public education, the creationism issue may have important indirect implications for a broader support base. If creationism can develop and then retain an aura of respectability, then it bolsters the argument that not only has God been excluded from ceremonial matters in public education, but also that public education has developed a biased curriculum which systematically excludes Christian principles.

The school prayer issue demonstrates the vulnerability of the legal and structural barriers to penetration by the NCR. Several recent public opinion polls have demonstrated that significant proportions of Americans do not accept the legitimacy of prohibiting prayer in public schools. For example, a national poll conducted earlier this month revealed that three-quarters of the American population think that prayer in school does not violate the separation of church and state. And 63 percent not only think prayer should be permitted, but that it should be encouraged (*The Daily Progress,* 14 October 1985: A6). These views, of course, stand in direct contradiction to several Supreme Court decisions, including *Wallace v. Jaffree* (1985) in the most recent court session.

Thus far, the New Christian Right has been held off by the courts and has been frustrated in its efforts to get a school prayer amendment before the full Congress for consideration. However symbolic the issue may appear, it seems to me to be an issue that stands a chance of eventually winning, either through progressive testing of the courts or by a Constitutional amendment.

Abortion is another issue about which the fundamentalists feel very deeply. It has not only proved to be an issue which has motivated action, it has also served to begin the process of building coalitions with other groups who share such concerns. Until only recently, fundamentalists have had a long history of animosity toward Roman Catholics and Mormons. On the issue of abortion, however, they are substantially together.

A critical indicator of developing movement maturity and strength is the ability to put aside ideological differences to work together on at least limited objectives with those who have otherwise been adversaries. Through the abortion issue, evangelicals, Catholics, Mormons, and members of other groups are now finding a broader range of common concerns and, as a result, their organizational alliances are beginning to extend into other areas of cooperation.

In summarizing the early years of the New Christian Right movement, I offer four observations.

First, this decade has been characterized by a broadening of the base of support among conservative Christians, large numbers of whom have not heretofore been engaged in the political process. We have no sensitive empirical indicators of just how extensive this type of activity has been, but there is an abundance of evidence that more and more people are shifting from indifferent bystanders to the category of adherents, and from adherents to constituents. Second, the number of New Christian Right organizations has increased precipitously, but again I am not aware of any systematic inventories of identity, memberships, or budgets. Third, and equally impressive, is the extent to which the New Christian Right leadership has been building organizational coalitions with groups that share common concerns on both broad fronts and limited social agendas.

Notwithstanding the potential of the New Christian Right to build a broader base of support for its critique of public education, its position on abortion, and perhaps several other matters as well, the fact remains that it appears to be swimming against the mainstream of American culture. (Cf. Hammond, 1983: 219). It seems out of step with emerging values about interpersonal relations between the sexes. Its long laundry list of personal "vices" covers a large proportion of matters that Americans feel ought to be left to personal choice.

A fourth observation in reviewing the NCR movement to date involves an assessment of their potential to develop issues that command national attention to a degree that requires collective resolution. The Civil Rights movement was of this character. It dramatically presented massive evidence of social inequality and mistreatment which demanded public attention and at least some sense of progress toward resolution.

Is there such an analogue in the burgeoning New Christian Right movement? The strongest critics of the New Christian Right argue that, if left unchecked, these Christian "zealots" will rewrite the laws and the Constitution to impose their pietistic moral code on the rest of the nation. Clearly, the New Christian Right stands sharply at odds with the general direction of American culture in some very important ways. My own sense, however, is that such thinking about the NCR locks us into a mind-set of the movement as a countermovement to the social movements of the 1960s. I think that this leads both to misunderstandings and to an underestimation of potential strength.

I began this paper by characterizing the heart of the New Christian Right movement as a crisis of dominion. Let me return to this theme. The past quarter of a century has sorely tested the American character. We have achieved technological accomplishments which were beyond the human imagination only a generation ago. We have taken giant strides to erase inequities and injustices inherited from our ancestors. And we have grown increasingly conscious of our planet, our place, and our requirement to be a good neighbor.

For all of our intentions at home and abroad, we seem to stumble. We have suffered the pain of assassination, the agony of defeat, the humiliation of impotence, the frustration of the inability to use strength, and the disgrace of failed leadership.

Domestically, the evidence for our having made lasting progress in eliminating discrimination against minorities and women seems ambiguous; poverty stubbornly resists our prescriptions for eradication; and drug use and crime seem out of control. The list of ills and frustrations, at home and abroad, goes on and on.

Others, in other times and places, have faced prolonged frustrations and humiliations and have learned to live with them. But the events of the past quarter century have not sat well with the American people because we have always thought of ourselves as a good, God-fearing people who, with his hand, have the ability to control destiny. As individuals, most of us are doing well. But as we look around at all that has gone wrong, these happenings seem to bear testimony to a much deeper and more fundamental cultural malady.

Sociologically speaking, if it were possible to step outside our world and objectively assess our cultural condition, it wouldn't matter. People act upon what they perceive to be real. Whether or not our problems seriously threaten our destiny as a people, we think that they do.

The liberal tradition in America does not stand in a strong position to direct us out of this perceived condition of cultural malaise. We stand too close in time to too many liberal programs that were supposed to help solve the very problems that now disturb us so.

The New Christian Right has offered us an old diagnosis—one that we have bought before. Our problems are of our own making. We must repent and make things right with our maker before we can resume our providential role in his divine plan.

What is required of us is not yet clear. Social movements never unfold in conformity with a master plan or blueprint. They are made up as they go. Falwell's vision of a repentant America has received a lot of media attention to date. Others, presently just off center stage, could soon move into the national spotlight.

My political theory leads me to believe that there are powerful forces which pull all movements toward the center of our culture. Within this framework, I find some hope that the movement will not take America to the extremes that many liberal groups fear. I also find hope in what I detect as a distinct turn from premillennial doctrine by some televangelists.[5] On the one hand, a return to postmillennial theology will likely give the social movement a great boost of energy. If this nation and the world are yet to be conquered before Christ's return, that could charge the movement with renewed zeal to restore God's dominion over America. The other side of postmillennialism, however, is that it could spell a much more responsible posture toward our tiny planet and all that dwells herein. And that, too, could be a source of hope. If Jesus isn't coming very soon, then it behooves all who are in positions of leadership and responsibility to recognize and protect our fragile interdependence on this planet.

Notes

1. An extended version of this paper was presented as the author's Presidential Address to the Society for the Scientific Study of Religion, 25 October 1985, Savannah, Georgia, and was published in the *Journal for the Scientific Study of Religion* (1987b). The author wishes especially to thank Razelle Frankl for critical insights that helped this analysis fall into place and Anson Shupe for helpful comments in an earlier draft.
2. Work in "resource mobilization" theory has been pioneered by Mayer N. Zald and John D. McCarthy. For a basic statement of the theory see McCarthy and Zald (1977). The best single source for an orientation to this perspective is their collection of essays (Zald and McCarthy, 1987). For a helpful example of how this perspective can be applied to the study of religious conflict, see Zald, 1982.
3. In *The Secret Kingdom,* Robertson writes: "At a point just ten miles from the site I had purchased [for CBN], the first permanent English settlers in America had planted a cross on the sandy shore and claimed the land for God's glory and for the spread of the gospel. After 370 years, the ultramodern television facility with worldwide capabilities began to fulfill these dreams" (1982: 196). Further providential significance is found in his creation of CBN University. These early Virginia settlers had planned Henrico College, a school to train young persons to teach and preach the gospel. Robertson traces his ancestry to these settlers.
4. I am indebted to Frankl for her brilliant analysis of how urban revivalism became an autonomous institutional form. See Frankl, 1987.
5. Since this paper was written, I have had the opportunity to discuss this issue with several televangelists, including Pat Robertson and Jerry Falwell. Both of these men reject the notion that their thinking is moving toward postmillenialism. However,

Robertson did admit to backing away from his sense that the second coming of Christ was imminent. Both assert that eschatology is not a significant variable in explaining the political engagement of the New Christian Right. On the basis of these interviews I have to conclude that explicit and dramatic rejection of pre-millenialism is not imminent. But I do think that this-worldly political success will gradually lead to a deemphasis of premillenialism.

References

Bellah, Robert N. 1975. *The Broken Covenant*. New York: Seabury.

Berger, Peter L. 1967. *The Sacred Canopy*. Garden City, NY: Doubleday.

Carnegie, Andrew. 1949. "Wealth." In *Democracy and the Gospel of Wealth*. edited by Gail Kennedy, 1–8. Boston: D.C. Heath.

Cherry, Conrad, ed. 1971. *God's New Israel: Religious Interpretations of American Destiny*. Englewood Cliffs, NJ.

Collins, Randall. 1979. *The Credential Society*. New York: Academic Press.

———. 1986. "Historical Perspectives on Religion and Regime: Some Sociological Comparisons of Buddhism and Christianity." In *Prophetic Religions and Politics*. edited by Jeffrey K. Hadden and Anson Shupe, 254–71. New York: Paragon House.

Cox, Harvey. 1984. *Religion in the Secular City*. New York: Simon and Schuster.

Falwell, Jerry. 1980. *Listen, America!* Garden City, NY: Doubleday.

Finney, Charles F., Jr. 1960. *Lectures: On Revivals of Religion*. Edited by William G. McLoughlin. Cambridge, MA: Belknap Press of Harvard University Press.

Frankl, Razelle. 1984. "Popular Religion and the Imperatives of Television: A Study of the Electric Church." Ph.D. diss., Bryn Mawr College.

———. 1985. "The Historical Antecedent of the Electric Church." Paper presented to the Annual Meeting of the Society for the Scientific Study of Religion.

———. 1987. *Televangelism: The Marketing of Popular Religion*. Carbondale, IL: Illinois University Press.

Hadden, Jeffrey K. 1980a. "Religion and the Construction of Social Problems." *Sociological Analysis*. 41: 99–108.

———. 1980b. "Soul-Saving via Video." *Christian Century*. 97 (28 May): 609–13.

———. 1987a. "Toward Desacralizing Secularization Theory." *Social Forces*. 65: 587–611.

———. 1987b. "Religious Broadcasting and the Mobilization of the New Christian Right." *Journal for the Scientific Study of Religion*. 26: 1–24.

Hadden, Jeffrey K., and Charles E. Swann. 1981. *Prime Time Preachers*. Reading, MA: Addison-Wesley.

Hammond, Phillip E. 1983. "Another Great Awakening?" In *The New Christian Right*. edited by Robert C. Liebman and Robert Wuthnow. New York: Aldine.

Harrington, Michael. 1983. *The Politics at God's Funeral*. New York: Holt, Rinehart and Winston.

Hofstadter, Richard. 1963. *Anti-Intellectualism in American Life*. New York: Random House.

Horsfield, Peter G. 1984. *Religious Television*. New York: Longman.

Hudson, Winthrop S. 1973. *Religion in America*. 2d ed. New York: Charles Scribner's Sons.

Marsden, George M. 1980. *Fundamentalism and American Culture*. New York: Oxford University Press.

McCarthy, John D., and Mayer N. Zald. 1977. "Resource Mobilization and Social Movements: A Partial Theory." *American Journal of Sociology*. 82: 1212–41.

Neuhaus, Richard John. 1984. *The Naked Public Square*. Grand Rapids, MI: Eerdmans.

Robertson, Pat. 1982. *The Secret Kingdom*. Nashville, TN: Thomas Nelson.

Smith, Timothy L. 1957. *Revivalism and Social Reform*. New York: Harper and Row.

Stark, Rodney and William Sims Bainbridge. 1979. "Of Churches, Sects and Cults: Preliminary Concepts for a Theory of Religious Movements." *Journal for the Scientific Study of Religion*. 18: 117–31.

Taylor, Frederick Winslow. 1911. *The Principles of Scientific Management*. New York: Harper.

Weisberger, Bernard A. 1958. *They Gathered at the River*. Chicago, IL: Quadrangle Books.

Zald, Mayer N. 1982. "Theological Crucibles: Social Movements in and of Religion." *Review of Religious Research*. 23: 317–36.

Zald, Mayer N., and John D. McCarthy. 1987. *Social Movements in an Organizational Society*. New Brunswick, NJ: Transaction Books.

15
Raison d'Église: Organizational Imperatives of the Church in the Political Order

John A. Coleman, S.J.

In any crucial situation the behavior of the Catholic church may be more reliably predicted by reference to its interests as a political organization than by reference to its timeless dogmas.

Gunther Lewy. *The Catholic Church and Nazi Germany*[1]

Organizational Analysis of the Church

IN THIS PAPER, I am going to ask about the organizational weight of the church in effecting its response to politics. Despite the general truth in the citation from Gunther Lewy with which I began this essay, *raison d'église* does not well or exhaustively explain all political responses of the church. But it is important that we attend to the institutional interests of the church and their impact in dictating or shaping its political stance.

Political scientists ordinarily enough refer to actions of governments by evoking the concept of *raison d'état:* the intractable self-interest of states in conducting a foreign policy, the action consequences of protecting state sovereignty, and the bottom-line organizational imperatives of national governments. Less attention is paid to the concept of *raison d'église,* the organizational imperatives of a church, its bottom-line, non-negotiable interests and institutional purposes.

252

Surprisingly, since the time of the early classic work of Max Weber and Ernst Troeltsch, sociology of religion has tended to rely more on ideas, belief systems, cultural ideologies, attitudes, and topologies of believers as explanatory variables than on organizational aspects of church polities. In the Catholic case, as the German sociologist F. X. Kaufmann contends, organizational problems tend to be submerged into theology. Burcaucratic organizational principles which emerged throughout history become rigidified and sacralized. Kaufmann states the point:

> The churches' existing view of themselves which in the Catholic Church, especially since the nineteenth century, has taken the form of ecclesiology, is "organization blind." This has two senses. First, the theory has no place for real weaknesses of the organization and second the organizational aspects of the church appear in the theory only in the mediated concepts of "office," "hierarchy," or "papacy." This theological blindfold blocks consideration of genuine and perduring problems within the church.[2]

We can note a number of distinct organizational problems of the Church to which theology often remains blind: (1) the lack of any responsible control over ecclesiastical administration (management review, financial accountability, efficiency studies); (2) failure to integrate the laity and give them voice within church organizations; (3) failure to improve human relations within the administration of the Church and between administrators and clergy who are on the line; (4) two-way communication distortion between administrative layers within the world church, between the Roman curia and national episcopacies, or between bishops and their service bureaucracy and line officers in pastoral work; (5) failure to protect individual rights of functionaries and employees of the church (including priests)—this involves not only financial rights and career security but other freedoms connected with due process; (6) the competence and sway of influence of lay councils at the parish, diocesan, or national levels as well as that of other groups such as International Synods of Bishops, episcopal conferences, or priests' councils within a diocese; (7) unclarity about role definitions and accountability structures of church service bureaucracies and various subordinate officers in the church; and (8) the fusion of religious concepts of authoritative leadership ("office" and "ordination" in the church) with de facto bureaucratic roles which have little direct binding with the New Testament notions of "office" (e.g., a chancellor, dean, or vicar within a diocese or a superintendent of Catholic school systems)—this fusion of a theological notion of "office" and bureaucracy lies at the root of Kaufmann's complaint about sacralizing purely organizational structures.[3]

I want to raise some questions, then, about the organizational weight of the church as an institution, how its bureaucratic structures and goals either lend flexibility or place limitations on the adaptive capacities of the church in the political order. We will be pursuing these questions against the backdrop of the larger issue, first strongly raised by Weber, of the relation of the church to processes of social change. We will want to tease out the conditions under which churches reenforce and converge with secular groups in promoting social change as well as the impediments to change, counterpoints of caution, which stem from the church's organizational structure.

The Church and Social Change

From certain vantage points, churches, and especially the Catholic Church, represent inherently conservative institutions. Sociologically, they usually represent the continuities of culture. Religions socialize new generations of recruits to carry on the meanings supplied by tradition. Churches act as moral agencies of social control or as symbols, as Durkheim argued, of societal unity against deviance. Nevertheless, as Peter Worsley has forcefully argued:

> Religion is neither intrinsically conservative nor revolutionary. It can be infused with any kind of social content, notably political; there are both religions of the oppressed and the kinds of religion that have been summed up in the label given to the Church of England as "The Conservative Party at Prayer." The relationship of beliefs, let alone movements and organizations, to the established power-system thus varies, and is not a matter for metaphysical pronouncement disguised as sociological generalization. It requires empirical investigation to see what the case is.[4]

We do better to inquire about the conditions under which religious groups support or oppose social change and their organizational limits as actors for social change than to generalize about religion and social change as a zero-sum game. Scott Mainwaring's summary of the three foundational interests of the Catholic Church can help to shape our inquiry into the conditions under which Catholicism supports or impedes social change: "The church, like other institutions, has interests it attempts to defend; the most relevant interests are the church's unity, its capacity to appeal to all social classes, and its identity as a fundamentally religious institution."[5]

Church Unity. The fundamentally Catholic form for preserving church unity resides in its hierarchical structure, which links the papacy to national episcopacies and derives the ecclesial mandate for priests or lay church elites from hierarchical approval. As Leonardo Boff has noted of this principle of hierarchy: "From a sociological perspective the church operates out of an authoritarian system."[6] Linkage to the world church represents, sociologically, both a resource and a concomitant limitation to national episcopacies. The papacy jealously guards its appointment powers over the episcopacy. Wherever possible, the Vatican seeks to break governmental power to nominate or veto episcopal appointments, as it successfully did in Argentina after 1966 and in Spain after the death of Franco.

The hierarchical principle in world Catholicism is the first and strongest nonnegotiable institutional interest of the Church. The Vatican will risk polarizing and splitting national churches, gutting their momentum and innovation, rather than yield power over episcopal appointment. At the level of national episcopacies, the Vatican seems to favor a divide-and-conquer strategy. It juxtaposes and mingles progressive and reactionary voices in the one bishops' conference to avoid any great local autonomy *vis-à-vis* the world church. This makes it difficult to achieve a local unified episcopal voice at the national level to accomplish a relatively unitary national pastoral plan, directionality, and prophetic strategies adapted to exert influence on a local context.

Where too much unity and pastoral directionality among local bishops has appeared—as, in recent years, in the Netherlands, the United States, or Brazil—the Vatican usually begins to appoint conservative or reactionary bishops. Indeed, recently Cardinal Josef Ratzinger of the Vatican Congregation of Doctrine and Faith has been trying to minimize as much as possible the importance and competency of episcopal conferences as a structure for local church unity. Ratzinger stresses, instead, the atomistic autonomous competence of each local bishop and diocese.

A Reactive Strategy. Concern for church unity within the local church, under these authoritarian structural principles of hierarchy, generally yields a church which appears very cautious institutionally. Notoriously, for example, neither the Catholic theory for the church (ecclesiology) nor its authoritative church-world strategies (social teaching) accord much positive value, despite good sociological evidence to the contrary, to cleavage, the creativity of tension, or conflict. Notoriously, as well, polities governed by unitary consensus and the lowest common denominator move cautiously, if at all.

One result of the Catholic organizational preoccupation (some might call it an organizational pathology) with unity, between papacy and local churches and within each national church, is that new pastoral initiatives or experiments generally are reactive strategies. The church marshals new imagination when it perceives threats to the organization's integrity, stability, expansion, or continuity. The church is likely to innovate only when faced with religious normative threats such as inroads by Protestant fundamentalists in Latin American countries or from leftist political parties. Several social scientists—Ivan Vallier, Thomas Bruneau, and Brian Smith—have stressed this essentially reactive character of Catholic pastoral innovation in responding to competition from new competing value movements in society. Vallier has argued that such value competition explains pastoral innovation in French Catholicism as opposed to Spanish or West German in the immediate post–World War Two period.

Bruneau points to similar perceived threats to explain shifts within the church in Brazil in the 1950s and 1960s, and Smith documents the rise of new value competition in Chile for the same period.[7]

Vallier expands on this argument for the Latin American continent:

> Two kinds of radical movements, both arising within the past half century, have helped to break the cultural monopoly of Catholicism: political movements of the left and salvation-oriented Protestant sects. Both movements preach a new reward system, assume a militant posture against the existing social order, and articulate a cohesive set of anti-Catholic values. The rapid growth of these movements between the first world war and 1970 severed the Latin American value system, at least in some countries, from the Catholic religious system.
>
> But the competition at the level of values turned out to be only one of the threats provided by these new value movements. Besides offering a whole new framework of "salvation," new meanings and new categories for evaluation, they also provided the adherents with a "program" and a "strategy of action" in society. Moreover, both the communist-socialist movement and the Pentecostals sponsored a lay ethic that provided both new and old members with roles that allowed full participation. . . . Consequently, the Catholic church found itself in competition with morally oriented action systems that were linked with society at the grass roots (among systems the church had not integrated) and that provided the membership with "opportunity structures" which, in most instances, served as effective bridging mechanisms between commitment and organizational participation.[8]

Faced with this new value competition, Latin American Catholic churches reacted by generating, for the first time, coherent programs, strategies for action, and movements to mobilize lay elites. They set in motion the grass-roots "base community movement" and gave birth to liberation theology. The presence or absence of competing religious value movements goes a long way toward predicting where a national church will be, comparatively, pastorally innovative (e.g., Chile, France, the Netherlands, and Brazil) and where not (e.g., Ireland, Colombia, and Argentina).

Elective Affinity. If a reactive strategy leads to change due to the threat to growth of the church, a strategy of elective affinity brings growth and change when the church joins its action to larger reforming or radical social movements in society. Weber spoke about an "elective affinity" between religious innovations and certain secular movements for change. In Weber's view, churches alone never generate social change. Indeed, inner church renewal itself always seems to be carried forward by linkage with important secular sociopolitical trends (e.g., the Protestant Reformation or the Second Vatican Council). Weber did not assume that the church is merely a reflection of context but argued rather that a religious system like any other complex organization interacts with its social situation at many levels. Exchange always takes place in both directions.

Political scientist Brian H. Smith makes much of the same Weberian point when he lists among the conditions that seem crucial for explaining the emergence of religious norms which can contribute significant legitimation for social and economic reforms, "the resonance between [progressive social positions inside a church] and those of a significant reform party" in secular society.[9] Smith also documents how, in the absence of significant secular allies, even progressive and prophetic church positions are unable alone to achieve a lasting structural impact on totalitarian or authoritarian regimes. The church cannot undermine such states or substantially alter their political economy. At best, in repressive regimes, the church represents an important holding operation, a locus of minimal resistance, in the absence of wider secular allegiance: "In no case . . . have churches been able, by themselves, to effect major changes in the political and economic structures underlying or causing the violations of civil, social, and economic rights."[10]

The churches, to be sure, sometimes make a positive, unique contribution to society but always in alliance with secular movements articulating alternative visions of the social order. In this Weberian view, religion's contribution to social change is never simply the work of the church but involves tactical alliances of elective affinity between religious groups and wider movements of social and cultural change. Religious social creativity, Weber argues, is never, in any simple sense, merely against the world. It always involves a conjoining of church and world. As an explanation for social change, Weber claimed that, in contrast to economic, political, and other powerful causal social variables, religion is generally (although not always) a reinforcing, even if independent, causal factor.

Together with other groups, the church lends its distinctive stamp to shaping the social order. The best historical examples of social creativity of the church point to these alliances of elective affinity, as in the combination of the Social Gospel movement in American Protestantism with the Progressive movement; a conjunction of the mainline Protestant churches with the secular Civil Rights movement in America in the 1960s; the Catholic Action and Christian Democracy in postwar Europe in alliance with other forces of resistance during the war; and the affinity of Latin American liberation theologians with movements of the secularist left and populism. Weber's point holds even in ostensibly Catholic countries. It is remarkable, for example, that in Poland and Lithuania increased church impact on the social order has coincided with a new openness in those settings to collaboration with "secular" dissident groups of workers, intellectuals, human rights activists, or nationalists.[11]

At best, the church can provide a decisive "tilt," a reinforcement and a shaping contour to larger movements of social change. Overriding institutional concern for the unity of the church severely restricts the amount of conflict or head-on confrontation and prophetic denouncement the church can absorb and tolerate. Churches will avoid overly partisan stands that

introduce secular political divisions into the national church. As evidenced by
the sharp institutional rejection by several national hierarchies of the Christians for Socialism movement and the persistent fears of a popular church
uncontrolled by the hierarchy, the church will very strongly reject leftist
progressive movements within the church which seem to question or threaten
the hierarchy's monopoly on teaching and discipline within the church. The
hierarchical principle militates against any alternative. Nevertheless, when
social messages from the center of the world church reinforce a relatively
unified episcopal conference, the national church can act in the political order
in ways that independently reinforce and favor secular movements of protest
and structural change. The Polish episcopacy's symbolic support for the Solidarity movement as well as the convergence of the moral message of the
American bishops with the goals of the secular groups in the nuclear protest
movement represent two salient contemporary examples of this principle of
elective affinity. As the Polish example illustrates, however, concern for the
institutional integrity and survival of the church will limit the extent to which
the hierarchy throws in its lot with wider social, cultural movements for
change.[12]

Social Class Universalism. Because of its nonnegotiable principle of social
class universalism, Catholicism characteristically opts for a "church" rather
than a sectarian mode of organization. This dichotomy, first elaborated by
Troeltsch, involves differences both in organizational type and religious orientation. Sects are often, although not always, in strong tension with society.
They frequently act as vehicles or catalysts for social dissent or change.
Churches exhibit less radical tension with their host societies. They are more
likely to pursue accommodation even if their purpose still envisions a reformist transformation of society. Sects can be revolutionary. Churches rarely move
beyond a stance of reform.

Sects, such as the Jehovah's Witnesses who sparked colonial rebellions in
Zambia and Malawi in the 1930s, are often class specific, drawing recruits
from the lower class or the declining middle class, from those who experience
perceived relative deprivation. Sects encourage *virtuoso* religion. The uncom-
promised ethic and ideal of religion becomes the primary diffused role norm
for everyday action. Churches typically allow greater role segmentation
between religious and secular roles, accord greater autonomy to the secular,
and tolerate different levels of religiosity within their organizations. They aim
at universalism, cradle-to-grave religious coverage of every social class. This
entails a tolerance of a compromised mass standard religiosity as, in some
minimal sense, religiously acceptable. The church seeks to open its doors to
the masses, not to limit itself to elites.

As many sociological studies have documented, the church absorbs and
segregates sectarian protest. As with the Franciscan movements of reform in
the thirteenth century or the Catholic Worker movement of Dorothy Day,

Catholicism's instinctive organizational strategy consists of taming and accommodating sects, turning them into specialized religious orders under hierarchical control or segmenting them from the wider church. Yet, as Troeltsch also clearly saw, the most creative moments of Catholicism have occurred precisely when the larger church has tolerated an acceptable maximum range of sectarian movements in its midst. If the church principle supplies law, order, form, and direction, a significant presence of sectlike groups, what Joachim Wach termed *ecclesiolae in ecclesia* ("little churches within the larger church"), provide the larger church, in its turn, with energy, motivated members, revitalization, capsule units for experimentation with new pastoral forms, and cultural accommodation.

Without a significant leverage for these revitalization movements within the larger church, the church form of organization runs the risk of becoming legalistic, moribund, and encapsulated in accommodation to prevailing social and cultural norms. The most innovative churches and dioceses in world Catholicism risk some greater leverage to the sect principle, such as the base community movement in Brazil, critical-experimental communities in the Netherlands, the Catholic Worker movement, charismatic Catholics, and peace and justice networks in the United States. An empirical variable in the comparative study of Catholicism and politics will look to the presence or absence (and number) of sectlike revitalization movements within a national church, their formal or informal linkages to the hierarchy and national or diocesan service bureaucracies, and the creative tension between sect and church organizational principles within the overriding church organizational structure. Without such movements, it remains highly improbable that a national church or diocese will engage in pastoral innovation or the forging of new church-world strategies which promise linkage with wider social movements of change. We urgently need comparative studies of instances of successful accommodation to *ecclesiolae in ecclesia* as opposed to cases of their total rejection or segmentation, in isolation from access to church decision makers, to give us a greater sense of just how much "give" the church mode of organization includes before nonnegotiable *raison d'église* moves in to expel the sect from the Catholic enclave.

Commitment to social class universalism imposes several crucial limitations upon the organizational flexibility of Catholicism in response to social change. The first limit lies in the way the principle of social class universalism entails a certain tolerance of weak membership commitment to the goals of the organization. The church's formal membership of more than 800 million baptized contains a wide spectrum of loyalties ranging from saints, nuclear participants, the irregularly practicing, and nominal members—all of whom differ in identification with the church and internalization and obedience to its teachings. In his ground-breaking studies of Catholic urban parishes in the United States, sociologist Joseph Fichter discovered that the membership roll of a typical parish includes adherents with widely different degrees of commitment, socialization into gospel values, and identification with the church.[13] Parishioners exhibit a range of allegiance from "marginal" to "nominal" through "passive regular participants" and active "nuclear" Catholics. Notoriously, in nominally Catholic countries such as Belgium, France, Italy, and Argentina, the level of weekly mass attendance rarely reaches much more than 10 to 15 percent of the Catholic population. The first organizational dilemma deriving from the principle of social class universalism, then, might well read: How many real bodies are there to support the church's religious aims and goals in the social order?

Overlapping memberships by Catholics simultaneously in the church and in their social class, political party, and other voluntary associations introduces into the church a second limitation which sociologists refer to as "cross-pressures." Cross-pressures refer to the conflicting loyalties that individuals feel when they identify simultaneously with several different social roles and reference groups. Cross-pressures, for example, where religious, political, and social class identification do not overlap but cancel each other out, can be contrasted with concerted and reinforcing group pressures from multiple groups. Typically, cross-pressures within a group reduce conflict and deep cleavages. They tend to neutralize behavior by cancelling one another out. By choosing a church mode of organization with an emphasis on social class universalism, Catholicism subjects itself to multiple cross-pressures. Catholicism's tilt of a social order will always remain somewhat muted by cross-pressures. Especially in churches such as those in the United States, Australia, Belgium, Canada, or the Netherlands, where the Catholic population almost perfectly mirrors the social class stratification of the nation, much, if not most, of the Catholic population will be influenced as much by class interests, social location, and their social class perspectives as by the religious factor. This seems unavoidable.

Mainwaring clearly states this principle of social class universalism as an issue of *raison d'église:* "The church has consistently marginalized movements which would threaten its capacity to appeal coherently to people from different classes and with a wide amalgam of religious and political beliefs." As Mainwaring sagely notes: "An effort to appeal to all individuals imposes a cautious character on the church."[14] From a decisive shock-troop dismantling of the priest-worker movement in post–World War Two France and contemporary tension with the "popular church of the poor" in Nicaragua, there are many examples of how the church mode of organization imposes serious limits on any preferential option for the poor. *Raison d'église* dictates that, in any social conflict between the classes, when push comes to shove, the hierarchy will continue to articulate a position similar to that of a Venezuelan bishop: "The church should be like Christ crucified—with its arms open to all people. With each arm open to a different part of the people. In other words, it should be a point of unification for all people, a point where all can collaborate."[15]

Quite obviously, since political parties, more than churches, can be more skewed to certain social classes, they are often much more effective instruments than churches to realize decisive structural change and to implement new social policies in society. Because of its option for social class universalism, the church eschews identification with political parties and their more narrow social class constituencics. It fcars thrcc major difficultics in ovcrly partisan identification. First, as Daniel Levine notes: "If politics becomes primary, then political commitments may be made the basic standard of Christian authenticity, gutting Catholicism of its transcendental content."[16] Secondly, the church wants to avoid introducing secular political divisions into its own always somewhat tenuous unity. Third, historical experience has taught the church to recognize the problem of personnel drainage due to politicization. Typically, for example, leftist political Christians, such as those in France and the Netherlands, have left the church to invest energies in maximal engagement in political parties as the more effective instrument when compared to the church for achieving political change. In the process, it becomes questionable whether their subsequent political engagement retains any vestiges of a distinctively Christian inspiration. Similarly, the Catholic bishops of Nicaragua became concerned after the Sandinista Revolution with declining interest in the church on the part of the laity and lay church leaders and with the government's ability to attract away from church-sponsored programs some of the church's best catechists.[17]

The Religious Nature of the Church. The ultimate objectives of any church are primarily religious, not political, even in the broad sense. Most people turn to the church for comfort. They seek in a religious tradition a place of loyalty where they can take a stand when faced with chaos and a crisis of meaning. Such people look for answers to personal hurts and ecstasies, tragedies, failures, joy, and travail. They look for the ultimate meaning of their lives and deaths, and, the strength to carry on their daily tasks. For most people, social justice issues and political stances of the church ride "piggyback," if at all, on these more personal religious issues.

Only a select few church people find in social justice causes the privileged locus for experiencing God. Survey research shows that most constituents of the church do not want an overly political or even social message in church preaching. In fact, this same sociological evidence also demonstrates that they get precious little of it.[18]

The church is a peculiarly religious organization. Fundamental conflicts over social policy issues within the church are often theological, concerning such questions as the church's appropriate mission and priorities, its relation to other religions and social groups, and what the limits of the church's political role should be. Divergent views of the church run deep. As a result of its fundamentally religious nature, the church, unlike political parties, gives only very part-time consideration to larger social and structural issues. Politically, in terms of focused action, it is no match for a well-organized political party, let alone a governmental regime, in effecting social structural change.

The church competes favorably with these more political organizations, however, in the depth of its symbols and in the diffused ways these symbols become linked with and touch personal identities. Sociologically, we must keep our expectations modest about church influence on social orders. But as Mainwaring notes, precisely because a church is fundamentally religious, "when an institution's fundamental end is nonrational, it may be willing to sacrifice some interests if it is convinced it has a calling to do so. . . . A church will renounce financial benefits, prestige, institutional expansion, and other interests, if it feels that its religious mission compels it to do so."[19] The church maintains an unmistakable yet powerful charismatic, prophetic, and utopian dimension which can have indirect political impact.

Raison d'église does not exhaustively explain all political responses of the church. There are some crucial limits to applying organizational analysis from sociology to the church. Donald Warwick makes this point tellingly. "The church could well become more efficient in its managerial operations without becoming more effective in reaching its overall goals. In fact, it might be argued that increasing efficiency may ultimately be harmful by prolonging the life of a moribund institutional structure."[20]

Finally, we should note that, since churches primarily focus on religious pastoral goals, the effect of religion on social development is not necessarily intentional. Mainwaring states this axiom in the form of a thesis: "Change in the church is more a product of inadvertent consequences of broader social change than of a conscious plan to change to protect its interests."[21] We should not overstate the extent to which the church can actually foresee the kinds of changes which will optimize its interests or influence.

Religion and Social Change

Sociologist Meredith McGuire suggests eight questions to bring as a focus to our comparative study of religion and social change.[22]

(1) Does the belief system contain a critical standard against which the established social system and existing patterns of interaction can be measured? In the Catholic case, gospel values and the social teaching of the church provide some critical leverage to judge social systems. Too great separation from the issues of the political order can lead to irrelevance and an inward-turning, otherworldly piety. Too great accommodation forfeits transcendent critical leverage.

(2) How does the belief system define the social situation? Some belief systems are fatalistic. They see the social system as God-given, unchangeable, or as the inevitable and intractable consequence of original sin. It is important to note whether the religious teaching indicates the need for serious structural

reform in society or restricts itself to suggestions of mere piecemeal legislation and ameliorist schemes. In his book *Religion and Politics in Latin America,* Levine argues that post–Vatican II social thought has shifted from a "moralist" to a "structuralist" analysis of social problems. Moralist approaches see the solution to social problems primarily in the reform of the heart of individuals. Structuralist analysis recognizes the reality of structural social sin and calls for both social analysis and structural change in combating social sin.[23]

(3) How does the belief system define the relationship of the individual in the social world? It is important to distinguish, following Levine, between programs of church political activism and programs of activation. Activism envisions a direct insertion of the corporate church into the partisan political order. It is almost always a mistake. Activation, more respectful of pluralism, points to "consciousness-raising" church education programs in relation to politics and social justice, programs to activate the laity, which then takes its own principled stand within the social order as autonomous Christians in action.[24] Religious programs of activation only make sense within belief systems which see human action in the social world as somehow salvific, a religious "vocation."

(4) Is the religious mode of action central to the cognitive framework of the culture? The church resists totalitarian or authoritarian cultures more effectively in Catholic cultures (such as Chile and Poland) where the inroads of secularization have been somewhat checked than in more secular authoritarian regimes where the religious mode of action is less central to the cognitive framework of the culture.

(5) Are religious roles and identification significant modes of individual action in a culture? McGuire asks: "Does it make sense in the culture for an individual to claim a religious identity or a special religious role?" Besides the belief framework of individual churches we need to pay attention as well to wider cultural belief contents, the "civil religion" of societies.

(6) Is religion relatively undifferentiated from other important elements in the society? The important search operations lying behind this question ask us to attend to both issues of culture and social structure. On the one hand, in societies where religion is relatively undifferentiated from other social institutions and social roles (e.g., Saudi Arabia, Iran, black South Africa), any change-oriented action is also likely to be simultaneously religious. Structurally differentiated religious institutions have greater instrumental capacity to effect political change. Paradoxically, however, their structural differentiation and autonomy may lead people to segment their expectations for these religious institutions, to see religious action as irrelevant to the political or economic spheres. They do not see it as an imaginative source for politics.

(7) If religion is relatively differentiated from other institutional spheres, do strong ties exist between religious institutions and other structures, especially political and economic ones? This question points our research attention to the social location of religion in various societies. Since so much of the

sociology of religion focuses primarily on individual religiosity (even if seen in the aggregate) and belief systems, the organizational power of religion in society can get lost. Statistics of church practice or individual religiosity are insufficient to tell us the actual social weight of religion in a given society. Thus, while weekly mass attendance in Uruguay and Chile are roughly similar, the organizational weight of the church in Chile is far and away stronger.

(8) Do other modes effectively compete with religion for the expression of human needs, the development of leadership, and the organization of effort toward social change? Where alternative modes offer value competition to religion or where alternate channels express efforts toward change, churches may lose their saliency in the political order. Several social science commentators have noted that in some Latin American countries, the Catholic Church has been such an effective vehicle for protest against repressive political regimes precisely because it is the only dissenting group with an established network of grass-roots organizations and commitments. Many Latin American bishops manifest a certain overconfidence that the church's current vitality will continue as repressive regimes give way to democracy.

The Dilemmas of Church Institutionalization

In what has become now a classic and much-cited essay, sociologist Thomas O'Dea speaks of "the dilemmas of the institutionalization of religion."[25] O'Dea explicates Weber's notion of "the routinization of charisma." Foundational charismatic breakthroughs become tamed and institutionalized as a way of perpetuating and protecting their originating insights and vitalities. The process of routinization for charisma provides order and continuity to an inherently unstable sociological form, the personal nexus between the original charismatic leader such as Jesus or Mary Baker Eddy and his/her followers. The following four of O'Dea's dilemmas throw light on our topic of *raison d'église*.

(1) *The dilemma of motivational engagement.* Passing on the original religious vitality to succeeding generations (the classic Puritan New England problem of the halfway covenant with those not truly "twice-born"), introduces watered-down commitments into the movement while it guarantees the perpetuation across generations of the original charismatic impulse. Not to institutionalize charisma, O'Dea argues, spells its death with the passing of the first generation. Institutionalization, however, entails an element of worldly compromise, a "taming" of the charisma. Insistence on purity of motive severely limits the number of potential recruits (and, therefore, the wider societal impact of the movement). But allowing "mixed motives" in a wider membership mutes concentrated motivational energies.

(2) *The dilemma of objectifying the transcendent*. In this second dilemma, O'Dea points to the need to find concrete embodiments of the religiously transcendent in culturally fixed norms, laws, and symbols. Although objectification is necessary, it runs the risk of relativizing the transcendent, thus fixating it in culturally determined and quite historically relative dogmas, rituals, and icons.

(3) *The dilemmas of goal achievement, goal specification, and goal displacement*. Movement effectiveness and a sense of religious achievement within charismatic and religious groups demands some attempt, however tenuous, to define the relatively diffuse, super-rational goals of religious organizations ("salvation," "eschatology," "faith") so that these do not remain empty, contentless ciphers. The very movement toward giving these goals greater specificity, however, entails several risks: (1) value competition stemming from competing religious or political groups; (2) drainage of personnel to these competing groups if the goals become so specific that alternative organizations appear to be more efficient in attaining the desired goal; and (3) goal displacement.

(4) *The dilemma of power and influence*. Because churches desire to exert influence upon cultural values, societal structures, and national or local elites, they construct formal or informal linkages with governments, elite structures, and national culture. If they do not become embedded in a national culture and structure, churches remain ineffective cultural forces, isolated, alien. The perennial danger naturally lies in state cooptation of churches for their own purposes or the adoption by churches of worldly forms of dominative power within their own polity.

The church needs, of course, like any group, a certain amount of internal, autonomous power to protect itself from both threats from within and from outside its boundaries. Yet this same, so-necessary power can be asserted against deviant and dissenting members *within* the church. External pressures and coercion may replace inner conviction and commitment to truth as a way to guarantee members' compliance.

In a certain sense, the O'Dea dilemmas are another way of stating issues of *raison d'église,* the cunning in the institutionalization of religion into church forms with their nonnegotiable principles of hierarchy, social class universalism, and the fundamentally religious nature of the church. Neither Weber nor O'Dea address, however, the characteristically religious tension in the processes of routinization of charisma. By their very propagation of the gospel and authoritative memory of early Christianity, churches paradoxically are constantly running the risk of spawning in their midst sectlike renewal movements carrying urgent reminders of the Reformers' dictum of the *ecclesia semper reformanda*.[26] As I suggested, churches probably depend sociologically on these countermovements for their own persistence, renewal, vitality, pastoral innovation, and the forging of new effective church-world strategies.

When the Church Reinforces Social Movements

Although at one level it is a book about a very particular national case study of the church and politics, Smith's brilliant social science investigation *The Church and Politics in Chile* represents equally a masterful specification of certain bottom-line, nonnegotiable, institutional interests of the church in whichever context or country it finds itself.[27] Smith summarizes a list of conditions under which the church effectively reinforces or checks societal movements for change. Here I want to borrow from Smith these more general principles about the political impact of the organizational church.

Smith substantially agrees with Mainwaring on the three factors of *raison d'église:* church unity, social class universalism, and the fundamentally religious nature of the church. He singles out, then, three key factors which dictate and shape *raison d'église:* "The general articulation of social norms so as to prevent official identification with partisan movements; hierarchical authority flows under the control of the Vatican and bishops; universal membership scope for all social classes."[28]

Using language redolent of O'Dea's terminology of dilemmas, Smith points to four central variables, which he calls "predicaments," to follow closely in charting comparative studies of Catholicism and politics. He stresses the importance of balancing various opposing values within the church.

Four Organizational Predicaments

(1) *First predicament: Greater church involvement in secular problems with, simultaneously, a greater neutrality in partisan disputes.* If the church genuinely wishes to implement, in local contexts, the directionality of its universal social teaching, it will need to find ways to integrate these social commitments without detracting from what is essential to its mission. This entails a rather delicate balance. Too great separation from the issues of the political order can lead to social irrelevance and an inward-turning, otherworldly piety. The delicate balance will consist of simultaneously specifying and implementing Catholic social values in the secular order and preserving the institutional church from too close identification with any one partisan group, ideological commitment, or political party.

Normative pronouncements can and sometimes should be very concrete in condemning certain abuses of power or violations of human rights such as torture, unjust tax laws and income distribution, the escalating arms race, and racism. The political power of the church, sociologically, lies in its ability to lend sacred legitimation, the aura of its charisma, to secular orders of society or to countermovements which embody new visions for the secular order. The church can achieve this effect only if it controls that charismatic power which depends, in turn, on its own institutional autonomy. Thus, for example, new strategies of extrication of the church from state cooptation in Latin America have enabled Latin American bishops, theologians, and laity to challenge with some effectiveness religious claims of national security ideologies. Where, however, the church in Latin America has achieved less autonomy from these political entanglements, e.g. Argentina and Colombia, its social voice has remained rather muted.

(2) *Second predicament: The challenge of implementing the values of collegiality and pluralism without undermining hierarchical authority*. Creative acculturation and the forging of effective church-world strategies in widely divergent social contexts demand some "give" to the nonnegotiable hierarchical principle and a greater structural implementation, beyond mere rhetoric, to the post–Vatican II pleas for collegiality. It also demands greater relative autonomy to local church units to diverge from liturgical or canonical norms not absolutely essential for unity (as opposed to legalistic uniformity) in the world church. Clearly, the enormous popularity and persistence in so many regions of the world church of theological slogans calling for greater decentralization, pluralism, collegiality, and participatory voice in decision making seem to reflect a sense that the world church exhibits at present a pathological overreliance on the hierarchical principle.

If autonomy of local church units *vis-à-vis* national governments is an important variable to pursue for the comparison of Catholic national units and politics, then the relative autonomy of the local church within the world church, its internal flexibility because of a relative unity among the episcopacy (e.g., Brazil) or the financial clout it exercises in the world church (e.g., West Germany, the United States) or its relative size (Brazil and the United States are the two largest Catholic units in the world church) are no less important causal factors to explain variations in pastoral innovation, role adaptation, and social impact.

There exists, indeed, a surprising convergence of sociological evidence showing that precisely those local churches which have engaged in internal church renewal toward collegial participation in the life and decisions, ministry, and mission of the church have also moved toward pastoral innovation and successful new church-world strategies. Thus, among Latin American churches, those in Brazil and Chile have perhaps gone the farthest in decentralizing their structures and in incorporating nonordained religious sisters and the laity into positions of pastoral leadership at the local level.[29]

In Western Europe, I argue in my book *The Evolution of Dutch Catholicism* that such internal church renewal in the directions of collegiality represented the indispensable precondition for a new church-world strategy which was the actual focus of my research in the Netherlands.[30] Similarly, within the Anglo-Saxon Catholic world, both the Canadian and United States churches have joined programs of inner church collegial renewal and new patterns of authority participation and collegial consultation with strikingly effective expansion of the wider social mission of the church.[31] In the Eastern European bloc, the

Yugoslavian church loses none of its limited capacity for wider societal leverage by allowing greater collegial renewal, comparatively, than other churches in the Eastern bloc.

Smith's study serves to remind us that the hierarchical principle has stood the church, organizationally, in good stead throughout the centuries and that it should never be lightly frittered away. I want to counter this argument, however. One-sided overemphasis on the hierarchical principle can actually impede the emergence of effective church-society strategies appropriately adapted to context. This second predicament forcefully states that inner church renewal and outer renewal of church mission to society tend to hang and fall together. The church will have no gift to society unless in its inner structures it represents another way to communicate, handle tensions, and exercise authority based on evangelical love and service.

(3) *Third predicament: Develop a widespread acceptance for new social emphases while still allowing a range of responses to normative teachings among different types of Catholics.* Smith's third predicament brings us back to Catholicism's option for social class universalism. As we have seen, Catholicism's choice of a "church" strategy permits a range of involvement and commitment and of membership across the social class spectrum. How can Catholicism maximize the potentialities for a social impact ingredient in a church organizational structure spanning the social classes? In the first place, it must target and direct specialized evangelizing programs toward nuclear-committed Catholics who will carry a disproportionate weight within the wider universalist social class membership. This will entail either (1) granting to such nuclear Catholics a special privileged access to church decision makers, or (2) tolerating the creation of some greater institutional space for the actions of sectlike revitalization movements within the wider church.

A number and range of specialized nuclear groups of deeply committed Catholics exist within dioceses, national churches, and in world Catholicism. Such groups include Opus Dei, Pax Christi, Foculare, Young Catholic Students, the Young Catholic Workers, The Catholic Worker Movement, Cursillo, the Christian Family Movement, and Encounter. Some of these groups of committed Catholics are mainly centered on a program of personal, inner-worldly piety. Other groups, such as Cursillo, Catholic Action, some bible groups, and the Christian Family Movement, combine intense religious deepening in Christian self-identity with a steadfast insistence on worldly service and action. I have argued that such groups represent essential "structural carriers" to implement a distinctively Christian vision in the world of work, professional life, and the political and social order. Elsewhere, I have called these groups "the pious lay conventicle ordered to work and service in the secular order."[32] With Karl Barth, they insist on reading, simultaneously, their bibles and the daily newspaper.

The important comparative issue for studying various church-world strategies will look to the varying presence of such "ginger" groups within the diocese and national churches. We should never underestimate the power of creative minorities to exercise wider influence in larger groups, beyond their comparative numbers, to give these larger groups a renewed shape and contour, an *esprit* and an *ethos*.

Smith does not deal, as I have dealt here, with the activation and support for *ecclsiolae in ecclesia*. In discussing his third predicament, he looks, instead, to educational strategies which cast a broader net. "To realize its new goals effectively, [the church] must generate stronger commitments to its socially progressive teachings among broad sectors of its membership and overcome apathy among rich and poor alike to its ethical demands for structural change in society."[33] It strikes me that Smith has cast his net too widely since he seems to suggest possible positive results from unfocused universal coverage. Yet good sociological evidence indicates that church renewal programs command a better probability of success if they target very definite subpopulations within the church (e.g., university youth, migrant workers, or Catholics in labor movements) for focused campaigns of pastoral evangelization.[34]

When the church reaches out in its pastoral mission to evangelize marginalized social groups, it is drawn to articulate religious norms that bear directly as well on the sociopolitical needs of the people involved. New pastoral outreach to targeted marginal groups previously neglected by the church draws the church to innovative pastoral strategies toward meeting new demands that are directly tied to the process of social change, for example, through literacy programs, organizing the poor in their base communities, and so on. In a profound sense, the church cannot really renew itself by this missionary outreach without becoming interested in social renewal.

In at least one respect, churches seem no different than broader national populations or political parties. A relatively small move, for example, in citizen activism in lobbying or participation in political groups will register on the national consciousness as a seismic shift. Thus, if a political party or lobbying group in a given set of several years were to succeed in shifting even 1 to 3 percent of its membership from relatively passive clients who merely vote for the party to greater activism (e.g., in financial and voluntary activity), the result will show up as seismic on the political map. Churches are no different. If they effect a greater involvement and commitment among even a minority, the results will seem seismic. Thus, the nearly one million members of the base community movement in Brazil (in a Catholic population well over one hundred million strong) give to the Brazilian church an innovative and even radical hue.

Smith lays great stress on avoiding the sectarian temptation in new programs to implement a new social emphasis in Catholicism. I want to suggest, however, that there is little evidence of any breakaway tendencies in the post–Vatican II Catholic sectlike groups (either in the Catholic charismatics of the United States or the base community movement in Latin America). The principle of hierarchy remains deeply rooted in the Catholic imagination. It is not under threat. The more important need, in my view, is for intensely focused strategies of evangelization and renewal among targeted groups of practicing nuclear Catholics and outreach to previously excluded social groups. The issue I am discussing here is sometimes referred to as the factor of a sufficient "critical mass" which, albeit a decided minority, changes an entire organizational climate.

(4) *Fourth Predicament: Balancing transnationalism and local inculturation*. In his fourth predicament, Smith argues that the church is, simultaneously, both a transnational actor and a conglomeration of subunits operating in a variety of national systems. As a transnational coordinating source, the Vatican has the capacity to transfer funds and personnel into local church settings. For example, aid from the first to the Third World has helped to launch and sustain new social programs (e.g., literacy projects, health programs, cooperative movements, and centers for social research) and to fund religious training programs for lay leaders.

Yet, resource transactions from the center to the periphery in the world church can be a mixed blessing. Foreign injections of money and personnel are sometimes resented by host governments who perceive sectors of the church trying to influence the course of political development within the country.[35] When the ideology or goals of the church and the state are at odds (as in the Philippines under Marcos), conflict can become overt. Foreign personnel may be expelled. Laws may restrict outside church funding. There have arisen, moreover, internal criticisms within the Third World churches which complain about negative consequences accompanying the influx of large amounts of foreign personnel into their countries. Support from outside sources can lead to a dependent church, almost totally reliant on foreign missionaries for its clergy.

Church Reinforcement of Social Change. Relying on the above four variables, we can distinguish several different sets of conditions of church reinforcement of or impediment to social change.

(1) "On a crucial public issue where (a) the dominant secular values coincide with important religious interests: (b) authority conflicts do not emerge inside the church; (c) a decision is binding on all Catholics uniformly, and (d) receives legitimating support from the Vatican, then the decision will be reached to the mutual satisfaction and advantage of both church and government, thus avoiding a major religiopolitical conflict."[36]

Smith illustrates this first case by recounting the history of the relatively smooth negotiations for a constitutional separation of church and state in Chile in 1925. Quite similar conditions held in postindependence Zambia, where the church freely handed over almost the entirety of its confessional school system to the state. Previous to Zambian independence, the churches held a near monopoly on education. Almost no new postrevolutionary government could tolerate the effective control by nonstate agencies of the education of its citizenry. The government of Zambia lacked sufficient financial resources to erect its own governmental network of state schools.

In postrevolutionary Hungary in 1948 the church also enjoyed a strong monopoly on education. The difference between the Zambian and the Hungarian cases, the latter of which involved considerable religiopolitical conflict on the school question, can be explained by the presence of the above-enumerated factors (a), (b), and (d) in Zambia and their absence in Hungary.

(2) The second set of conditions facilitating church reinforcement of social change reads: "If there are serious differences between religious values and structures and those guiding the process of societal change, but sufficient overlapping concerns to prevent prolonged conflicts, then peaceful coexistence and even limited cooperation might occur between religious and secular groups. In such a context, the church, while not being a major contributor to change, would not also be a significant obstacle to it."[37]

Smith appeals to these considerations to explain relations between church and state during the leftist Popular Unity government of Salvador Allende in Chile. We should not automatically assume that the church will *ipso facto* come into conflict with Marxist leftist governments. Thus, church and state have found relatively benign accommodation in Castro's Cuba, largely due to a shrewd Vatican *pro-nuntius* and the siphoning off through migration of Catholic militant antisocialists. The sort of acrimonious church-state conflict which has typified the official church reaction to the Sandinista regime in Nicaragua (where sharp opposition is more likely to originate from the side of certain sectors of the church) cannot be universalized into a general organizational law. At no point were diplomatic relations, for example, ever severed between the Vatican and Castro's Cuba.[38]

(3) In his treatment of church-state interaction in Chile under the Pinochet military regime, Smith generalizes a third set of conditions for reinforcing or impeding social change in authoritarian regimes:

> Finally, in a situation where the church is a surrogate for other social institutions curtailed by an authoritarian regime, its capacity to act as a consistent opposition force to the state will also be determined by the interaction of its key normative, structural, and behavioral components with secular forces. If it can articulate norms that are sufficiently forceful to delegitimate public authority, maintain authority flows and protect its structures, preserve unity among its formal adherents, and maintain autonomous resource bases, then it could be a crucial factor in blunting repression. If, however, its leadership or membership is seriously divided or its resources can be curtailed by the state, its impact on public policy will be limited and the willingness of the hierarchy to risk sustained and open confrontation with the state diminished.[39]

Sometimes military dictators in Latin America, following rather self-consciously the lead of General Banzer of Bolivia in the 1970s, have played upon the organizational conditions for resistance that Smith outlines. Banzer shrewdly sought to divide the church and tame its opposition to his repressive regime by pitting the hierarchy and the minority native Bolivian clergy against the majority of foreign priest missionaries, thus diminishing leadership unity within the church. Other military groups have lent support to divisive, reactionary corporatist Catholic groups such as the Tradition, Family and Property movement, which can be found in several Latin American countries. In Eastern Europe during the Stalinist period, regime authorities attempted to introduce a wedge between the hierarchy and the lower clergy by sponsoring and favoring with state subsidies regime-loyal "peace priests." As the Eastern European case in countries such as Czechoslovakia or Hungary vividly demonstrates, Catholic principles of hierarchical control over appointment policy and unity among the hierarchy remain bottom-line organizational values to protect the institution against subversive and divisive tactics of authoritarian regimes.

There are several other ways in which *raison d'église* determines and limits church behavior *vis-à-vis* authoritarian regimes. In national settings as diverse as Brazil, Bolivia, El Salvador, Rhodesia, and the Philippines, bishops as a group remain initially cautious in taking on the systematic abuse of human rights by authoritarian regimes. It is only after the repression of a regime systematically begins to touch bishops personally (by restricting their preaching, movement, or publication of church messages, or by arresting one of their number) or touches their priests (by expelling foreign priests or arresting or killing local pastors) or key lay elites close to the bishops that national episcopacies begin to issue unambiguous condemnations of systematic repression.

Internationally famous and consistently courageous bishops, such as Archbishop Hurley of Capetown or Brazil's Dom Helder Camara, do not well represent their brother bishops who remain, typically, cautious in attacking regime injustices. Thus, for example, during the funeral mass of André Jarlan, a French missionary priest murdered in Santiago by security police agents during the time of my field visit to Chile, the sermon of Cardinal Fresno of Santiago made no direct reference to the manner in which Jarlan died. From his homily, Jarlan could have died in his sleep! Later, however, Fresno (who had won the sobriquet among social activists in Chile of *"Freno"* (i.e., the one who puts on the brakes) was moved to sharp public rebuff of the Pinochet regime because it exiled his close collaborator, the Vicar for Soli darity, the seventy-two-year-old Reverend Ignatio Gutierrez, S.J. Smith underscores the power of *raison d'église* as an explanatory variable in the study of Catholicism and politics: "Only when [bishops in Latin American authoritarian regimes] considered core interests of the church to be under attack (usually the lives or safety of the clergy) have they spoken out clearly and critically against the wider structures of oppression affecting the whole of society."[40]

The very same institutional realities which allow the church to provide alternative space as a holding maneuver against dictatorships and which check the sway of their repression simultaneously seriously mute the prophetic capacities of the church at the normative level. The church remains anxious to preserve for itself at least a minimal institutional reality, to protect the church against a persecuting power. This institutional burden of the church weighs especially heavily on bishops who, by reason of their office, perceive their first responsibility to be the preservation, at all costs, of church structures so that the church's primary religious mission of preaching the gospel and administering the sacraments can be continued.

Conclusion

I have coined a new phrase, *raison d'église,* to speak about the fundamental religious commitments and organizational slant which set parameters on the church's range of flexibility and adaptability in political situations. Clearly, the church can have enormous reinforcing and even channeling power and impact on politics in national settings. The mission of the church and its message (its social teaching) is progressive and bold in support of the poor, open in its sense of a range of allies.[41] But sometimes the church follows a logic of maintenance of the organization more than its logic of mission. It would take another essay to draw out the political implications of the church's logic of mission. What I have attempted here is to draw out, however, the logic of maintenance. Some might object to the term I have coined, seeing in *raison d'église* a pretentious parallel to the state and its *raison d'état*. But claims against the church that it, at times, seems to act like a state within the state would only reinforce my usage.

The three bottom-line principles of *raison d'église* are (1) commitment to the hierarchical principle as the mode of social authority and organization; (2) commitment to social class universalism and a church rather than a sect mode of organization; and (3) commitment to the fundamental religious mission of the church. Woe to the secular politician or church reformer who neglects to pay attention to these bottom-line organizational imperatives! As Smith notes: "While variations (and even inconsistencies) in the functioning of these components have occurred over time, the history of the church also indicates that Rome and the hierarchy will firmly resist developments that in principle challenge or undermine any of them."[42]

Raison d'église sets sociological parameters and limits to the contextual specification of the church's mission to the world. Within these parameters and limits, however, the church can be a powerful force for social change as much as for more conservative social stability. While its political moves are sometimes unpredictable, *raison d'église* helps us chart some of the outer limits and contours under which church action on the social and political orders always takes place.

Notes

1. Gunther Lewy, *The Catholic Church and Nazi Germany* (New York: McGraw-Hill, 1965), 326.
2. F. X. Kaufmann, "The Church as a Religious Organization," in *The Church as Institution*, edited by Gregory Baum and Andrew Greeley (New York: Herder and Herder, 1974), 77. Cf. also F. X. Kaufmann, "Religion et Bureucratie: Le Problème de l'Organisation Religieuse," *Social Compass* 21(1) (1974): 101–7.
3. Kaufmann, "Religion et Bureucratie," 103.
4. Peter Worsley, *The Trumpet Shall Sound: A Study of Cargo Cults in Melanesia* (New York: Schocken, 1968), xxix.
5. Scott Mainwaring, "The Church and Politics: Theoretical notes," Kellogg Institute working paper, University of Notre Dame, 1.
6. Leonardo Boff, *Church, Charism and Power* (London: SCM Press, 1985), 40.
7. Ivan Vallier, *Catholicism, Social Control and Modernization* (Englewood Cliffs, NJ: Prentice-Hall, 1970); Brian Smith, *The Church and Politics in Chile* (Princeton, NJ: Princeton University Press, 1982); Thomas C. Bruneau, *The Political Transformation of the Brazilian Catholic Church* (New York: Cambridge University Press, 1974).
8. Vallier, 58–59.
9. Smith, 155.
10. Brian Smith, "Churches and Human Rights in Latin America," In *Churches and Politics in Latin America*, edited by Daniel Levine (Beverly Hills, CA: Sage Publications, 1979), 183.
11. For evidence of new alliances in Lithuania, cf. V. Stanley Vardys, *The Catholic Church, Dissent and Nationality in Soviet Lithuania* (New York: Columbia University Press, 1978); for Poland, cf. Leszek Kolakowski, "The Church and Democracy in Poland," *Dissent* 57 (Summer 1980) and Timothy Garton Ash, *The Polish Revolution* (London: Jonathan Cape, 1983).
12. Cf. Ash, 231.
13. Joseph Fichter, *Southern Parish* (Chicago, IL: University of Chicago Press, 1951) and *Social Relations in the Urban Parish* (Chicago, IL: University of Chicago Press, 1954).
14. Mainwaring, 4.
15. Cited from an interview with Daniel Levine, *Religion and Politics in Latin America: The Catholic Church in Venezuela and Columbia* (Princeton: Princeton University Press, 1981), 177.
16. Ibid., 94.
17. Cf. Michael Dodson and Tommi Sue Montgomery, "The Churches in the Nicaraguan Revolution," in *The Nicaraguan Revolution*, edited by Thomas Walker (New York: Praeger, 1981) and Philip Berryman, *The Religious Roots of Rebellion* (Maryknoll, NY: Orbis, 1984), 226ff.
18. For failures to preach to social issues cf. Ernst Campbell and Thomas Pettigrew, *Christians in Racial Crisis: A Study of Little Rock's Ministry* (Washington, DC: Public Affairs Press, 1959) and Charles Glock et. al., *Wayward Shepherds* (New York: Harper and Row, 1975).

19. Mainwaring, 17.
20. Donald Warwick, "Personal and Organizational Effectiveness in the Roman Catholic Church," *Cross Currents* 17 (Fall 1967): 402–3.
21. Mainwaring, 1.
22. Meridith McGuire, *Religion: The Social Context* (Belmont, California: Wadsworth, 1981), 196–203.
23. Levine, 179–80.
24. Ibid., 183.
25. Thomas O'Dea, "Five Dilemmas in the Institutionalization of Religion," in *Sociology and the Study of Religion*, edited by Thomas O'Dea (New York: Basic Books, 1970), 240–55; cf. also Thomas O'Dea, "Pathology and Renewal of Religious Institutions," in *The Church as Institution*, edited by Gregory Baum and Andrew Greeley (New York: Herder and Herder, 1974), 127.
26. For the notion of a dangerous memory ingredient in religious organizations leading to an *ecclesia semper reformanda*, cf. J. B. Metz, *Faith in History and Society* (New York: Herder and Herder, 1984), 127.
27. Smith, *Church and Politics in Chile.*
28. Ibid., 85.
29. For more recent developments in Brazil, cf. Thomas C. Bruneau, *The Church in Brazil: The Politics of Religion* (Austin, TX: University of Texas Press) and Scott Mainwaring, *The Catholic Church in Brazil* (Palo Alto, CA: Stanford University Press, 1987).
30. John A. Coleman, *The Evolution of Dutch Catholicism* (Berkeley and Los Angeles: University of California Press, 1978).
31. For American Catholicism, cf. John A. Coleman, *An American Strategic Theology* (Macawah, NJ: Paulist Press, 1982).
32. Coleman, *American Strategic Theology*, 38–56.
33. Smith, *Church and Politics in Chile*, 45.
34. Bruneau in *The Church in Brazil* makes the point that the Brazilian church focused its pastoral strategies on targeted groups (cf. 50).
35. For difficulties in relying on outside church sources for funds and personnel, cf. Ivan Illich, "The Seamy Side of Charity," *America* 221 (January 1967): 89–91. For an account of claimed West German church manipulation in Third World countries, cf. David Mutchler, *The Church as a Political Factor in Latin America With Particular Reference to Colombia and Chile* (New York: Praeger, 1968), chapters 1, 17.
36. Smith, *Church and Politics in Chile*, 63.
37. Ibid.
38. For a nuanced treatment of religion and politics in Castro's Cuba, cf. Margaret Crahan, "Salvation Through Christ or Marx: Religion in Revolutionary Cuba," in *Churches and Politics in Latin America*, edited by Daniel Levine, 238–66.
39. Smith, *Church and Politics in Chile*, 64.
40. Ibid., 70.
41. For a good general treatment of social teaching of the church, cf. Donal Dorr, *Option for the Poor* (Maryknoll, NY: Orbis Press, 1984).
42. Smith, *Church and Politics in Chile*, 62.

16
Religion and Patriotism: Poland, France, Great Britain, and the United States

Barbara Strassberg

Introduction

THIS PAPER is based on a broader study of the relationship between religion[1] and national identity. The aim of my study was to contribute to the explanation of this well-known relationship by finding the factors which determine or modify its character and changes. In fact, initially I was interested in research related exclusively to the American sociocultural context. With the course of time, however, I realized that in order to discover some more general determinants of this relationship, it might be helpful to make a comparative sociohistorical study of different cultural contexts. For this purpose, I selected two countries in which the Roman Catholic culture traditionally predominated, Poland and France, and two countries in which the Protestant culture predominated, Great Britain and the United States. The patterns of general social and cultural development of these four countries were different to such an extent that we may speak about four different contexts for the relationship between religion and patriotism.

In the course of my study, it appeared possible to distinguish three levels of the analytical relationship. The first one is the relation between the religious culture of a given nation and national consciousness. The second one is the relation between religious identity and national identity. And the third one is the relation between religiosity and patriotism.

The concept of national religious culture, which may be called a national religious dialect, appears to be very helpful. It permits an analysis of the specific variants of a given religious system on a national level (e.g., the differences in the religious cultures of Poland and France in spite of the same base, the Roman Catholic religious system). National religious dialects are developed as a result of the process of the intermingling of various elements of religious faith with elements of national culture, within the context of general social development of a nation.

Based on the definition of religion accepted for this study, we can define national consciousness as a historically created and changing set of beliefs, symbols, meanings, and values shared by members of a society living in a given territory conceived as the homeland, and participating in a given cultural and social heritage, which has developed on this very territory; as a set of ideals, patterns of behavior, acts, and actions connected with those beliefs that unite into one community, called a nation, all who actualize them.[2] The crucial process for the development of this consciousness is, in my opinion, the creation by a society of its own specific "central zone." This "central zone" is "the center of order of symbols, of values and beliefs, which govern the society. It is the center because it is the ultimate and irreducible . . ." in the sense that it is "intimately connected with what the society holds to be sacred. . . ." It is also "a structure of activities, of roles and persons, within the network of institutions. . . . The central value system is not the whole of the order of values and beliefs espoused and observed in the society." It "is constituted by the values which are pursued and affirmed by the elites of the constituent subsystems and of the organizations which are comprised in the subsystems. . . . These values are the values embedded in current activity."[3] In the majority of societies "there are some elements of the common culture which are widely shared, such as language, the name of the nation, the territory, the division of labor, and system of authority, and which generate a sense of affinity with those who share that culture and the sense of difference from those who do not share it."[4]

Beside this cultural "central zone," in every society there are cultural "peripheries," and the social and cultural integration of the whole society (though it is always relative) depends on the extent to which the "peripheries" approach the "central zone." This, in turn, depends upon the degree to which the economic system is unified, political democracy accepted, urbanization and education developed, and so forth.

Among various components of the cultural "central zone," there is also the "core" of the national religious dialect. I assume that the "zone" functions as the main frame of reference for national consciousness, national identity, and patriotism. The processes which lead to the creation of the central cultural zone and the national consciousness simultaneously play the role of causes and effects, and they comprise the interplay between the national religious culture and national consciousness. The process of development of national consciousness modifies the national religious culture. In the sphere of religious symbols, this entails the modification of their meaning; in the sphere of values and norms, the modification of their hierarchy. The aims, methods, and techniques applied in religious activities and roles also undergo transformations. Finally, the religious institutions change their structure and functions to adapt themselves to the demands of members. On the other hand, the religious culture functions as one of the modifying factors of the process of development of national consciousness. By justifying and "sanctifying" the central cultural zone of a nation, religion influences the general attitude toward the nation. In the doctrinal dimension, the religious myths mix with the national ones and thus the "National Messianisms" are created. In the dimension of knowledge about nation, the knowledge of religious symbols and myths, as one of the components of cultural heritage, influences the knowledge of the remaining components. In the sphere of experience, the religious experience in its various forms leads to the increase of the predispositions to react emotionally to those elements of cultural heritage which are more or less directly included in the religious and national myth. In the social aspect, religious rituals become the components of the "national style of life" and of national rituals. The membership in a religious community becomes a form of membership in the national community. And, finally, the religious morality defines the core of the national one. Obviously, the influences presented above have rather the character of a model.

I conceive of national religious culture and national consciousness as potentials that provide the bases for religious and national identity and for religiosity and patriotism.[5] I call them "potentials" because they are as if "given" to the people who are brought up within their context. Obviously, every subsequent generation introduces certain changes of these potentials. The "new," however, can be built only on the bases of the "given old."

I see national and religious identity as more "active," more pragmatic, dimensions of religious culture and national consciousness. People may know their national religious dialect, they may be conscious of their nationhood, but they do not have to self-identify with this culture or with their nation. According to definite interests, they may build their religious or/and national identity on the basis of only some selected elements of these "potentials" linking them with elements of other "potentials" available to them, or they may find a completely different cultural central zone for the frame of reference of their identity.

Finally, at the third level, we have religiosity and patriotism, which I conceive of as actual manifestations of religious and national identity. It appears, then, that for the relationship between religion and patriotism, the most crucial factors are identity, the frame of reference for this identity, and its dimensions. Certain selected aspects of identity and its structure will be the main topic of the analysis presented hitherto.

My general assumptions are: (1) The character and changes of the relationship between religiosity and patriotism, considered as actual manifestations of religious and national identity, depend upon the distance between the central cultural zone and cultural peripheries, and on the contents of this zone. The contents and the scope of the central cultural zone depend, in turn, on the political system, the economic system, the social stratification, and the systems of education and information. I assume that the smaller the scope of the central cultural zone and the larger the distance between this zone and cultural peripheries, the greater the significance of the religious factor for patriotism. (2) The national identity is composed of social, cultural, and political identities. If the frames of reference for all three of these components are included in the central cultural zone, then the national identity is fully integrated and patriotism is also three-dimensional. I assume that the more the components of patriotism are integrated into the cultural zone, the smaller the significance of the religious factor for patriotism.

I wish to test these hypotheses by referring to the four selected sociocultural contexts. Limited by the scope of the paper, I will focus only on post-World War Two situations, although I am fully conscious of the extent to which these are determined by more distant historical factors.

The Polish Context

In the Polish case, we deal with a relatively small scope of the central cultural zone as well as a far distance between this zone and the cultural peripheries. This situation is determined by a number of factors. First of all, for the last three centuries (with the exception of the relatively short interwar period), the Polish nation was governed by foreign powers. Also, after World War Two, the political system was imposed on this nation by external forces; it has no support of the nation as a whole. Contrary to the theoretical ideals upon which it is based, this system is characterized by lack of democracy, lack of political liberty, and lack of equality of rights. The communist ideology, however, gives the foundations not only for the political system but also for the economic system. The latter appears to be unfavorable for the development of industry and urbanization. Although both these processes are observable, they do not occur in a way or at a speed that would contribute to the neutralization of deep social inequalities. Everybody has the right to work, and therefore a specific attitude toward work has developed: Work is not a value in itself. The lack of competition for employment has definite negative consequences for the effectiveness of work, especially because greater efforts do not bring extra rewards. The political and economic systems, in turn, shape the social stratification. Polish society is still relatively "closed," and intergenerational social mobility is rather slow. The hierarchy of social categories is very well defined, and the social distance between the lowest rung (i.e., peasants) and the highest rung (i.e., intellectuals), is quite large. The educational system does not help in this respect. Although, in theory, all people have equal access to education and, although, moreover, the curricula are uniform for every level of teaching, the difference between the actual level of education of people representing different social classes and strata is very significant. These inequalities and differences also cannot be neutralized by the system of mass media. This system, carefully controlled by the political authorities, does not contribute to the extension of the central cultural zone. Other institutions that fill in the social space between the family and the nation do not evoke any respect, and therefore they are not able to pursue or affirm the values that might have become the components of the central cultural zone.

In sum, the undemocratic political system which lacks the support of the nation, the "social vacuum" between the institution of the family and the institution of the nation, the inefficient economic system, limited social mobility, the system of education, and the situation wherein mass media work in favor of the elite as opposed to folk culture, or a nationwide culture are the main factors hindering the development of the central national cultural zone in Poland. The existing central cultural zone comprises, then, besides common language, common territory, and some common features of the everyday life, mainly symbols, ideas, and ideals which do not stand for any empirical reality. A large part of this zone is made of beliefs, symbols, values, patterns of behavior, and types of social bonds having their roots in the Roman Catholic religion. It is a well-known fact that the religious symbols are a reality themselves and that they do not reflect anything empirical. In the Polish context, national cultural, social, and political symbols, acquire the same character, and therefore both religious and nonreligious symbols belong to the same category. In this situation, religion is an important frame of reference for identity on the national level. On other levels, very strong identities are still built by referring to cultural peripheries: regional, ecological (cities vs. small villages), and, most importantly, socio-occupational categories.

The definition of the central zone comprises one more important element. It says that this zone "is central because it is espoused by the ruling authorities of the society."[6] In Poland, symbols and values comprised by the central zone are not espoused by ruling authorities, and this reinforces the negative attitude toward these authorities of people for whom this zone is "sacred." The separation of the church and state since World War Two, which in fact has entailed all possible attempts made by the state to control the church, means that the only institution accepted by the nation and able to espouse the values of the central zone is the institution of the church.

It becomes clear that in Poland the national identity is strongly related to Roman Catholic identity. What are the consequences of this fact for the relationship between religiosity and patriotism? They are quite obvious. Religiosity, which in the Polish context should be called rather "ecclesiasticy,"[7] in-all its dimensions—cultural, social, and institutional—is the manifestation of patriotism. If you define yourself as a Roman Catholic and you participate in religious practices and, above all, you declare respect for the church and the church's teaching in all possible spheres, then, undoubtedly, you are a Polish patriot. As a Polish patriot, you do not have to be especially attached to those symbols or values which have an empirical equivalent, such as the territory of the homeland; if you manage to emigrate, you are simply "lucky." You do not have to be especially attached to the Polish language; the more fluent you are in any of the Western languages, the better for you, because this gives you a chance to settle in the Free World. Moreover, and this might seem paradoxical, you prove your patriotism if you are ready to leave your homeland, because this means that you do not accept the ruling authorities and the "empirical" principles on which they try to build up the economic, social, and cultural reality of Poland. It appears that as a Polish patriot you may give up all the "empirical" elements comprised by the cultural central zone. What you have to maintain is the Polish national Roman Catholic dialect.

The above observations make it clear that in the Polish case there is no balance between the three components of identity: social, cultural, and political. The national identity finds its frame of reference in fact only in the cultural, mainly religious, dimension. The social identity is still of a peripheral character, and there is no political identity. The Polish people do not feel attached to the state in the sense of political authorities; they do feel attached to social subsystems which are their direct groups of reference, and, on the national level—just as it was at the times of the partition of Poland—they are all Roman Catholics. Obviously, this is not entirely true: Not all Poles are Roman Catholics! However, the proportion of those who belong to non–Roman Catholic Churches is relatively very small, and therefore the stereotype that to be a Pole means to be a Roman Catholic is quite strong.[8] Moreover, the members of religious minorities in Poland enter into a distinct type of relationship with political authorities, but this question may be the subject of a separate paper.

In consequence, Polish patriotism is unidimensional; it is only cultural. It lacks the social and political dimensions. It refers to symbols, ideas, and ideals without empirical equivalents. Nowadays, therefore, it manifests itself almost exclusively in loyalty to the Roman Catholic Church, in defending this church against the communist attempts to minimize the church's influence on the society, and in the maintenance of the Polish national religious dialect.

The French Context

In France, there is a relatively broad central cultural zone and a small distance between this zone and cultural peripheries. The political system of a democratic republic has been developed gradually by the French nation since the end of the eighteenth century. The economic system, based mainly on small, family businesses, was already quite well developed in the second half of the nineteenth century. The degree to which processes of urbanization and industrialization have advanced was sufficient to neutralize economic and social differences. The well-organized system of education, which is compulsory til the age of sixteen, and the system of mass media have contributed to the creation of the national mass culture. The institutions, including political ones, are accepted and respected by the majority of the members of the nation.

In sum, the political system supported by the French people for almost two centuries, the development of institutions respected by the nation, the economic system favoring economic and social rise, the system of education, and the mass media working in favor of the nationwide culture are the factors which contributed to the development of the central national cultural zone of France. This zone comprises such values as common language, common territory, common features of everyday life, and, very importantly, the values of "liberty, equality, and brotherhood," promoted at the time of the French Revolution, on which contemporary political and economic systems are believed to be based. The fact that the national values are seen as having empirical reflection in the political, economic, and social reality evokes a specific type of pride in being a member of the French nation, of the first European nation which devoted itself to the actualization of these fundamental humanistic principles. In consequence, the national identity of the French people finds a very broad frame of reference in the central zone of the national culture. The religious core comprised by this zone is rather small, and religious identity does not play any significant role in the national one. The processes of secularization of the French nation were already well advanced in the early 1940s, when French sociologists initiated empirical studies of the religious life in their country, which they considered "the country of mission." The separation of church and state was introduced in France at the time of the Revolution, and since then the French nation has not expected the political authorities to support or defeat religion. The state and the church are supposed to function as two separate institutions, the state promoting national values and the church promoting religious values.

In this context, religiosity has nothing to do with patriotism. People are patriots irrespective of whether they are religious or not. The type of national identity observed in France is characterized by the balance between social, cultural, and political factors. This identity refers to the national central cultural zone in which both cultural values and social and political ideals are included, all of which are believed to be more or less fully actualized in the life of the nation. In consequence, French patriotism is three-dimensional, and a French patriot is expected to be loyal to and to defend the political system, French society as a whole, and French culture. The rejection of the Roman Catholic culture which traditionally dominated in France does not diminish the strength of the national identity or patriotism of a Frenchman.

The British Context

The British context is also different, and it is determined by certain features characteristic of the English component of the British State. In England, from the sixteenth century on, political and religious authorities became united and subsequent kings and queens have led not only the state but also the Church of England. The political system of a monarchy combined with the rules of a parliament is accepted and respected by the nation to a very high degree. With regard to the economic system, we have to remember that the English society was the first to experience the industrial revolution and all of its consequences. The processes of industrialization and urbanization are much further advanced than in France, and the farms have also turned into industrial enterprises. As a result, the differences between people who live in the country and in the cities are relatively insignificant. Both the political and the economic systems favor economic and social mobility. The systems of education and of the mass media work for the creation of the new nationwide culture of common behavior and thought. Together with other institutions, they promote the development British national values. It has to be added, however, that the central cultural zone of Great Britain is different from that of France, and the distance between this zone and the peripheries is larger. This is mainly due to the fact that Great Britain comprises four major cultural subentities: England, Scotland, Wales, and Ireland. Therefore, the central zone comprises social and political ideals first of all, and only a limited degree of common cultural values.

In this context, the national identity is mainly referred to the society and state. Patriotism appears to be primarily two-dimensional—social and political—and, to a smaller extent, cultural. Cultural identity of members of the British nation is still peripheral, in the sense that it is related to the values comprised by cultural subzones.

Obviously, in this situation, the function of the religious factor for national identity and patriotism has to be very specific. Due to the foundation of the Church of England, religion acquired the national dimension. The fact that the highest political and religious authority is represented by the same person means that the attitude of the English people toward the Church is similar to their attitude toward other institutions. However, Great Britain, as opposed to Poland or France, is characterized by religious pluralism. Besides the Church of England, there are other Protestant churches, as well as the Roman Catholic Church. The religious factor appears, then, on two different levels, and it has two different, but supplementary, meanings. Within the national identity and patriotism, it can be traced to some extent as a factor included in the political aspect. In a different sense, it is also observed as one of the components of the cultural identity on the peripheral level. In general, however, although its significance is greater than in France, it is possible to state that the process of the secularization of the British nation, understood among other phenomena to be represented by the decline of the importance of religion for the national identity, is well advanced. A British patriot accepts and respects the political order established for centuries, including its religious dimension. He respects his society, and he is proud of being its member. He maintains the values comprised by the central cultural zone, but, at the same time, he preserves a quite significant part of the values included in the cultural subzone to which he belongs.

The American Context

In contrast to the situation in Poland, France, and England, where people first developed the sense of nationhood and then, little by little, created the basis for the new countries and their independence, in the United States, the state was founded first and the nation has developed next. The ideas of democracy, equality of rights, and political liberty, on which the political system was based, have been accepted and respected since colonial times. The principles of free market and competition, on which the economic system was built, have been seen as the only ones giving opportunities for mobility "from rags to riches." The processes of urbanization and industrialization, which began rapidly in the second half of the nineteenth century and have continued til the end of World War Two, led to economic prosperity with no parallel in the world. In consequence, after the war, around the time of the 1970s, the United States experienced its transformation into a postindustrial society. The immigrant origin of the nation, the constant influx of people ready to fight for the betterment of their lives, contributed to the development of a specific ethos of work within the American political and economic systems. Work as such became a value, because "money changes everything" and "a better job means a better life." All of these factors contributed to the development of its social stratification, which is flexible enough to promote not only economic but also social mobility.

The people who created the United States cared for education, and therefore they developed the private (including denominational) and public systems of education. These systems, in spite of all criticism which they face, contribute to the development of the American central cultural zone. Also, the system of mass media, and the entire net of social institutions filling up the "social space" between the family and the nation, worked for the development of symbols, ideas, ideals, values, norms, and patterns of behavior which are shared by all members of the American nation. The American central cultural zone became larger and larger, and it comprises such components as common language; common civil rights; access to education and information; ethos of work; hope for a better future; common features of everyday life; common life aims, such as money; common values, including pluralism itself and freedom of choice; and so on. It also includes the "core" of American religious culture built up on the initial denominational pluralism. The main factor here is the American National Messianism—the belief that "Americans are the first *nation* who devoted itself to the actualization of fundamental moral and philosophical principles, according to which all people were created as equal and endowed with equal rights to life, liberty and drive to happiness."[9] Political and religious institutions, based on the principles of American democracy, evoked the belief that they make the actualization of American ideals included in the central zone easier and that they protect them. Therefore, they gave rise to a very strong sense of loyalty and, at the same time, the conviction about their exclusive perfection. On this basis, the conviction that American ideals should be passed not only to subsequent generations but also to members of other nations appeared well justified. And this, in turn, through a feedback loop, reinforced the belief of members of the American nation in the "extraordinary" character of their own country and nation as a whole, in spite of multisided inner differentiations which have often led to very acute conflicts.

In sum, the American national identity is related to the American central cultural zone, and the fact that Americans also feel affiliated to some peripheral regional, state, racial, ethnic, socioprofessional, or companionate cultural subzones only plays the role of a supplementary factor and not a contradictory one. Since World War Two, when the American central zone gradually started to increase, the significance of the religious factor for national identity and patriotism began to decline. The national values are also more and more important for the American National Messianism.[10] The religious factor still exists, however, as one of the components of the central zone, in the form of the core of American religious culture. It also functions, to a larger extent, in a very differentiated way on the peripheral level. We may say, then, that it is as if the American situation were a combination of the French and British patterns—of the French because American patriotism is three-dimensional and since the social, political, and cultural frames of references are comprised by the central zone; of the British because the peripheral identities are relatively very strong and they play a supplementary function in relation to the national one.

Conclusions

The above remarks on the relationship between religion and patriotism in the four selected contexts lead to the following general conclusions. First, the analyzed relationship is independent of the dominating religious system. Second, it depends very heavily on the political system, on the level to which this system is accepted and respected by members of a nation, and on the relationship between political and religious authority. Third, it depends on the contents and scope of the central cultural zone: The higher the extent to which the national symbols and values are believed to be actualized in the life of the nation, "to be embedded in current activity," the smaller the importance of the religious factor for national identity.

Notes

1. I understand religion as a historically developed and changing set of beliefs, symbols, meanings, values, and norms related to the differentiation between the empirical and extraempirical reality and the subordination of the empirical reality to the extraempirical one; as a system of ideals, patterns of behavior, acts, and actions shared by individuals who accept this set of beliefs and who create communities of a different level of organization and institutionalization. This definition is based on the one formulated by R. Robertson. I am fully aware of the importance of functions performed by religion; however, I do not like the functional definitions of religion. The latter permit the conception of various "isms," including patriotism, as religions. I think that the essence of religion consists of the belief in real existence of a reality which even potentially cannot be empirically tested.

2. In the national consciousness understood in this way, it is possible to single out dimensions analogous to the ones of religion: (1) general attitude toward the nation; (2) national doctrine, that is, national myths; (3) knowledge about the nation and about its social and cultural heritage; (4) experience of the nation, in the sense of given predispositions to react emotionally to given elements of the social and cultural heritage; (5) national rituals, that is, patterns of behavior, acts, and actions resulting from the general attitude toward the nation, such as participation in the celebration of national holidays; (6) national community, that is, a given type of social bonds and relations; and (7) national morality or ethics understood as historically created set of rules, evaluations, ideal patterns of behavior in relation to one's own nation, and a set of beliefs that justify them, for example, readiness to defend the territory conceived as the homeland at the price of one's life.

3. E. Shils, *The Constitution of Society* (Chicago, IL: University of Chicago Press, 1982), 9.

4. Ibid., 36–37.

5. P. L. Berger, in *Facing Up to Modernity: Excursions in Society, Politics and Religion* (New York: Basic Books, 1977), speaks about an "abstract" patriotism as opposed to a "communal" one which has as its frame of reference the peripheral subzones. On patriotism, see also M. Janowitz, *The Reconstruction of Patriotism: Education for Civic Consciousness* (Chicago, IL: University of Chicago Press, 1983).

6. E. Shils, 9.

7. "Ecclesiasticy" is more accurate than "religiosity" because the institutional dimension of religious identity is the most important.

8. It is so strong that during the "Solidarity" movement of the early 1980s, the Polish Tartars who belonged to the Roman Catholic Church burnt down the church building of another group of Polish Tartars who were Muslims. Because the latter had not joined the Roman Catholic Church which fought for the political and civil rights of Poles, they were accused of being traitors to Polish national interests.

9. This is a quotation from Jimmy Carter's speech delivered on 15 July 1976, quoted after P. McWilliams, "The Myth of America's Civil Religion: An Essay Concern-

ing the Religious Foundations of America's Social Order," paper presented to the Annual Meeting of the Society for the Scientific Study of Religion, 28 October 1977.

10. Notice that the American nation is no longer the one "chosen by God" to actualize the fundamental moral and philosophical principles, but it is the "nation who *devoted itself*" to this purpose.

17
Religion and the Political Order: The Case of Norway

John T. S. Madeley

THE NORWEGIAN CHRISTIAN PEOPLE'S PARTY (CPP) is a curious anomaly on a number of grounds. Although it has gained imitators in other Nordic countries, it is still the only major Christian Democratic party in Scandinavia. In the Norwegian context, its very right to exist is still contested by the other major parties on the grounds that it exploits its Christian label to gain a dishonest electoral advantage by implicitly claiming to be the sole representative of Christian values in a country where more than 90 percent of the population (and a majority of the supporters of each of the major parties) remain members of the national church. The other parties insist that religion is a private matter which should be kept out of politics, but the CPP, representing an activist religious minority, argues its relevance to a whole range of issues, in addition to promoting the views and interests of its constituency in those areas of public life where religious and moral issues have an obvious relevance. The CPP is part cause, part consequence, of a situation in which the press accords great news value to such items as conflicts over the appointment of bishops, the ordination of women priests, local licensing regulations, and even, in one celebrated episode in the 1950s, theological arguments over the doctrine of eternal damnation in hell.

In a broader European context, the CPP also presents an anomaly. Christian Democracy is largely a Catholic phenomenon (although in the Netherlands it is also represented in the Calvinist population). Indeed, while the religious factor has been of continuous importance since the French Revolution in those societies with majority or large minority Catholic populations, it has been conspicuous by its relative absence in the overwhelmingly Protestant countries of Britain (i.e., The United Kingdom minus Northern Ireland) and Scandinavia since World War One. The political culture of the latter has often been taken to exemplify high degrees of homogeneity and secularization, generally untroubled by intersubcultural conflict, and at one time these countries were seen as harbingers of a new age of nonideological politics.[1] The major political parties, as representatives of the principal economic interest blocs, mediated a rational, consensual system of bargaining which had produced mature and successful models of social democracy. In this context, the Norwegians' periodic obsession with conflicts over religion and morals could only be seen as a puzzling exception to the rule. One British commentator even suggested that they only quarreled over such issues because no real conflicts divided them and it was therefore necessary to invent artificial ones![2]

A number of Norwegian students of politics have attempted to provide more thoroughgoing accounts of the phenomenon. Henry Valen and his various collaborators, in their work on electoral behavior and the spatial modeling of the party system, have shown that it is necessary in order to describe adequately voters' perceptions of party distance to add a crosscutting "moral-religious" dimension to the conventional left-right dimension.[3] Similarly, Rokkan's more historical analysis has emphasized the partly coinciding and partly crosscutting territorial, sociocultural, and religious dimensions in the nation's developing cleavage system, in addition to the better-understood cross-local functional bases of cleavage.[4] While this work, which has attracted considerable international attention by its quality, has highlighted the importance of the religious factor, it has been more concerned with relating it to other factors and to its place in the system as a whole than with explaining how it came to be important in the first place. Such explanations as are given tend to represent the religious element as just one vehicle, among a number, of peripheral "countercultural" protest against the nation's historic center. This paper reports a piece of research that attempts to supplement this view with an analysis of the considerable amount of material relating to the context of a unique set of church-state-society relations and the development of a particular religious cleavage system with its distinctive patterns of conflict. By concentrating more directly on the specifically ecclesiastical and religious aspects of the Norwegian case, it is hoped that light will also be thrown on general questions relating to the varying incidence of the religious factor in the politics of different countries and the role of religion in the construction and management of the political order.[5]

The Reformation in Norway was entirely successful in eradicating loyalty to the Roman See: No pockets of Catholic resistance remained to be mobilized at a later date, as occurred in other parts of Protestant Europe. The change of church regime was imposed by royal fiat throughout both parts of Denmark-Norway when the resolution of an early-sixteenth-century dynastic succession struggle issued in the success of a Lutheran candidate. The church and its property were taken over by the crown, and the clergy was reduced to the status of royal ecclesiastical servants under the supervision of reformed bishops appropriately retitled superintendents.[6] A new vernacular liturgy was introduced, and the Lutheran fashion for preaching (also, of course, in the vernacular) reinforced a new identity between crown, church, and people. This vernacular of the new Lutheran Bible, liturgy, and preaching was closer to the Danish of the court, the university, and officialdom than to the various dialect forms used by the mass of the Norwegian population, and at no time did the Danish monarchy manage to impose its linguistic standard with anything approaching the success with which it imposed the new religious standard. This fact was to be of considerable importance in the nineteenth century when Norwegian romantic nationalism coincided with a new literacy on the one hand and the growth of movements of religious revivalism on the other.[7]

The Eidsvoll constitution, which remains as a monument to the attempt in 1814 to seize national independence, did not introduce the same degree of change to church-state relations as it did to relations between crown and people within the state. Despite the impact of Enlightenment ideas about the sovereignty of the people and the division of powers, the church remained within the sole jurisdiction of the (hitherto, and in this respect continuing, absolute) monarchy. Special financial provision was made for its upkeep and all powers relating to organization, liturgy, and doctrine were reserved to the crown, which was bound to uphold "the Lutheran-evangelical religion." Nor was the church provided with any representative machinery that might have mitigated the crown's absolute authority within the church; it was to remain, as it had been since the Reformation, an ecclesiastical bureaucracy (albeit with many civil functions) subject to crown supervision. Finally, through some curious mischance which historians have since puzzled over, guarantees of freedom of religious belief and observance were omitted from the constitution. The long-established threefold religious monopoly of Lutheranism within the country, of the crown within the church, and of the clergy within society were thus confirmed.

This anomalous heritage of the threefold monopoly of a confessional state accounts for many of the ecclesiastical and religious-cum-moral controversies which have periodically occupied Norwegians since 1814. The repeal of the conventicle ordinance (an eighteenth-century measure which had prohibited the holding of religious meetings not sanctioned by the local clergy) provided the first focus of conflict in the 1840s. Since then, conflicts have tended to revolve around, on the one hand, the liberalization of church government, in particular the provision of organs of self-government for the church with all of the implications of this provision for the powers of the crown, the authority of the popularly elected *Storting*, and the standing of various religious groups; and, on the other hand (and more recently), the defense or promotion of religious values to which the state remains constitutionally committed through its remaining connection with the established church. The origin and course of these conflicts can only be fully understood, however, by paying attention as well to the nature of the religious groups that have been mobilized to engage in them. The paper now turns to this aspect of the record, with particular attention to the three major "translations" of religious conflicts into politics: the Haugians in the early nineteenth century, the moderate and radical revivalists in the 1880s, and the groups associated with the rise and development of the Christian People's Party in the twentieth century.

Hans Nielsen Hauge (1771–1824) was the first major figure in a strong native tradition of Lutheran revivalism which has constituted an important pole of attraction and repulsion ever since his day. In 1795, Hauge underwent an intense conversion experience in which he believed he had received a divine call "to confess God's name to men" and "exhort them to repent." Although he had been baptized, confirmed, and brought up in a decent, respectable peasant household and had not indulged in any extraordinary youthful excesses, he came to regard his life prior to 1795 as having been steeped in depravity and sinfulness. Only through a conversion wrought directly by God without the agency of the church had he been brought into full possession of Christ's saving grace, and he felt constrained to answer the divine call irrespective of any considerations of respectability or of the restrictive regulations of the old church order. His subsequent missionary travels around Norway during the eight years preceding his final imprisonment brought him up against the civil and ecclesiastical authorities on many occasions. The conventicle ordinance was used frequently to put a stop to his activities in particular parishes, and his typical response was simply to move on to other localities to continue his work as opportunity allowed.

The network of "friends" he established became the nucleus of a subculture of religious revivalism which has retained its vitality ever since. In the early period up to the 1840s, the Haugians eschewed formal organization. Although in any one locality a group of elders, generally the heads of leading families, exercised leadership by undertaking correspondence with their counterparts elsewhere and imposing a patriarchal form of discipline within their own groups, they did not adopt any of the marks of a separatist community. They had no formal membership rolls, no heterodox creed, no headquarters. Hauge's testament enjoined them to remain within the church and to submit themselves to the clergy in the proper exercise of their liturgical functions. The Haugians, in following these injunctions, became the most assiduous group of church attenders, while nevertheless maintaining a separate identity.

The Haugians were able to form *ecclesiolae in ecclesia* (small churches within the church) largely because of the response of the ecclesiastical authorities. Although Hauge was hounded by local priests and magistrates, and spent almost all of the years from 1804 to 1814 in prison, the attempt to repress the movement he had founded was eventually given up. The charges on which he was imprisoned were concerned more with his various commercial ventures and the proposal to set up a "holy fund" for the benefit of his "friends" than with his repeated breaches of the conventicle ordinance. Some churchmen, for example Bishop Brun of Bergen, had adopted a lenient line early on, arguing that his activities, which arose from religious enthusiasm, should go unpunished in an age that tolerated the publication of freethinking tracts. And in the last ten years of his life, when his damaged health prevented him from traveling and preaching as before, Hauge enjoyed the respect of many who had little sympathy for his teachings. This effective toleration, even accommodation, of Haugianism within the church, contrasted greatly with the treatment of religious dissent and nonconformity in some other Protestant countries, and accounts for many of the contrasts in the structure and culture of religious affiliation in Norway as opposed to other parts of the Protestant world. It meant that in Norway religious revivalism could continue to claim to be the carrier of the true national religious tradition. Not cut off from the state church by the action of the authorities and not distinguished by attachment to an alternative creed, they could struggle to advance their own values and ethos within the framework of the nation's own religious organization, the Lutheran-evangelical state church.

The eventual toleration of Haugianism occurred despite the fact that it resonated social as well as religious tensions within Norwegian society and was regarded by many members of the official estate as deeply subversive. In some of his early tracts, Hauge made bitter attacks on the greed and corruption of the clergy as well as on their rationalistic style of religion. He presented them as hireling shepherds unconcerned with their flocks' spiritual welfare—more concerned, indeed, as the contemporary term "potato priests" indicates, with the improvement of agriculture, when they were not engaged in maintaining their own privileges. In a country where the official estate, which included the clergy, represented the social, cultural, and political elite, these assaults were feared as much as resented, particularly when the Haugians became embroiled in politics.

The involvement of the Haugian movement in politics might at first sight seem strange. Conversionist religious movements that maintain, as the Haugians did, their overwhelming emphasis on the importance of individual conversion and the cultivation of godliness have typically deemphasized secular concerns. They have often foresworn involvement in political affairs, regarding them as worldy impediments to concentration on the one thing needful (*det ene fornødne*), namely, the salvation of individual souls. It is a matter of some interest, therefore, that the Haugians, represented as they were at the first national convention in 1814 and later in the Storting, came to be an important political force in the first half of the nineteenth century.

One explanation for this involvement is that they were forced to engage in politics in order to obtain the repeal of the conventicle ordinance, an objective not achieved until 1842. Thus Kaartvedt wrote: "The Haugian movement wished first and foremost to be a religious movement. But under the old, strict state church system it was clearly impossible for a lay movement which was denied free development, to distinguish between religion and politics, least of all between religion and church politics."[8] This seems an inadequate explanation, however, since the repeal of the ordinance did not become an issue until 1833 and even when it was raised in that year this was not done by a Haugian.

An alternative explanation rests on a broader view of Haugianism in its context. First, Hauge placed great emphasis on the Lutheran doctrine of the calling, the idea that the Creator had placed every man in a particular position in society and laid upon him the duty to work conscientiously to the glory of God and for the betterment of the community of believers. There was thus a positive acceptance of this-worldly activity reminiscent of Weber's inner-worldly asceticism. Second, in early-nineteenth-century Norway, with its relatively broad suffrage and new *Storting,* a new calling with its associated duties had arisen, namely, to involve oneself conscientiously in the government of the state, a state which was after all committed to the protection of the Lutheran faith. For those, such as many Haugian "elders," who were fitted by their position and their talents to undertake the role of representative for their locality, the calling to be a member of the Storting was as honorable as any other, and where alternative candidates were less worthy, perhaps by virtue of their blindness to the cause of salvation, the call itself might take on the aspect of a positive duty. Third, the Haugians' history of resistance to officialdom, their rejection of the fashionable rationalistic religion of the day, and their organizational resources made them admirable candidates for a peasantry which had historically resented the exactions of officialdom but which had lacked any cross-local organizations. Therefore, in the early 1830s, when the first stirrings of a self-conscious peasant mobilization at the polls arose, a number of prominent Haugians were among the organizers.

The importance of the Haugians for the later history of the religious factor in Norwegian politics is twofold. Firstly, by remaining within the state church, they laid the foundation for a tradition of religious revivalism which maintained a fertile source of tension between different cultural tendencies *within* the national community. Had they left or been forced out of the established church and formed a separate religious community, as many small sects were to do, it is likely that they and subsequent revivalist movements would have become marginalized. Secondly, by rejecting the option of withdrawal from political life they established a tradition of involvement and concern, legitimated by the doctrine of the calling with its implied duty to work for the moral welfare of the whole community, which has contributed much to the character and content of Norwegian political life.

In the middle decades of the nineteenth century, Haugian revivalism underwent important changes. In the 1850s, Professor Gisle Johnson of the university theological faculty became the central figure in a pietist revival in Christiania (Oslo) which recruited to the cause of revivalism many young men who were to become priests in the church. Whereas Haugianism had been the property of sections of the peasantry, the Johnson revival now brought members of the middle and upper classes into the movement. At the same time, there developed a new framework of organization in the form of associations for the support of missionary work at home and abroad. It is significant that although almost the entire population was baptized into, and under the spiritual supervision of, the state church, Johnson and others, like Hauge before them, regarded the Norwegian populace itself as a prime target for mission work. Nor were the inner mission organizations primarily concerned with social problems; these engaged relatively little of their energies compared with the business of spreading the gospel and propagating revival, in the by-then time-honored manner of the Haugians. Apart from serving these particular purposes, they also provided the principal form of association between the converted believers.

The Johnson revival had a strong conservative aspect. Johnson himself regarded the mission organizations as a necessary device in the absence of a reform of the church (to which the authorities refused to commit themselves) for harnessing revivalist forces and subjecting them to some sort of overarching discipline. He was particularly concerned with insuring that the Haugian tradition of lay preaching, which not only breached the clerical monopoly of religious functions but which was also in breach of the Lutheran confession, should not lead to fanaticism and false doctrine. By means of his "emergency principle" (which was based on the argument that an exceptional need or emergency existed because of the lack of properly trained clergy), he justified the use of laymen as "emissaries" for the spreading of the gospel. He hoped that by exercising unofficial supervision over the recruitment and activity of such "emissaries" or "bible messengers" that the fears of the more conservative clergy, on the one hand, and the desire for lay preaching among the converted believers, on the other, could be met. In this he was largely disappointed. The conservative clergy continued to attack Johnson's Luther Foundation (designed to provide central coordination for the inner mission associations) as constituting a breach of church order, while the more radical lay revivalists continued to attack it as representing an attempt to deprive the old Haugian tradition of its birthright of independence and to subject it to clerical supervision. Although Johnson eventually lost out to those who wanted full endorsement for the irregular practice of lay preaching (the "emergency principle" was finally abandoned in 1890), there remained a division between moderate and radical lay revivalism which was to have important repercussions.

After the 1840s, the Haugians disappeared as a distinct group within the Storting. Although individual Haugians such as Ueland remained prominent within the peasant opposition, autonomous movements of peasant mobilization, which owed little, if anything, to the Haugians, now provided the principal vehicles of opposition to the entrenched privileges and power of the official estate. Indeed, it was only after Ueland's departure had removed an obstacle to the development of party organization in the Storting that the left alliance of peasant leaders and urban radicals was formed. And it was only as the fifteen-year constitutional struggle (which reached its climax with the dramatic breakthrough to parliamentarism in 1884) and the associated polarization between the parties of the left and right that the structure of religious cleavages again impinged significantly on politics.

The intense and protracted conflict between the partisans of the regime of the officials with its reliance on the royal veto, and the forces of the left with their call for all power to be gathered into the hands of the Storting majority, brought in its wake a bitter conflict among revivalists. In the closing stages of the struggle, Johnson closely associated himself with an "Appeal to the Friends of Christianity in our Country." The Appeal claimed to be motivated solely by a desire to safeguard the position of Christianity against "the danger which we are convinced now threatens this nation's greatest treasure from the side of *political radicalism*." The radicalism of the left (the party's name was not mentioned throughout, but the implication was clear) had its root in "free-thinking, the modern apostasy" and its aim was to destroy Christianity in Norway: "It treads truth and right underfoot and by its conduct more and more destroys respect for everything that is high and holy." All friends of Christianity must combine and work to ensure its defeat: May God "lead this work . . . so that all might be done in His name, all be to the nation's gain and to His great and holy name's honor and praise!"[9]

This attempt to mobilize the forces of the right in a holy war against the left in the name of religion caused a great sensation, not least because the left coalition included a significant number of men associated with radical lay revivalism. Prominent among these was Jakob Sverdrup, the nephew of the leader of the left, and Lars Oftedahl, the pioneer of a large number of missionary enterprises in the southwest and a leading figure within the more radical revivalist camp. Oftedahl's own newspaper, among its many responses to the Appeal, retorted that Christianity was indeed in danger but not from the left, rather from the right with its lukewarm priests who stood opposed to popular religious revivalism. Among the aims of the religious leaders associated with the left was the introduction of parish councils which would subject the clergy to control by the laity and so repeat, at a local level within the church, the same subjection of officialdom to the will of the people that parliamentarism was intended to effect at the national level in the state.

The left did not long survive the achievement of the immediate goals which had kept it united, and the first major split occurred over two issues associated with religion. First, on the issue of a stipend for the writer Kielland, who had lampooned leading lay religious figures (not least Oftedahl), the moderates (as they came to be called) sided with the right to defeat the proposal. Secondly, the proposal for parish councils, which had been a particular point of interest for the moderates, was resoundingly defeated, and, when Sverdrup, the minister responsible, refused to resign, the split between the moderate and pure wings of the Left became bitter and irreversible. In the 1888 election, the moderate left, which drew much of its support from the radical revivalists of the south and west, emerged as a largely regional party more or less closely associated with radical revivalism. The party was little more than a vehicle for individual representatives, however, and never developed a distinctive program. After the public disgrace of Oftedahl (he confessed to improper relations with one of his female servants), many revivalists adopted the view that politics had become a dangerous occupation for believers, and, in the absence of political issues directly affecting the church and religion, tended to concentrate instead on work within the missionary organizations. The moderate left declined, and by the late 1890s was little more than a regionally based ally of the right.

In the religious field, the impact of the political division remained, and attempts in the 1890s to transcend the differences between moderate and radical revivalism, which Johnson had done so much to embitter, failed when the inner mission movement was split between two major organizations—a national one, which superseded Johnson's Luther Foundation, and a west-country one, which continued the more radical traditions of revivalism in the "dark coastal strip," Norway's Bible Belt. Among foreign mission organizations, too a similar differentiation in terms of degrees of ecclesiastical radicalism occurred, as some organizations introduced new practices, such as ordaining their own missionaries and holding their own communion services, both in defiance of church regulations. Despite these developments, no major organization (or the members of such) was expelled from the church, which consequently came to embrace an ever-broader range of religious traditions, each in turn claiming to be the bearer of the nation's true religious identity.

The emergence of new proposals for church reform and other issues affecting the church continued to produce occasional alignments between religious and political groups. After the introduction of parliamentarism had given power within the church as well as the state to the Storting majority, clerical conservatives and moderate revivalists combined in an effort to wrest independence for the church by equipping it with its own synodal constitution. In 1907, a renewed attempt issued in the foundation of the Church Party. This body, more a pressure group committed to switching votes to those candidates of the established parties who favored its reform program than a party in its own right, achieved some success particularly with the right/conservatives. The more radical revivalists saw in the campaign yet another attempt to reinstate clerical authority within the church, and they were, through their representative on a subsequent royal commission, partly responsible for scotching the attempt. They were by then themselves split over whether or not to pursue their own former aim of introducing local parish councils and other piecemeal reforms, but the adoption of these proposals by the liberals insured that they were introduced.

While religious activists of different persuasions within the church tended to be divided over issues of church reform, they found themselves on common ground over one issue which surfaced very dramatically in 1905. In that year, the government appointed to the chair of dogmatic theology at the university a modernist scholar whose views were anathema to all orthodox believers whatever their church politics; such a man would after all be responsible for teaching Lutheran dogmatics to all intending priests in the church. In response, an orthodox front, represented by the leadership of the different mission organizations, combined to organize the establishment of an alternative theological faculty to be funded independently and privately. The orthodox also committed themselves in 1919 to noncooperation with all modernists within the church. For the first time, orthodox revivalism transcended the differences which previous conflicts over their relationship with the church and proposals for church reform had provoked, and emerged as a more-or-less united force. This new sense of unity among orthodox revivalists is reflected in their increasing adoption of the term *kristenfolket* to describe themselves. The term can best be rendered in English as "Christianfolk" and is used to distinguish them from nominal Christians and theological liberals as well as from atheists. The pejorative term used by their opponents, particularly in the press, is "the pietists." It is this emerging collectivity with its strong network of organizations and its increasing influence in the life of the church in the twentieth century that has provided the core constituency for the major contemporary vehicle for the translation of religious concerns into politics, the Christian People's Party (CPP).

The party was founded in the province of Hordaland, western Norway, shortly before the 1933 election. Proposals to form a separate political party to represent the views and aspirations of the Christianfolk had been discussed on a number of occasions (e.g., in 1919, the national conference of missionary organizations had raised the issue). In Hordaland itself, a decision to run a separate Christian list had been made by a group associated with the more radical revivalist organizations in 1927 and frustrated only by the adventitious failure of the person deputed to hand in the nomination papers to do so. In 1930, those who favored working through the established parties succeeded in getting the general secretary of the radical Western Inner Mission Federation, Nils Lavik, nominated to a position on the liberal list (in this connection, he appeared as alternate twice in the succeeding Storting period). It was their failure to get him nominated to a secure place on the same list in 1933 that finally precipitated the foundation of the CPP.

In the 1920s, the liberals had succeeded in attracting the support of the Christianfolk by adopting a positive attitude to Prohibition, a cause that they, along with secular teetotalers, supported strongly. After six years, however, prohibition had been defeated in a second referendum, and in certain areas, for example Bergen (immediately adjacent to Hordaland), the liberals had presided over the reopening of liquor outlets. For the Christianfolk, other derelictions on the part of the liberals helped to bring about the breach in Hordaland.

In particular, the staging of what was taken to be a blasphemous play at the National Theater in Oslo early in 1933 brought the dissatisfaction of the Christianfolk with the liberals to a new pitch. A storm of protest had greeted the announcement of the play and led to its cancellation. One closed showing was nonetheless arranged, and it was the presence at this of the prime minister (a leading liberal from Bergen) that was taken by the Christianfolk as demonstrating beyond doubt the unreliability of the Liberal party. This incident occurred at a time characterized by intense polarization between cultural radicalism and cultural conservatism, as evidenced by the storm around the blasphemy trial, also in early 1933, of the author Arnulf Øverland. For the Christianfolk, it was the Labor party, with its Marxist heritage and rhetoric, that represented the greatest threat to traditional Christian values, particularly since the contemporary economic dislocation and political turmoil were encouraging more and more working people to turn to it. It was in this context, then, that the Christianfolk discovered that the broad-based liberals with their important "European radical" wing were as unreliable as any of the nonsocialist parties in the fight against "antichristian propaganda" and moved to establish their own political alternative.

The CPP's first program commitment was "to protect Christian and national values in the church, the school, the workplace, and in our cultural life as a whole."[10] With little more than a month between the date of its foundation and election day, the party's success in taking more than 17 percent of the vote in Hordaland was remarkable; it clearly owed much to the already-existing network of communications which characterized the Christianfolk subculture, particularly in that part of the country.

It was in 1945, in the aftermath of World War Two, during which Norway had been under Nazi occupation, that the CPP made the transition from a regional to a national party. In so doing, it set out to become the voice of the Christianfolk of the whole country and not just of its more radical elements in the southwest. It was assisted in this task by a small but important group whose identification with the Christianfolk had not previously been accepted on either side—a number of individuals associated with the Buchmanite Oxford Group, or Moral Rearmament, which had, during the closing stages of the war, discussed plans for a nationwide Christian political forum with a supporting press. Despite hurried preparations and inadequate financing, the CPP surprised most observers of the 1945 election by taking 8 percent of the vote and by establishing itself for the first time as a significant electoral force nationwide. In subsequent elections, its average level of electoral support settled at approximately 10 percent, although in 1977 it achieved more than 12 percent following the final breakup of the Liberal party, which had until then retained the loyalty of some sections of the Christianfolk. Despite its relatively modest size in percentage terms, the CPP since the mid-1970s has been the third largest party in a system dominated by the Labor and Conservative parties; as such, it has led the group of three or four minor parties in the center of the spectrum.

As is the case with most Christian Democratic parties (which emerged around the same time), the CPP's ideological profile was, and is, rather indistinct. Its dual attachment to liberal democracy and Christian values, broadly conceived, fails to distinguish it from either the modern conservative or social democratic traditions. Unlike most of its continental counterparts, the CPP cannot be seen as an extended arm of the church, however. The institutional church in Norway is regarded by the vast majority of its members as little more than the branch of the welfare state that offers public services (the ambiguity of the term conveys the point nicely) in connection with the ceremonial marking of birth, marriage, and death. For the Christianfolk who have a tendency to regard themselves as the embodiment of the true church, the state church represents not so much something which must be defended as an arena of contestation in which the demands of moral and doctrinal discipline must continually be pressed in connection with such issues as the ordination of female priests, the appointment of theological liberals to positions of authority, the marriage of divorcees, or the content of religious education in the public schools. In these as much as in other issues less directly related to the church, the CPP has been much less a church-interest party than a party committed to the defense and promotion of particular religious and/or moral values. These values, to which Norway is committed, according to the Christianfolk, by virtue of its constitution, are those of the dominant tradition of Lutheran revivalism—temperance or total abstinence in the matter of intoxicants and nonmedical drugs, strict sexual morality in matters related to family law, pornography, homosexuality, and so forth, and (most recently) an intensely restrictive approach to abortion. These "politics of morality" issues have provided the main agenda for the CPP in the postwar years, as attempts have been made by more secular forces to remove the last elements of the traditional bias of the law in favor of traditional Christian morality. The party has on the whole fought a losing battle and consequently has been faced with the predicament of whether, or how best, to compromise. Thus, in 1981, it refused to join what would, with its cooperation, have been a majority nonsocialist coalition government because the other parties would not commit themselves to a radical reform of existing liberal abortion legislation. Such unbending attachment to particular value commitments at the expense of a share in the fruits of office confirmed the picture of the CPP as a rather unusual political party.

The CPP is of interest, then, not only because it provides the exception to the Scandinavian rule of a secular politics of material interest bargaining, but also because, in a wider comparative context, it deviates from the normal patterns of Christian Democracy in a number of respects. As has been indicated, its origins and much of its continuing vitality are associated with a tradition of religious revivalism in an overwhelmingly Lutheran context, which elsewhere, since the eighteenth century, has been marked by a tendency to political quietism. Further, unlike its Catholic and Calvinist counterparts in Continental Europe, it has never been a protagonist of the institutional church as such. Indeed, its origins are to be found among groups which have tended to be rather anticlerical, or at least aclerical, despite their continuance within the ambit of the state church. Finally, it has retained the character of a party oriented almost exclusively to the defense or promotion of a set of religious or moral values which are held to derive directly from attachment to a particular form of religion. While other Christian Democratic parties have tended to become actual or potential "parties of government" concerned with the whole range of state policy and to seek support on different grounds from assorted population groups, the CPP has concentrated almost exclusively on its core issues and on the mobilization of support in connection with these.

As has been seen, the party is only the most modern representative in Norway of a religiopolitical tradition which goes back to the early nineteenth century. Any attempt to assess its origins, development, and nature must therefore span a considerable period. It has been necessary to go back at least as far as to the Reformation in order to account for one set of contextual factors without which the case would remain inexplicable. These are the factors affecting church-state-society relations, which have in important respects remained almost unchanged since that early date. Just as, even further back, at the end of the Viking period, the principal actors in church and state entered a compact which created the earliest foundations of Norway as a distinct territorial unit, so at the Reformation the particular resolution of then-existing church-state conflicts set a pattern which undergirded the structure of the developing nation-state and left a legacy which still marks the political complexion of the country. The established state church remains today as a constant reminder of the close mutual articulation of the religious and political orders that was once typical of all early modern Europe but nowadays makes Norway exceptional within Western Christianity.

Notes

1. S. M. Lipset, *Political Man* (London: Heinemann, 1960), chapter 13.
2. George Mikes, "The Largest Little Country in the World," *Encounter*. (April 1954): 41–2.
3. H. Valen and W. Martinussen, *Velgere og Politiske Frontlinjer* (Oslo: Gyldendal, 1972).
4. S. Rokkan, *Citizens, Elections, Parties*. (Oslo: Universitets forlaget, 1970) and elsewhere.

5. For comparative treatments of the same theme in the Scandinavian and the wider European contexts, respectively, see my "Scandinavian Christian Democracy: Throw Back or Portents," *European Journal of Political Research.* (1977): 267–86; and "Politics and the Pulpit: The Case of Protestant Europe," in *Religion in West European Politics,* edited by S. Berger (London: Frank Cass, 1982).

6. The term "superintendants" never entered popular parlance, however. Similarly, ministers of the church continued (and continue) to be called priests.

7. I do not deal here with the language conflict, which only partly crosscuts the lines of religious cleavage. Although Rokkan et al. group together religious revivalism (they call it fundamentalism), temperance, and support for *landsmal* as the characteristics of the rural "counterculture" of the south and west, these phenomena are in many ways distinct; in Norway there was never the degree of identity between the religious and language issues that characterized, for example, Welsh nonconformity.

8. Alf Kaartvedt, "Det Norske Storting gjennom 150 ar" (Oslo, 1964): 130.

9. The Appeal is printed as an appendix to C. F. Wisløff, *Politikk og Kristendom.* (Oslo: Lunde, 1961).

10. The manifesto is printed in "Kristelig Folkeparti 1958–1965" (Oslo, 1965).

Contributors

Allison Alexander, Department of Communication, University of Massachusetts, Amherst, Massachusetts

Nancy T. Ammerman, Assistant Professor, Candler School of Theology, Emory University, Atlanta, Georgia

John A. Coleman, S.J., Jesuit School of Theology, Berkeley, California

Karel Dobbelaere, Professor of Sociology, Catholic University of Leuven, Leuven, Belgium

Jeffrey K. Hadden, Professor of Sociology, University of Virginia, Charlottesville, Virginia

Barbara Hargrove, Professor of Sociology, Illiff School of Theology, Denver, Colorado

Benton Johnson, Chairman and Professor of Sociology, University of Oregon, Eugene, Oregon

Stephen W. Littlejohn, Department of Speech, Humboldt State University, Arcata, California

John T. S. Madeley, Lecturer in Political Science, London School of Economics, London, England

W. Barnett Pearce, Professor and Chairman, Department of Communications, University of Massachusetts, Amherst, Massachusetts

Daniel Pipes, Director, Foreign Policy Research Institute, Philadelphia, Pennsylvania

Roland Robertson, Professor of Sociology, University of Pittsburgh, Pittsburgh, Pennsylvania

Richard L. Rubenstein, Professor of Religious Studies, Florida State University, Tallahassee, Florida

Mark A. Shibley, graduate student at the University of California, Santa Barbara, California

Anson Shupe, Chairman and Professor of Sociology, Indiana/Purdue University, Ft. Wayne, Indiana

John H. Simpson, Professor and Chairman, Department of Sociology, University of Toronto, Toronto, Canada

Barbara Strassberg, Institute for Advanced Study, University of Chicago, Chicago, Illinois

Thomas Walsh, Director, International Religious Foundation, New York, New York

William M. Wentworth, Associate Professor of Sociology, Clemson University, Clemson, South Carolina

Index

305